D0464776

MAY 22 '96

Tracking Skill
and
Manual Control

Tracking Skill
and
Manual Control

E. C. Poulton

Medical Research Council
Applied Psychology Unit
Cambridge, England

ACADEMIC PRESS
New York   San Francisco   London   1974
A Subsidiary of Harcourt Brace Jovanovich, Publishers

BF
295
P68
1974

COPYRIGHT © 1974, BY ACADEMIC PRESS, INC.
ALL RIGHTS RESERVED.
NO PART OF THIS PUBLICATION MAY BE REPRODUCED OR
TRANSMITTED IN ANY FORM OR BY ANY MEANS, ELECTRONIC
OR MECHANICAL, INCLUDING PHOTOCOPY, RECORDING, OR ANY
INFORMATION STORAGE AND RETRIEVAL SYSTEM, WITHOUT
PERMISSION IN WRITING FROM THE PUBLISHER.

ACADEMIC PRESS, INC.
111 Fifth Avenue, New York, New York 10003

United Kingdom Edition published by
ACADEMIC PRESS, INC. (LONDON) LTD.
24/28 Oval Road, London NW1

Library of Congress Cataloging in Publication Data

Poulton, E. C.
    Tracking skill and manual control.

    Bibliography: p.
    1.   Perceptual—motor learning.   I.   Title.
BF295 .P68   620.8′2   73-5299
ISBN 0−12−563550−8

PRINTED IN THE UNITED STATES OF AMERICA

Contents

Chapter 3 Recommended methods of scoring

Chapter 4 Not recommended methods of scoring

Part 2 Tracking

Chapter 5 Tracks with single steps

Chapter 6 Tracks with many steps

Contents

Chapter 7 Ramp tracks

Chapter 8 Sine wave tracks

Chapter 9 Pursuit and compensatory displays

Chapter 10   Augmented displays

Chapter 11   More display variations

Chapter 12   Display sampling

Chapter 13   Displays using alternative visual dimensions

Chapter 14   Nonvisual displays

Chapter 15   Controls

Chapter 16 Orders of control system

Chapter 17 Other control system variations

Preface

This is the only book to provide a systematic coverage of the whole field of tracking skill and manual control. The book is written primarily for psychologists and engineers with interests in skill, tracking, information processing, and engineering psychology. It should be of value also to graduates and undergraduates in departments of physical education. With its numerous illustrations and simple explanations, it can be read and understood by any intelligent person without special knowledge of psychology or physics. It will provide him with an understanding of the skills which he has acquired, and of how the equipment which he uses can be designed to make the best use of his skills.

The tracking literature contains many contradictory results. In the past arbitrary selections have been made from the results, and theories have been put forward to fit the selections. Here the author follows a new and revolutionary approach. The contradictions in the literature are shown to be due to asymmetrical transfer and range effects produced by the within subjects experimental designs which are used. Strategies learned in one condition are carried over to conditions for which they are less appropriate, or in some cases quite unsuited. Once the biased results are discarded, there emerges a clear and sensible description which differs in many respects from current views and practices.

An example is the tendency to go for quickened relative motion displays. It is clear from the evidence reviewed in this book that true motion predictor displays are likely to be far easier and safer for people to use. The evidence has been available for over 10 years. Yet it has been neglected because it contradicts Birmingham and Taylor's design philosophy (1954), which has dominated the thinking of human factors experts for the last 20 years. The fashions of design engineers are perhaps not very different from the fashions of designers in other fields. However they may cost lives when they lead to wrong design decisions.

Part 1 of the book is concerned with experimental method, which is crucial to the understanding of the contradictions in the literature. The early chapters of Part 2 describe the principles of skilled performance. They show how the principles can be derived from the study of simple skills like reaching for something, or pointing at a moving object. The later chapters progress to the more complex skills which are demanded in the modern highly technical world, such as driving an automobile, steering a boat, or flying an aircraft. These chapters show how the principles of skilled performance derived from simple skills can be used to describe the performance of these more complex tracking tasks. Design recommendations are given at the end of most chapters, based upon the experimental results reviewed in the text.

Acknowledgments

It is a pleasure to acknowledge the help of the many people without whom this book could not have been written. The research workers listed below have helped by answering letters and questions, and by granting permission to reproduce their results as figures or tables. I am particularly grateful to my colleague Dr. A. Carpenter. He prepared Figure 11.10, and his extensive knowledge has been invaluable in writing many of the chapters. Mr. P. D. McLeod commented on a draft of the manuscript. Dr. Paul W. Fox was a helpful and effective reviewer. Dr. P. M. Altham and Dr. B. J. T. Morgan helped with statistical problems. My son Mr. C. Poulton helped with some of the mathematics. Mrs. D. H. Attwood typed the first 2 drafts of the manuscript. Mrs. A. Copeman typed the last 2 drafts. Mrs. C. H. Frankl drew the figures. Mr. D. C. V. Simmonds photocopied them.

Adams, J. A.	Burke, D. L.	Gordon, N. B.
Bahrick, H. P.	Burrows, A. A.	Griew, S.
Battig, W. F.	Campbell, F. W.	Hahn, J. F.
Bekey, G. A.	Chernikoff, R.	Hammerton, M.
Bergeron, H. P.	Christ, R. E.	Hartman, B. O.
Bergum, B. O.	Cooper, G. E.	Helson, H.
Bernotat, R. K.	Elkind, J. I.	Hick, W. E.
Bice, R. C.	Ellson, D. G.	Hofmann, M. A.
Birmingham, H. P.	Forbes, T. W.	Holland, J. G.
Briggs, G. E.	Fuchs, A. H.	Howland, D.
Broadbent, D. E.	Garvey, W. D.	Huddleston, H. F.
Brogden, W. J.	Goldman, A.	Hudson, E. M.
Buck, L.	Goldstein, D. A.	Hunt, D. P.

Jackson, K. F.	Muckler, F. A.	Simon, C. W.
Jex, H. R.	Naish, J. M.	Simon, J. R.
Keele, S. W.	Newhall, S. M.	Slack, C. W.
Kelley, C. R.	Newton, J. M.	Smith, K. U.
Knowles, W. B.	Noble, M. E.	Smith, S.
Krendel, E. S.	Notterman, J. M.	Speight, L. R.
Lathrop, R. G.	Pew, R. W.	Thornton, G. B.
Lean, D.	Platzer, H. L.	Tickner, A. H.
Levine, M.	Posner, M. I.	Tipton, C. L.
Levison, W. H.	Regan, J. J.	Todosiev, E. P.
Lincoln, R. S.	Ritchie, M. L.	Trumbo, D. A.
McConnell, D. G.	Rockway, M. R.	Vallerie, L. L.
McLeod, P. D.	Rolfe, J. M.	Vince, M. A.
Meiry, J. L.	Roscoe, S. N.	Wargo, M. J.
Micheli, G. S.	Russell, R. W.	Warren, C. E.
Miller, D. C.	Sadoff, M.	Warrick, M. J.
Milnes-Walker, N. D.	Sampson, P. B.	Welford, A. T.
Milton, J. L.	Schori, T. R.	Wortz, E. C.
Monty, R. A.	Senders, J. W.	Young, L. R.
Morgan, C. T.	Shackel, W. B.	Ziegler, P. N.
Moss, S. M.	Sheridan, T. B.	

I am grateful to the British Medical Research Council for generous support over the last 25 years. Many of the experiments described in this book would not have been possible without the facilities provided by the British Royal Navy. Equipment and funds have been made available through the Royal Naval Personnel Research Committee. The greatest asset has been the regular supply of naval ratings for use in experiments.

Tracking Skill
and
Manual Control

Part

1

Introduction
and method

Chapter

1

Tracking skills

Summary

Tracking is concerned with the execution of accurate movements at the correct time. Tracking may involve true motion or relative motion. The man may have to track along a contour, or acquire a target. The eyes and the voice track as well as the hand. Most everyday tracking tasks are selfpaced, but paced tasks are generally studied in the laboratory. Driving an automobile involves tracking with a control system of high order. Tracking skills are well remembered. Aircraft pilots are a selected group, highly trained at tracking.

Choice and action

Every activity can be said to involve deciding what to do and then doing it. In studying activities such as talking or typing, the principal emphasis is put on selecting responses. The talker has to decide what words to use. The typist has to decide which keys to press.

Talking and typing do require skill for their execution. The talker has to speak so that he can be understood. This is not easy if he has to use a foreign language. The typist has to press the correct key sufficiently hard to type the letter, and not so hard that the typeface perforates the paper. But the activities are usually studied as decisions. The person's choice of a word or of a key is related to the other choices which he or she could have made.

In studying activities such as reaching for an object or steering an automobile, the principal emphasis is put on the execution of responses. In reaching for an object, the person has to move his hand the correct distance in the correct direction. The automobile driver has to turn his steering wheel through the correct angle at the correct time.

Reaching and steering do require decisions before they are carried out. The person has to decide what to reach for. The driver has to decide where he wants to go to. But the activities are usually assessed in terms of the timing and precision of the movements, not in terms of the choice of movements.

The distinction between choice and action has been a useful abstraction in sketching out and limiting fields for research and teaching in psychology. But the distinction must not be allowed to become so rigid that choices and actions are treated in isolation from each other.

In studying tracking, it is essential to know what choices the man makes, what strategy he uses, what he tries to do. A simple description of tracking behavior which takes no account of strategy and choice, cannot easily explain the wide variety of experimental results reported in the literature. A man's use of a number of different strategies in tracking distinguishes his behavior from the behavior of automata.

True motion and relative motion

The left side of Figure 1.1A illustrates a simple true motion or pursuit tracking task. The spot moves up and down, following a program which can be called a track. The man's task is to keep the horizontal line superimposed on the spot, so that it moves up and down like the spot. The man may do this by moving a control like the control stick of an aircraft. A simple block diagram representing the task is given on the right of the figure.

The critical features of the task are that the man can see the movements of the spot which he has to copy. And he can see the movements of the horizontal line which represent the effects of his control movements. An example of a pursuit or true motion task is keeping a spotlight aimed at an actor as he moves around a stage. The pursuit rotor (Ammons, 1955) presents a simplified version of pursuit tracking, which

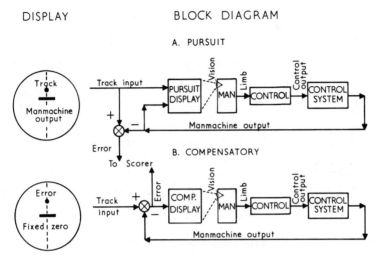

DISPLAY · BLOCK DIAGRAM

Figure 1.1. Pursuit and compensatory tracking.

The tracking error is computed by the device marked with a cross. It subtracts the manmachine output from the track input. With the pursuit display the man does not see the resultant error voltage which is scored against him. So if there is an error in the subtracting device itself, the man cannot compensate for it. With the compensatory display the man sees the resultant error directly. He corrects for an error in the subtracting device during the normal course of tracking.

In compensatory tracking tasks intended to represent flying an aircraft, the track is sometimes mixed with the output of the man's control and fed into the control system. This is done because external disturbances such as gusts of wind and sudden changes in pressure are shaped by the aerodynamic characteristics of the aircraft before they change the readings on the instruments. The block diagram looks different from the block diagram of **B**.

is sometimes used in elementary psychology classes. It has had to be omitted from this book.

The left side of Figure 1.1B illustrates the corresponding relative motion or compensatory tracking task. Here the horizontal line is fixed in the middle of the display. The spot moves up and down as before, following the track program. The man's task is to hold the spot on the fixed line. His control moves the spot, not the line. The movement of the spot is a combination of the effect of the track program and of the man's responses. A simple block diagram representing the task is given on the right of Figure 1.1B.

The critical features of the task are that the man does not see directly either the track movements or the effect of his own control movements. He sees only the error. This represents the difference between the track movements and the output of the control system, or their relative motion.

An example of a compensatory or relative motion task is holding the needle of the speedometer of an automobile at a fixed point corresponding to a speed limit. Changes in the slope of the road change the distance which the gas pedal has to be depressed in order to hold the speed constant.

Compensatory tracking is a good deal more difficult than pursuit tracking. When the man tracks perfectly with the compensatory display, the spot rests on the fixed line. The man cannot see what he is doing, nor what he is supposed to be doing. Whereas when the man tracks perfectly with the pursuit display, the spot and the line move up and down together. The man can still see the movements produced by the track program, and also the effects of his own control movements.

Tracking along a contour

Figure 1.2 illustrates a pursuit or true motion task in which the man can see the track ahead. The paper tape moves up the figure at a fixed speed. The pen at the bottom draws a wiggly track on the paper. The man holds the ballpoint pen, and moves it across and back in the slit. He attempts to keep the tip of the pen on the wiggly line.

Preview of the track ahead can be varied by altering the position of the screens. When preview is abolished, the task resembles the pursuit task of Figure 1.1A. The main difference is that the man writes directly on the display with a pen, instead of controlling a display marker at a distance by moving a lever.

An example of tracking along a contour is steering an automobile along a wiggly road. Except in fog and sometimes at night, the driver can see the road some distance ahead. When vision ahead is restricted, the task becomes more difficult.

Target acquisition

Most tracking tasks involve 2 stages. First the target has to be acquired, and then it has to be held. On the left of Figure 1.1A the spot representing the track may start as illustrated some distance above the line. The man has to acquire the spot by superimposing the line on it.

Acquisition can be studied without continuous tracking. The spot suddenly jumps up or down in the display, and then stays at rest. The man has to restore alignment as quickly as possible. A track with sudden jumps can be called a step track. Acquisition occurs in taking a photo-

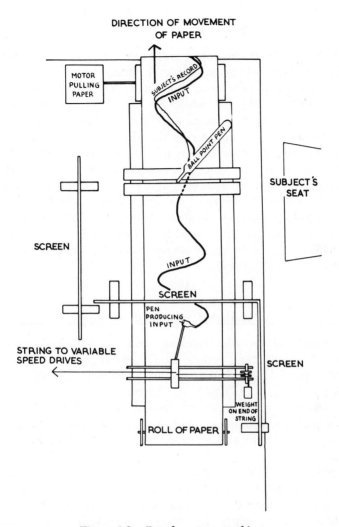

Figure 1.2. Paced contour tracking.
The experimental arrangement is seen from above. The drum which pulls the paper tape is illustrated at the top of the figure attached to the motor. To prevent the pen from tearing the paper, it should be placed directly above the drum, so that it writes on the rotating surface of the drum. The man should be seated at the top of the figure, so that the paper tape moves directly towards him. He tracks more accurately like this. (From Poulton, 1964.)

graph. The photographer gets the person or object of interest into the center of the field of view of the camera before he presses the shutter release.

Tracking by eye and by voice

As a person looks at one object and then at another, the eyes acquire the objects in turn. When an object is being looked at directly, the image of the object falls upon the fovea. This is the most sensitive part of the retina of the eye, where fine details can be perceived most easily. The eyes have to acquire an object in this way in order to be able to transmit information on its fine details to the brain. The eyes face the same difficulties in tracking moving objects as the hands do.

People track with their voice when they pronounce unfamiliar words in a foreign language. In speaking and reading aloud a person has to maintain the correct intensity of the voice, and to check on its clarity. This also involves tracking. So does singing or whistling in tune, and playing in tune on a string or reed instrument such as a violin or oboe. Unfortunately very little experimental work has been carried out on these everyday tracking skills.

Paced and selfpaced tracking

The majority of everyday tracking tasks are selfpaced. There is no rigid time limit, although people usually prefer to spend as little time on a task as possible. Rigid pacing occurs practically only when a moving object has to be tracked. This is the aircraft tracking problem of World War II, which supplied much of the impetus for the early laboratory studies of tracking. It represents only a small proportion of today's tracking tasks, yet practically all laboratory experiments on tracking are rigidly paced.

In controlling a vehicle a man can usually select his own speed, although it may not be easy to change speed rapidly. In using pens, pencils, and hand tools the man can almost always go at his own speed. Acquisition is usually unpaced, although time may be limited. It is virtually only in the experimental laboratory that people are instructed to complete an acquisition task as quickly as possible, and are rewarded or penalized for the time which they take.

Tracking becomes more difficult as the degree of pacing is increased. The most difficult part of an airline pilot's control task is while he is coming in to land. This is because he has to keep his aircraft on a closely defined glide path. His air speed also has to be held within close limits. One of the more difficult tracking tasks is aiming at a fast low flying object. Another is hitting a fast moving ball. Both these tasks are rigidly paced.

Control systems of various orders

The tracking tasks considered so far all involve position or zero order control. There is a direct relationship between a bodily movement and the movement of whatever is being controlled.

Controlling the speed of an automobile with the gas pedal is a more complex kind of tracking. On a level road the speed of the automobile depends upon the distance which the gas pedal is depressed. But there is a time lag. The automobile only gradually reaches the speed which corresponds to the position of the pedal. The gas pedal is called a rate or first order control, because it controls the rate of the automobile. It is a lagged rate control, because there is a time lag between a change in the position of the pedal and the full corresponding change in the speed of the automobile.

In positioning an automobile on a road, the steering wheel is an acceleration or second order control. The angular position of the steering wheel determines the side to side acceleration of the automobile. The front wheels turn through an angle which is proportional to the amount of rotation of the steering wheel. The angle of the front wheels determines the rate at which the automobile changes direction. And the direction in which the automobile points determines the rate at which it moves over towards the side of the road. Thus rotating the steering wheel 30° gives the automobile an acceleration toward the corresponding side of the road.

The engineering variables

A difficulty in discussing tracking is that many different tracking tasks are carried out. It is not possible to state categorically which task is the most typical. In studying tracking in the experimental laboratory, the experimenter has to decide what kind of track he is going to use, what kind of display, what kind of man, what kind of control, and what kind of control system. These independent variables are represented in the block diagrams of Figure 1.1.

In an experiment simulating the tracking of aircraft, Speight and Bickerdike (1968, Table 1) list 18 physical characteristics of the tracking equipment. In each case the experimenter has to select from a number of possible alternatives. His experimental results will be determined by his choices.

Memory for tracking skills

Once a person acquires a tracking skill, he retains his skill for months or years. Evidence for this is listed in the last 4 columns of Table 1.1.

Table 1.1
Memory for tracking skills

Author(s)	Year	N	Display	Track
Ammons, Farr, Bloch, Neumann, Dey, Marion, and Ammons	1958	41 to 58 per condition	Compensatory 3 dimensions	Irregular
Battig, Nagel, Voss, and Brogden	1957	3	Compensatory 2 dimensions	Irregular
Fleishman and Parker	1962	7 to 10 per condition	Compensatory 3 dimensions	6 cpm in 1 dimension only
Mengelkoch, Adams, and Gainer	1958 & 1971	13 13	Compensatory aircraft	Aircraft maneuvers
Noble, Trumbo, Ulrich, and Cross	1966	45	Pursuit 1 dimension	Steps ranging between fully predictable and random
Trumbo, Noble, Cross, and Ulrich	1965	40 or 50 per condition	Pursuit 1 dimension	

$$* \frac{\text{Last training trial} - \text{First memory trial}}{\text{Last training trial} - \text{First training trial}} \times 100$$

$$\dagger \frac{\text{Number of trials to reach performance of last training trial}}{\text{Number of training trials}} \times 100$$

The training time is given in the seventh column. It is rarely more than a few hours. The time after which retention is tested is given in the next column. It is often a number of months. In the Ammons experiment listed in the top part of the table, the learning during 1 hour of practice has not been forgotten completely after 2 years.

The measures of performance are given in the ninth column. Unfortunately Ammons, Farr, Bloch, Neumann, Dey, Marion and Ammons (1958) use time on target. The Battig experiment just below shows that memory assessed by time on target need not correspond very well to memory assessed by a more adequate measure such as modulus mean

Control System	Training time (hr)	Retention interval (mo)	Measure of performance	Percent loss of memory*	Percent trials to relearn†
Position	1	1		8	26
		6		40	33
		12	Time on target in	50	42
		24	3 dimensions	68	43
	8	1	simultaneously	9	4
		6		9	5
		12		30	6
		24		38	10
Position	19	8	a Modulus mean error	a 10 to 13	
			b Time on target	b 31	
Simulated aircraft	6	9		12	1
		14		8	5
		24	Weighted average	31	>21
		1	modulus mean	1	1
		5	error	0	0
		9		3	3
		14		3	4
Aircraft	4	4	Average modulus	53	64
	8		mean error	15	30
Position	3	3	Modulus mean error	22	
Position	1	1		26	
	2	5	Modulus mean	36	
		1	error	29	
		5		43	

error. Battig, Nagel, Voss and Brogden (1957) report memory losses for the modulus mean error in the vertical and side to side dimensions of 10% and 13% respectively, whereas time on target gives a memory loss of 31%. The exact size of the memory loss assessed by time on target depends upon the size of the target. The disadvantages of time on target as a measure are discussed in Chapter 4.

It used to be thought that tracking tasks are remembered better than other tasks. This is not necessarily so. An exact comparison cannot be made between a tracking task and a procedural or verbal task. This is because it is not possible to equate the tasks for difficulty. Also it is not possible to tell how much learning of one task corresponds to a fixed degree of learning of the other task.

Ammons and his colleagues (1958) give their college students a simple 3 dimensional tracking task, the Airplane Control Test. Other groups of about 40 college students are given a procedural task to learn instead. A vertical panel has 17 controls mounted on it. The students have to learn to operate 15 of them in the correct order. If anything, the tracking task is remembered better than the procedural task, but both tasks are remembered pretty well.

Mengelkoch, Adams and Gainer (1958, 1971) give a simulated flying task to students from the Reserve Officers Training Corps with no flying experience. In addition to learning to fly the simulated aircraft, the students have to learn the operating procedures. In the test 4 months later, the experimenters report a reliable amount of forgetting of all classes of procedures. All 6 statistical tests show reliable decrements. Whereas on the measures of tracking proficiency, only 5 out of the 10 statistical tests show reliable decrements. Thus the acquired tracking skill is, if anything, retained better than is memory of the operating procedures. But as Mengelkoch and his colleagues point out, this could be because the students spend more time flying the simulator than they spend on the operating procedures.

Clearly, some memory of both tracking tasks and of other tasks can be shown to survive for many months, probably for many years. It is not possible to conclude that tracking tasks are remembered the best.

Differences between aircraft pilots and nonpilots

Most of the experiments described in this book are performed either by college students, or by ordinary enlisted men. The students and enlisted men are usually not selected because they are good at tracking. Most of them are not trained trackers. Their tracking ability ranges from high to low.

Aircraft pilots are used in some experiments. Pilots differ from ordinary people in being trained to perform tracking tasks with control systems of second and higher order. The less skilled trainees tend to drop out during training. This leaves pilots as a selected and highly trained group.

An advantage of using pilots is that they usually require less practice than ordinary people in order to master a tracking task of high order. But there may also be a disadvantage. Pilots tend to be best at the kinds of task which they are used to. If pilots perform one condition better than another, it is not possible to conclude that ordinary people will do so too. The biases introduced by transfer of training are discussed in Chapter 2.

In evaluating the results of a tracking experiment, it is important to know whether pilots or ordinary people serve in it. In this book it is always stated where pilots are used, if the information is available.

Chapter

2

The design and evaluation of experiments

Summary

A balanced treatment design can produce asymmetrical transfer and range effects which bias the results. If less than 6 people are used in an experiment, it is not possible to tell how representative the results are likely to be. A typical experiment is described. What appear to be negligible differences between conditions can increase greatly in size when a man is working under difficulties.

Controlling for transfer

In comparing 2 conditions **A** and **B**, the same people may perform both. Whichever condition is performed second may benefit from practice in the condition performed first. This is referred to as positive transfer.

Transfer need not be positive. The condition performed second may be at a disadvantage as a result of the condition performed first. People may learn strategies in the first condition. The strategies are carried

Table 2.1
A balanced treatment design

	Condition on:	
	Trial 1	Trial 2
Group 1	A	B
Group 2	B	A

over to the second condition, where they are inappropriate. This is called negative transfer.

A common way of controlling for practice is for half the people to perform condition **A** before condition **B**, while the other half perform the two conditions in the reverse order. The experimental design is illustrated in Table 2.1. Both conditions are performed first by half the people and second by the other half.

The experimental design is adequate only if transfer is symmetrical. The effect on **B** of performing **A** first must be equal to the effect on **A** of performing **B** first. Probably the two effects are never exactly equal, except by chance. In tracking experiments, the effects are often reliably different. Sometimes **A** benefits **B**, while **B** has no effect upon **A**. In other cases **A** benefits **B** while **A** is at a disadvantage after **B**.

Asymmetrical transfer

If transfer between the 2 conditions is asymmetrical, only the results of the first trial can be used. It is not valid to combine the scores from the 2 trials. This is illustrated in Figure 2.1. Gordon (1959) compares tracking with a pursuit or true motion display and with a compensatory or relative motion display. Except for the difference in the display, the 2 tasks are identical. In the figure, the average error with the pursuit display is represented by the filled points. The unfilled points represent the average error with the compensatory display.

Each function represents the performance of a separate group of 10 sailors. The group indicated by the filled circles practices throughout the experiment with the pursuit display. The group indicated by the unfilled squares practices throughout with the compensatory display. The pursuit display gives reliably the smaller average error. These 2 groups are the reference groups for the asymmetrical transfer.

The experimental design of Table 2.1 is illustrated by the 2 remaining groups. The group indicated by the triangles practices with the pursuit display for the first 9 trials, and then switches to the compensatory

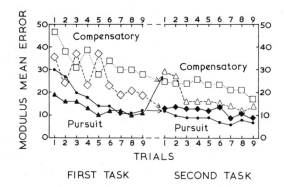

Figure 2.1. Asymmetrical transfer between pursuit and compensatory tracking.
Tracking is in 2 dimensions. The track is an irregular sine wave with an average of 15 reversals in direction per min. The displacements in the horizontal dimension lag about 45 sec behind the displacements in the vertical dimension. The man uses the 2 cranks illustrated on the left of Figure 11.16, and the 2 dimensional display in the center. Each crank controls the position of the display marker in one dimension. (Results from Gordon, 1959.)

display. The group indicated by the diamonds has the 2 conditions in the reverse order. For the first 9 trials the differences between the 2 groups are about as large as the differences between the groups represented by the circles and squares. But for most of the second 9 trials the differences between the triangles and diamonds are small. Switching displays reduces the sizes of the differences between the displays.

On the middle 3 trials of the second task, the unfilled triangles lie reliably below the unfilled squares. This means that practice with the pursuit display benefits subsequent performance with the compensatory display more than does practice throughout with the compensatory display. The filled diamonds lie above the filled circles, although here the difference is not reliable. This is one way asymmetrical transfer (Poulton and Freeman, 1966).

The differences illustrated on the left side of Figure 2.1 reflect the true differences between the 2 displays. So do the differences on the right side of the figure between the circles and the squares. But the differences on the right between the filled diamonds and the unfilled triangles do not reflect the true differences. The true differences are reduced by the asymmetrical transfer.

For the groups indicated by the diamonds and by the triangles, it is not valid to combine the results of the 2 halves of the experiment. If the results of the 2 halves are combined, they will unfairly favor the compensatory display at the expense of the pursuit display. Asymmetrical transfer can actually change the direction of a difference (Poulton, 1969).

To avoid the risk of asymmetrical transfer, it is necessary to use separate groups of people for each experimental condition. This is equivalent to using the scores only from trial 1 in the experimental design of Table 2.1.

Range effects with multiple comparisons

An engineer may have a number of design variables which he wishes to optimize. Each variable may have several values which ought to be included in the experiment. Here the experimenter may be tempted to choose a balanced treatment or latin square design. The same people receive all the conditions in different orders. The orders are balanced so that each experimental condition is performed an equal number of times in each serial position.

An advantage of a balanced treatment design is that it does not need a lot of people. If the differences between the experimental conditions are large, 6 people may be enough. Also it is possible to remove from the analysis the differences in the average levels of performance of the different people.

The major disadvantage of a balanced treatment design is that there may be asymmetrical transfer. There is no known way of finding out whether this is the case, except by repeating the experiment with separate groups of people. Asymmetrical transfer influences to an unknown extent the sizes of the differences between the experimental conditions. It means that the results apply for certain only to people who have been trained on all the conditions included in the experiment. The results cannot be generalized to people who have not been trained in this particular way.

Where a number of values of a variable are included in the experiment, asymmetrical transfer usually favors the values in the middle of the range (Poulton, 1973). Figure 2.2 (Slack, 1953b) illustrates a range effect for sizes of step. Steps of 10 different sizes are presented in an irregular order in different directions at fixed intervals of time. The fixed time interval between the steps within a series is changed after 12 series. The figure shows the average error of overshooting or undershooting, taking account of the sign. The error is for the first response to each step, before it is corrected. The average error is smallest for steps of intermediate size. Small steps are overshot on average, while large steps are undershot.

It is not valid to conclude from the results in Figure 2.2 that first responses to steps of about 1 in always have the smallest average error.

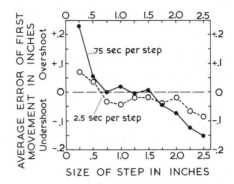

Figure 2.2. A range effect for 10 sizes of step.
The experimental arrangement is similar to the one illustrated in Figure 1.2. A horizontal paper tape moves at a constant speed of 3.5 in per sec. A track containing steps is drawn on the paper tape with a felt tip pen. The paper tape is completely covered by a sheet of aluminum except for a slit 3.5 in long and .25 in wide which lies across the paper tape. The undergraduate has to keep the tip of the pen on the track in the slit.

The 10 sizes of step are always presented in the same irregular order, but the directions vary from series to series. The time interval between steps is fixed at .75, 1, 1.5, 2 and 2.5 sec in different conditions. Only the conditions with the shortest and longest time intervals are shown in the figure. The 10 undergraduates receive the 5 conditions in an irregular order. There are 12 series under each condition before proceeding to the next condition. The results of the last 10 series under each condition are shown in the figure. Unfortunately statistical tests do not appear to have been carried out to determine how repeatable the results are likely to be. (After Slack, 1953b, Figure 2.)

The range effect is less marked at the slow speed represented by the unfilled points. This is because at the slow speed the man is able to make use of his knowledge of the order of sizes of step. The order of sizes is always the same, and can be learnt, even though the direction of the steps varies from trial to trial. At the fast speed, the man has less time to prepare himself for any except the average size of step. As a result, he shows a more characteristic range effect.

They have the smallest error in the figure only because they happen to lie near the middle of the range of sizes of step chosen by the experimenter. If the experimenter chooses a different range of sizes of step, the step with the smallest average error will lie near the middle of the new range.

In some experiments everyone practices all the conditions before the experiment starts. If so, asymmetrical transfer can produce its bias during the practice, before the experimenter starts to collect his experimental results. Once the transfer occurs, the results are likely to remain biased by the transfer throughout the experiment. There may then be no suggestion in the results that they are biased by transfer.

For tracking experiments in which transfer is likely to be asymmetrical, the author of this book strongly recommends separate groups. Complex multifactorial designs using the same people are almost certain to introduce biases of unknown sizes and directions.

The biases can perhaps be reduced by using a number of separate groups, each of which receives a separate limited number of experimental conditions. The conditions performed by a group should be those which are likely to produce the smallest amount of asymmetrical transfer. The top part of Table 2.2 lists combinations of conditions which should not

Table 2.2
How to avoid asymmetrical transfer and range effects

A. Combinations of conditions which should not be given to the same group of people	Where the conditions are dealt with
Tracks	
Step tracks with different sizes of step	Figure 2.2, Figure 6.5
Step tracks with different time intervals between steps	Chapter 6.
Step tracks with different directions of step	Table 6.1
Ramp tracks with different lengths of ramp	Chapter 7, last section
Ramp tracks of different orders	Figure 7.6
Displays	
Pursuit and compensatory displays	Figure 2.1, Figure 9.6
Quickened and unquickened displays	Figure 10.5
Displays with different durations of preview	Chapter 10, last section
Displays with different magnifications	Figure 11.2
Control systems	
Control systems of different orders	Figure 16.4, Figure 16.5
Control systems with different aiding ratios	Figure 16.7
Control systems with continuous and stepped inputs	Table 17.2
Control systems with different kinds of cross coupling	Chapter 17, one from last section
Control systems with different directional relationships between control and display movements	Chapter 17, last section

B. Combinations of conditions which can perhaps be given to the same group of people	Where the conditions are dealt with
Tracks	
Sine wave tracks of different amplitudes	Chapter 8, first section
Control systems	
Control systems with different gains	Chapter 17, first section

be given to the same group of people, if asymmetrical transfer and range effects are to be avoided. The list is probably not complete. Other combinations may have to be added.

The bottom part of the table indicates the changes which are probably the easiest to adapt to, although they do produce asymmetrical transfer. Changes in track frequency (Chapter 8) are perhaps the next easiest to adapt to, provided the man has a pursuit display which allows him to see the changes directly. But there is always a risk of asymmetrical transfer when a group performs more than one condition.

The extent of the bias can be estimated by adding a second stage to the investigation. The 2 or 3 key combinations of values of the experimental conditions are checked separately. Each combination is given to a fresh group of people.

The results of these separate groups are not biased by the original comprehensive experimental design. If the order of the experimental conditions is found to be the same in both stages of the investigation, then the bias introduced by the original comprehensive experimental design cannot be the major determinant of the results. The results of the original experiment can therefore be accepted with reservations (see Poulton, 1973).

It can be argued that experiments with biased results should not be mentioned. This would leave more space for the remaining experiments. The suggestion is not followed here, because the published results of biased experiments are often accepted by readers at their face value. To prevent this, it is necessary to point out the source of the bias, and to show how the bias is responsible for the results.

There are not a great many tracking experiments which are certainly unbiased. If the book were restricted to experiments which are certainly unbiased, a number of topics could not be mentioned. In these areas all the experiments possibly contain bias.

The minimum number of people

Experimenters often assume that their results apply to people whom they do not test. To be reasonably sure that experimental results can be generalized to other people, it is usually necessary to test a minimum of 6 people.

An experimenter may use only 1 person in his experiment. In order to obtain sufficient results for statistical tests, he may compare 2 conditions on each of 6 days. If 1 of the 2 conditions is consistently better than the other condition on each of the 6 days, the difference is reliable statistically. This is a perfectly legitimate use of statistics. The difficulty is that one cannot be sure that another person would give a similar result. In order to be able to generalize from the people used in an experiment to the people who could be used but are not used, it is necessary to use more than 1 person.

An experimenter may give 2 conditions to 2 or 3 people. If the difference between the 2 conditions is sufficiently large, the difference may be reliable on a parametric statistical test. The result can be generalized to the population from which the 2 or 3 people are drawn, but only if the performance measured in the experiment has a Gaussian or normal distribution in the population. This is because parametric statistical tests assume that the scores have a Gaussian distribution. The author of this book believes that it is not a reasonable assumption to make. Many distributions are not Gaussian.

Nonparametric statistical tests (Siegel, 1956) are preferable to parametric statistical tests, because they do not assume a particular shape of distribution of scores. Nonparametric tests assume only that, whatever the shape of the distribution, it does not change from one condition or person to another. To give a reliable difference, nonparametric tests require a minimum of 6 people. So 6 people is the smallest number to use in order to be able to generalize the results with reasonable certainty. More than 6 people are necessary if 1 or 2 people perform very differently from the rest.

Unfortunately a large number of the experiments on tracking use less than 6 people. If this book were restricted to experiments on 6 or more people, a number of topics could not be discussed. In these areas all the published experiments use less than 6 people. The experiments are included, provided they use more than 1 person. But it is stated that too few people are used for it to be possible to tell how repeatable the results are likely to be with other people.

A typical experiment

Each student or untrained enlisted man sits at a comfortable distance from the display, with his eyes about 30 in away. The display is presented on the face of a cathode ray tube (CRT) with a diameter of about 5 in. Tracking is in 1 dimension. The man uses a lever or joystick which is spring centered. Soon after World War II the controls were usually about 15 in long. Today they are more likely to be about 4 in long. The control rotates about $\pm 45°$ from its central position. When the control is moved in one direction, the display marker moves a corresponding distance in the same direction.

Trials last about 1 min. Figure 2.3 shows that if trials last too long,

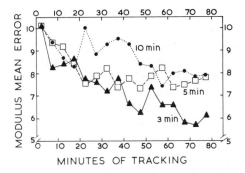

Figure 2.3.   Learning curves for trials of different durations.
The 3 groups of enlisted men track for a total of about 20 min on each of 4 days. The 6 men represented by circles have 2 trials daily each lasting 10 min, separated by a rest of 4 min. The 6 men represented by squares have 4 trials daily each lasting 5 min, separated by rests of 2 min. The 12 men represented by triangles have 7 trials daily each lasting 3 min, separated by rests of 1 min. The 3 functions have been adjusted so that they all start from the same point during the first 5 min. At the end of 80 min the group with 3 min trials has improved reliably more than the group with 5 min trials.
The display is compensatory. The track contains 2 fairly rapid U shaped out and back excursions, one to each side. The excursions last about 5 sec each. They are separated by an interval of about 10 sec. The track repeats every 30 sec. In other respects the experiment resembles the typical experiment described in the text. (After Shackel, 1954, Figure 9.)

the man does not improve so rapidly. The trials are separated by short rest periods during which the man receives some idea of how well he is tracking. The experimental conditions are presented to different men using a balanced treatment design. This controls for the order of presentation, but not for asymmetrical transfer. Before the experiment each man practices all the experimental conditions.

Experiments which are like this typical experiment will not be outlined in detail in the text. Instead emphasis will be placed upon the deviations from the typical experiment.

Evaluation of experimental results

An experiment like that of Figure 2.1 may show that people are likely to perform better with a pursuit display than with a compensatory display. The result may then be evaluated by an engineer who is attempting to design the most efficient combination of a man and a machine. He may be willing to accept the worse human performance with the compensatory display for the sake of other advantages. He may predict that the overall system will function more efficiently, even though the man himself cannot work so efficiently.

This is unwise. A man may have to work in difficult circumstances (Poulton, 1970). A difference between 2 conditions which is reliable under normal circumstances, may increase enormously when working under difficulties. Even a small difference between 2 experimental conditions which is hardly noticeable in normal circumstances, may become unacceptably large in difficult circumstances.

An example is given by Garvey and Taylor (1959, Experiment 3). They compare a position control system with an acceleration control system, using separate groups of 8 enlisted men. The acceleration control system gives less accurate tracking early in practice, and takes longer to learn. But eventually tracking is about as accurate as with the position control system. The 2 control systems are then compared when the men are subjected to 7 different difficulties, or task induced stresses as Garvey and Taylor call them. Under each difficulty, performance with the acceleration control system deteriorates reliably more than performance with the position control system.

Four of the difficulties produce large differences between the 2 control systems. One of the 4 difficulties involves a change in the relationship between control movements and display movements. The man has to move the control to the right in order to make the error marker move to the left. Other difficulties involve tracking with both hands simultaneously, and tracking in 2 dimensions simultaneously. The fourth difficulty involves having to report the range and bearing of targets on a visual display, which is placed directly above the tracking display. When the man's job is made more difficult in any of these 4 ways, performance with the acceleration control system suffers over twice as much as performance with the position control system.

It can be argued (Poulton, 1966, pages 187–188) that it is quite unrealistic for a design engineer to accept a result which is not reliable statistically as indicating no difference, unless the conditions are compared under difficulties. For the design engineer cannot easily predict the difficulties under which people will have to operate his equipment. A design which is as good as any under normal circumstances, may be quite unacceptable when people have to operate the equipment under difficulties.

Recommended experimental design and evaluation

Separate group designs should be used. If not enough groups are available, each group may have to be given a separate limited number of experimental conditions. The conditions allocated to a group should be those which are known to produce the least asymmetrical transfer.

At least 6 people should be used in an experiment.

Test trials should be short. They should be separated by adequate rest periods, during which the man is told how well he is doing.

Design engineers should use the condition which is easier for the man, even if the difference found in the laboratory is small under ordinary conditions.

Chapter

3

Recommended methods
of scoring

Summary

Overshoots and undershoots at reversals of the track can be measured directly. So can the errors in time at various positions on the track. Frequency analyses of the amplitude and phase of the response function are illustrated in Figures 3.3 and 3.4.

Overall measures of error are illustrated in Figure 3.6 and Table 3.1 The root mean squared (RMS) error may correlate almost perfectly with the modulus mean error. An overall pattern analysis can be made by human judges.

Errors in position at reversals

This chapter and the next are concerned principally with the tracking of sine waves, because performance with sine waves has been scored in more ways than has performance with steps or ramps. But most of the methods can be used also for step and ramp tracks.

MALASPINA UNIVERSITY-COLLEGE LIBRARY

Figure 3.1 illustrates a section of paper record obtained from tracking. A record of this kind is obtained directly from an experimental arrangement like that illustrated in Figure 1.2.

A similar record can be obtained if the man tracks with an electronic display like that illustrated in Figure 1.1. A 2 channel oscillographic recorder is needed. The voltage representing the track is fed into one channel of the recorder. The voltage representing the output of the man's control system is fed into the other channel. The 2 channels of the recorder need to be calibrated together to ensure that both respond identically to changes in voltage. It is also necessary to know the point on one chart which corresponds to a point on the other chart representing the same time and voltage. It is then possible to superimpose the 2 charts. They can be viewed by transmitted light.

In Figure 3.1 the tracking error is represented by the distance between the track and the response. At some reversals of the track the man goes too far and overshoots. At other reversals the man does not go far enough and undershoots. These errors are clearly errors of positioning. Their sizes are indicated by the heights of the shaded areas in the figure.

Some of the error in positioning at reversals can be caused by the man's response having a bias in one direction or the other. His response record in Figure 3.1 may tend to lie a little below the track record. He then tends to undershoot the reversals like that marked R which point upward. He tends to overshoot reversals which point downward. By making measurements at a number of reversals, it is possible to calculate the average constant error in this up and down dimension. It is also possible to calculate a standard deviation for errors in the up and down dimension. The standard deviation represents the man's variability in this dimension at the reversals.

Overshooting and undershooting

A usually more relevant source of positioning error at reversals is the tendency to overshoot or undershoot. An average constant error of overshooting or undershooting can be calculated. It is also possible to calculate a standard deviation for errors in the overshoot and undershoot dimension (Carriero, 1964).

A man often tends to undershoot reversals of the track when they are located far out on either side. This is because when the track approaches the edge of the display, it is bound to return toward the center. The man may be tempted to anticipate its return. The man may overshoot reversals when they occur near the average position of the track in the center of the display. This is because when the track approaches the center of the display, it usually continues toward the other side. The man does not expect it to stop near the center and reverse direction.

This range effect can be checked from a record like that in Figure 3.1. Reversals can be classified as falling for example between +.5 and —.5 in on the scale of the ordinate, or falling further from the center. The average degree of overshooting of reversals in the inner and outer zones can be compared.

It may be possible to describe the man's behavior equally well by saying that when the distance on the display between 2 reversals is large, he tends to undershoot. When the distance between 2 reversals is small, he tends to overshoot. The man learns the average distance between reversals, and tracks on the assumption that the distance will be about average.

This behavior also can be checked from a record like that in Figure 3.1. The average distance between reversals can be determined. Reversals can then be classified as further than average from the previous reversal, or less far than average. The average degree of overshooting or under-shooting can be compared for reversals of the 2 kinds.

In general a reversal which is far from the previous reversal is likely to be fairly near to the edge of the display. While a reversal which is close to the previous reversal is likely to be somewhere near the

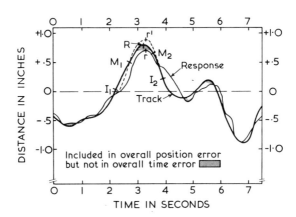

Figure 3.1. A paper record of tracking with preview.
The experimental arrangement is illustrated in Figure 1.2. The preview is 2.5 sec. I_1 and I_2 indicate points of inflection on the track. **R** indicates where the track reverses direction. **r** indicates where the man's pen reverses direction. **r'** on the broken line indicates where the man's pen may reverse direction if he overshoots the bend. M_1 and M_2 are points on the track half way in time between **R**, and I_1 and I_2 respectively. (After Poulton, 1962.)

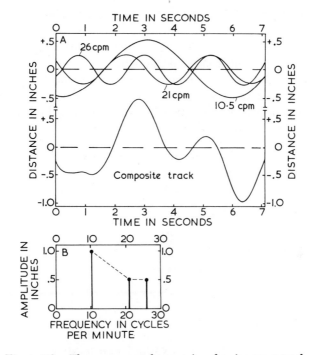

Figure 3.2. The component frequencies of a sine wave track.
The sum of the heights of the 3 sine waves at the top, taking account of the signs, produces the composite track below. The frequency analysis is shown at the bottom. Here the 3 points representing the 3 frequencies are connected by broken lines, to match Figures 3.3 and 3.4. This is not strictly correct, because there are no intermediate frequencies in Figure 3.2.

center of the display. If the man's tracking corresponds to one of the 2 descriptions, it is likely to correspond also to the other description.

It is possible to determine which description best fits the man's tracking behavior by looking for reversals which are fairly close to the previous reversal, but are located toward the edge of the display. The other key reversals are those which are further than average from the previous reversal, but are located somewhere near the center of the display. The average degree of overshooting or undershooting at these 2 key kinds of reversal should indicate which is the better description of the man's tracking behavior.

Response amplitude analyzed by frequency

Any continuous function like the track or the response in Figure 3.1 can be analyzed by frequency. Figure 3.2A shows how the track of Figure 3.1 is composed of 3 sine waves. The 2 smaller sine waves have

frequencies of 26 and 21 cycles per min (cpm). The third sine wave
has twice the amplitude of the other 2, and a frequency of 10.5 cpm.
The composite track below is constructed by summing the heights of
the 3 sine waves, taking account of the signs.

Figure 3.2B illustrates a frequency analysis of the track. Each point
indicates the amplitude of one of the 3 frequencies. The response in
Figure 3.1 contains these 3 frequencies, and also some higher frequencies
which correspond to the wobbles in the response.

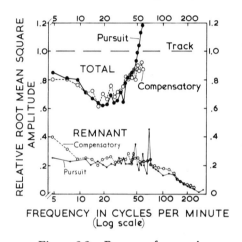

Figure 3.3.   Response frequencies.

The larger points represent the relative amplitude of the total response at the
track frequencies. The smaller points labeled remnant represent the frequencies
in the response which do not correlate with the track. A logarithmic scale is used
on the abscissa in order to include frequencies up to 300 cpm without crowding
up the low frequencies. This is a little misleading when, as here, there is equal
energy per cycle. Over half the energy in the remnant is in fact contributed by
frequencies above the top track frequency at 58 cpm.

The figure should not be taken to indicate that the man responds separately
to each frequency. This is not so. The figure illustrates simply the technique of
analysing the man's response by frequency.

The man looks at the vertical face of a CRT. He moves a stylus over the
horizontal face of another CRT which is let flush into the top of a desk. Movements
of the stylus in a left and right direction move a circle of light in the same
direction across the display. The target is a spot of light. The electronic linkage
between the stylus and the display is called a pip trapper.

The track which supplies the results in the figure extends up to 57.5 cpm.
It contains 48 frequencies of about equal amplitude, spaced at equal intervals
of 1.2 cpm. Tracks with lower and higher top frequencies are also included in
the experiment. All the pursuit conditions are completed before any of the compensatory conditions are started. Unfortunately the results are from only 3 men. Thus
it is not possible to tell how representative they are likely to be. (Results from
Elkind, 1956, Figures 4-8a and d, and 4-10a and d.)

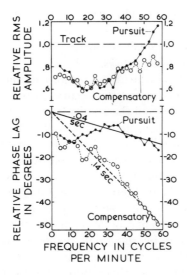

Figure 3.4.   Closed loop transfer functions.

The upper part of the figure is a rather different way of presenting the results of Figure 3.3. It shows only the part of the response which correlates with the track. When the remnant is included, the functions become the top functions of Figure 3.3. The heights of the functions are hardly affected, because the remnant is small, and the amplitudes are measured in RMS units. RMS amplitudes are combined by squaring them and taking the square root. A remnant with a small RMS amplitude hardly affects the combined amplitude, because its value when squared is so small.

The lower part of the figure shows the average difference in phase between the response and the track. The 2 sloping lines represent constant time lags. (After Elkind, 1956, Figures 4-8a and b, and 4-10a and b.)

A frequency analysis usually requires a computer, and a sample of tracking lasting between 1 and 4 min. The track and response are recorded on magnetic tape, instead of on the paper tape of Figure 3.1. The frequencies are divided into frequency bands by means of narrow bandpass filters. In Figure 3.3 (Elkind, 1956) a bandwidth of 1.2 cpm. has been used. The top of the figure shows the total amplitude of the response at each track frequency. The amplitude is given in root mean square (RMS) units, which are discussed later in the chapter. The RMS amplitude at each frequency is plotted relative to the RMS amplitude of the track at this frequency, which is called 1.0.

The small points at the bottom of the figure, labeled remnant, show the part of the man's response which does not correlate with the track. Above the top track frequency of 58 cpm all the energy in the man's response is in the remnant. The remnant tends to be large when the man uses the nonlinear strategies discussed at the end of Chapter 8. The remnant tends to be small when the man successfully predicts the track and preprograms his responses.

Figure 3.3 does not indicate the positions of the reversals at which most overshooting or undershooting occurs. In order to analyze by frequency, it is necessary to pool the results from a relatively large number of consecutive reversals. The figure shows only the pooled results.

It is not even easy to tell from a plot of this kind whether on average the man overshoots or undershoots. The man will overshoot more often than he undershoots if the total energy in his response exceeds the total energy in the track. In Figure 3.3 the total energy in the response is obtained by calculating the energy represented by the large points up to the top track frequency of 58 cpm. To this must be added the total energy represented by the small points at frequencies above 58 cpm. If the summed energy in the response exceeds the total energy in the track, the man must overshoot more often than he undershoots.

If the summed energy in the response is a little less than the total energy in the track, the man may still overshoot more often than he undershoots. This is because the response contains frequencies above the top track frequency. Any high frequency response peak which crosses the track near a reversal counts as an overshoot. Thus the man may tend to overshoot more often than he undershoots, although on average the response stays closer to the center of the display than the track does.

Errors in time

In Figure 3.1 errors in time are measured horizontally. Usually the thin line which represents the man's response lies to the right of the thick line which represents the track. This indicates that the man tends to lag behind the track.

The time error at reversals is measured by comparing the time at which the track reverses direction with the time at which the man reverses direction. Fortunately both points can usually be specified unambiguously. If the man pauses at a reversal before returning, it is possible to take the average of his time of arrival and time of departure.

Between reversals it is not usually possible to determine which point on the response function corresponds to a particular point on the track. The points of inflection of the track can often be specified reasonably easily, for example I_1 and I_2 in Figure 3.1. But a wiggly response function may supply a number of corresponding points of inflection to choose from. This is because it contains higher frequencies than the track does.

It is not possible to decide which point of inflection in the response function corresponds to the point of inflection of the track.

Between reversals the errors in time at points on the track can be assessed only by measuring the horizontal distance between the track and the response function. The measure reflects 2 separate sources of error in the man's tracking. The man may be early or late. On the other hand the man may be on time, but he may have positioned himself incorrectly. If he has gone too far, he may be early. If he has not gone far enough, by the time he passes the correct position he will be late. Figure 3.5 illustrates the average time error measured at a number of points corresponding to I_1, M_1, R, M_2, and I_2 in Figure 3.1.

Suppose the man undershoots at a reversal. There is then no response

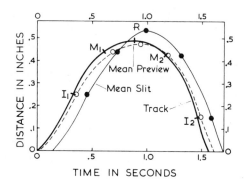

Figure 3.5.   Average response lags.

The thick line represents a theoretical loop of track like that illustrated in the center of Figure 3.1. The frequencies in the track are illustrated in Figure 3.2. The points represent the average of 10 measurements taken from each of the same 12 young enlisted men. The curves have been fitted to the points by eye.

The unfilled points and broken line are for tracking with a preview of 2.5 sec. The man tends to slow up more than the track before the reversal labeled **R**. He falls further behind in time, and tends to undershoot the reversal. He lags in time twice as far behind the track at the reversal as he does at the points of inflection labeled I_1 and I_2. The difference is reliable statistically. Approaching reversals more slowly than departing from them, is characteristic of aiming at targets which can be seen ahead (see Figure 5.5).

The filled points and unbroken line are for normal pursuit tracking without preview. The almost constant time lag of about .12 sec indicates that the man does not predict the track ahead for as long a time as he could. This is presumably due to the balanced treatment experimental design. With a preview the man does not need to predict. When the preview is removed, he tends to carry on in rather the same way without predicting much. Range effects with different durations of preview are discussed in the last section of Chapter 10. (Results from Poulton, 1962, Table 1.)

function to use in measuring the time error on either side of the reversal. When the man overshoots at a reversal, there is no corresponding track against which his time error can be measured. The difficulty is illustrated by the shaded areas in Figure 3.1. They are bounded on each side either by the track or by the response function, but not by both track and response function. Sections of record like these have to be omitted in measuring the average time error between reversals.

Errors in phase

The average errors of timing can be investigated by frequency. Both the man's response function and the track are passed through a narrow bandpass filter. With a filter setting of 15 cpm, the filtered response and track may look much like those at the top of Figure 11.4. The amplitude of the filtered response at each point in time is then compared with the amplitude of the filtered track, and the size of the crosscorrelation is calculated. The crosscorrelation can be increased in size by advancing the response, because the response tends to lag in time behind the track. The filtered response is advanced perhaps .01 sec, and again correlated with the filtered track. The filtered response is then advanced another .01 sec, and the process is repeated.

The crosscorrelation will be largest when the filtered response is advanced in time so that the average time lag is zero. If the filtered response is advanced in time further than this, the crosscorrelation will become smaller again, because the advanced response will be on average too far ahead of the track. The man's average time lag at the frequency of the bandpass filter is represented by the time which the filtered response has to be advanced in order to give the maximum crosscorrelation. The average time lag is converted to an average phase lag. The whole procedure is repeated for a number of selected bands of frequency.

The phase lags at various frequencies are illustrated in the lower part of Figure 3.4 (Elkind, 1956). The upper part of the figure illustrates the relative RMS amplitude of the response to which the phase lags apply. The whole figure is called a closed loop transfer function. The remaining amplitudes of response, which do not correlate with the track, form the remnant illustrated at the bottom of Figure 3.3.

The phase lags on the extreme left of Figure 3.4 may not represent the true values. Frequency analyses are likely to be inaccurate at low frequencies, because a sample of tracking lasting between 1 and 4 min contains so few cycles of low frequency. L. W. Taylor (1970, Figure 1) gives 3 independent frequency analyses of the same experimental results. At a frequency of 4 cpm one frequency analysis shows a small lead in phase. A repeat analysis shows a lag in phase of 140°. Both the functions in the lower part of Figure 3.4 have to start at the point representing zero phase lag at zero frequency. But it is not possible to be sure exactly how they get there.

The average error in phase can be measured only for frequency bands which are represented in the track. The average phase angle of the band of frequencies in the man's response has to be compared with a standard phase of the same frequency. If the track does not contain the particular frequencies, no standard is available. The track of Figure 3.4 contains frequencies only up to 58 cpm. The phase angle of response frequencies higher than this cannot be measured.

Overall measures of error

An experimenter may not wish for 2 separate measures of error, one for amplitude and one for time. He may want a single measure which represents the overall efficiency of performance. In Figure 3.1 the error is the area between the track and the response function. It is measured most easily by drawing a series of vertical lines between the 2 curves at fixed intervals of time, and calculating their average height, as in Figure 3.6.

With an electronic tracking apparatus, it is possible to integrate automatically the difference in voltage between the track and the response. If the display is linear, the integrated voltage is proportional to the average distance between the 2 display markers. This is the vertical distance in Figures 3.1 and 3.6 between the track and the response. The automatic scorer may or may not switch the sign of the error each time the response crosses the track. Switching eliminates the sign of the error.

On the left side of Figure 3.6 the sign of the error has been counted, as in conventional statistical calculations. The constant position error, or average error, corresponds to the mean in statistics. In tracking, it indicates only the extent to which the response is on average above or below the track. With tracks which vary in direction, it is usually of little interest. This is because when the constant position error is integrated over a period of time, the errors with a positive sign tend to cancel the errors with a negative sign.

The other conventional statistical measure on the left of Figure 3.6 is the standard deviation of the error. In the figure and in Table 3.1, the standard deviation is computed by subtracting the constant position error from each individual error value before squaring. There is a different and usually quicker method of computing the standard deviation,

which is described in textbooks of statistics. It is this variable error
which best indicates how well the man is performing. Most of the area
between the 2 functions in Figure 3.1 represents variable error in
position. Even constant time lags produce variable errors in the position
dimension.

The right side of Figure 3.6 shows the 2 corresponding overall measures which are traditionally used in tracking. Here the sign of the
error is neglected. The average error with the sign neglected is called
the modulus mean error, or average absolute error. It represents mainly
the variable error, although it usually includes a small constant position
error.

The root mean squared error, or root mean square error without the
d at the end of squared, is usually abbreviated to RMS error. It is
illustrated at the bottom on the right of the figure. It is computed by
squaring the uncorrected error values. The methods of calculating the
4 overall measures of error are shown in the upper part of Table 3.1,
using numbers.

Unfortunately it is the relatively uninformative constant position error
which is most compatible with parametric statistical tests. This is because
the amplitudes of the error, counting the signs, are most likely to have
the approximately Gaussian or normal distribution (Fitts, Bennett &
Bahrick, 1956, Figure 6) which parametric stasistical tests require.

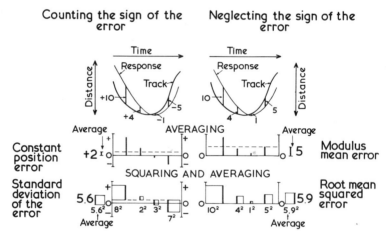

Figure 3.6.   Overall measures of error.

Time is represented horizontally from left to right. The vertical error between
the response and the track is measured 4 times, at intervals of .25 sec. On the
left the errors are averaged taking account of their signs. The average is subtracted
from each value before squaring. On the right the errors are averaged without
taking account of their signs. They are squared as they stand. The calculations
are given at the top of Table 3.1.

Table 3.1
Overall measures of error

Measure of error	Calculation
Constant position error (average error)	$\dfrac{10 + 4 - 1 - 5}{4} = \dfrac{8}{4} = 2$
Modulus mean error (average absolute error)	$\dfrac{10 + 4 + 1 + 5}{4} = \dfrac{20}{4} = 5$
Root mean squared (RMS) error	$\sqrt{\dfrac{10^2 + 4^2 + 1^2 + 5^2}{4}} = \sqrt{\dfrac{142}{4}} = \sqrt{35.5} = 5.9$
Standard deviation of the error	$\sqrt{\dfrac{(10 - 2)^2 + (4 - 2)^2 + (-1 - 2)^2 + (-5 - 2)^2}{4}}$
	$= \sqrt{\dfrac{8^2 + 2^2 + 3^2 + 7^2}{4}} = \sqrt{\dfrac{126}{4}} = \sqrt{31.5} = 5.6$

Measure of error	Coefficient of correlation*		
	CE	RMS	SD
Constant position error (CE)		+.48	+.50
Root mean squared error (RMS)			+.82
Standard deviation of the error (SD)			

* Results from Fitts and colleagues (1956, Table 1), given also by Bahrick and Noble (1966, Table 16–3).

The modulus errors have only half the Gaussian distribution, since they have no negative values. The distribution is approximately J shaped. The distribution of means is less skewed than the distribution of modulus errors, but it is certainly not Gaussian. Modulus mean errors are therefore not as compatible with parametric statistical tests as constant position errors are.

Sometimes the mean squared error is used directly, without taking the square root. Mean squared errors are less compatible with parametric statistical tests than modulus mean errors are, because squaring the errors increases the length of the tail of the J shaped distribution.

Taking the square root of the mean squared errors gives the RMS errors. The square root transformation reduces the skewing of the means, and makes the distribution more Gaussian. The standard deviation of the error is similar to the RMS error in this respect. The order of compatibility with parametric statistical tests is therefore: 1. constant position error, 2. RMS error and standard deviation of the error, 3. modulus mean error, and 4. mean squared error.

Correlations between overall measures of error

The constant position error and the standard deviation of the error are statistically independent measures. Whereas the modulus mean error and the RMS error are related to each other, and also to both the independent measures.

The 2 statistically independent measures of error can be correlated in the results of a group of trackers. The lower part of Table 3.1 (Fitts & colleagues, 1956; Bahrick and Noble, 1966) is based upon the results from a group of 100 students. The constant position error and the standard deviation of the error correlate $+.50$. This is because poor trackers tend to have a large constant position error and also a large variable error. While good trackers tend to have a small constant position error and a small variable error.

The correlation between the related measures constant position error and RMS error is $+.48$. If anything, this is slightly smaller than the correlation between the 2 statistically independent measures. Thus the statistical relationship between 2 measures of error does not necessarily indicate the size of the correlation between them in a group of people.

The size of the correlation between the RMS error and the modulus mean error depends upon how the changes in the average size of the errors are related to the simultaneous changes in their variability. Conditions with larger errors may have the same shape of distribution of errors as conditions with smaller errors. For example, all the distributions could be Gaussian or normal. If so, the correlation will be $+1.0$. This is because the individual errors found in each condition are proportional to the individual errors found in the other conditions.

The point can be illustrated using the hypothetical errors in the upper part of Table 3.1. If all the errors are multiplied by a constant k, the modulus mean error becomes $5k$, and the RMS error becomes $5.9k$. As k is given different values, the 2 measures increase or decrease in the same proportion. They are therefore correlated $+1.0$.

A practical example comes from Obermayer, Swartz, and Muckler (1962, Table 3). These authors report the average RMS errors and average modulus mean errors (average absolute errors) for 18 separate experimental conditions. Each average represents 20 trials by 6 people. The correlation between the average RMS errors and the average modulus mean errors is $+.9996$. It is possible to calculate the average modulus mean errors fairly accurately from the average RMS errors by multiplying the RMS errors by $.77$.

If the RMS error and the modulus mean error are almost perfectly correlated, the RMS error should be used. This is because the average

RMS error can be calculated more precisely from a section of record than can the average modulus mean error. As a rule it takes 15% more tracking time to give as good an estimate of the modulus mean error as it does of the RMS error (Kelly, 1969a, Table 2).

The RMS error and the modulus mean error need not correlate so highly. The correlation decreases when people do not track well (Muckler, personal communication). The 2 measures then reflect rather different aspects of the error. The modulus mean error penalizes errors strictly according to their average size. The modulus mean of a pair of errors will be 5 whether both modulus errors are of size 5, or whether one error is of size 9 and the other error is of size 1. The RMS error penalizes a mixture of large and small errors more than a mixture of average sized errors. The RMS of a pair of errors will be 5 if both modulus errors are of size 5. But if the modulus errors are of size 9 and 1, the RMS error will be $\sqrt{\dfrac{9^2 + 1^2}{2}} = \sqrt{41}$ or 6.4.

An advantage of RMS errors is that they are easily combined. The overall RMS error of a system containing men and machines can be estimated by squaring and summing the component RMS errors and taking the square root of the total. The estimate is reasonably accurate provided the constant errors which are included in the RMS errors are small, and vary in direction from one part of the system to another.

But if the constant errors are large, and are always in the same direction, combining RMS errors underestimates the overall system error. This can happen if time errors are being measured, because errors in time are almost always lags. Constant lags of 5 in 2 consecutive parts of a system produce a total lag of 10. The modulus mean errors are 5 and 5, which sum to 10. The RMS errors of the 2 parts of the system are also 5 and 5. But squaring and summing the RMS errors and taking the square root gives an overall RMS error for the system of only $\sqrt{5^2 + 5^2} = \sqrt{50}$ or 7.1. This underestimates the overall lag in the system.

Relative errors

In this book RMS errors and modulus mean errors are expressed where possible relative to the error produced by the track when the man does not respond at all. The no response error is called 100. The errors are given as a percentage of this value.

There are advantages in using relative errors. Relative RMS errors and relative modulus mean errors are more comparable than are raw RMS errors and raw modulus mean errors. In the experiment by Obermayer and his colleagues (1962, Table 3) the average modulus mean errors are only .77 of the size of the average RMS errors. Using the relative RMS errors and relative modulus mean errors eliminates this difference.

Relative errors are also an advantage in comparing separate experiments with rather different track amplitudes. Here again relative errors are more comparable than are the raw errors.

Overall pattern analysis

When an experimenter believes that he has an adequate understanding of a man's performance, he may program a computer to mimic the man. Both the man and the computer are given the same tracking task to perform. If the computer model is good enough, it should not be possible to distinguish between the paper records of the 2 performances.

Stone (1961) suggests a simple way of testing this. Each of a number of judges is given a scrambled set of records like that in Figure 3.1, half of which come from the man and half from the computer model. He is told to sort the records into 2 equal piles, classing together the records which look most alike. If this method does not discriminate between the man and the computer model at better than the chance level, the computer model can be said to mimic the man adequately (Poulton, 1967a).

Recommendations on scoring

To study a man's strategies, it is necessary to measure his errors in position and time at particular points on the track.

A frequency analysis is required to show the amplitude and phase of the response at various frequencies.

RMS error should be used as the measure of the overall adequacy of tracking.

Sorting by judges can be used to compare the performance of a man and of a computer programed to mimic him.

Chapter

4

Not recommended methods of scoring

Summary

The high frequencies in the man's response are reflected in the number of reversals in direction, or changes in rate, of the response function over and above the number required to match the track.

Measures made on the error function reflect the interactions between the track and the man's responses. The phase relationships of the error depend upon both the phase and the amplitude of the response. Autocorrelating the error is a complicated procedure which produces little information.

There are nonlinear relationships between times on target with different sizes of target. Consistency can be measured without knowing the correct track. Subjective estimates of the difficulty of tracking are likely to be biased.

Overall estimates of high frequencies

A rough overall estimate of the high frequencies in the response can be made when the track and response are recorded simultaneously, as in Figure 3.1. Count the number of reversals, both for the response and for the track. The difference gives an indication of the extent to which the frequencies in the response are higher than the frequencies in the track. The difference per minute can be divided by 2 because a cycle includes 2 reversals. It is then called an excess frequency count (Poulton, 1963a, Table 4).

An excess frequency count can be made even when the response does not reverse direction more often than the track. In Figure 3.1 the response contains more changes in rate than the track does. If the voltage corresponding to the response function is differentiated and recorded on an oscillograph, the points of inflection of the response function will appear on the chart as reversals in direction. Counting the number of reversals on the chart corresponds to counting the number of points of inflection in Figure 3.1. An excess frequency count can be obtained in this way (Poulton, 1963a, Table 4).

An excess frequency count gives no indication of what the frequencies in the response are, nor of their amplitude. This information requires a frequency analysis like that in Figure 3.3. If a frequency analysis is available, an excess frequency count is unnecessary. But if the facilities for carrying out a frequency analysis are not available, a quick excess frequency count may be worth making.

Overall estimates of high frequencies in the error

Only the tracking error may be recorded, instead of the response and the track. Reversals of the error function are more difficult to interpret than reversals of the response function, because they depend upon both the response and the track. If the man does not respond at all, the reversals in the error function correspond to the reversals in the track. If the man responds perfectly, there are no reversals in the error function.

If the man responds less well, some reversals in the error function may correspond to loops of track which the man has not followed perfectly. Other reversals may have been inserted by the man by mistake. From a record of the error function alone, it is not easy to tell which are which. Shelly (1963) reports the number of reversals in the error functions of 2 practiced people, and also the number of inflections. The results are hard to interpret.

The frequency of crossing of zero error corresponds to the number of times that the response function crosses the track in Figure 3.1. Like the number of reversals of the error function, the number of zero error crossings reflects both the frequencies in the track, and the frequencies in the response function.

Wobbles of a particular amplitude in the track and in the response will produce zero error crossings only when the average error at the time is smaller than they are. Thus the number of zero error crossings depends partly upon the average size of the error. Practice usually reduces the average size of the error. After practice the frequency of zero error crossings should not be much smaller than the frequency of reversals of the error function.

The number of reversals of the track can be subtracted from the number of zero error crossings. The difference represents largely the high frequencies in the response. The difference per minute can be divided by 2 because a cycle crosses the zero twice. It is then called a wobble score (Poulton, 1963b).

After practice the wobble score derived from the error function correlates fairly highly with the excess frequency count made on the response function. This is because both represent the high frequencies in the response. For the 6 experimental conditions of Poulton (1963a) the tau coefficient of rank correlation ranges from +.60 to +.97, with a median of +.73.

None of the measures discussed so far in this chapter is an adequate substitute for a frequency analysis like that in Figure 3.3. But if a frequency analysis cannot be made, and only the tracking error has been recorded, it may be worth counting the number either of reversals or of zero crossings of the error function.

A measure rather similar to the number of zero error crossings is the number of times that the tracking error leaves a target zone of a particular size, and crosses into a target zone which tolerates larger errors (Fitts and colleagues, 1956; Bahrick and Noble, 1966). Other fairly simple measures which can be made on the error function are described by Shelly (1963). A measure of error rate is described by Lathrop (1964). Like all measures made on the error function, they are difficult to interpret.

Frequency analyses involving the error

It is possible to analyze by frequency the record of the error in the same way as the response record is analyzed in Figure 3.4. Unfortunately the RMS amplitude of the error at a particular frequency does not indicate the sign of the error. A response function with too small an

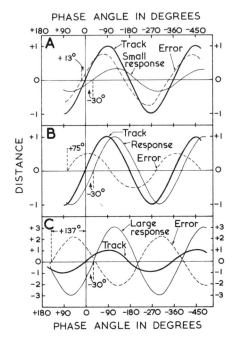

Figure 4.1. The phase of the error.

The figure shows the phase relationships between a simple sine wave track, a theoretical sine wave response of the same frequency but lagging 30° in phase, and the resultant error. In **A** the amplitude of the response is only one third the amplitude of the track. In **B** the 2 amplitudes are the same. In **C** the response amplitude is 3 times the track amplitude. The scale on the ordinate has been reduced.

The phase of the error ϵ with respect to the track can be calculated at the point where the response crosses the track, and so has the same numerical value. Here

$$\mathbf{T} \sin \epsilon = \mathbf{R} \sin(\epsilon + \lambda),$$

where **T** and **R** represent respectively the amplitudes of the track and response, and λ represents the phase lag of the response. This can be written

$$(\mathbf{T}/\mathbf{R}) \sin \epsilon = \sin \epsilon \cos \lambda + \cos \epsilon \sin \lambda$$

or

$$\sin \epsilon \, ((\mathbf{T}/\mathbf{R}) - \cos \lambda) = \cos \epsilon \sin \lambda.$$

Hence

$$\tan \epsilon = \frac{\sin \lambda}{(\mathbf{T}/\mathbf{R}) - \cos \lambda}.$$

It follows from **B** that if the response is a reasonable copy of the track, and lags in phase just over 90° behind the error, it will almost synchronize with the track.

amplitude at the frequency can give the same RMS error amplitude as a response function with too large an amplitude. To distinguish between the 2 alternatives it is necessary to compare the RMS amplitude of the response with the RMS amplitude of the track, as in Figure 3.4.

The relationship between the phase of the error and the phase of the track is illustrated in Figure 4.1. The thick sine wave represents the track. The thin sine wave represents a theoretical response with a phase lag of 30°. The error is the difference in height between the response and the track. It is represented by the broken line. In **B** the response has the same amplitude as the track. The error is advanced in phase relative to the track by 90° minus half the phase lag of the response. The phase advance is therefore 90° — (30°/2), or 75°.

If the man does not respond at all, the error is identical with the track. It then has a phase angle of zero with respect to the track. If the man responds with a phase lag of 30°, but his amplitude is less than the amplitude of the track, as in **A**, his error has a phase advance of a size lying between 0 and 75°. In **A** the phase advance is 13°.

If the man responds with an amplitude very much larger than the amplitude of the track, the phase advance of the error approaches 180° minus the phase lag of the response. With the 30° response lag of Figure 4.1C, the phase advance of the error is 137°.

It follows that the phase advance of the error can be varied between 0° and almost 180° simply by varying the amplitude of a lagging response. The phase of the error depends also upon the phase lag of the response, as indicated in the caption to Figure 4.1. The phase of the error with respect to the track is therefore not easy to interpret. It is simpler to examine separately the phase and amplitude of the response with respect to the track, as in Figure 3.4.

Open loop frequency analyses

In tracking with a compensatory display, the man does not see the track unless he stops responding. He sees only the error function. The frequencies in the man's response function can be compared with the frequencies in the error function which he sees. In the closed loop transfer function of Figure 3.4, the amplitudes and phases of the response frequencies are shown relative to the track frequencies. Instead, the response frequencies can be shown relative to the error frequencies. The plot corresponding to Figure 3.4 is then said to represent the open loop transfer function.

The open loop transfer function looks quite different from Figure 3.4. At low frequencies the amplitude of the error is relatively small compared with the amplitude of the track. The response amplitude is therefore about twice as large as the error amplitude (Elkind, 1956, Figure 4-12a).

The estimate of the ratio is not very accurate, because the man's error at low frequencies is only a small proportion of his total error. Dividing the amplitude of the man's response at low frequencies by the small inaccurate error estimate, produces a still more inaccurate ratio. Taylor (1970, Figure 1) gives 3 independent values of the amplitude of the response relative to the amplitude of the error calculated from the same experimental results. At a frequency of 4 cpm one ratio is over twice as large as a repeat ratio.

At the high frequencies of the track of Figure 3.4, the amplitude of the error is almost as large as the amplitude of the track. Since the response amplitude is also about as large as the amplitude of the track, the response amplitude is about the same size as the error amplitude (Elkind, 1956, Figure 4-12a).

The bottom part of the open loop transfer function also looks different from the bottom part of Figure 3.4. Figure 4.1 indicates that the phase of the error is ahead of the phase of the track. Relative to the error, the man's response lags further behind in phase than it does relative to the track in the bottom part of Figure 3.4.

The exact phase lag depends upon the amplitude of the response. Figure 4.1C shows that the phase lag will be relatively large when the response is larger than the track. This is the case with the pursuit task for the top track frequencies on the right of Figure 3.4. Figure 4.1A shows that the phase lag will not be so large when the response is a good deal smaller than the track, as at the intermediate frequencies in Figure 3.4.

Closed loop transfer functions are reasonably easy to follow and to interpret, provided the amplitude of the track and response function are shown separately. Open loop transfer functions are not easy to interpret. The amplitude at each frequency depends upon the amplitude of the error, as well as upon the amplitude of the response. The phase at each frequency depends upon the amplitude of the response, as well as upon its phase. Closed loop transfer functions are therefore preferable.

It is only in the very early stages of practice with a compensatory display that the man responds purely to the error which he sees. He soon learns some of the statistical characteristics of the track. Eventually he responds primarily to the track. He may use the error only as an indication of his deficiencies in reproducing the track. It is usually necessary to train the man up to this point before computing his transfer function, because his performance tends to be too variable before this.

At this stage the closed loop transfer function which relates his response to the track, is more appropriate than the open loop transfer function which relates his responses to the displayed error.

Autocorrelation of the error

The error function can be correlated with itself after shifting one of the 2 versions a fixed amount in the time dimension. The amplitudes of the 2 versions are then compared perhaps every .01 sec. When the time interval between the 2 identical versions of the error function is zero, the coefficient of correlation will be +1.0. As the time interval is increased, the autocorrelation falls.

The autocorrelation falls more rapidly if the error function consists of high frequencies, than it does if the frequencies are lower. The study described by Fitts and colleagues (1956, Table 1) and by Bahrick and Noble (1966, Tables 16-2 and 16-3) reports the time interval required to reduce the autocorrelation to +.5. The interval is used as a measure of the relative amplitude of the high frequencies in the error.

If the track is a simple sine wave of 15 cpm, it will repeat exactly every 4 sec. The autocorrelation of the track will be 1.0 when the time interval between the 2 identical versions of the track is 4 sec. If the man's average response amplitude is too large or too small, the error function will contain some of the track frequency. The autocorrelation of the error will then increase as the time interval between the 2 identical versions of the error approaches 4 sec. A larger error in the average amplitude of the response produces a larger autocorrelation of the error at the times which correspond to the periodicity of the track (Fitts and colleagues, 1956, Table 1; Bahrick and Noble, 1955, Tables 16-2 and 16-3).

Autocorrelating the error is an elaborate way of finding out very little. We have already seen that the frequencies in the error function are hard to interpret. The information which can be obtained from a plot like Figure 3.3 includes all the useful information which can easily be obtained by autocorrelating the error. If a plot like Figure 3.3 can be made, there seems little point in autocorrelating the error.

If the facilities for making a plot like Figure 3.3 are not available, information similar to that given by autocorrelating the error can be obtained more simply by an excess frequency count, and by measuring the amplitude error at reversals. Clearly if a facility for autocorrelation is available, it will be used. But if a facility for autocorrelation is not available, there seems little point in making the effort to obtain one.

Overall average time lags

The overall average time lag of the response function can be determined by crosscorrelating the complete response function with the complete track. The procedure is similar to the procedure described in Chapter 3 for determining the errors in phase. The main difference is that the response and track are not crosscorrelated in each of a number of separate frequency bends. The overall crosscorrelation gives a simple overall time lag (Elkind, 1953, Figure 4; Fitts and colleagues, 1956, Figure 14B).

Unfortunately an overall average time lag is not always an adequate description of the man's time lags in tracking. The differences in time between the track and the broken line function in Figure 3.5 cannot be described adequately by an overall average time lag. The time lag at reversals is reliably larger than the time lag at the points of inflection. The difference is about two thirds of the size of the overall average time lag.

Representing performance in the time dimension by an overall average time lag is misleading. The results are described more adequately in Figure 3.5. Asymmetrical nonlinearities of this kind are represented in a frequency analysis by even numbered harmonics. They go in the remnant illustrated at the bottom of Figure 3.3, perhaps at frequencies above the top track frequency.

If the facilities are available for a crosscorrelation, it should be carried out for each of a number of bands of frequency. This produces results like those in Figures 3.3 and 3.4. The overall average time lag can be obtained quite simply from the results in the lower part of Figure 3.4. Figure 3.4, and the remnant of Figure 3.3, also indicate the ways in which an overall average time lag fails to fit the results. Thus Figures 3.3 and 3.4 present a more complete picture of the results than can be obtained from an overall crosscorrelation of the response function with the track.

Time on target

Time on target was a popular measure soon after World War II, because it is suited to electrical methods of scoring with simple equipment. The target, and response marker or stylus, can both be made of metal. When they are in contact, an electrical current can pass between them. The hand of an electric clock can be made to rotate whenever the current flows.

However time on target is not a very suitable measure of a man's tracking performance. Errors just large enough to leave the target area are not much worse than errors which are just small enough to stay within the target area. Yet time on target does not penalize the slightly smaller errors at all, whereas it places the maximum penalty on the slightly larger errors.

Time on target need not be used with electronic tracking equipment. There are available voltages proportional to the displacements of the track and of the response function. These voltages provide more information than time on target does.

Figure 4.2 (Bahrick, Fitts, and Briggs, 1957) illustrates the theoretical relationship between time on target and RMS error for targets of different sizes. In computing the shapes of the functions, it is assumed that the distribution of the tracking errors is Gaussian or normal. This is not strictly true for people who are poor at tracking. Also it is not strictly true for an unassorted group of good and poor trackers (Fitts and colleagues, 1956, Figures 6 and 7).

As a man practices and so learns a tracking task, his RMS error becomes smaller. Usually there is a rapid decrease in error at first. There is then a more gradual decrease as the man approaches the point, perhaps .25 volts in Figure 4.2, where further improvement is virtually impossible. The figure shows that if time on target is used as the measure of performance, the shape of the learning curve will depend upon the size of the target selected.

With a large target of size 50, the man will approach the point of

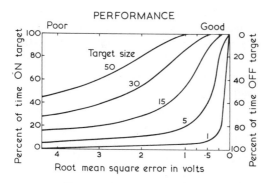

Figure 4.2. Time on target.
The figure shows the theoretical relationships between RMS error and time on or off target, for different sizes of target. With a target of size 100, the man is never off target provided he does not touch his control. The sizes of target have been expressed as a percentage of this. Target sizes of 100, 50, 30, 15, 5, and 1% correspond respectively to voltages of ±5.0, ±2.5, ±1.5, ±.75, ±.25, and ±.05. The theoretical relationships hold only if the errors in tracking have a normal or Gaussian distribution. (After Bahrick and colleagues, 1957, Figure 4.)

little further improvement relatively rapidly. With a small target of size 5, he may appear to improve more rapidly in the late stages of practice. With a very small target of size 1, the man may never appear to improve much if his RMS error does not fall below .25 volts.

It follows from Figure 4.2 that the proportion of time on target depends upon the size of the target. Yet the size of target selected may be an arbitrary decision made by the experimenter. For this reason experiments which use time on target are not often emphasized in this book. Of 2 similar experiments, the experiment which does not use time on target is likely to receive the more extended treatment.

Unfortunately the criticism of time on target applies in some degree to all measures of performance. The measures of tracking performance described in this chapter and Chapter 3 are not necessarily related linearly to each other. Learning curves plotted using one measure will not necessarily resemble learning curves plotted using another measure. None of the measures need necessarily be related linearly to the learning process in the man's brain. The choice of measures made by the experimenter is necessarily arbitrary. He might as well choose the measures which are most suited to his particular purpose.

Figure 4.2 shows that there is not a single optimal size of target for all purposes. When an experimenter is studying the effect of practice while the RMS error lies between 4 and 2 volts, he should not choose a target of size 1. If he does, most people are not going to show much change in their times on target. When the experimenter is studying the effect of practice while the RMS error lies below 1 volt, he should not choose a target of size 50. If he does, not many people are likely to leave the target area. Again his measure of performance will not reflect the learning which is taking place.

If time on target is used, medians and nonparametric statistical tests should also be used. This is because if the RMS errors have a distribution which is more or less Gaussian or normal, the average times on target will not do so. When a distribution is very different from a Gaussian distribution, it is not valid to use the usual parametric statistical procedures like calculating the mean and testing it for reliability. Nonparametric statistics are required.

It is possible to convert times on target to RMS errors using the theoretical curves of Figure 4.2. Kelley (1969a, Table 3) gives the conversion factors for various times on target. It is necessary to know only the size of the target. Unfortunately it has to be assumed that the errors in tracking are distributed normally. This is likely to be true only for good trackers (Fitts and colleagues, 1956).

Measuring the time on target and converting it to RMS error throws away much of the precision which can be obtained by measuring the RMS error directly. At least 50% more tracking time is required to give as good an estimate of RMS error by the indirect method. Kelley (1969a, Table 2) gives the exact values of the extra tracking time required for different proportions of time on target. Clearly it is preferable to compute the average RMS error directly, rather than to estimate it from the proportion of time spent on a target of a known size.

Consistency

In driving an automobile round the corners of a race track, it is not possible to specify the correct route very precisely. The best route to take depends upon the design of the automobile, and upon the level of skill of the driver. But if the test driver drives round the track a number of times, his performance can be assessed by its consistency. The assumption is that the man drives at what he considers to be the limit of safety. If he corners very much more steeply or more quickly, the automobile will leave the race track. As long as the man continues to drive at his limit of safety, his route will be much the same on each circuit.

Consistency can be measured by superimposing the routes on each circuit. At each point on the race track the average position of the automobile can be calculated. The average position is taken as the correct position. Deviations from the average position on each circuit are treated as errors.

Unfortunately, consistency in driving is not necessarily the same as good driving. It is possible for a driver to drive consistently but inappropriately. The driver may have a particular error of technique which he displays with alarming consistency. However a measure of the consistency of deceleration of an automobile in cornering on a test track, is reported to distinguish reliably between good and poor drivers. The good drivers tend to be consistently good. The poor drivers are less consistent from trial to trial (Lewis, 1956).

Subjective estimates of difficulty

Experimenters sometimes ask the people who serve in their experiments what they think of the task which they have been given. The answers may suggest hypotheses about performance which can be tested. Hypotheses may also be suggested by watching people performing the task, and by the experimenter performing the task himself. Subjective information of this kind is not usually given as much weight as objective measures of performance.

However it is possible for a well human engineered aircraft to be assessed subjectively by 1 or 2 top Air Force test pilots. If they do not like the handling qualities when they fly it, the Air Force may refuse to buy the aircraft. As long as there is a risk that this can happen to a new aircraft, design engineers have to try to defend themselves and their new aircraft. It is done by relating the ratings of test pilots to the aerodynamic handling qualities of the aircraft. This is illustrated in Figure 4.3 (Sadoff, McFadden, & Heinle, 1961). From results of this kind it is possible to predict acceptable and unacceptable handling quali-

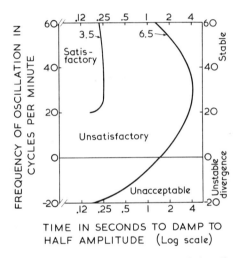

TIME IN SECONDS TO DAMP TO
HALF AMPLITUDE (Log scale)

Figure 4.3.   Subjective estimates of aircraft handling qualities.
The oscillations represent the longitudinal oscillations of a high performance aircraft. The subjective estimates satsifactory, unsatisfactory, and unacceptable are made by 6 test pilots during simulated trials in a centrifuge. The pilots are practiced at flying aircraft with different handling qualities, and at using simulators representing variable stability aircraft. They use the original Cooper (1957) scale of aircraft handling qualities. It has since been replaced by the revised scale of Table 4.1. In the original scale the descriptions are shorter and rather different.
The contour above on the left represents an average rating of 3.5. The contour on the right and at the bottom represents an average rating of 6.5. The negative frequencies at the bottom of the figure represent a pure divergence. The pilots' ratings do not correlate very highly with their tracking performance during the trials. The ratings of the different pilots vary by up to 4 points. The ratings of the same pilot can vary at different times (Cooper, 1957). To obtain the smooth functions in the figure, the average ratings have to be faired. Moderately similar results are reported in flight tests using 1 of the same 6 pilots. (Results from Sadoff and colleagues, 1961, Figure 8.)

Table 4.1
Revised Cooper scale of aircraft handling qualities
(To be used only after designating the flight phase and/or subphases
with the accompanying conditions.)

1. Excellent. Highly desirable. Pilot compensation not a factor for desired performance.
2. Good. Negligible deficiencies. Pilot compensation not a factor for desired performance.
3. Fair. Some mildly unpleasant deficiencies. Minimal pilot compensation required for desired performance.

4. Minor but annoying deficiencies. Desired performance requires moderate pilot compensation.
5. Moderately objectionable deficiencies. Adequate performance requires considerable pilot compensation.
6. Very objectionable but tolerable deficiencies. Adequate performance requires extensive pilot compensation.

7. Major deficiencies. Adequate performance not attainable with maximum tolerable pilot compensation. Controllability not in question.
8. Major deficiencies. Considerable pilot compensation is required for control.
9. Major deficiencies. Intense pilot compensation is required to retain control.

10. Major deficiencies. Control will be lost during some portion of required operation.

Ratings	
1–3	Satisfactory without improvement
4–6	Deficiencies warrant improvement
7–9	Deficiencies require improvement
10	Improvement mandatory

After Cooper & Harper, 1969, Figure 7.

ties. Aircraft which are likely to have unacceptable qualities can be modified or scrapped in the early stages of design.

Relying on the subjective estimates of test pilots may seem a sensible method of assessing a new aircraft. Test pilots ought to know how difficult an aircraft is to fly. All you have to do is to ask them. Unfortunately it is not quite as simple as this. By asking people, it is possible to find out which of 2 objects such as aircraft has more of a particular quality. But it is not possible to determine by questioning exactly how much more of the quality the preferred object has. The exact size of the estimated difference depends upon the exact form of the question asked.

The estimate depends also upon the size of the range of qualities which has recently been experienced. A person who has recently experienced a wide range of qualities is likely to judge differences as smaller than a person who has recently experienced only a restricted range of qualities (Poulton, 1968).

In addition, people vary in their estimates of magnitude. Anxious people judge differences to be larger than less anxious people do (Stephens, 1970). People who have had a lot of practice at making subjective estimates are like less anxious people. They judge differences to be smaller than less practiced people do (Eyman, 1967). These problems are met when test pilots assess the handling qualities of aircraft (Cooper, 1957).

It is possible to reduce the variability in subjective estimates of magnitude by using always the same standardized method. The same test pilots can be used for all subjective estimates. The same existing aircraft can always be used as a standard against which new aircraft are judged. The assessment can be restricted to certain standard maneuvers.

The test pilots can be asked to assess the handling qualities twice. A first assessment can be made when they first fly the aircraft. A second assessment can be made when they have had more practice, and have learned how to master its peculiarities (Cooper, 1957). A standard rating scale can be used to express the magnitude estimates, like the revised Cooper scale of Table 4.1 (Cooper and Harper, 1969).

But this does not eliminate all sources of bias. At best the subjective estimates of 1 or 2 test pilots can provide only approximate estimates of the sizes of the differences between the handling qualities of different aircraft. The author of this book believes that objective measures of performance are preferable when they are available.

Part

2

Tracking

Chapter

5

Tracks with single steps

Summary

Reasonably large quick movements have an average error of about 5% of their size. Very small quick movements are a good deal less accurate. To achieve greater accuracy, movements have to be made more slowly, so that they can be monitored visually and corrected if necessary. In step tracking, an initial quick preprogramed movement may merge into a slower monitored movement.

A low control gain increases travel time if the man has to turn a knob several full rotations. A high control gain increases adjustment time. The optimal control gain lies somewhere in between.

Step tracking

An example of step tracking is using a slide rule. A mark on the slider has to be positioned exactly opposite a fixed mark. Other examples of step tracking are plotting the position of a ship or aircraft on a map or chart, reaching over to and placing a finger on a push button, aiming a camera on an object, focusing the camera, and changing lanes while driving along a multilane highway.

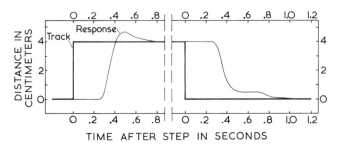

Figure 5.1. **Responses to single steps.**

The man overshoots the first step and has to make a second response. He undershoots the second step. (After Craik & Vince, 1944, 1963b, Figure 10.)

Overshoots tend to be corrected rather more quickly on average than undershoots.
This is because the man can tell a little sooner after the start of the movement
that a correction is necessary. The point is illustrated in the lower part of Figure
6.5.

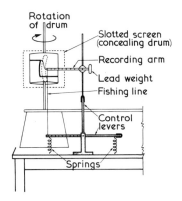

Figure 5.2. **An early tracking apparatus.**

Smoked paper is fixed to the drum of a kymograph. The track represented by
the thick line is drawn on it using the recording arm. The step is produced by
stopping the kymograph and changing the position of the recording arm. A slotted
screen is placed between the drum of the kymograph and the recording arm. The
man sees only the part of the track in the slot. This gives him a warning
of about .05 sec before a step.

The man has to keep the tip of the recording arm on the track, using one
of the 2 control levers illustrated. The vertical and horizontal control levers are
both 20 cm long, the same length as the recording arm. In the figure they are
restrained by light springs, so that they return to the central position when released.
The lever unit is connected to the recording arm by a piece of fishing line. A
lead weight counterbalances the light recording arm. It ensures that the arm follows
the movements of the control lever. A longer piece of fishing line is required
to connect the recording arm to a foot pedal on the floor. The positions of attachment
of the fishing line determine the ratio between the movement of the handle of
the control and the movement of the tip of the recording arm. The ratio in the
figure is 1 to 1. (After Craik & Vince, 1944, 1963b, Figure 12.)

Figure 5.1 illustrates an example of step tracking from the experimental laboratory. The steps in the figure can be drawn on a horizontal paper tape like the track in Figure 1.2. The man sees the track only through the slit in which he moves his pencil. When the track suddenly jumps to a new position, the man has to superimpose his pencil on the new position of the track as quickly as he can. Craik and Vince (1944, 1963b) used an arrangement of this kind, and also the kymograph with smoked paper illustrated in Figure 5.2. Here the man holds a lever. The lever controls the position of a pointer which writes on the smoked paper.

Speed of quick movements

In Figure 5.1 there is a delay after each step in the track before the man starts to respond. This corresponds to the man's reaction time in a visual reaction time experiment. The squares in Figure 5.3 (Craik and Vince, 1944, 1963b) show that the average reaction time is about the same length whether the size of the step is .7 or 11.4 cm.

Searle and Taylor (1948, Figure 7) also report that both small and large steps give about the same average reaction time. But their 6 people

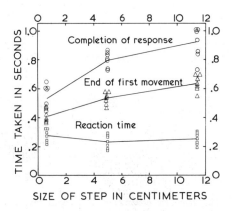

Figure 5.3.   Reaction times and movement times for steps.
The 7 points in each stack represent the averages of the same 7 people. A track with steps like those illustrated in Figure 5.1 is drawn on a paper tape in black pencil. The paper tape is fixed to a rotating drum like that illustrated in Figure 5.2. The drum is covered by a vertical screen which contains a straight vertical slit. The man holds a pencil. He has to try to keep the point of the pencil on the track which he can see in the slit. The slit gives him about .05 sec warning of each step.
After a certain amount of practice, the man tracks a number of steps of one of the 3 sizes. He then goes on to the next size of step, and finally on to the third size of step. The order of the 3 sizes of step is varied from person to person. (After Craik & Vince, 1944, 1963b, Figure 13.)

react .02 sec more quickly to steps of intermediate size. The difference is reliable statistically. This is because Searle and Taylor vary the sizes of steps within a series. They attribute their result to a range effect, like those discussed in the next chapter. The man prepares himself for a step of average size. Responses to unexpectedly small and unexpectedly large steps sometimes take extra time to get started. This slightly increases the mean reaction time.

Figure 5.4 (Taylor & Birmingham, 1948) illustrates separately the distance traveled, and the rate, acceleration, and delta acceleration or jerk of a selected quick movement. The movement ends rather more slowly than it starts. This is characteristic of practiced quick movements which have to end accurately on a target.

Figure 5.5 (Craik & Vince, 1944, 1963b) shows that the responses to larger steps are made faster, and accelerate and decelerate more rapidly. This result from a single person is confirmed by the statistically

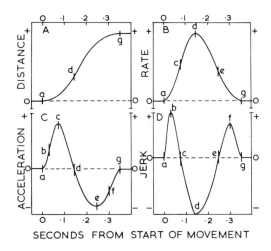

SECONDS FROM START OF MOVEMENT

Figure 5.4.   The acceleration pattern of a quick response to a step.
The short vertical lines labeled with lower case letters indicate corresponding points on the 4 functions. The **d** in **D** need not be at the lowest point on the function.
The man looks at a CRT with his right eye through an eyepiece, which focuses the display at infinity. A dot has to be returned to a verticle hair line each time it jumps away from the hairline either to the right or to the left. Moving a horizontal lever to the right moves the dot to the right. There are 3 sizes of step in each direction. They present angles of 1.5°, 3° and 6° respectively at the man's eye. The 6° step calls for a control movement of 9 in. The movement illustrated in the figure is of this size. There are 6 ways of combining 3 sizes of step with 2 directions of step. Every combination is presented in random order 10 times to each of 10 people. There are 2 practice trials with each combination before the test trials. (After F. V. Taylor & Birmingham 1948, Figure 2.)

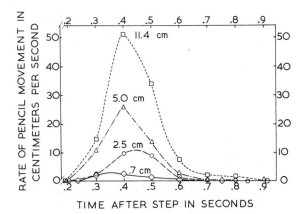

Figure 5.5.   Rate of movement and size of step.
The average rate of movement of a man's pencil point is shown at various times after a step in a track. The 4 functions are for the 4 different sizes of step indicated. Each point represents the average of 4 movements by the same one person. The movements tend to end more slowly than they start. The experiment is described in the caption to Figure 5.3. (After Craik & Vince, 1944, 1963b, Figure 14.)

reliable results of Searle and Taylor (1948, Figure 5) for a group of 5 people, and of Taylor and Birmingham (1948, Figure 3) for a group of 10 people.

In spite of faster rates, large movements take reliably longer to make and to complete than do small movements (Searle & Taylor, 1948, Figure 7; Taylor & Birmingham, 1948, Figure 3). This can be seen from Figure 5.3 by comparing the movement times for step sizes of 11.4 and .7 cm. All 7 people take longer to make the large movement. Part of the difference found by Searle and Taylor (1948) and by Taylor and Birmingham (1948) is likely to be due to a range effect.

Size of quick movements and accuracy

Figure 5.6 (Craik & Vince, 1944, 1963b) shows that for quick movements greater than about 2 cm the average size of the error is roughly proportional to the size of the movement. This can be called Craik's ratio rule.

In the experiment, the man has to move the recording arm illustrated in Figure 5.2 quickly from a horizontal reference line drawn on the drum to a horizontal target line drawn a fixed distance below. He uses a foot pedal. Depressing the pedal extends a spring. The spring and the counterbalancing lead weight on the further side of the recording

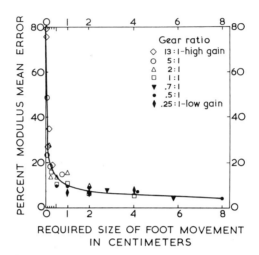

REQUIRED SIZE OF FOOT MOVEMENT
IN CENTIMETERS

Figure 5.6.   Size of quick movements and accuracy.
The man has to depress a pedal quickly various distances with his foot. The error is expressed as a percentage of the correct size of movement. The order of the experimental conditions varies for each of the 6 people. A force of 6 lb is required to depress the pedal 8 cm. (After Craik & Vince, 1944, 1963b, Figure 24).

Part of the large proportional error with very small movements is due to the fishing line which connects the foot pedal to the recording arm. The variable error produced by the fishing line is probably about the same average size whatever the size of the control movement. With very small control movements it may be almost as large as the movement itself. It may account for much of the 80% error with control movements of .02 cm. If the experiment is repeated with an accurate electronic link betwen the control and the display, a curve of similar shape will no doubt be found. But the average proportional error with the very small movements will not necessarily be so large.

Unfortunately statistical tests were not carried out on any of Craik and Vince's results. Thus it is not possible to tell how repeatable they are likely to be, except for Figure 5.3 where individual means are shown.

arm return the arm to the reference line when the man releases the foot pedal at the end of his movement. To prevent him from correcting his quick movement after he makes it, the recording arm is screened from him as it approaches the target line. He is not allowed to see his recorded response movement until the recording arm returns to the reference line.

Craik's ratio rule is not quite correct, even for quick movements of between 2 and 8 cm. Figure 5.6 shows that quick movements of 2 cm have average errors of about 7%, while movements of 8 cm have average errors of about 4%. We shall see in the next section that accuracy is increased by increasing the time taken by a movement. The man probably takes slightly longer to make the large movements of Figure 5.6, and this slightly increases their proportional accuracy. But as a first approximation, quick movements of a reasonble size can be said to have an average error of about 5%.

Craik's ratio rule breaks down for very small movements. Movements of less than 1 mm have average errors of between 30% and 80%. The errors are of course larger with the larger movements, because 4% of 8 cm is .3 cm, whereas 80% of .02 cm is still only about .02 cm. But in proportion to the size of the movement, the average errors are smaller with movements of a reasonably large size.

With each gear ratio except for the lowest gain, the reference line and target line on the drum are 5 different distances apart: 4, 2, 1, .5 and .25 cm. The points in the same vertical column of Figure 5.6 represent the different distances between the 2 lines. The points all lie fairly close to each other. The distance between the 2 lines does not matter very much, as long as it is sufficiently large for the man to be able to see the directions and sizes of his errors reasonably easily.

The results in the figure are for depressing a foot pedal like the gas pedal of an automobile. A similar curve is obtained for quick movements of the hand (Craik & Vince, 1963b, Figure 20). The man always makes 10 practice movements of the required size, and then 20 movements which are scored.

When quick movements of different sizes have to be made one after the other in irregular order, the average size of the error is about 3 times as large for the foot. For the hand the increase in the size of the error is about 25% (Craik & Vince, 1963b, page 438). Under these conditions small movements tend to be a little too large, and large movements tend to be a little too small. This is a range effect which is discussed in the next chapter.

Speed of movements and accuracy

The results in Figure 5.7 (Fitts, 1954) show that movements of between 2 and 16 in take longer to make on average when they have to end within a small target area, than when the target area is larger. Two target plates are placed a fixed distance apart. The man has to tap them alternately as quickly as he can. The ratio of the width of the target to the size of the separation is given on the abscissa.

The figure shows that the average time taken by a movement depends upon the ratio of the size of the target to the size of the movement. Halving the width of the target has the same effect upon the average time taken as doubling the size of the movement. Within the range

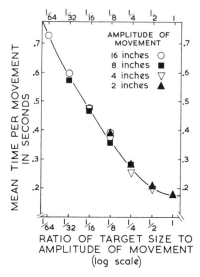

Figure 5.7. Speed of movements and accuracy.
Two targets of the same width are mounted side by side like a Roman II.
The targets are rectangular with a height of 6 in. Their widths are 2, 1, .5 or
.25 in. The separation between their centers is 16, 8, 4 or 2 in. The ratio of
the width of the targets to the distance between them is given on the abscissa.
The man sits comfortably with his right arm half way between the 2 target plates.
He holds a stylus weighing 1 oz. He has to tap the 2 target plates in turn as
many times as possible in 15 sec. He is instructed to concentrate on accuracy
rather than speed. He is told after each trial if he has made any errors.
   The 4 distances between the 2 target plates combined with the 4 widths of target
make a total of 16 conditions. Sixteen right handed college men perform each
of the 16 conditions according to a balanced experimental design. The 16 conditions
are then repeated in the reverse order. The experiment is repeated on a subsequent
day with a stylus weighing 1 lb. The ratio rule is again found to apply. Fitts'
mathematical formulation of the rule is sometimes referred to as Fitts' law. Unfortunately no indication is given of the extent to which people vary, and there are
no statistical tests. (Poulton, 1972, Figure 11.5, showing results from Fitts, 1954.)

of 2 to 16 in it makes little difference how large the movement is, provided the size of the target is adjusted proportionally. This can be called
Fitts' ratio rule.

   Fitts' ratio rule does not hold for very small movements. But it does
apply to single prepared movements, provided they are reasonably large.
For single prepared movements, the times are only about 60% of the
times illustrated in the figure (Fitts & Peterson, 1964, Figure 2).

   Fitts' ratio rule can be related to Craik's ratio rule, which was discovered 10 years earlier. Figure 5.6 shows that reasonably large quick
movements have an average error which is roughly proportional to their

size. Figure 5.7 shows that when this is so, the average movement time is constant. It suggests that the reasonably large quick movements of Figure 5.6 must all take about the same time. This does not quite agree with the average movement times illustrated in Figure 5.3 for movements of 5 and 11.4 cm. The larger movements take a little longer on average. The extra time may account for the slightly greater proportional accuracy of the larger quick movements in Figure 5.6.

Fitts' ratio rule is not quite correct. In the experiment of Figure 5.7, the average proportion of errors increases from .4% with the 2 in target to 3.3% with the .25 in target. This shows that the students do not slow down their movements with the narrower targets quite as much as they should do in order to maintain the same degree of accuracy as with the wider targets. The result is confirmed by Welford, Norris, and Shock (1969). It probably represents another range effect. A similar range effect is found with single prepared movements (Fitts & Peterson, 1964, Table 4). If the students were to adjust their speed to hold accuracy constant, the points in each column for the small movements with the narrow targets would tend to lie a little above the points for the larger movements with the wider targets.

Visual guidance of quick movements

Movements which last much less than .3 sec. are not guided by eye. This is because the man cannot see what correction is wanted until the movement has started. Two possible corrections may then be required, one for an overshoot and one for an undershoot. A 2 choice visual reaction time takes an average of about .3 sec. Thus movements which last much less than .3 sec do not benefit from visual guidance. This is illustrated by the results in Figure 5.8 (Keele & Posner, 1968).

The student has to tap 1 of 2 small circular targets with a stylus. The targets are placed to the right and to the left of the resting position of the stylus. As soon as a circle of light appears around one of the 2 targets, the student has to lift his stylus from its resting position and tap the target. Lifting the stylus brakes an electric contact. This extinguishes the circle of light round the target. In half the trials it also extinguishes the light above the apparatus, leaving the student in the dark.

As soon as the student touches the target, or the metal plate in which it is mounted, the light comes on again. The student is told in advance how long his movement is supposed to take. The figure shows the average movement times for hits and misses, both in the light and in the dark. Printed below the figure are the percent of hits in each condition.

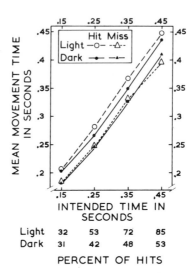

Figure 5.8. Visual guidance of quick movements.

The 4 points in a column together represent 96 trials by each of 8 men under-graduate or graduate students. The man starts by holding the tip of the stylus against an electrical contact. Two circular metal targets, each with a diameter of .25 in, are mounted 6 in to the right and left of the home electrical contact. A ring of translucent plastic about .05 in thick surrounds each target. The ring round one of the targets lights up. The man has then to touch the target with the tip of the stylus, taking one of the 4 specified times on the abscissa. Misses are signaled by a red light.

After each movement the man is told how long he has taken to make it. The movement time represents the time during which the tip of the stylus is not making an electrical contact. The man starts with 2 practice sequences of 24 trials, taking his own time. He then has 3 sequences in succession with each of the 4 intended times given on the abscissa. The results in the figure represent the last 2 of each 3 sequences. The experiment is repeated on a second day. (Results from Keele & Posner, 1968. The separate times for hits and misses are kindly given in a personal communication.)

On the left of the figure the time set for the movements is .15 sec. The movements average about .19 sec. There is no difference in either the speed or the accuracy of movements with the light on and with the light off. Hits, represented by circles, take an average of about .02 sec longer than misses, represented by triangles. This is probably because misses tend to undershoot the target, and so finish sooner (Keele & Posner, personal communication). The movements must be prepro-gramed, because being able to see the stylus and target throughout the movements does not increase their accuracy. There is no time to guide or correct them.

When the time set for the movements is .25 sec, the man takes an average of about this length of time. On trials with the light off, he scores 42% of hits. This is rather more than the 31% of hits when his average movement time is about .19 sec.

The man is reliably more accurate still when the light stays on. He scores 53% of hits. Thus visual guidance must enable him to change a certain number of potential misses into hits. The successful corrections are presumably made on some of the trials with the longer movement times, because here more time is available for detecting and correcting an error.

With an intended movement time of .25 sec, the unfilled circle for hits in the light lies almost .02 sec above the filled circle for hits in the dark. Unfortunately the reliability of the difference is not reported. But for hits and misses combined, the average movement time is reliably longer in the light. This cannot be due to the misses, since they have about the same average movement time in the light as in the dark. It suggests that changing a potential miss into a hit in the light increases the movement time. The correction presumably occurs toward the end of a movement. It is probably responsible for the slow average rates toward the ends of the movements illustrated in Figure 5.5.

This experiment is more satisfactory than a previous experiment by Vince (1948a, Experiment 2). Vince's 10 people (not 20 as stated) make a series of 20 rapid movements in time to the tick of a metronome. Each time they have to try and stop the tip of the recording arm illustrated in Figure 5.2 on a horizontal target line. Trials with the eyes open are compared with trials in which the eyes are closed at the start of each movement. The eyes are not opened again until the movement has been completed.

The eyes cannot easily be opened and closed at rates above 100 times per min. At this and slower rates aiming is reliably more accurate with the eyes open. But the result could be due to the distraction caused by the additional task of blinking in the condition with the eyes closed. The detrimental effect of intentional blinking is discussed at the end of Chapter 12.

Reaction time for a correction

Experimenters who attempt to measure the reaction time for the correction of a movement, report times ranging from longer that .3 sec down to almost no time at all. Long reaction times are found when the man is not expecting to have to make a correction (Poulton, 1950a). Very short times are found when the man incorporates the correction in his response before the response starts.

Reaction times are long in an experiment reported by Chernikoff and Taylor (1952) for correcting movements like the movement illustrated in Figure 5.4. After the man has practiced a number of quick movements in response to steps, a switch is thrown which unexpectedly reverses the direction of movement of the error marker next time the man responds. When the next step appears, the man makes a typical response in the usual, but now inappropriate, direction. The response is eventually followed by a response in the reverse direction, when the man sees that he has moved the marker the wrong way. The experiment indicates that movements like the one illustrated in Figure 5.4 can be made without visual guidance. But the reaction time for the correction is longer than it need be, because the man is not expecting to have to make a correction.

Hick (1949) reports an average reaction time of about .3 sec, for a correction. The man holds a lever which directly controls the movement of the pen of an oscillograph. When he hears a click, he has to move the pen over to a mark on the oscillographic chart which he can see. This requires a force on the lever of about 3 oz, increasing to about 4 oz. A selected response is shown at **A** on the left of Figure 5.9. **S** on the abscissa indicates the time of the click. R_1 indicates when the pen starts to move.

In rather less than one quarter of the trials a solenoid comes on as soon as the lever starts to move. This increases the force required to move the

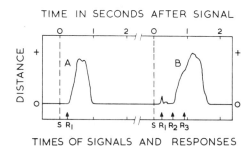

Figure 5.9.   Reaction time for a correction.
The man responds to the click of an electrically operated pen, which places a mark on the chart at time 0. Three different limb movements are used on different days. The first movement to be tried involves the whole arm. The second movement involves bending only the wrist. The third movement involves twisting with the fingers. It is the second and third kinds of movement which are represented in the figure. Between about 60 and 160 pulls or twists are made in each condition. Unfortunately only 3 research workers serve in the experiment. One is the experimenter, another is the author of this book. It is not possible to tell whether other people would perform in a similar way. (After Hick, 1949).

lever to about 20 oz. If the man's response involves flexing the wrist or twisting with the fingers, it is not powerful enough to overcome the extra load. The man has to make a new and more forceful response. This is illustrated at **B** on the right of the figure. Here R_1 indicates the start of the unsuccessful movement. R_2 indicates the start of the new and more powerful movement.

On the average it takes .21 sec to start to move the pen. This is represented by the horizontal distance in the figure between **S** and R_1. It takes an average of .30 sec to make the new and more forceful response. This is represented by the horizontal distance between R_1 and R_2. The 3 men used in the experiment all take reliably longer on average to amend their responses than to make their initial responses.

When the man expects to have to amend his first response as soon as it starts, he can change the kind of response which he makes. Instead of making a light hand movement appropriate to the usual force of 3 or 4 oz, he can make a massive arm movement which will do for whichever of the 2 forces turns out to be necessary. His problem then is to restrain his arm when it is moved against only the light spring. This can be done by a preprogramed movement in which the force increases gradually from 3 or 4 oz to 20 oz. If 3 or 4 oz turns out to be enough to start to move the display marker, the remainder of the preprogramed response can be cut out before the target is overshot.

When Hick allows the strategy of the massive response to be used, the measured reaction time for the amendment is often shorter than the reaction time of the first movement. But it is not a true reaction time. It is simply the time for the arm to increase its force from 3 or 4 to 20 oz as it has been preprogramed to do. This artifact probably accounts for the rather short reaction times reported by Vince (1948a, Experiment 1) when a first response has to be amended on half the trials.

Reaction time for the correction of direction

When the direction of a movement starts to be corrected within about .1 sec, the correction must be incorporated in the initial response without reference to a sensory input signal. There is a fairly simple method of producing a correction of this kind. The method was discovered by Gibbs (1965). It is used by Angel (Angel & Higgins, 1969; Higgins & Angel, 1970; Angel, Garland and Fischler, 1971) and by Buck (1972).

The man has to move a marker sometimes to the right and sometimes to the left in an unpredictable order. He is given a control with an incompatible directional relationship. A movement of the control to the right moves the marker to the left. This is a confusing task when it is first practiced. The man becomes confused from time to time and starts off in the wrong direction. When he spots his error, he moves the control in the opposite, correct direction.

At the start of training the man usually does not spot his error until he sees that the marker is moving in the wrong direction. After he has responded in the wrong direction once or twice, he is partly on the lookout for responses in the wrong direction. He takes an average of .24 sec from the start of the response in the wrong direction before he amends it. After 70 steps, responses in the wrong direction are amended in an average of .11 sec. About 10% are amended in .05 sec or less (Gibbs, 1965, Figure 2).

When the amendment time is very short, the man must incorporate the amendment in the response before the response starts. Some people start quick movements fairly consistently with a twitch in the opposite direction (Trumbo, personal communication). A person who starts off in the wrong direction only occasionally may be confused about the correct direction of his output selector switch. In his haste to respond, he makes a mistake and programs the switching to occur during the movement, instead of before the movement.

Figure 5.8 shows that movements cannot be amended as quickly as this in response to a visual signal. The average simple reaction time to a visual signal is not often shorter than .18 sec. The average simple proprioceptive reaction time is somewhat shorter, about .12 or .13 sec. (Chernikoff & Taylor, 1952; Higgins & Angel, 1970). But even these times are over twice as long as 10% of Gibbs' (1965) amendment times.

Aiming by successive approximation and by monitoring

When a large quick movement has to end at a precise target, it is unlikely to end at the target first shot. The man usually has to make a correction subsequently, as illustrated in Figure 5.1. Figure 5.6 shows that the first quick movement is likely to finish on average about 5% of the distance from the correct position. A subsequent quick correction may also be accurate on average to within about 5%, provided the error left at the end of the first movement is a reasonably large one.

Figure 5.6 shows that final, very small, quick corrections are likely to have proportional errors which are a good deal larger than this. The man will soon be at the stage when any quick correction which he makes will be as likely to increase the distance from the target as to reduce it. Extensive trial and check will sometimes be necessary in order to achieve reasonably perfect alignment.

A more sensible strategy when close to the target is to approach it at a more or less constant slow rate. A final decision to stop the movement is made a reaction time before the target is reached. If alignment has to be very accurate, the final movement needs to be very slow. Then an error in deciding exactly when to stop still leaves an acceptable alignment. Something of this kind may have happened with the later parts of the movements illustrated in Figure 5.1. The figure shows only one correction following each first quick movement. The correcting movement gradually approaches the target without any obvious additional trial and check.

A slow monitored movement of this kind can be contrasted with a quick preprogramed movement. The end point of a quick preprogramed movement is determined before the movement starts. Whereas the end point of a monitored movement is determined only a reaction time before the movement stops. A quick preprogramed movement is likely to have an accuracy which is proportional to its size. Whereas the accuracy of a monitored movement is likely to be proportional to its rate just before the final decision to stop.

If a person is told to be both quick and accurate, he may respond in a way which is neither completely preprogramed nor completely monitored. He may start with a quick preprogramed movement and slow it down as the target is approached. A correction may begin before the first movement has been completed, so that it is not possible to tell exactly where the first movement ends and the correction begins. The last part of the movement may be monitored. Its rate then depends upon the criterion of accuracy which the person adopts.

Control sensitivity and acquisition time

The results in Figure 5.10 (Jenkins & Connor, 1949) illustrate 2 components of the time taken to line up a marker accurately against a target marker. The man holds a control knob. By rotating the knob he can move a response marker along a horizontal scale. The marker has to be moved as quickly as possible along the scale, and lined up accurately within a small target area.

The curve on the right labeled adjustment represents the time taken to make the final fine adjustment. When the control sensitivity or gain is high, the final fine adjustment takes a long time. Rotating the control knob as little as .3° moves the response marker from one side of the target area to the other.

The curve for adjustment corresponds to the curve in Figure 5.6 for single quick movements. Both curves rise steeply when very small movements are required. Very small quick movements have a large average

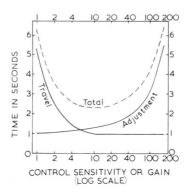

Figure 5.10.   Travel and adjustment time.

The control knob has a diameter of 2.75 in. It is connected by string and pulleys to a response marker. Rotating the knob moves the marker along a horizontal scale. The scale has 20 target positions, which are arranged symmetrically along its length at distances ranging from .2 to 5.5 in. The man starts with the response marker in the center of the scale. As soon as a target lights up, he has to move the marker across and line it up with the target. When the marker arrives within .1 in of the target, the clock which measures his travel time stops, and the clock which measures his adjustment time starts.

The marker had a width of .025 in. It has to end completely within the target area which has a width of .032 in. As soon as the man is satisfied, he presses a switch with his other hand. This stops the second clock, and disconnects the knob control from the response marker. Settings are almost always accurate. When they are not accurate, the readings are discarded.

There is a good deal of friction to be overcome in moving the control knob. It is tolerated in order to remove backlash, and ensure that the marker responds accurately to small movements of the control. Friction increases the difficulty of making slow accurate movements (see Chapter 15). Unfortunately there is no indication of how the final fine adjustment is made. Thus the effect of the friction is difficult to assess. Also with only 3 people, it is not possible to tell how repeatable the results are likely to be, especially with the high gain where the 3 people behave rather differently. (Results from Jenkins & Connor, 1949, Figure 2.)

error in proportion to their size. The man may make several attempts before he is fortunate enough to land on the target. The alternative strategy of approaching at a slow constant rate also takes extra time. Thus fine adjustments take a longer average time to complete when the control sensitivity or gain is too high.

The curve in Figure 5.10 for travel shows the calculated time required to move the response marker 3.1 in. With a control sensitivity of 1, it takes 14 full rotations of the control knob. As the sensitivity or gain of the control is increased, fewer rotations are required. Travel time is therefore shorter.

The average travel time in the figure does not fall below about 1 sec even with a high control sensitivity. Two of the 3 people show reductions in travel time to less than 1 sec with the high gain. But the other person shows an increase in travel time to about 2.2 sec (Jenkins & Connor, 1949, Figure 2).

An increase in travel time when a very precise movement is required at the end of the travel, is in line with the results of Hecker, Green and Smith (1956). The man starts on the final slow task of adjustment before his limb crosses the arbitrary boundary set by the experimenter between travel and adjustment (Annett, Golby & Kay, 1958).

The broken U shaped curve labeled total shows the sum of the travel and adjustment times. It is lowest at a control sensitivity of about 10, but it does not change height very much over its middle third. Any control sensitivity in this region will do.

When a joystick or lever is used instead of a control knob, the curve in Figure 5.10 for travel time is almost a horizontal straight line. A control stick does not normally move as far as 90° on either side of its central position. It is almost as quick to move a stick through 180° as through a smaller angle. There is nothing to correspond to the numerous full rotations of the control knob which are required in Jenkins and Connor's (1949) experiment.

Thus, with a joystick or lever, the relationship between acquisition time and control gain is J shaped, like the function for adjustment time on the right of Figure 5.10 (Jenkins & Olson, 1952). The optimum gain is obtained by equating maximum stick travel with the maximum required travel of the response marker. This leaves more stick movement available for the final adjustment.

The J shaped curve for adjustment time with a joystick or lever, can be related to Fitts' (1954) ratio rule for tapping with a stylus. In Figure 5.7 acquisition time remains constant provided the size of a movement is changed without altering the ratio of movement size to target size. Changing the size of a movement while holding the ratio constant, corresponds to changing the control sensitivity or gain of Figure 5.10. Thus Fitts' ratio rule gives a horizontal line instead of the curve for adjustment in Figure 5.10.

This is because Fitts' movements are all relatively large. His results correspond to the almost horizontal part of the function for adjustment on the left of Figure 5.10. Figure 5.6 shows that quick movements have to be reduced to less than 2 cm before their size affects their proportional accuracy very much. Fitts' smallest movement of 2 in, or about 5 cm, is considerably larger than this.

Recommended control sensitivity

The optimal sensitivity of a rotary control with several full rotations has to be a compromise between the high sensitivity required to reduce travel time, and the low sensitivity required for quick accurate adjustments. The optimum should be checked by experiment for each application.

With a lever or joystick position control, the largest stick movement should be equated with the largest display movement.

Chapter

6

Tracks with many steps

Summary

When 2 steps follow closely one after the other, the response to the second step is likely to be delayed. This reflects the psychological refractory period. If the man expects 2 steps in rapid succession, he may delay his response to the first step and make a combined response to the pair of steps. When he responds quickly and correctly to the second step, it may be simply because he has guessed correctly. If his expectations are wrong, he may fail to respond, respond too soon, or respond in the wrong direction.

In tracking many steps, the man learns the average time interval between steps, and the average direction and size of the next step for various positions on the display. His responses deviate in the direction of these average values. This is a range effect.

Tracking many steps

A track with many steps is produced by a rotating radar aerial, which picks up the positions of ships or aircraft once every rotation. On a plan position indicator display like that illustrated in Figure 9.3, the echoes which represent the ships or aircraft jump from one position to the next at each rotation. A man who has to keep a response marker superimposed over an echo, follows a track with many steps in it.

In the experimental laboratory the steps usually vary in direction. This is sometimes done in order to be able to distinguish between the responses to 2 steps which follow quickly one after the other. If both steps are in the same direction, the man may make what appears to be a single response to the 2 steps. It is not possible to tell whether the man sees that there are 2 steps, or thinks that there is only a single step.

Interactions between responses to pairs of steps

A step may follow quickly after another step. Figure 6.1 (Vince, 1950) shows that the man's responses to the pair of steps can be classified in 1 of 3 ways:

1. The first response may be the proper size, in which case the second response will usually be delayed.
2. Both responses may be too small, and usually delayed.
3. The pair of responses may be unscorable because a response is omitted, is in the wrong direction, or starts before the step appears.

On this once controversial topic we follow Craik (1948) and Vince (1948b). These authors believe that responses classified in the first 2 ways represent 2 alternative strategies. The 2 strategies are illustrated in the 2 top rows of Figure 6.2. Both strategies may be used by the same man at different times. Which strategy he uses depends upon when he expects the second step of the pair to arrive.

Vince (1950) presents pairs of steps using an experimental arrangement rather like that illustrated in Figure 5.2, except that the slit is straight instead of curved. The steps are drawn on a moving paper tape, which appears from behind a screen. The man follows the steps with a pencil, which he moves up and down in the slit. The steps are of 3 sizes. Each size of step follows every other size an equal number of times. The second step is always in the opposite direction to the first step. The time interval between steps is varied between .05 and 1.6 sec.

Responses of proper size:
the psychological refractory period

Figure 6.3 shows the average reaction times for the shorter intervals between pairs of steps. The circle on the left hand ordinate represents the average reaction time to an isolated step, about .23 sec. The unfilled

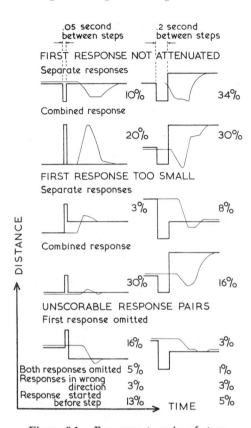

Figure 6.1. Responses to pairs of steps.
The responses are selected to illustrate the classification used by Vince (1950, Figure 3). On the left of the figure the time interval between the 2 steps of a pair is .05 sec. On the right the interval is .2 sec. At each time interval the percentages add up to 100. They indicate the proportion of response pairs which fall into each category. The first response is classified as too small when its amplitude is less than 75% of the amplitude of the first step.

circles show that when the response to the first step of a pair is about the proper size, it has about the same average reaction time. The filled circles indicate the average reaction times to the corresponding second steps. The filled circles all lie reliably above the unfilled circle on the left hand ordinate for an isolated step.

Responses to the second step are delayed most on average when the interval between the 2 steps is shortest. This reflects the psychological refractory period (Vince, 1948b; Welford, 1952, 1967; M. C. Smith, 1967). It is illustrated in the top row of Figure 6.2. The man cannot start to react to the second step during his reaction time to the first

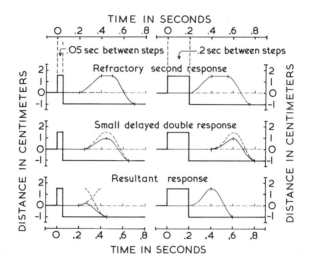

Figure 6.2.   Alternative models for responses to pairs of steps.
The 2 strategies described by Craik (1948) and by Vince (1948b) are illustrated in the top 2 rows. The model favored by Ellson and Hill (1948) is illustrated in the bottom row. For simplicity it is assumed that the uncomplicated reaction time is .2 sec, and that movements in each direction also take .2 sec.

The reaction times for the second responses in the top row are taken from the filled circles of Figure 6.3, .45 sec when the interval between steps is .05 sec and .35 sec when the interval between steps is .2 sec. The reaction times are longer than they need be because the man is usually not expecting a second step so soon. When he expects a second step soon after the first, he usually waits for it and adopts the strategy in the middle row. When he uses the strategy of the delayed double response, he tends to underestimate the size of the first step because he cannot see it once the second step has appeared.

The model in the bottom row assumes that the man responds to each step of the pair a reaction time after the step appears. The resultant response on the left is the algebraic sum of the 2 hypothetical responses, which are indicated by broken lines. People cannot behave like this, but it is difficult to demonstrate conclusively using responses to pairs of steps.

step. The average delays in the figures are between .1 and .15 sec longer than they need be. This is probably because the man adopts the strategy when he does not expect a second step so soon (Poulton, 1970, Figure 5).

Delayed attenuated responses

When the first response is less than 75% of the size of the step, the average reaction time is represented in Figure 6.3 by unfilled squares. For steps separated by intervals of .05 or .1 sec, the average reaction time of small first responses is about .25 sec. For steps separated by

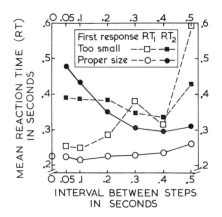

Figure 6.3. Reaction times to the steps of a pair.
   The circles show the average reaction times when the response to the first step is about the right size. The squares show the average reaction times when the response to the first step is less than 75% of the size of the step. There are 10 different time intervals between pairs of steps, .05, .1, .2, .3, .4, .5, .6, .7, 1.2 and 1.6 sec, but only the 6 shortest intervals are represented in the figure. Steps are of 3 sizes, 1.5, 2.5 or 3.5 cm. There are 9 ways of combining pairs of steps of 3 possible sizes. All combinations are used. The first step of a pair can move in either direction, unless the track happens to be near the top or bottom of the slit. The second step of a pair is always in the opposite direction to the first step.
   The 10 time intervals between the steps of a pair, and the 9 combinations of sizes of step, are combined in apparently random fashion. Single steps are inserted occasionally between pairs of steps. A trial includes 3 pairs of steps using each of the 10 time intervals, and 3 single steps. Each of 12 people have 3 trials. No practice is given before the experiment. All scorable responses are used in the results. (Results from Vince, 1950.)

an interval of .2 sec, the average reaction time of small first responses is .29 sec. Both averages are reliably longer than the average of .23 sec for responses to isolated steps.

   For steps separated by intervals of .3 sec and longer, the average reaction time of small first responses is greater than .3 sec. As the time interval between the 2 steps increases, the average reaction time of small responses to the first step of the pair also increases, as if the man tends to wait for the second step before responding to the first step.

   The filled squares in the figure represent second responses which follow small first responses. They behave rather differently from the filled circles for second responses which follow first responses of about the right size. The height of the filled squares does not vary much with the duration of the interval between the pair of steps. The second responses are always delayed by an average of between .35 and .4 sec. For intervals of both .05 and .1 sec between steps, the filled squares lie reliably below the filled circles.

The results represented by the squares in Figure 6.3 indicate that when the response to the first step is too small, the man tends to delay initiating his response to the step because he expects the second step almost at once. He eventually initiates a combined response to the pair of steps, either just before or just after the second step appears. This is illustrated in the second row of Figure 6.2.

The first response is delayed while waiting for the second step to appear. The second response is delayed by the more or less constant time taken to make the first response. The amplitude of the combined response is too small because the man can no longer see how large it should be. By the time he comes to respond, he can see only the line on which he has to terminate the combined response.

Unscorable responses

The lower part of Figure 6.1 shows that when the time interval between the 2 opposing steps is short, the man sometimes omits to respond to the first step, or to both steps. In some cases he may not see the steps. He may not be expecting a step and may be blinking (see the last part of Chapter 12). He may be expecting a step in the other direction, and so be looking in the slit for the step on the wrong side of his pencil. The first step may then simply alert him for the second step, to which he duly responds.

In other cases the man may see the first step, but may not initiate his response to it by the time the second step arrives. So he simply responds to the difference in amplitude between the first and second steps. When the 2 steps have the same amplitude, he does not respond at all. The man is not told what to do when a second step arrives before he has responded to the first step. He is told simply to try and keep his pencil on the track.

The bottom of Figure 6.1 shows the proportion of responses which either start before the man can see the step, or are made in the opposite direction to the step. These responses can be regarded as examples of the range effect for time, which is discussed later in the chapter. The man knows that a step must be due, and makes a premature or false reaction as it is called in experiments on reaction time.

When quite a high proportion of false reactions occur, some short reaction times must indicate false reactions. It is not possible to be certain in any individual case that the man does wait for the step before he responds.

This applies to some of the delayed combined responses represented in Figure 6.3 by squares. When the combined response is not initiated until the second step is seen, the first response must be delayed by the sum of the interval between the 2 steps plus a reaction time. The unfilled squares show that the average delay is less than this. It suggests that the man must sometimes initiate his combined response before he sees the second step. He can do this with a certain degree of confidence, because he always knows the direction of the second step, and 55% of steps are followed by a second step within .5 sec.

Difficulties of interpretation

The selected results in Figure 6.1 illustrate some of the difficulties of attempting to infer the man's strategies in individual cases from his recorded responses. When 2 steps follow each other in close succession, it is not always possible to distinguish between a preprogramed double response and 2 separate responses which run into each other.

Figure 6.4 shows that a rather similar confusion can occur when the man corrects his first response by a movement in the same direction as the direction of a simultaneous second step. A correlation of this kind may occur before step 4 in Figure 6.4. If the next step appears during the man's reaction time for the correction, his response to the second step will be delayed. Yet the correction may run on into the response to the second step. The double response then looks like a single response to the second step with a very short reaction time.

The confusion can also occur if the man's hand drifts in the direction of the expected step a little before the step appears. In Figure 6.4 possible drifts in the expected direction are illustrated before steps 1 and 5. Drifts may be more marked in Gibbs' (1965) experiment, which is discussed later in the chapter, because the target marker disappears for 1 sec before it reappears in its new position. During this time the man does not know where his response marker is supposed to be.

When drifts occur, it may sometimes look as if the man starts off early with a gradually accelerating response. Drifting hand movements may be easier to spot when they happen to be in the wrong direction. In Figure 6.4 possible drifts in the wrong direction are illustrated before steps 2 and 3. Drifts in the wrong direction need to be distinguished from a twitch in the wrong direction at the start of a response. Some people start fairly consistently with a quick twitch in the wrong direction (Trumbo, personal communication).

In step tracking the visual stimulus to which the man responds can be defined precisely, both in extent and in time. This does not mean

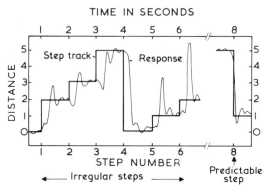

Figure 6.4.   Responses to steps in a series.

A track marker steps from side to side over the face of a CRT once every second, at the times indicated on the abscissa. In this experiment by Trumbo and colleagues (1968) there are 6 possible positions, .8 in apart, for the track marker to jump between. They are indicated on the ordinate. The man rests his arm on a lever which is pivoted at his elbow. A horizontal rotation of 11° moves the response marker 1 in in the corresponding direction. Before responding to steps 1 through 6, the man responds to about 400 random steps.

The response to step 8 on the extreme right of the figure illustrates the optimal strategy when the man knows the time, direction and size of a step. The aim is to minimize the modulus mean error, which is represented by the area between the track and the response. This is done by starting to respond before the track steps to its new position, and reaching the new position an equal time after the step. The response function then crosses the step near its midpoint. With the irregular series of steps illustrated on the left of the figure, this strategy will not often pay. For even when the man knows for certain the direction of the next step, he cannot be sure of its size. (From an oscillographic chart kindly lent by Dr. Trumbo.)

that the man's individual responses must be equally easy to specify. Interpretation is simplest when the man is waiting ready for the step. If he is not ready, or if he is doing something else when the step arrives, it may not be possible to interpret his response unambiguously.

The difficulties of interpretation with step tracks enable different experimenters to give different interpretations to rather similar recorded results. Craik (1948) and Vince (1948b) use results rather like those in Figure 6.1 to support the view which has just been presented. They hold that when 2 steps follow each other in close succession, the 2 possible outcomes are illustrated in the 2 top rows of Figure 6.2.

Ellson and Hill (1948) use rather similar recorded results to support their theory of simultaneous responses. They hold that when 2 steps follow in close succession, the man's resultant response is the algebraic sum of the 2 separate responses, as illustrated at the bottom of Figure 6.2 on the left. This is how a linear servomechanism behaves. A man does not behave like a linear servomechanism, but the distinction cannot be made unambiguously from results like those in Figure 6.1.

The range effect for sizes of step

Range effects were so named by Searle and Taylor (1948). A range effect reflects the tendency to make responses which deviate in the direction of the average of the series. This is sometimes called the central tendency of judgment. It is pointed out in Chapter 2 that range effects are common with balanced treatment experimental designs. They are characteristic of many kinds of decisions. A range effect is found in making subjective estimates like those illustrated in Figure 4.3.

In tracking many steps, there are range effects for the sizes of the steps, for their times, and for their directions. Once the man has learned the statistical characteristics of a step track, he makes use of the knowledge in his tracking.

The upper part of Figure 6.5 (Ellson and Wheeler, 1949) illustrates the range effect for sizes of step. One group of 25 undergraduates tracks steps of .25, .5 and 1.0 in. Another group tracks steps of 1.0, 1.5 and 2.0 in. Steps of 1.0 in are the largest steps tracked by one group, but the smallest steps tracked by the other group. The steps vary irregularly in direction, right or left. They are presented at irregular intervals of time.

The upper part of the figure shows the average error of overshooting or undershooting, taking account of the sign. The error is for the first movement in response to each step out from the central position. Both groups of undergraduates tend to overshoot their small steps and to undershoot their large steps. The group with the small range of steps makes an average first movement of .96 in to the 1.0 in step. The group with the large range of steps averages 1.07 in to this same step. The difference of .11 in is highly reliable. A similar range effect for 10 sizes of step is illustrated in Figure 2.2.

The lower part of Figure 6.5 (Craig, 1949) shows the average time to the end of the first movement. Both groups tend to take rather less time when the steps are smaller. This is in line with the times illustrated in Figure 5.3. The group with the small range of steps takes an average of .57 sec after the appearance of the 1.0 in step to complete the first movement. The group with the large range of steps averages .49 sec for this same step. The difference of .08 sec is highly reliable.

The difference is in the opposite direction to the difference predicted from Figure 5.3. The larger overshooting responses to the 1.0 in step take less time to complete than the smaller undershooting responses.

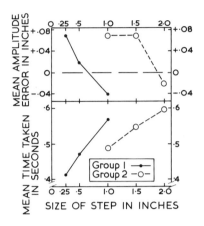

Figure 6.5.   A range effect for 3 sizes of step.
The ordinate at the top shows the error of overshooting or undershooting by
the first movement in response to each step. The ordinate at the bottom shows
the average time to the end of the first movement. This represents the sum of
reaction time plus movement time. The filled points are for a group of 25 men
undergraduates who have steps ranging from .25 to 1 in. The unfilled points are
for another group who have steps ranging from 1 to 2 in.

The experimental arrangement is fairly similar to that of the experiment of Figure
2.2, but here the paper tape is mounted vertically. Also the man uses an almost
frictionless stylus, which slides along a rail beneath the slit. He tracks 54 steps
out from the center. There are 18 steps of each of 3 sizes, 9 to the right and
9 to the left. The order of the directions and sizes is randomized. The steps out
from the center occur irregularly, probably at intervals of 2, 3 or 4 sec after
a step back to the center (Ellson & Coppock, 1951). They are followed .7, 1.0
or 1.3 sec later by a step back to the center, which is not scored. (Results from
Ellson & Wheeler, 1949; Craig, 1949.)

This is because the measured time of completion of the first response
depends upon the time of initiation of the subsequent correction. Overshoots are corrected more quickly than undershoots because the man
can tell sooner that a correction is necessary. There is no need to introduce a 2 factor theory as Craig (1949) does.

After the man has tracked steps of various sizes, he prepares himself
each time for a step of average size. If the step happens to be smaller
than this, his response tends to be a little too large, and so is corrected
relatively quickly. If the step happens to be larger than average, the
man's response tends to be a little too small, and so is corrected more
slowly.

It is pointed out early in Chapter 5 that reaction times are slightly
but reliably shorter for steps of average size, when the exact times of
appearance of the steps are not known (Searle & Taylor, 1948, Figure

7). If the step happens to be smaller or larger than average, the man takes an extra .02 sec on average to prepare himself before he initiates his response. Even then, Figure 6.5 shows that he does not adapt fully to the size of the step.

A range effect for step sizes of unequal probability

In the experiment of Figure 6.5, steps of the 3 sizes occur equally often. Trumbo (1970; Trumbo, Noble & Quigley, 1968) describes the range effect for size of step when the probability of the commonest size is varied between .92 and .5. Separate groups of 6 or 8 male students serve in each condition. The steps occur at regular intervals of 1 sec.

Here we are concerned only with choices when all the possible steps are in the same direction, and the student's reaction time is less than .15 sec. Under these conditions the student must guess the size of the step, and initiate his response to the step before he sees it. The conditions are quite different from the conditions of the experiment of Figure 6.5. In the conditions of Figure 6.5 the man cannot respond until he sees the step, because he does not know its direction.

When the probability of the commonest size of step is .92, the anticipatory first movements of all 16 students tend to be of the commonest size. This strategy is called maximizing.

When the probability is only .7 or .62, two thirds of the students tend to alternate between anticipatory first movements of the various sizes, making about the correct proportion of the commonest size of movement. This strategy is called probability matching. The remainder of the students either maximize, or else tend to make anticipatory first movements of the average size.

The strategy of averaging corresponds most closely to the range effect for sizes of step illustrated in Figure 6.5. The strategies of maximizing and of probability matching can be elicited only by using step sizes of unequal probability, and by encouraging people to initiate their responses before they see the steps.

The range effect for times of step

A simple predictable series of steps may be presented with varying intervals of time between the steps. After practice, the man learns the average time interval before the next step. He tends to respond early when the time interval is a long one. He responds late when the time interval is short. The time at which he responds tends to be a little too close to the average time between the steps. The range effect is about as marked for 18 students who have a fixed learnable sequence of time intervals between steps, as for 12 students who have random sequences of time intervals (Trumbo, Noble, Fowler & Porterfield, 1968, Experiment 1).

Noble and Trumbo (1967, page 10) describe an experiment by K. Cross which compares the range effect for times of step with the range effect for sizes of step. Both range effects reduce the average modulus mean error by about the same amount, but they do so in different ways. The 7 students who show the range effect for times of step, track known steps at varying times. Their errors of timing are large and variable. But they have a compensatory advantage from knowing the directions and sizes of the steps. The sizes of their first movements are therefore reasonably accurate.

The 7 students who show the range effect for sizes of step, know the times and directions of the steps. They can start off in the correct direction just before the steps appear, even though they do not know how far to move. The greater accuracy in timing of the first movements, makes up for their less accurate size. The 2 range effects thus reduce the average modulus mean error by about the same amount.

Cross does not find range effects when the man knows only the value of 1 of the 3 variables: size of step, time of step, or direction of step. The man has to know the values of at least 2 of the variables (Noble & Trumbo, 1967).

The range effect for directions of step

Suppose a step track in 1 dimension has 5 possible positions which are equally likely, like the track used by Gibbs (1965). The top 2 rows of Table 6.1 show the proportion of possible directions of the next step for each position of the track marker. When the track marker is left of center, the next step is likely to be toward the right. When the track marker is on the extreme left, the next step is certain to be toward the right. The bottom 2 rows of part **A** of the table show the proportion of probable and improbable directions of movement for each position of the track marker. The last column shows that the overall average ratio of probable to improbable directions is 80 to 20, or 4 to 1.

For the step track with 15 possible positions used in the experiments described by Noble and Trumbo (1967), the overall average ratio is 3.3 to 1. Once the man has learned the statistical characteristics of the track, he can on average predict the direction of the next step a good deal better than chance, especially when the track marker is near either edge of the display.

Part **B** of Table 6.1 (Gibbs, 1965) shows that the average reaction

Table 6.1
A tracking task with 5 positions

A. Percent of directions of next step

Direction of next step	Position of track marker					Average for all positions
	Left outside	Left inside	Center	Right inside	Right outside	
Left	0	25	50	75	100	50
Right	100	75	50	25	0	50
Probable direction:	100	75	50	75	100	80
Improbable direction:	0	25	50	25	0	20

B. Reaction time (seconds) for correct and incorrect directions

	Direction of step				
	Certain (100:0)	Probable (75:25)	Equiprobable (50:50)	Improbable (25:75)	Impossible (0:100)
Correct direction:	.23	.25	.30	.36	—
Incorrect direction:	.33	.30	.28	.27	—

C. Percent of incorrect directions

	Direction of step				
	Certain	Probable	Equiprobable	Improbable	Impossible
Incorrect direction	5	18	42	70	—

(Results from Gibbs, 1965.)

times to steps which occur regularly every 2 sec, depend upon the probability of their directions. The first row is for responses made in the correct direction. The average reaction time of Gibbs' 12 people ranges from .23 sec. when the direction of the steps is certain, to .36 sec. when the direction is improbable. The difference is reliable. Buck (1972) confirms this tendency for reaction times to increase as the direction becomes less probable.

The second row is for responses made in the wrong direction. Here the probabilities have to be reversed. When the correct direction is improbable (25:75), the wrong direction is the probable direction. Average reaction times are shortest for the probable direction errors, and largest for the impossible direction errors (100:0). However this result is not confirmed by Buck (1972). Buck finds that responses in the wrong direction always tend to have rather shorter average reaction times than responses in the correct direction. Presumably the man initiates his response a little too soon, before he is certain of the correct direction.

Part **C** of the table gives the average percent of errors. When the correct direction is improbable (25:75), there are 70% of errors. The percent of errors is very nearly as large as the probability of 75 that the track marker will step in this direction.

As the incorrect direction becomes less probable, the percent of errors decreases. The percent of errors remains almost as large as the probability that the track marker will step in the incorrect direction. This represents slightly conservative probability matching.

When the correct direction is certain (100:0) there are 5% of errors in the impossible direction. These errors must represent confusions made by the man in the direction of the control movement. Confusions occur in the experiment because the man has to move the control always in the direction opposite to the direction in which he wishes to move the response marker. Occasionally the man becomes confused and responds in the wrong direction.

A range effect for the directions of step can reduce the modulus mean error in tracking. In one condition of the experiments described by Noble and Trumbo (1967), the track steps every second between 15 equiprobable positions. With practice the modulus mean error falls by about 15%. This is accompanied by a reduction in the average reaction time of the 9 students from .16 to .12 sec (Noble and colleagues, 1966, Figure 2c).

At the start of the experiment a group of 30 students makes an average of about 10% of responses with reaction times of less than .15 sec. In these cases it can be assumed that the student initiates his response before the step appears. At the end of the experiment the proportion of these beneficial anticipations increases to almost 30% (Trumbo and colleagues, 1965, Figure 3c). Presumably most of the beneficial anticipations occur when the track marker is near one side of the display or the other, and the direction of the next step is therefore highly probable.

The point is investigated by Trumbo (1970; Trumbo and colleagues, 1968) in the experiments used to investigate also the range effect for step sizes of unequal probability. The probability of the most likely direction of step is varied from .92 to .50 for separate groups of 8 or 16 students. When the probability of the commonest direction is .92, all the anticipatory first movements of 14 of the 16 students tend to be in the commonest direction. When the probability of the commonest direction is only .77, half the students maximize like this. The other half tend to match probabilities, by making about 77% of anticipatory first movements in the probable direction.

Strategies with fully predictable steps

Slack (1953a) describes 2 extreme strategies with fully predictable steps. His steps have a fixed amplitude, and are alternately to the right and to the left every 1.25 sec. Some undergraduates start to move before each step appears, and finish moving about an equal time after the step has appeared. Their responses resemble the response to step 8 in Figure 6.4. Slack (1953a) calls this locking in.

Other undergraduates clearly know the pattern of steps, but do not take advantage of their knowledge. They always wait until a step has appeared before reacting to it. However Slack (1953a) notes that their performance is partly determined by their knowledge of the track. After they have learned the track, he presents them with a surprise step of a different direction or amplitude, or delayed in time. The first time this happens, the undergraduates often respond to the expected step, not to the surprise step. This behavior is related to the anticipatory responses to pairs of steps, which are listed at the bottom of Figure 6.1 (Vince, 1950). Unfortunately Slack (1953a) gives no indication of the proportions of undergraduates who use the 2 strategies.

How a person responds to fully predictable steps, depends upon what he thinks he is supposed to do. The instructions used by Noble and Trumbo (1967) encourage people to lock in. They are told to minimize their modulus mean error. The effect of quick anticipatory movements in minimizing the error is demonstrated to them. The training procedure follows the procedure used earlier by Adams and Creamer (1962c).

In another series of experiments Adams and Creamer (1962a) use various forms of pretraining, instead of explicit instructions. During pretraining the student has to synchronize a response with signals presented at regular intervals of time. Successful pretraining is found to result in a reliably longer average time on target than uninstructed practice at the task, but not all methods of pretraining are successful. Unfortunately Adams and Creamer (1962a) do not run a reference group with explicit instructions. Thus it is not possible to tell how the best methods of pretraining compare with explicit instructions.

Tracks with mixed predictable and unpredictable steps

Many of Noble and Trumbo's (1967) experiments include groups of students who receive a series of mixed predictable and unpredictable steps like those listed in Tables 6.2. There may be 12 steps in a series,

Table 6.2

Predictable and less predictable series of steps

Time in seconds	Fully predictable		Intermediate 5		Intermediate 3		Intermediate 2		Intermediate 1		Random	
	Track position	Step	Track position	Step	Track position	Step	Track position	Step	Track position	Step	Track position	Step
0	10	L6	x	Variable	x	Variable	x	Variable	x	Variable	x	Variable
1	4	L3	4	L3	4	L3	4	L3	4	Variable	x	Variable
2	1	R10	1	R10	1	R10	1	Variable	x	Variable	x	Variable
3	11	L1	11	L1	11	Variable	x	Variable	11	Variable	x	Variable
4	10	L6	10	L6	x	Variable	10	L6	x	Variable	x	Variable
5	4	R3	4	Variable	4	R3	4	Variable	4	Variable	x	Variable
6	7	L6	x	Variable	7	L6	x	Variable	x	Variable	x	Variable
7	1	R14	1	R14	1	Variable	1	R14	1	Variable	x	Variable
8	15	L10	15	L10	x	Variable	15	Variable	x	Variable	x	Variable
9	5	L1	5	L1	5	L1	x	Variable	5	Variable	x	Variable
10	4	R1	4	R1	4	R1	4	R1	x	Variable	x	Variable
11	5	R5	5	Variable	5	Variable	5	Variable	5	Variable	x	Variable
12	10		x	Variable	x	Variable	x	Variable	x	Variable	x	Variable

(After the experimental design described by Trumbo and colleagues, 1965.)

1 step every second. A fully predictable series is shown on the left of the table. The 15 positions of the track marker are spaced at equal intervals along the display. Position 1 is on the extreme left of the display, position 15 is on the extreme right.

The direction and size of a step can be deduced from the change in position. At time 0 the track marker is in position 10 toward the right of the display. A second later it jumps to position 4 toward the left of the display. The step is therefore to the left, and of 6 units in size, or **L6.**

A random series of steps is shown on the extreme right of the table. x indicates that the position of the track marker varies from series to series. The direction and size of each step is herefore variable.

The intermediate conditions are shown in the center of the table. In the condition called Intermediate 5, there are 2 random positions of the track marker, one after 6 sec, the other at the end of the series after 12 sec. The table shows that a single random position results in 2 steps of variable direction and size. One of the variable steps is to the random position. The other is from the random position to the next fixed position.

In the condition called Intermediate 1, every second position of the track marker is random. Thus every step in the series is variable in direction and size. The Intermediate 1 condition gives if anything a rather larger modulus mean error than the random condition (Trumbo and colleagues, 1965). The students may be well aware of the alternate predictable positions of the track marker. But in order to use the information, they have to compute the direction and size of the step between their present variable position and the subsequent fixed position. Apparently they are unable to do this in the 1 sec which is available between steps.

In the random condition the students make use of the probable direction of the next step. It follows from part A of Table 6.1 that when the track marker is near either end of the range, it generally jumps in the direction of the middle of the range. The students tend to use this information to initiate a response in what is usually the correct direction before the step appears. In the Intermediate 1 condition the students do not do this so often. The alternate fixed marker positions may direct their attention away from the statistical characteristics of the series as a whole.

In order to benefit from predictable positions of the track marker, there have to be predictable steps. The Intermediate 2 condition in the table has 4 predictable steps in the series of 12. In one experimental condition it gives a just reliably smaller modulus mean error than the random condition (Trumbo and others, 1965). The Intermediate 3 and Intermediate 5 conditions have respectively 6 and 8 predictable steps in the series of 12. As one would expect, these 2 conditions give reliably smaller modulus mean errors than the random condition. Intermediate 5 is of course worse than the fully predictable condition, but the difference is not reliable (Noble and colleagues, 1966).

In the Intermediate 3 and Intermediate 5 conditions, the first movements toward the variable marker positions have the largest average errors after practice. The first movements from the variable marker positions to the subsequent fixed marker positions have the next largest average errors (Noble and others, 1966, Figure 4). This is what one would expect. Unfortuntely the differences do not appear to have been subjected to statistical tests.

Chapter

7

Ramp tracks

Summary

In tracking a velocity ramp, the man corrects the error no more often than 2 or 3 times per second, whatever the rate of the ramp. With practice the intermittent corrections are superimposed upon a rate which more or less matches the rate of the ramp. Doubling the rate of the ramp doubles the average error, except in cranking at moderate speeds.

A range effect is found when a man is switched between rate and delta acceleration ramps, and when he tracks irregular multiple ramps. Irregular multiple velocity ramps are tracked more accurately than the comparable irregular sine wave track.

Tracking at a constant rate

Figure 7.1 (Garvey, 1960) illustrates velocity, acceleration, and delta acceleration or jerk ramps. What the man sees can be appreciated by covering the whole figure except for a vertical slit. As the slit is moved toward the right at a constant rate, the ramp tracks move upward with a constant velocity, acceleration, or delta acceleration. The experimental arrangement is illustrated in Figure 1.2. Ramp tracks can also be pro-

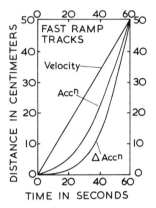

Figure 7.1.   Velocity, acceleration and delta acceleration ramps.
The ramps are the fast tracks used by Garvey (1960) in the experiment of Figure 7.6. All 3 tracks move the error spot of the compensatory display a distance of 50 cm in the 60 sec trials. The fast rate is .8 cm per sec. The fast acceleration is .03 cm per sec^2. The fast delta acceleration or jerk is .0015 cm. per sec^3.

duced electrically, as Garvey does for his experiment. In most experiments the ramp tracks have a constant velocity. Garvey's (1960; Garvey & Mitnick, 1957) experiments are unique in including ramp tracks with a constant acceleration or delta acceleration.

Ships and aircraft usually move at constant rates. They produce constant rate tracks on a map display, although not when they are viewed directly by a fixed observer. From the viewpoint of a fixed observer, ships and aircraft moving at constant rates accelerate as they approach and decelerate as they go away. The horizontal angular rate is illustrated in Figure 8.1.

There are few examples of constant rate tracks from the viewpoint of a fixed observer. One example is a newsman with a television or movie camera located at the center of a circular race track. Horses or automobiles racing round the track at a constant speed present a constant angular rate at the camera. In order to keep a horse or automobile in view, the newsman rotates his movie camera at the correct constant angular rate.

The theoretical importance of ramp tracks with constant rates is that they set the man a constant unchanging problem. Changes in his responses must therefore be determined by his limitations, and by the strategies which he uses to overcome his limitations. Experiments with ramp tracks can thus indicate the nature of the man's limitations and strategies. Similar limitations and strategies presumably operate with more complex tracks, but they are not so easy to study.

First responses to velocity ramps

The first responses of 10 adults to constant velocity ramps are described by Young (1951). A dot is centered over a hairline in the center of a CRT. After a warning signal, the dot starts to move either to the right or left at a constant angular velocity of 2, 4, 8 or 16° per sec. The man has to return the dot to the hairline as quickly as possible, by moving a lever in the direction in which he wishes the dot to go. The dot then continues on its constant velocity track. The man is instructed to let it do so.

The man's average reaction time decreases reliably from about .32 sec at the slowest angular velocity of 2° per sec, to .24 sec at the fastest angular velocity of 16° per sec. Presumably it takes the man less time to see that the dot is moving when the angular velocity is greater. The average amplitude, rate and acceleration of the man's first response movement increases reliably as the dot moves more rapidly. There is a range effect for rates of ramp, like the range effect for sizes of step discussed in Chapter 6.

The average time taken by the first response movement increases from about .24 sec when the dot moves at its slowest rate, to about .29 sec when the dot moves at its fastest rate. The times are about .05 sec shorter than the movement times reported previously by Taylor and Birmingham (1948) for first movements of comparable size in response to steps. This is presumably because a fast first response is an advantage in tracking ramps of various rates with a compensatory display, but a disadvantage in tracking steps of various sizes.

Figure 5.8 shows that in tracking steps a fast response provides less opportunity for visual guidance during the movement than does a slower response. Thus for steps, a fast first response is a disadvantage.

The position is different for the first response compensating for ramps of various rates. Here quick visual guidance is probably not very effective, because the man sees only the difference between his first response movement and the movement of the track. He does not see his response movement unmasked by the track movement. In the brief time available, the difference information is probably too complex to use to adjust the first response successfully. So a fast first response is not a disadvantage.

The advantage of a fast first response movement is that it leaves the dot in much the same final position, even when the man slightly misjudges the speed of the ramp. The response is complete before the misjudgment in the speed has time to introduce much of an error in position. Whereas when the first response movement is slower, there is more time for an error in position to develop.

It follows that in Young's (1951) experiment with ramps, quick first movements are an advantage. Whereas in Taylor and Birmingham's (1948) experiment with steps, slower first movements are an advantage. This probably accounts for the difference in the time taken by the first movements in the 2 experiments.

Response frequency and rate matching

The left side of Figure 7.2 illustrates how a man tracks a constant rate ramp with a lever position control. The figure follows the description given by Craik (1947) shortly before his death in 1945. The thick sloping line represents a ramp track which starts moving at time 0 on the abscissa. The thin wavy line in the upper part of the figure represents the man's response. The man corrects the error which he sees on average about once every .5 sec. The time interval between corrections ranges from about .25 to 1.0 sec.

Craik and Vince (1943, 1963a) show records of this kind, and also error records like that illustrated in the lower part of the left figure. The start of each response has been indicated by the letters **A** through **F**. There is 1 response for every 2 reversals of the error function. This can be described as 1 response per cycle, since 1 cycle of a sine wave contains 2 reversals. The basic frequency of the error function is 2Hz, or 120 cpm. If the rate of the ramp track is doubled, the man still corrects

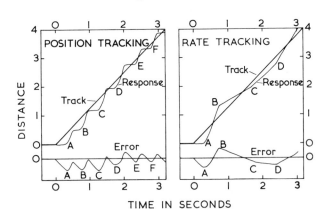

Figure 7.2. Position tracking and rate tracking.
The theoretical paper records illustrate how the error function is related to the man's response function in tracking a ramp of constant speed. There are many possible compromise strategies between the pure position tracking and the pure rate tracking.

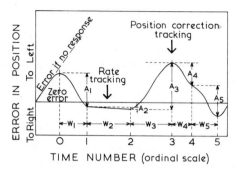

Figure 7.3.   The error in position tracking and in rate tracking.
The track is a ramp of constant speed. The times along the abscissa numbered **0** through **5** indicate the points on the record used to separate error half waves W_1, through W_5. A_1 through A_5 show the amplitudes of the error half waves. Zero error is indicated by the horizontal line. If the man does respond at all, the error runs parallel to the sloping broken line on the left. The experiment is described in the caption to Figure 7.4.

The events are not easy to interpret because the peaks in the error record lag in time behind the start of the man's corrections. On the left, the constant rate of the track marker produces an error of increasing size as the man's response marker is left behind. A little before time **0** the man starts to correct the error in position by a movement which is faster than the track marker is moving. After time **1** the man moves at about the same rate as the track. After time **2** in the middle of the figure, the response marker gradually comes to a halt, and so falls behind the track marker. Before time **3** the man therefore responds again. A little before time **4** it becomes clear that the first response is not large enough to catch up with the track marker. The man therefore makes a correction which places his response marker at time **5** some way ahead of the track marker. (Modified from Ellson and colleagues 1947, Figure 2.)

the error at about the same frequency. The modulus mean error is therefore about twice as large.

The average interval of about .5 sec between responses comprises a reaction time of about .25 sec, followed by a movement taking the remaining .25 sec. The man does not initiate his next movement until he has seen the outcome of his last movement. When the ramp stops, the man stops.

Craik (1947) compares the man with his reaction time of about .25 sec to a hypothetical servomechanism with a transmission lag of .25 sec. The servomechanism responds continuously to its error .25 sec previously. With a constant rate ramp, the servomechanism oscillates at a frequency of .5 sec per cycle, or 2 Hz, just like the man. But when the ramp stops, it continues to oscillate at the same frequency. The amplitude of the oscillation corresponds to the size of the error at the instant the ramp stops.

The servomechanism would do better to wait like the man until it has corrected the error which it has sensed, before sensing the next error to correct. When the ramp stops, there will then be no next error. It is a sensible strategy to adopt for any person or machine with a reaction time. People presumably learn it in infancy. Machines usually work on a different principle. The residual oscillation is damped, so that it gradually dies away.

Craik (1947) also describes how after practice the man's intermittent corrections of the error have superimposed upon them a constant rate of movement. The man as it were produces a rate of response which more or less matches the rate of the track, and intermittently corrects the error between the two.

The programmed rate element in the man's response is clearly apparent when the ramp stops suddenly without warning. The man continues to respond at the same rate for a reaction time. He does not stop until he sees the error which his now inappropriate rate anticipation is producing (Vince, 1948b, Figure 1C). The error corresponds to the response described in Chapter 6 (Slack, 1953a) to the expected step, instead of to the surprise step.

Rate anticipation is complicated by momentum or inertia. Craik (1947) uses the example of a man turning a crank to compensate for a constant rate ramp. With fast ramps the man has to turn the crank all the time. His arm and the crank together acquire angular momentum, like a heavy flywheel. They cannot be stopped instantaneously, even after the man sees the need to stop.

The right side of Figure 7.2 is a theoretical example of pure rate tracking. The man changes his rate at the times marked **A** through **D**. The changes in rate occur only about once every .75 sec. The changes at **A** and **B** produce only 1 reversal each in the error function shown in the lower part of the figure. After **C** the error function does not reverse. It takes 3 changes of rate, **B**, **C** and **D**, to produce 1 cycle in the error function. This occupies about 2 sec.

The basic frequency here is only .5 Hz, or 30 cpm. This is one quarter of the basic frequency for position tracking illustrated on the left of the figure. If the man is rate tracking well, the basic frequency need not be as high as this, because he does not have to correct his rate so often.

Error frequency

Ellson, Hill and Gray (1947) arrive at rather similar conclusions to Craik (1947) from a study of error records like that illustrated in Figure 7.3. In this experiment, a track marker moves to the right or to the left at a fixed speed. Ten practiced students have to keep a second marker in line with it, by flexing or extending the right elbow joint. If the student tracks perfectly, he produces the horizontal straight line in Figure 7.3 labeled zero error.

Ellson and his colleagues divide the error record into half waves as indicated along the abscissa of the figure. They measure the amplitude and time of each half wave. The divisions are bound to be somewhat arbitrary, but the method is specified in detail, and is presumably standardized.

After practice most trials produce sections of record like that labeled W_2. Ellson and his colleagues call it rate tracking. They define rate tracking as a section of error record in which the error is small, and changes by a size corresponding to less than .5° of elbow movement. The remainder of the time is spent in the development of misalignments between the 2 display markers, and in their correction. This is called position correction tracking.

In different trials Ellson and his colleagues increase the speed of the track from 5° of elbow movement per sec to 25° per sec. This produces a corresponding fivefold increase in the average amplitude of each half wave in the error function.

Half waves with amplitudes of .5° of elbow movement and above by definition represent position correction tracking. Their average duration hardly changes with changes in the speed of the track. Increasing the speed from 5 to 25° per sec decreases the duration of the average W only from .48 to .41 sec. The reduction is not reliable statistically. Practically 90% of the W's have durations which lie between .3 and .6 sec.

The results suggest that the timing of the man's position correction responses is almost independent of the speed of the ramp track. In this they support Craik (1947). But the average duration of the error half waves of Ellson and his colleagues is not quite as long as the average interval of .5 sec between responses, which is reported by Craik (1947) and by Vince (1948b).

Unfortunately it is not easy to tell from error records like those in Figure 7.3 just how frequently the man responds. The changes in error after times 2 and 5 could be due to the man changing the rate of his response for a response rate which is too slow as at B on the right of Figure 7.2. Or they could be due simply to the control handle coming to rest at the end of the response, as in the descending parts of the error functions on the left of Figure 7.2. The man could respond once for each W in Figure 7.3, or only once for each pair of W's. Most likely he responds at some intermediate rate. But it is not easy to ascertain the rate from a simple error record. It is preferable to record the track and the response function separately, as in the upper parts of Figure 7.2.

However there is a conclusion which can be drawn from the distributions of error half wave lengths reported by Ellson and his colleagues (1947). This is that even with fast ramps which produce large errors, the man does not respond more frequently than about once every .35 sec. This is the weighted average duration of the error half waves of all amplitudes with the fastest ramp. It sets an upper limit to the average response rate. If 2 **W**'s like those in Figure 7.3 often represent a single response, the average response rate may not exceed about 1 response every .5 sec, as reported by Craik (1947) and by Vince (1948b).

Average error and rate of ramp track

Figure 7.4 (Ellson and colleagues, 1947) shows that doubling the rate of a ramp track approximately doubles the modulus mean error

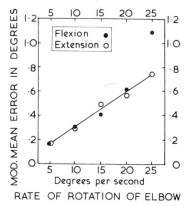

Figure 7.4.   Performance in rate matching.

The figure shows the average modulus mean error in tracking a constant rate ramp, for various rates of flexion and extension of the right elbow joint. The straight line has been fitted by eye. No statistical tests appear to have been carried out on these particular results.

Tracking is pursuit. A horizontal slit about 18 in long and 1 in tall reveals 2 black markers against a white background. Each of 10 practiced university students holds a hand grip mounted near the rim of a bicycle wheel with a radius of 14 in. The position of the hand grip is adjusted so that the student's elbow joint is in line with the axis of rotation of the wheel. A 5° rotation of the elbow joint moves the response marker about 1 in left or right.

A trial starts with the track marker 2.5 in further to the side than the response marker. As the track marker reaches the response marker, the man starts to track. He continues until he has rotated his elbow through about 60°. (After Ellson and colleagues 1947, Figure 5.)

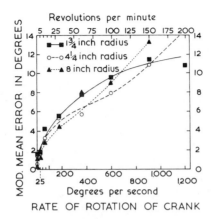

Figure 7.5. Performance in cranking at a fixed speed.
The squares, circles and triangles are for handles respectively 1.75, 4.25 and 8.0 in from the center of rotation. The forces required to rotate the handles are 3.0, 1.2 and .7 oz respectively. The display is compensatory. Each point represents the average of the same 4 people. The curved functions are fitted by eye. The experiment was conducted during World War II, and the details of the experimental procedure are not now available. No statistical tests were carried out. (After Craik & Vince, 1943, 1963a, Figure 25.)

over most of the range of rates tested. The only exception is at the fastest rate. Here the proportional average increase in error when the man flexes his elbow is rather larger than the proportional increase in rate. This may be because flexion involves raising the forearm. Probably the man has not time to attain the correct response rate before the 2.2 sec of test ramp is finished.

There are a number of reasons why doubling the rate of the ramp track should double the modulus mean error. If the man responds with a constant time lag, doubling the rate of the track doubles the distance which he lags behind. This doubles his modulus mean error.

Another reason is suggested by Craik (1947). We saw in the last section that the man responds at about the same average frequency, whatever the speed of the ramp. Doubling the speed of the ramp might be expected to double the average error which develops between one response and the next. This could well double the modulus mean error.

A contributary reason follows from Craik's ratio rule, which is illustrated in Figure 5.6. For individual movements larger than some minimum value, the average error is roughly proportional to the size of the movement. We have just seen that doubling the speed of the ramp might be expected to double the average error which develops between one response and the next. Since individual corrections have errors which are roughly proportional to their size, this also doubles the average size of the error left after the correction.

These explanations treat the rate tracking illustrated in Figure 7.3 exactly like the position correction tracking. They assume that what Ellson and his colleagues (1947) call rate tracking is simply the position correction tracking of the small errors. This may well be true. The 5 fold increase in the rate of elbow rotation which increases the modulus mean error by about 5, reduces the time spent in rate tracking to almost one fifth, from about 60% to about 15% (Ellson and others, 1947, page 18). It is what could happen if rate tracking represents simply the durations of the error record with the small errors.

The straight line in Figure 7.4 reaches 0° per sec on the abscissa (not shown) when the average error is about .05°. It suggests that there must be a minimum variable error with very slow ramps. A very slow ramp calls for very small movements. Figure 5.6 shows that very small movements have relatively large proportional errors. There is probably a minimum variable error for very small movements, and hence for very slow ramps.

Average error in cranking at fixed speeds

Figure 7.5 (Craik and Vince, 1943, 1963a) illustrates the accuracy with which people can turn a crank at a fixed speed. Over the middle range of rates the relationship between speed and accuracy is approximately linear. Increasing the rate of winding from 30 to 150 revolutions per minute (rpm) is a 5 fold increase. It about doubles or trebles the modulus mean error, depending upon the radius of the crank. In proportion, the size of the error increases less rapidly than the rate of winding.

This is because the man is not very good at winding the crank at a slow fixed speed. His hand tends to move too quickly in one part of the cycle, and too slowly in another part of the cycle. As the rate of winding increases up to perhaps 150 rpm, the variability in the rate becomes proportionally smaller. Thus the size of the error is proportionally reduced. The reduction is more marked after practice (Garvey and Mitnick, 1957).

This finding was used during World War II to increase the accuracy of tracking aircraft. A gearbox is inserted between the crank and the equipment, to gear down the crank. The man may have to turn the crank twice as fast in order to move the tracking sight at the same rate. His average error in the rate of turn is somewhat larger, but this is halved by the gear box before it reaches the sight. He therefore tracks more accurately (Helson, 1949, Figure 3).

Figure 7.5 shows that as the rate of winding increases, the increase in average error is larger with the large 8 in crank. The large crank is more accurate at the slower speeds, but less accurate at the fast speed of 150 rpm. When using the 8 in crank, the hand has further to move in order to move the display marker a given distance. The increased ratio of control movement to display movement is an advantage at slow and moderate rates of winding.

However at 150 rpm it is difficult to crank fast enough with the 8 in crank, because the hand has such a long distance to move. When the man happens to fall behind the track, it takes him quite a time to catch up again. At 150 rpm the 1.75 in crank is still some way from its upper limit of speed. Thus the 1.75 in crank is the more accurate at this speed. Helson (1949, Figure 3) reports similar results.

Figure 7.4 can be regarded as a large scale version of the lower left corner of Figure 7.5. The errors are slightly smaller in Figure 7.4 for comparable rates of rotation. This is probably because Ellson and his colleagues (1947) use a radius of rotation of about 12 in between the student's closed hand and his elbow joint. A larger radius produces rather more accurate tracking at slow rates.

The straight line drawn through the points in Figure 7.4 corresponds to the steep rise in average error on the left of Figure 7.5. In both cases the increase in average error is roughly proportional to the increase in the rate of movement. In the last section this relationship is accounted for partly by the frequency and accuracy of individual movements. However over the middle range of the functions in Figure 7.5 there is a smaller proportional increase in error as the rate of winding is increased. Here individual responses are replaced by a continuous rotation of the crank, which becomes relatively more accurate at faster rates of rotation.

Lag and lead errors with ramp tracks

Figure 7.6 (Garvey, 1960) illustrates a range effect when men are switched between rate, acceleration, and delta acceleration or jerk ramps. There are 2 ramps of each kind, 1 twice as fast as the other. The fast ramps are illustrated in Figure 7.1. The man has a pressure stick and a rate control.

A rate control differs from the position controls which have been considered so far. With a position control, the display marker moves a distance which is usually directly proportional to the distance moved by the control. With a rate control, it is the rate of the display marker which is proportional to the distance moved by the control. With the pressure stick which Garvey (1960) uses, the rate of the display marker is proportional to the pressure exerted by the man on the control. A

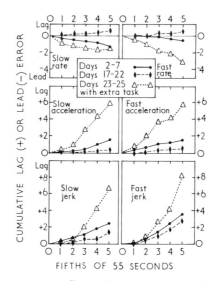

FIFTHS OF 55 SECONDS

Figure 7.6.   A range effect with ramp tracks of different orders.
The figure shows the cumulative constant position error, either lag or lead, for
6 different ramp tracks. Rising functions indicate lags. The falling functions at
the top indicate leads. The man has to keep a dot over a hairline in the center
of an 8 in CRT. The 3 fast tracks are illustrated in Figure 7.1. The 3 slow
tracks have half the values of the 3 fast tracks.
The 6 enlisted men have 6 trials daily with each of the 6 tracks. Trials last
60 sec. The 36 conditions are arranged irregularly in a balanced treatment design.
The design varies from day to day for 22 days, but the man is always told in
advance which condition he is to receive next.
The 6 men then track for 3 days while performing the 3 additional tasks listed
after Garvey (1960) in Table 12.7. They are told to perform the additional tasks
as well as they do when they are not tracking. The subtraction task is always
performed on the first day, the reporting task on the second day, and the lights
task on the third day. The results for tracking with the 3 additional tasks are
pooled. (After Figures 6 and 7 of Garvey, 1960.)

pressure of 1 lb to the right gives the display marker a rate of 10 cm
per sec to the right.

The unbroken lines represent performance early in training. With the
slow rate ramp the man runs reliably ahead of the track. The cumulative
lead increases at a more or less constant rate. This means that on average
the man leads the track by the same amount of time throughout the
trial.

The lead reflects a range effect like those discussed in Chapter 6
(Garvey, 1960, footnote 3). The 2 acceleration and the 2 delta accelera-
tion ramps all start moving very slowly, and get faster during the trial.
This happens on average in 4 out of every 6 trials. The man appears

to get used to the acceleration, and to expect it to some extent with the slow rate ramp. The range effect is less marked in a rather similar previous experiment by Garvey and Mitnick (1957, Figure 4), probably because only 3 out of the 6 ramps accelerate, and there are no delta acceleration ramps.

Early in training the man lags reliably behind with the acceleration, and delta acceleration or jerk ramps. The figure shows that with the acceleration ramps the cumulative lag increases at a more or less constant rate. This means that on average the man lags behind by the same amount of time throughout the trial.

With the delta acceleration ramps the cumulative lag accelerates reliably. The man tends to lag further and further behind during the trial. The accelerating lag also reflects the range effect. The man responds to the delta acceleration ramps rather as if they are simple acceleration ramps.

Marked range effects are to be expected with the balanced treatment design which Garvey (1960) uses. It is possible that the man would learn not to lag behind one of the delta acceleration ramps, if he were to practice with it all the time, and not be exposed to the rate and acceleration ramps. The experiment needs to be repeated using separate groups of people for each track.

The broken lines connecting the diamonds in the figure represent performance after training. Now only the delta acceleration or jerk ramps result in a reliable lag. The lag increases at a more or less constant rate, instead of at an accelerating rate. There is no longer a lead with the rate ramps. Presumably the man has learned to discriminate between the rate ramps and the acceleration ramps, although not between the delta acceleration ramps and the acceleration ramps. The unfilled triangles show that the range effect is exaggerated when the man is subsequently given an additional task to perform while tracking. Additional tasks are discussed toward the end of Chapter 12.

Side to side errors with velocity ramp tracks

When tracking a target which moves with a constant rate, the accuracy of angular aim depends upon the direction of the movement, not upon the speed. In the experiment, the man has to keep a stylus above a target which travels at a fixed rate along a narrow horizontal alley 35 cm long. The alley is laid on a flat table top with the near end directly in front of the man.

In some trials the far end of the alley is also directly in front of the man. The direction of the alley is then defined as 0°. In other trials the far end is at an angle of up to 90° to the left or right. The man tracks from the near end of the alley to the far end, or in the opposite direction. Contacts between the stylus and the edges of the alley are recorded as errors.

Corrigan and Brogden (1948) use a target rate of 3 cm per sec. Their 80 undergraduates track most accurately with the right hand when the hand moves forward and to the left at an angle of about 45°, or back in the reverse direction. They call the directions 315° and 135° respectively. For the left hand the most accurate directions are forward and to the right at an angle of about 45°, and back in the reverse direction. The most accurate directions for the left hand are the least accurate directions for the right hand (Briggs & Brogden, 1953).

Thompson, Voss and Brogden (1956) give separate groups of 16 undergraduates target rates which range between 2.5 and 4.5 cm per sec. They report that the man touches the sides of the alley about as many times at all speeds. This indicates that the sizes of the man's errors of angular aim are unrelated to the speed of the target. Increasing the speed does not change the average distance traveled before the stylus hits the edge of the alley. It simply reduces the average time taken to hit the edge.

Tracks with multiple ramps

Range effects with multiple ramp tracks

Range effects occur for the positions of the reversals in multiple ramp tracks, just as they do for sizes of step. In one study the man holds a pencil which carries a mask, as illustrated in Figure 7.7. In the experimental conditions the man can see the track only through the small circular window round the pencil. The tracks consist of 12 ramps, usually of different lengths, but always with the same slope upward or downward. In half the tracks the lines are arranged in repeating patterns. The remaining tracks are random. The man is told to take about 10 sec to traverse the 60 cm of track.

The positions of reversals can be classified as predictable if they occur in the patterned tracks after the pattern had started to repeat. The positions of the remaining reversals can be classified as unpredictable. Predictable and unpredictable reversals can each be subdivided by whether they are located toward the center of the display or toward the top or bottom edge of the display.

Each of these 4 classes can be subdivided again into 4 subclasses by the length of the ramp at the end of which the reversal comes, and

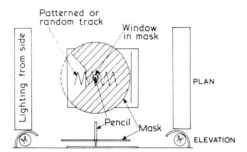

Figure 7.7. An apparatus for selfpaced tracking.
The pencil projects 2.2 cm beneath the clear celluloid disk, which has a diameter
of 25 cm. The man has to hold the pencil almost vertical. He moves it forward
and back to trace the track from left to right. The tracks all comprise 12 ramps.
The ramps all slope at an angle of 13.5° to the vertical but usually vary in length.
All tracks have a total length of 60 cm. The man is told to take about 10 sec
to trace the track. After tracking, he is told how long he has taken and he can
see how accurately he has tracked.

In 2 experimental conditions the clear celluloid disk carries a circular opaque
mask. The mask allows a view of the track only through the central window
2 cm in diameter round the pencil. The pencil blocks the central .7 cm of the
window. The lighting is from the sides, but transmitted light from below is preferable.
In one of the 2 conditions the man is allowed to see the full track for as long
as he likes before starting. In the other condition he is not allowed to see the
track first.

In a third experimental condition the opaque mask is shaped as illustrated in
the figure. In a reference condition there is no opaque mask. In both these 2
last conditions the man is allowed to see the track before he starts. There are
16 tracks, 8 patterned and 8 random. Two patterned and 2 random tracks are
presented to the same 16 young enlisted men under each of the 4 conditions.
(Poulton, 1957a.)

by the length of the previous ramp. The effect of each variable can
thus be examined independently of the effect of all the other variables.
In the series of tracks, ramps follow ramps of about the same length
twice as frequently as they follow ramps of very different length.

The man shows 2 distinct kinds of range effect. He always tends
to overshoot at reversals. But he overshoots reliably less when the
reversals are located far out towards the top or bottom of the display.
He overshoots to a greater extent when the reversals are located near
the center of the display. The man presumably learns to expect reversals
toward the top or bottom of the display, not near the center of the
display.

The second kind of range effect is determined by the previous one
or more ramps of the same track. The man overshoots reliably less at
the end of a ramp when it follows a ramp of about the same length,

than when it follows a ramp of very different length. The man presumably learns to expect ramps of about the same length to follow each other, as they tend to do.

There is another range effect of this second kind. The man overshoots reliably less at the predictable reversals of the patterned tracks, than at the unpredictable reversals. Here he is again making use of the recent structure of the track. This second kind of range effect varies in its nature from time to time, because it depends upon the recent structure of the track. It is more transient than the first kind of range effect, which is based upon the unchanging overall average position of the reversals.

Irregular multiple velocity ramp and sine wave tracks

An irregular multiple velocity ramp can be tracked more accurately than the comparable irregular sine wave track. Heinemann's (1961) ramp tracks contain ramps of different rates. The positions of the reversals in one of the tracks (Problem A) match the positions of the reversals in one of Heinemann's irregular sine wave tracks (Problem D). The amplitudes of the various excursions of the 2 kinds of track are identical. Each ramp represents the average velocity of the corresponding half cycle of the sine wave track between 2 reversals.

The modulus mean error is about 1.5 times as large with the sine wave track as with the multiple ramp track. The difference is probably highly reliable, although it does not appear to have been tested.

The man's difficulty with the ramps is confined largely to the positions of the reversals. Between reversals he can soon discover the rate of the ramp, and more or less match it. Whereas the irregular sine wave track changes its rate all the time. It presents the man with a more difficult tracking task.

Chapter

8

Sine wave tracks

Summary

Doubling the amplitude of a sine wave track about doubles the average error. The theoretical relationship between the top track frequency and the average error is S shaped.

As the top frequency of a quasirandom track is increased, the average amplitude of the response decreases, the average time lag increases, and the average amplitude of the remnant increases. Attenuating the high frequencies in the track to one tenth in a single step increases the remnant at the low frequencies, and increases the phase lag at the high frequencies. This does not happen if the high frequencies are attenuated by lowpass filters.

Nonlinear strategies are represented in the remnant. A small remnant indicates successful predicting of the track and preprogramming of responses.

Tracking an object whose rate varies

Most objects move in a straight line at a more or less constant speed. But Figure 8.1 shows that to a fixed observer, the angular rate of an

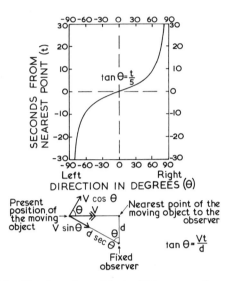

Figure 8.1.   The direction of an object which moves at a constant speed.
The object moves in a straight line from left to right. It might be a bicyclist riding at 10 ft per sec at a distance of 50 ft, or an aircraft flying at 1000 ft per sec at a distance of 5000 ft. What a fixed observer sees can be appreciated by covering the whole figure except for a horizontal slit. As the slit is moved upward at a constant rate, the track of the object moves to the right. The angular speed of the object increases until the object reaches its nearest point directly ahead. The angular speed then decreases again. A constant angular rate is represented by a sloping straight line.

The direction θ of the object at time t is given by $\tan \theta = Vt/d$, where V is the velocity of the object and d is its nearest distance. The diagram at the bottom of the figure shows that the angular velocity at any point is $V \cos \theta$ divided by the distance $d \sec \theta$. This can be written as

$$\frac{d\theta}{dt} = \frac{V \cos \theta}{d \sec \theta} = \frac{V}{d} \cos^2 \theta$$

or

$$\frac{1}{\cos^2 \theta} d\theta = \frac{V}{d} dt$$

Integrating,

$$\tan \theta = Vt/d$$

as indicated above.

object increases as it approaches. The angular rate decreases when the object has passed and is going away. An aircraft rises in the sky at an increasing rate as it approaches. It descends at a decreasing rate as it flies away toward the horizon. The accelerating and decelerating

track of a moving aircraft is representative of many of the tracks which
people meet in everyday life.

Sine wave disturbances occur in flying aircraft. The gusts of wind
and pockets in the air which buffet an aircraft result in S shaped displacements of the aircraft. A pilot who is attempting to keep the aircraft
on a straight and level course, has to null the S shaped displacements.

The aerodynamic characteristics of high performance aircraft may
make them undergo longitudinal damped oscillations after they have
been buffeted by a pocket in the air. Longitudinal damped oscillations
may also occur following a maneuver made by the pilot to change height.
The pilot is usually expected to track out the disturbances as far as
he can.

Amplitude of sine wave tracks

Figure 8.2 illustrates the relationship between the amplitude of a sine
wave track and the sizes of the control and display movements. Doubling

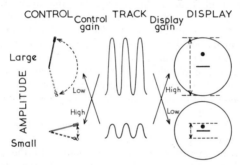

Figure 8.2.   Amplitude of track, control, and display.
The large amplitude track at the top produces large control and display movements.
The small amplitude track at the bottom produces small control and display movements. A large amplitude track can be paired with small control movements by
increasing the control gain. The resulting display movements can be reduced in
size by reducing the display gain. Similarly a small amplitude track can be paired
with large control and display movements by changing the gains. What matters
to the man is the sizes of the control and display movements, not the amplitude
of the track as such.

As a general rule, doubling the amplitude of the track more or less doubles
the RMS or modulus mean error in tracking. The exact size of the effect depends
upon the control gain and upon the display gain. If the control gain starts too high
or the display gain starts too low, doubling the amplitude of the track gives the
man the advantage of control or display movements nearer to the optimum size.
His tracking error is then a little less than doubled. If the control gain starts
too low or the display gain starts too high, doubling the amplitude of the track
makes the control or display movements still further from the optimum size. The
man's tracking error is then a little more than doubled.

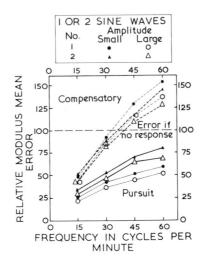

Figure 8.3. Performance with tracks of various amplitudes and frequencies.

The tracks consist of 1 or 2 sine waves. For the tracks with 2 sine waves, the frequency of the larger sine wave is indicated on the abscissa. The smaller sine wave has half the amplitude of the larger, and a frequency 1.37 times as high. With the pursuit display, the maximum amplitude of the large 1 and 2 sine wave tracks is 3 in. The small 1 and 2 sine wave tracks have half the amplitude. The maximum required amplitudes of the control movements are the same as the maximum amplitudes of the tracks. The gain of the compensatory display is only half the gain of the pursuit display, although both displays call for control movements of the same size (see Figure 8.4).

The 3 pilots and 13 young enlisted men receive all the 32 conditions once. The points in the figure represent the last 30 sec of the 60 sec periods of tracking. In the balanced experimental design all conditions with the pursuit display are performed either before or after all the conditions with the compensatory display. The 4 frequencies of each function in the figure are always presented one immediately after the other in order of increasing frequency. To be reliable, differences in relative modulus mean error must be at least 12. (Results from Poulton 1950b, 1952a.)

the amplitude of a sine wave doubles both its rates and its accelerations. The man sees the greater amplitude of the track, unless the gain of the display is reduced. He has to double the amplitudes, rates and accelerations of his control movements, unless the gain of the control is increased.

In Figure 8.3 doubling the amplitude of a sine wave track does not quite double the modulus mean error. The error if the man does not respond at all is taken as 100 for all the tracks. The ordinate shows the modulus mean error relative to this value. If doubling the amplitude of the track doubles the modulus mean error, the unfilled points for twice

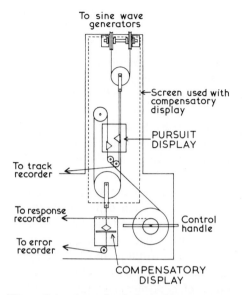

Figure 8.4. A mechanical tracking apparatus.
The apparatus is designed to compare pursuit and compensatory displays. The sine wave track is fed in at the top from behind. It is generated by fishing line attached to rotating arms. The sine waves are summed and halved in amplitude by the top pulley. Control movements are fed in from the control handle on the right. The pursuit display with its track and response markers is illustrated in the middle. The man holds the right side of the control handle, so an upward movement raises the response marker. A certain amount of friction is required to prevent the control from moving spontaneously whenever the track marker is pulled upward. Track movements and control movements are recorded separately on the same paper tape at half amplitude.

The large pulley below the pursuit display subtracts the control movements from the track movements, and halves the difference. The compensatory display is located below the large pulley. The position of its single error marker above or below the fixed reference line indicates the direction and size of the halved error. The man holds the left side of the control handle so that an upward movement raises the error marker. The halved error is recorded separately on the same paper tape as the half amplitude track and control movements. A paper record is illustrated in Figure 8.8. (After Poulton, 1950b, 1952a, Figure 1.)

amplitude would be superimposed upon the corresponding filled points for normal amplitude. This is not so. The unfilled points all lie a little below the corresponding filled points.

The experimental arrangement is illustrated in Figure 8.4. The same people serve in all the experimental conditions. But the relative advantage of the larger amplitude track cannot be due to transfer, because a similar result is reported by Fitts, Marlowe and Noble (1953) when separate groups of students serve in each experimental condition. Hartman and Fitts (1955) report similar results for tracks comprising 1, 2 and 3 sine waves.

The effect of doubling the amplitude of a sine wave track can be related to the effects of doubling the size of a step, and of doubling the rate of a velocity ramp. Figure 5.6 shows that for quick movements above a certain minimum size, the average error of the movement is approximately proportional to its size. Figure 7.4 shows that for constant rates of movement of reasonable size, the average error is proportional to the rate. As a first approximation, doubling the amplitude of a sine wave track should therefore double the average error.

The slight relative advantage of the track of larger amplitude in Figure 8.3 is due to the way in which experiments on track amplitude are usually set up. When the control and display gain are both held constant at 1:1, Figure 8.2 shows that the largest amplitude of the track is limited by the size of the display, and by the range of control movements. The largest track covers most of the display, and requires most of the available range of control movements. This is the optimal condition.

Reducing the size of the track reduces both the size of the display and the size of the control movements. As the size of the display is reduced, small errors become more difficult to see. As the size of the control movements is reduced, correcting small errors becomes relatively inaccurate, as illustrated on the left of Figure 5.6. Relative to the amplitude of the track, the average tracking error is therefore usually a little larger with the smaller track.

This need not happen if the experiment is set up differently. Suppose the smaller track covers most of the display, and requires most of the available range of control movements. The larger track then makes the display marker disappear off the edge of the display from time to time, or rest against the stops at the edge of the display. Also the largest available control movement is insufficient to match the extreme movements produced by the track. Here the smaller track should produce the smaller relative average error. It does not usually happen in practice, because experiments are not set up this way.

Frequency of sine wave tracks

Doubling the frequency of a sine wave doubles the rates and quadruples the accelerations. The effect which this has upon the average error in tracking depends upon the number of frequencies in the track, and upon what the frequencies are. Doubling moderate frequencies may

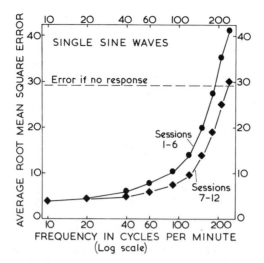

Figure 8.5. Performance with single sine wave tracks.
The display is pursuit. The man rests his forearm on a horizontal lever which is pivoted beneath his elbow. He has to move his forearm through a horizontal arc of 20°. Before the experiment each man has between 500 and 1000 min of practice with sine waves of between 30 and 90 cpm. A session consists of 2 consecutive trials of 1 min at each of the 10 frequencies in the figure. The order of the frequencies is randomized. Each man has 7 practice sessions before the results in the figure are collected. Sessions are always on separate days. To be reliable, differences in height must be at least 10. Unfortunately with only 3 people in the experiment, it is not possible to tell how representative the results are likely to be. (Results from Noble & colleagues 1955.)

more than double the average error. But doubling very low or very high frequencies has only a relatively small effect. The complete theoretical relationship between average error and frequency is S shaped, like the functions in Figure 8.7.

Figure 8.5 (Noble, Fitts, & Warren, 1955) shows that with single sine waves doubling the frequency does not as much as double the average error, except at frequencies of 100 cpm and above. However, the filled points in Figures 8.6 (Chernikoff & Taylor, 1957; Obermayer and colleagues, 1962) and in Figure 8.7 (Elkind, 1956) show that for tracks comprising 3 or more sine waves, the average error can be doubled by doubling top frequencies well below 100 cpm.

Tracks with top frequencies of 10 cpm and below are easy to follow with a position control. Below 10 cpm doubling the frequency does not increase the average error very much. Practice makes the task easier for the man. Figure 8.5 shows that practice raises the frequency at which the average error starts to rise steeply. Practice therefore raises the fre-

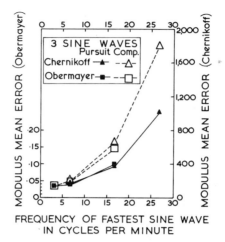

Figure 8.6.   Performance with tracks comprising 3 sine waves.
The frequencies of the sine waves have ratios of 15:10:6. The amplitudes are inversely proportional to the frequencies. The triangles and scale on the right hand ordinate represent the original experiment by Chernikoff and Taylor (1957). The squares and scale on the left hand ordinate represent the partly repeat experiment by Obermayer and colleagues (1962). The 2 scales are adjusted to superimpose as far as possible the pairs of corresponding points at the common top frequencies of 6.7 and 16.7 cpm. The results are for a position control system.

Chernikoff and Taylor (1957) use a separate group of 6 enlisted men for each track frequency. The results for rate aided and rate control systems are not shown. Pursuit and compensatory displays are paired with each of the 3 control systems. The 6 combinations are arranged in a latin square design. A practice trial of 1 min on each condition is always given before 3 test trials. There are 14 days of practice on each experimental condition before the results are collected.

Obermayer and colleagues (1962) use the same 6 graduates for all conditions. Different track frequencies are presented on separate days, in balanced order. The results for rate and acceleration control systems are not shown. Only either the pursuit or the compensatory display mode is used in a single experimental session. Within each of 2 sessions using a single display mode, there are 10 consecutive 1 min trials with each control system. The first 5 of the 10 trials are for practice only. There are also 13 practice trials on each condition before the experiment, using a single sine wave with a frequency of 2.2 cpm. The practices are reported separately by Obermayer, Swartz and Muckler (1961). Neither research report provides sufficient details of the statistical calculations to determine the exact precision of any of the plotted points in the figure.

quency at which doubling the frequency first doubles the average error.

Figure 8.7 shows that with high top track frequencies, the average error may cease to increase with increase in frequency. This happens once the error exceeds the average error which occurs when the man does not respond at all. The man may realize that his efforts are tending

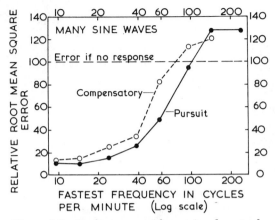

Figure 8.7. Performance with quasirandom tracks.
    The tracks consist of between 40 and 80 sine waves of about equal amplitude, spaced at equal intervals of frequency. The results are from 3 practiced men. The details of the experiment are described in the caption to Figure 3.3. Unfortunately statistical tests do not appear to have been carried out on these particular results. (From Elkind, 1956, Table 4-6.)

to increase the average error rather than to reduce it. If so, he may cease to respond altogether, or respond with a very reduced amplitude. The complete relationship between average error and top track frequency is then **S** shaped, as illustrated in the figure.

Lag and lead errors with single sine wave tracks

Predicting single sine waves of low and medium frequency

Single sine waves are relatively easy to predict. The man does not need to follow the track a reaction time behind. He can make his response function synchronize with the track, apart from small errors which reflect lack of skill either in prediction, or in the execution of responses.

In one experiment each of 11 young enlisted men sits in turn in front of the experimental apparatus illustrated in Figure 8.4. Six of the men have never tracked before. The men are told to move the control lever up and down a few times to see how it controls the response marker of the pursuit display. As soon as the track marker starts to move, they have to keep the 2 markers of the pursuit display in line. The track has a frequency of 15 cpm.

Within the first cycle, or early in the second cycle, 10 out of the 11 men get ahead of the track in position at least once (Poulton, 1950b).

The other man does not get ahead in position for almost 4 cycles. He reports afterwards that he has been trained always to follow behind. In some cases the first anticipatory error probably results from the assumption that the track marker moves at a more or less constant rate. When the track marker slows down before it reverses, the man is not expecting it to slow down so quickly, and tends to get ahead in position.

Figure 8.8 illustrates consistent anticipation. The figure represents a selected paper record of a sine wave of 60 cpm, tracked with a pursuit display. Paper records like this suggest that the man generates a function something like a sine wave of the correct frequency and amplitude. To do so he has to make a nonstop series of alternate up and down control movements. This programed response is body oriented or closed (Poulton, 1957b). It can continue for brief periods without vision.

The programed response is adjusted visually from time to time to make it match the track better in phase, in average amplitude, or in average position on the display (Poulton, 1950b; Noble and colleagues, 1955). After practice the median interval between adjustments is about 4 sec (Poulton, 1957c). In Figure 8.8 adjustments probably occur at a to correct a lag in phase, and at c to correct an error in the average height of the response.

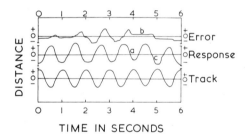

Figure 8.8.   A paper record of tracking a sine wave of 60 cpm.
The man uses the pursuit display and the simple lever control of Figure 8.4. The error function at the top is derived by adding the response function below it to the track function at the bottom, paying attention to the sign. As time passes the man's response function tends to lag further and further behind the track. This is reflected by the increasing amplitude of the error function shown at the top. The error function is about 90° ahead of the track in phase. It appears to be 90° behind the response, because the response has been recorded with a phase reversal of 180°.

After 4 sec the man introduces a correction by reducing the amplitude of the downward response labeled a. This eliminates the time lag, but leaves a constant position error on the display, labeled b on the error funtion. A second later the man over corrects it by making a downward response of unduly large amplitude labeled c. (After Poulton, 1950b, Figure 6.)

During the first 4 sec of the paper record, there is no clear evidence that the man adjusts his programed response. He may make an adjustment which is too small to detect. More likely he simply makes decisions from time to time not to change his programed response.

A comparable experiment indicates that the man can often track as well for 5 sec with his eyes closed, as he can with his eyes open. In this other experiment 12 young enlisted men practice the task of Figure 8.8 for a few minutes alternately with their eyes open and closed, until they do not appear to be improving any further with their eyes closed. In the experimental condition they then have to track for alternate 5 sec periods with their eyes closed. In the reference condition they track all the time with their eyes open.

Eight of the 12 men track as accurately or more accurately in at least one 5 sec period with their eyes closed, as in a 5 sec control period with the eyes open. About 30% of all attempts with the eyes closed are indistinguishable from control periods with the eyes open (Poulton, 1957c). Thus the programed response illustrated in Figure 8.8 may well not be adjusted during the first 4 sec.

Lag and lead errors with single sine waves of high frequency

Ellson and Gray (1948) describe the tracking of single sine waves of between 30 and 240 cpm with a pursuit display. The track and response are recorded separately, as in Figure 8.8. The 4 not very practiced people are able to keep more or less in time with the track up to frequencies of 120 cpm. But at frequencies of 180 and 240 cpm they succeed in keeping more or less in time on only about one third of the trials. When they do so, their errors in timing are usually lags of not more than about 35° in phase.

In the remaining two thirds of the trials at frequencies of 180 and 240 cpm, the man is unable to keep his response in time with the track. He responds with about the correct amplitude, but the frequency of his response is too high. Periods of being out of phase alternate with short periods of being in phase as the response becomes 1, 2, or more complete cycles ahead of the track. Sometimes the man is able to keep in phase once his response has climbed into the correct phase again. But usually the drift in phase continues uncorrected.

At these high frequencies the man can see that he is out of phase. But it is difficult for him to decide whether his response frequency is too high or too low. Ellson and Gray (1948) do not tell the man when his response frequency is too high. He must assume that he cannot keep up with the track, and so does not reduce his response frequency.

In 2 trials out of every 7, the frequency of the track increases from 60 cpm to 240 cpm over a period of 22 sec. In these speeding up trials the man learns to increase his response frequency when he appears to be losing synchronization with the track marker. This strategy must transfer to trials with a high constant frequency.

If this is so, it accounts for the inconsistent performance shown by Ellson and Gray's people from trial to trial. When the man happens to start at the correct frequency, he remains at the correct frequency. When he happens to start at a frequency which is too low, he tends to speed up until he reaches the correct frequency. But when he happens to start at too high a frequency, he tends to respond at a still higher frequency, and so stays out of synchronization with the track marker.

Noble, Fitts, and Warren (1955) repeat the experiment on 3 highly practiced men, but without any speeding up trials. At frequencies above 120 cpm, one man consistently goes too fast like Ellson and Gray's people. Another man does not respond faster than about 160 cpm, even with the sine wave of 240 cpm. There are similar individual differences in the amplitude of the response. One man responds with too large an amplitude, another man responds with too small an amplitude.

These results suggest that there are no characteristic kinds of errors when people track single sine waves of frequencies up to 240 cpm. Different people make different kinds of errors, unless they receive an experimental condition which predisposes them to a particular kind of error, like Ellson and Gray's (1948) speeding up trials.

The irregularity of tracks with 2 or more sine waves

A combination of 2 sine waves can produce a track which appears fairly random at a brief glance, provided the ratios of the frequencies and amplitudes are carefully selected. A frequency ratio of 1 to 1.37 is used for the tracks represented by triangles in Figure 8.3. The pattern does not quite repeat every 3 cycles of the slower sine wave, because there is a phase shift of 40°. It takes 27 cycles before there is a more or less perfect repeat.

The amplitude of the slower sine wave should be the larger. A ratio of 2 to 1 is used for the tracks in Figure 8.3. If the faster sine wave is the larger, its reversals tend to dominate the timing of the track reversals.

In spite of these precautions, a track with only 2 sine waves produces sections of paper record which look much like other sections. Figure 8.3 shows that the track is responded to much like a single sine wave. The functions represented by triangles are not very different in shape from the corresponding functions represented by circles. They are simply shifted up or down.

With the pursuit display, the triangles lie above the circles. This is due mainly to the greater irregularity of the tracks composed of 2 sine waves. It is not due simply to the higher frequency of the smaller of the 2 sine waves. This follows from the results of an experiment in which the smaller of the 2 sine waves has the lower frequency. The experiment uses the 3 pilots and 5 of the enlisted men who have served in the experiment of Figure 8.3, and the same pursuit display.

When the larger and smaller sine waves have frequencies respectively of 60 and 15 cpm, the relative modulus mean error is 62. When both the sine waves have frequencies of 60 cpm, the relative modulus mean error is reliably smaller, only 50 (Poulton, 1957d). The difference of 12 in the relative modulus mean error corresponds to the difference of 15 between the unfilled circle and unfilled triangle at the bottom on the right of Figure 8.3 for a frequency of 60 cpm. Thus most of the increase in modulus mean error in Figure 8.3 produced by the second small sine wave of different frequency, is due to the greater irregularity of the track. It is not due simply to the higher frequency of the second small sine wave.

Tracks with 3 sine waves

The repetitiveness of a track with only 2 sine waves can be reduced by adding a third sine wave. However the unfilled points and broken curve in Figure 8.9 show that a track comprising 3 sine waves can be predicted ahead better than chance for an average of rather more than .5 cycle of its top frequency. In the experiment the man uses the pursuit display of Figure 8.4. In some conditions an electric hammer sounds every second. At this signal the man has to move his response marker quickly to the position which he estimates that the track marker will reach .5 sec later when a bell rings. The man then has .5 sec before the tap of the hammer calls for his next response.

In other experimental conditions the man has to predict 1.5 or 3.5 sec ahead. Since the man's response has to synchronize with the tap of the hammer, the spans of prediction are about .7, 1.7 and 3.7 sec respectively. With the 3 different top track frequencies indicated in the figure, this gives the 9 unfilled points. As is to be expected, the accuracy of prediction depends upon the amount of track cycle in the prediction span, not upon the duration of the span.

The tracks composed of 3 sine waves in Figure 8.9 have frequencies with ratios of 10:7:5. Thus the irregular patterns repeat after every 70 cycles of the top frequencies. The tracks of Figure 8.6 all comprise

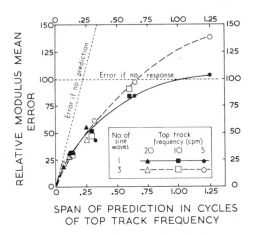

SPAN OF PREDICTION IN CYCLES
OF TOP TRACK FREQUENCY

Figure 8.9. The span of prediction.
The man has to predict the position of a track marker at various times ahead. The abscissa gives the span of prediction in cycles of the fastest sine wave in the track. The filled points and unbroken curve represent single sine wave tracks. The unfilled points and broken curve represent tracks comprising 3 sine waves of equal amplitude, with frequencies in the ratios of 10:7:5. The 2 curves are fitted by eye. The 12 men make all their predictions with one track before changing tracks. In each experimental condition the men make 40 predictions, the first 20 for practice.

The straight broken lines indicate the average performance if the man does not predict. For the horizontal broken line running through 100 on the ordinate, the man always leaves his response marker in the center of the display. For the sloping broken line, the man always leaves his response marker where the track marker was at the start of the prediction span. To be reliable, differences must be at least 16.

The relative modulus mean error is not much smaller with the single sine waves than with the tracks composed of 3 sine waves. This is because the experimental technique is not suited to single sine waves. With single sine waves prediction is best measured when the man is tracking all the time, because prediction is assisted by the rhythm of the man's regular to and fro limb movements. (After Poulton, 1952b, Figure 3.)

3 frequencies with ratios of 15:10:6. Here the irregular patterns repeat after every 30 cycles of the top frequencies.

With a good deal of practice, the man may be able to learn some parts of the irregular patterns. It is not known to what extent the man's performance can benefit from this. People improve with practice. Part of the improvement reflects greater skill at handling the control. In pursuit tracking with a position control system, the remainder of the improvement reflects the learning of the track. This may include learning parts of the irregular patterns. Unfortunately it is not possible to tell from a learning curve what aspects of the task are being learned.

In practical experiments comparing engineering variables, it may not matter if the track has repeating patterns which can perhaps be learned. But if the experimenter wishes to make inferences about the man's strategies, he needs to know the characteristics of the track which have and have not been learned. If so, it is preferable to stick to single sine waves which are fully learnable, or else to use tracks comprising many sine waves or filtered noise, because they do not contain repeating patterns.

Tracks comprising many sine waves or filtered noise

An irregular track cannot be really random if it is to be tracked successfully. Very high frequencies of large amplitude make tracking virtually impossible, and have to be excluded. One way of producing an irregular track without high frequencies is to use tracks consisting of white noise with the high frequencies attenuated by one or more lowpass filters. White noise contains all frequencies, and has equal energy per cycle. The amplitudes have a Gaussian or normal distribution. The phase relationships are random. The behavior of a lowpass filter in attenuating high frequencies is illustrated in Figure 11.10.

Another way of producing an irregular track without high frequencies is to synthesize low frequency noise, using many low frequency sine waves. The quasirandom tracks of Figure 8.7 (Elkind, 1956) each have between 40 and 80 components with random phase relationships. The components are of about equal amplitude. They are evenly spaced every .15 to 6 cpm, depending upon the top frequency in the track.

There do not appear to be any direct experimental comparisons between filtered noise tracks and the corresponding quasirandom tracks filtered to match them. It appears to be assumed that the results would be almost identical. This has still to be determined by experiment.

Some of the learnable characteristics of any irregular track are probably the average position on the display, the average and approximate maximum amplitude, the average frequency of reversals, and the average and approximate maximum rate of movement.

When the highest frequency in a track has a large amplitude, it tends to determine the average frequency of the reversals. This is what happens with Elkind's (1956) quasirandom tracks of Figure 8.7, where the highest frequency has about the same amplitude as all the lower frequencies. The man then tends to predict reversals at the top track frequency. Figure 8.11 shows that the frequencies in his response function have their largest amplitude here, unles the top frequency is too high.

When a track consists of filtered noise, its top frequency does not determine the average frequency of the reversals. This is because the top frequency is the most attenuated.

At frequencies well above the break frequency of a lowpass filter (see Figure 11.10), the amplitudes of sine waves become inversely proportional to their frequencies. This inverse relationship between amplitude and frequency is sometimes used for tracks comprising only 3 sine waves, like the tracks of the experiments of Figure 8.6. It ensures that the top frequency does not dominate the other frequencies in the track.

Response frequencies with sine wave tracks

Figure 8.10 (Pew, Duffendack & Fensch, 1967a) shows that in tracking a single sine wave, the man's response contains frequencies which are outside the narrow band of frequencies around the track frequency. The extra frequencies represent the man's failure to copy the track perfectly, and the strategies which he uses to make his copy as accurate as he can. For each track in the figure, the average RMS error amplitude at the track frequency is called 1.0. The RMS amplitudes at other frequencies are shown as a proportion of this.

The filled circles in the figure are for a sine wave of about 6 cpm The man's response contains a broad band of frequencies tailing off above about 120 cpm. The response at 120 cpm probably represents occasional corrections of position separated by about .5 sec. Consistent behavior of this kind is illustrated on the left of Figure 7.2. The results in Figure 8.10 are from 3 highly practiced people. Most of the time they do not need to correct their response as often as twice per second. This is indicated by the quite large amplitude of the frequencies lying between 6 and 120 cpm.

The response at 8 cpm may correspond to some changes of rate separated by about 3.7 sec, or about 16 changes of rate per minute. But it can equally well correspond to some corrections of position separated by about 7.5 sec, or about 8 corrections of position per minute. The rather different effects upon the error frequency produced by changes in rate and by corrections of position are illustrated in Figure 7.2. In Figure 8.10 the response amplitudes represented by the filled circles at frequencies of from 12 through 75 cpm probably correspond to some corrections of position and some changes of rate.

The points on the functions for the sine waves of 30 and 120 cpm can be interpreted in a similar way. The points to the left of the peaks of the functions represent frequencies of correction below the track frequency. Here the corrections change the phase of the response, or

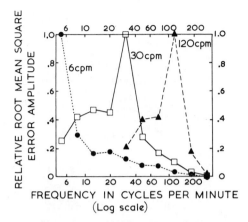

Figure 8.10. Response frequencies with single sine wave tracks.
The RMS amplitude of the error is shown on the ordinate relative to the RMS
amplitude of the error in the frequency band containing the track frequency, which
is called 1.0. The RMS amplitude is measured at 10 frequencies, spaced at equal
logarithmic intervals.

The task resembles the task of Figure 8.5. The display is pursuit. The man
has to rotate his horizontal forearm through an angle of 42° to track sine waves
with amplitudes of 8 cm. The control is spring centered. It requires a force of
1.4 lb to move it 21° to either side of its central position. Each function in the
figure represents the average of the same 3 people.

During each 2 min trial the 3 people hear all the time a tone whose pitch
indicates their error integrated over the last 2 sec. At the end of the trial they
are told their average integrated error for the trial. They practice for a total of
32 daily 1 hr sessions. The practice includes a number of conditions other than
those in the figure: sine waves of 14 and 220 cpm, a compensatory display,
a display gain half as large, a control gain twice as large, and a spring centering
one third as large. After this much practice, the differences between the 3 people
and the 2 display modes are small. Unfortunately with only 3 people it is not
possible to tell how representative the results are likely to be. (Results from Pew
and colleagues, 1967a.)

its absolute position in the display, like the corrections illustrated in
Figure 8.8.

Response frequencies with tracks comprising
many sine waves

When a track is composed of many sine waves, the frequencies in the
man's response do not correspond perfectly with the frequencies in the
track. The match is best when the top frequency of the track is low.
It becomes less good as the top track frequency increases.

Figure 8.11 (Elkind, 1956) illustrates closed loop transfer functions
for tracks with top frequencies of 38, 96 and 144 cpm. The frequencies

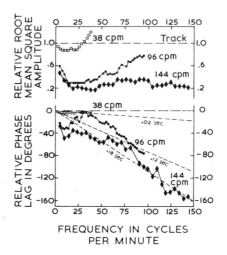

Figure 8.11. Closed loop transfer functions with quasirandom tracks.
The top track frequencies are printed against the functions. The sloping broken lines represent constant time lags. The details of the experiment are described in the caption to Figure 3.3. (After Elkind, 1956, Figures 4-9a and b, and 4-10a and b.)

in the response are given relative to the frequencies in the track. A closed loop transfer function represents the part of the man's response which correlates with the track. It includes his predictions and his pre-programed responses, in so far as they are successful and reproduce the track. Most of the energy in the response function of Figure 8.8 goes in the closed loop transfer function.

The filled points in Figure 8.13 show the closed loop transfer functions for tracks with top frequencies of 29 and 86 cpm. The filled circles in Figure 3.4 show the closed loop transfer function for a track with a top frequency of 58 cpm. All the functions are for the same 3 highly practiced people, tracking with a pursuit display.

When the top frequency in the track is increased, the man is not able to predict the track so accurately (see Figure 8.9) because there is more track movement during a fixed interval of time. Figures 8.11 and 8.13 illustrate 2 systematic trends in performance as the top frequency in the track is increased. The upper parts of the figures show that there is a decrease in the average amplitude of the closed loop transfer function. For the track with a top frequency of 29 cpm, the filled circles in the upper part of Figure 8.13 have a RMS amplitude of .9 or more of the track amplitude at all frequencies. For the track with a top fre-

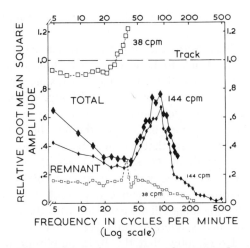

Figure 8.12. Response frequencies with quasirandom tracks.
At each frequency the total RMS amplitude is calculated by combining the RMS amplitude of the remnant with the RMS amplitude of the corresponding closed loop transfer function of Figure 8.11. (Results from Elkind, 1956, Figures 4-9a and d, and 4-10a and d.)

quency of 144 cpm, the diamonds in the upper part of Figure 8.11 have a RMS amplitude of only about .3 of the track amplitude.

The large diamonds in Figure 8.12 show that when the RMS amplitude of the remnant is added, the total RMS amplitude of the response increases to between .3 and .7 of the track amplitude. But this is still only a moderate proportion.

The reduction in the amplitude of the response could be because the track tends to correct the errors which it produces before the man can correct them. Or it could be due to a deliberate strategy by the man to avoid RMS errors much larger than those produced by the track alone. Figure 8.7 shows that when the highest frequency in the track is 144 cpm, the man's RMS error is larger than the RMS error produced by the track alone. If the man were to increase the amplitude of his response, he would increase his RMS error still further.

The lower parts of Figures 8.11 and 8.13 show that the average time lag increases with increases in the top track frequency. For the track with a top frequency of 29 cpm, the filled circles in the lower part of Figure 8.13 have an average time lag of about .01 sec. For the track with a top frequency of 144 cpm, the diamonds in the lower part of Figure 8.11 have an average time lag of about .18 sec.

An average time lag of .18 sec is about the same as the average reaction time to an expected visual signal in a single choice reaction time experiment. It is less than half the average reaction time of .4 sec to a sudden unexpected step in an irregular sine wave track (Gottsdanker, 1956a). Thus with the top track frequency of 144 cpm, the man must expect the track to behave more or less as it does. But he presumably cannot predict the track movements at all accurately an appreciable time ahead. So he waits for a change before he responds to it, like a man in a single choice reaction time experiment.

With the top track frequency of 96 cpm, the man has a shorter average time lag, .12 sec. This means that he must be able to predict the track reasonably accurately about .06 sec ahead. He therefore initiates his responses an average of .06 sec early, according to his predictions. With lower top track frequencies, the man can predict the track reasonably accurately a longer time ahead. This is in line with the results illustrated in Figure 8.9. The man's average time lag is therefore shorter.

Figures 8.12 and 8.14 show that the RMS amplitude of the remnant increases with increases in the top track frequency, and with the consequent decrease in the man's ability to predict the track. For the track with a top frequency of 29 cpm, the small circles at the bottom of Figure 8.14 have a RMS amplitude of only about .1 of the amplitude of the track. For the track with a top frequency of 144 cpm, the small

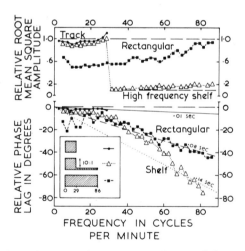

Figure 8.13. A closed loop transfer function with a track having a high frequency shelf.

The frequency spectrum of each track is illustrated at the bottom on the left. The sine waves are all spaced at intervals of .6 cpm. Some of the details of the experiment are described in the caption to Figure 3.3. (Results from Elkind, 1956, Figures 4-21a and b.)

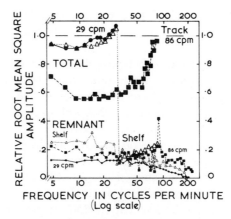

Figure 8.14. Response frequencies with a track having a high frequency shelf. The 3 tracks are those of Figure 8.13. (Results from Elkind, 1956, Figures 4-21a and d.)

diamonds in Figure 8.12 have a RMS amplitude at the track frequencies of from about .2 to .6 of the track amplitude.

Response frequencies with tracks having attenuated high frequencies

We have just seen that increasing the top track frequency reduces the average amplitude of the closed loop transfer function, increases the average time lag, and increases the average size of the remnant. Figures 8.13 and 8.14 (Elkind, 1956) show that there are similar, but less marked, effects upon the closed loop transfer function if the added high frequencies are attenuated to one tenth in a single step. The unfilled triangles represent a track with equal amplitudes up to a frequency of 29 cpm. Between 29 cpm and the highest frequency of 86 cpm, the amplitude is only one tenth as large. A comparison between the triangles and the circles indicates the effect of this high frequency shelf.

The upper part of Figure 8.13 shows that the high frequency shelf reduces the amplitude of the closed loop transfer function below 29 cpm. The lower part of the figure shows that the high frequency shelf increases the phase lag at low frequencies. The lower part of Figure 8.14 shows that adding the high frequency shelf increases the remnant at low frequencies. The high frequency shelf produces a noisy track. Its effects upon the low frequencies in the response are probably similar to the effects upon the response of masking a track by mixing it with noise of low amplitude (see Figures 11.12 and 11.13).

Figure 8.13 shows that a high frequency shelf does not affect the low frequencies of the closed loop transfer function as much as when the high frequencies are left unattenuated. The filled squares represent the response to a track with a rectangular spectrum extending up to 86 cpm. The upper part of the figure shows that the low frequencies of the closed loop transfer function are attenuated to between .7 and .5 of the track amplitude. Whereas the closed loop transfer function for the track with the high frequency shelf still has an average amplitude of about .9.

The lower part of the figure shows that the phase lag of the squares at low frequencies averages between 10° and 20°, whereas the triangles have a phase lag at low frequencies of only about 5°. Thus a high frequency shelf has similar effects upon the low frequencies of the closed loop transfer function as unattenuated high frequencies have, only the effects are smaller.

However Figure 8.14 shows that the high frequency shelf has a greater effect upon the remnant at low frequencies, than does the unattenuated track with a top frequency of 86 cpm. Up to 29 cpm, the small triangles in the lower left part of the figure have an average RMS amplitude of about .25, whereas the small squares have an average of rather less than .2. The remnant at low frequencies does not increase if the high frequencies are attenuated gradually by lowpass filters (Elkind, 1956, Figure 4-14d).

It is misleading to state as McRuer, Graham, Krendel, and Reisener (1965, page 74) do that a high frequency shelf does not materially affect the operator's behavior. The statement overlooks the increase in the size of the remnant. Also it is based upon an incorrect comparison which gives a conveniently good match. McRuer and his colleagues (1965, Figure 23) take Elkind's (1956) track B6 with a top unattenuated frequency of 29 cpm, and a high frequency shelf extending up to 86 cpm. They compare it with Elkind's (1956) track R.40, which has a top frequency of only 24 cpm.

The correct comparison is with track B7, which has a top frequency of 29 cpm. Elkind (1956, Figures 4-24a and b) illustrates the corresponding comparison between tracks B6 and B7. The match is not nearly so good. The amplitudes differ by about 4 decibels (dB) at all frequencies. The phase lags differ by at least 5°, except between 18 and 29 cpm.

McRuer and his colleagues are concerned with compensatory displays and with open loop transfer functions. In an open loop transfer function, the frequencies in the response are related to the frequencies in the error. The difficulties of interpreting open loop transfer functions are discussed in Chapter 4. Closed loop transfer functions are easier to interpret, because the frequencies in the response are related to the frequencies in the track.

This book is concerned principally with pursuit displays and with closed loop transfer functions. Figure 8.13 and 8.14 illustrate the closed loop transfer functions and remnants for Elkind's (1956) tracks B6 and B7 with a pursuit display. The tracks are represented, respectively, by triangles and circles. Figure 8.13 shows clearly the effect of the high frequency shelf upon the transfer function at lower frequencies. Figure 8.14 shows the increase in the size of the remnant.

There is another curious effect of reducing the amplitude of the high frequencies in a single step. It increases the man's phase lag at the high frequencies. At a frequency of 80 cpm, the triangles in the lower part of Figure 8.13 have a phase lag of 70°. While the squares for the rectangular spectrum have a phase lag of only 40°.

This result also is not found if the high frequencies in the track are attenuated by lowpass filters. The lower part of Figure 8.16 (Elkind, 1956) shows the phase lag which results from attenuation by filters. The phase lag is smaller when the high frequencies are more attenuated. At a frequency of about 60 cpm, the triangles for the heavily filtered track have a phase lag of 60°, while the squares for the lightly filtered track have a phase lag of 70°.

High frequencies of low amplitude are sometimes added to a track. This is done to enable the man's phase lags at the high frequencies to be measured without giving him an impossibly difficult task. Figures 8.13 and 8.16 show that the phase lags which are measured by the method depend upon the shape of the spectrum of the attenuated high frequencies. Attenuation to one tenth in a single step increases the phase lag at the high frequencies. While attenuation by lowpass filters reduces the phase lag in proportion to the number of filters. This finding reduces the generality, and hence the usefulness, of the measured phase lags at high frequencies. It means that the shape of the spectrum of the high frequencies in the track must be held constant, in order to obtain comparable phase lags under different conditions.

Human describing functions

Control engineers have a technique for describing the behavior of nonlinear control systems (Graham & McRuer, 1961). The technique has been used to describe compensatory tracking behavior. It involves fitting the linear open loop human transfer function by a describing function. The nonlinear remnant is dealt with separately.

In 1957 (McRuer & Krendel, 1957; 1959a, b) the complete human

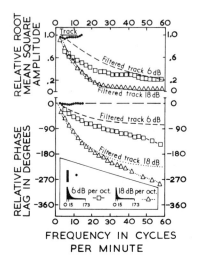

FREQUENCY IN CYCLES
PER MINUTE

Figure 8.15. Closed loop transfer functions with filtered tracks.
The frequency spectrum of each track is illustrated at the bottom. The rectangular track comprises 48 sine waves spaced every .3 cpm. The 2 filtered tracks comprise 144 sine waves spaced every 1.2 cpm. The break frequency (see Figure 11.10) of the lowpass filters is 15 cpm. The amplitudes of the tracks are indicated by the broken and dotted lines in the upper part of the figure. The phases of the tracks are indicated by the broken and dotted lines in the lower part of the figure. Some of the details of the experiment are described in the caption to Figure 3.3. (Results from Elkind, 1956, Figures 4-14a and b.)

describing function had 5 components. They are illustrated in Figure 8.17. The figure shows 3 representative values of each of the components. By selecting appropriate values it is possible to fit most open loop human transfer functions. Since 1965 (McRuer and colleagues 1965; McRuer, Graham & Krendel, 1967a, b) 3 extra lowpass filters and 1 extra highpass filter are sometimes added.

Describing functions have not been fitted to closed loop human transfer functions, which include the man's successful predictions and preprogramed responses. Describing functions have been fitted only to open loop transfer functions, which are not considered in this book because they are difficult to interpret. The difficulties are pointed out in Chapter 4. The values of the components of the open loop describing function cannot be related in a meaningful way to the man's strategies. The attempts made to do so will not be discussed.

However describing functions can be fitted to closed loop transfer functions. The closed loop transfer function represented by the unfilled points in Figure 3.4 (Elkind, 1956) comes from one of the compensatory

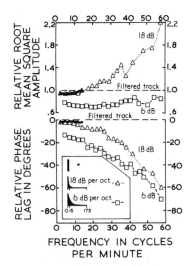

FREQUENCY IN CYCLES
PER MINUTE

Figure 8.16.   The same closed loop transfer functions as in Figure 8.15.
The functions are plotted with the amplitudes of the filtered tracks at all frequencies
called 1.0, and the phase lags of the filtered tracks called 0°. The upper part
of the figure is misleading. The response represented by the triangles appears to
have a considerably larger amplitude than the response represented by the squares.
The true relationship is illustrated in the upper part of Figure 8.15.

The lower part of the figure is easier to follow than the lower part of Figure
8.15. The phase of the track at each frquency is independent of the phase at
every other frequency. The phases after filtering are also independent. Thus it
is not necessary to give the phase of the filtered track, and to show the phase
of the response relative to it as in Figure 8.15. (After Elkind, 1956, Figures 4-14a
and b.)

tasks considered by McRuer and Krendel (1957, 1959a, b). The points
are replotted in Figure 8.19. The relative amplitudes at the top of the
figure average about .7, and slope up to the right. The figure shows
that they can be fitted reasonably well by a gain of .63 and a highpass
filter with a time constant of .15 sec.

The relative phase lags in the bottom part of the figure are fitted
reasonably well by a transmission time lag of .14 sec. The figure shows
that the time lag has to be increased to .26 sec. to counteract the lead
produced by the highpass filter. The approximate fit involves 3 components: a gain, a transmission time lag, and a highpass filter.

Figure 8.18 illustrates what happens when a lowpass and highpass
filter are connected in series. Part A of the figure shows that when
the highpass filter has the longer time constant, the amplitude of the
combined output increases with frequency. The phase of the combined
output at first increases and then decreases, producing an inverted U.

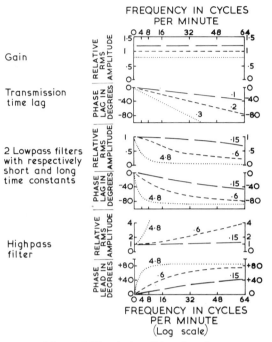

Figure 8.17. A describing function.
The first open loop describing function for compensatory tracking has the 5 components listed on the left (McRuer and Krendel, 1957, 1959a, b). The components are illustrated on the right. More components of the same kind are now sometimes added. The numbers printed against the functions on the right represent seconds. The values of the components can be selected to fit the closed loop transfer functions illustrated in this and other chapters. The gains at the top are 1.2, 1.0, and .8.

The open loop describing function is often written with the 5 components in their Laplace transforms:

$$\frac{Ke^{-ts}(1 + T_LS)}{(1 + T_NS)(1 + T_IS)}$$

where **K** is the gain, e^{-ts} is the residual transmission time lag, T_L is the time constant of the highpass filter $(1 + T_LS)$. T_N and T_I are the time constants of the lowpass filters $1/(1 + T_NS)$ and $1/(1 + T_IS)$ (see the caption to Figure 11.10).

Part **B** of the figure shows that when the lowpass filter has the longer time constant, the effects are reversed. The amplitude of the output decreases with frequency. The phase of the output at first decreases and then increases, producing a **U** the right way up.

The 2 functions represented by the circles in Figure 8.11 are for pursuit tracking with a top track frequency of 96 cpm. The function at the bottom is a kind of inverted **U**. However at zero frequency the function

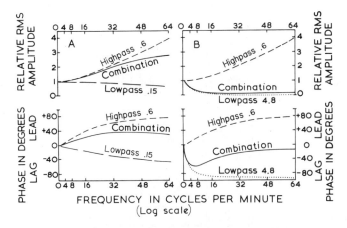

Figure 8.18. Combined lowpass and highpass filters.
In **A** on the left the highpass filter has the longer time constant. In **B** on the right the lowpass filter has the longer time constant.

has to reach the origin. Thus the complete theoretical function is like an S on its side: ∽. The first U part can be fitted by the combination of a lowpass and a highpass filter, as in Figure 8.18B. The lowpass filter has the longer time constant. The inverted U part can be produced by a transmission time lag.

The top part of Figure 8.18B shows that this combination produces a relative amplitude which decreases with frequency. Whereas the relative amplitude of the function represented by the large circles in the top part of Figure 8.11 at first decreases and then increases with frequency. The increase in amplitude at the higher frequencies requires a second highpass filter with a time constant of about .6 sec. This makes 2 highpass filters with time constants of about .6 sec, and a lowpass filter with a time constant of about 4.8 sec. The gain has to be increased to about 1.1.

The increase in phase, which the second highpass filter produces at the higher frequencies in the bottom part of Figure 8.11, has to be counteracted. It can be done by increasing the transmission time lag to about .25 sec. The approximate fit has involved 5 components: a gain, 2 highpass filters, a lowpass filter, and a transmission time lag.

The 5 components illustrated in Figure 8.17 can be given any suitable values. When they are combined with 3 extra lowpass filters and an extra highpass filter as required, it is possible to fit almost any human transfer function, whether open loop or closed loop.

Unfortunately the flexibility of the describing function makes it incap-

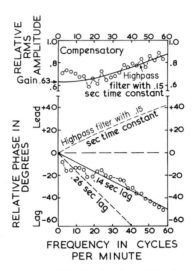

Figure 8.19. The fit of a describing function.

The closed loop transfer function is replotted from Figure 3.4 (Elkind, 1956). The relative amplitude at the top is fitted by the combination of a gain of .63, and a high pass filter with a time constant of .15 sec. The gain determines the height of the fitted function. The time constant determines the slope up to the right.

The relative phase at the bottom is fitted by the combination of the high pass filter with its .15 sec time constant, and a transmission time lag of .26 sec. The resultant phase lag approximates closely to the .14 sec transmission time lag shown.

able of precise prediction. "There is a common saying that an equation with two constants in it can be made to fit an elephant and one with three constants can make its tail wiggle" (Morgan & Stellar, 1950, p. 156). A describing function contains 5 constants, perhaps 9. At present the exact numerical value of each constant has to be calculated from the transfer function. The exact values cannot be predicted in advance.

A more serious criticism of a human describing function is that it can be misleading. The transmission time lag of the describing function is not the man's transmission time lag. It is the residual time lag after fitting the highpass and lowpass filters. In Figure 8.19 the man's transmission time lag is .14 sec. It is not .26 sec. Calling .26 sec the man's reaction time lag conceals this fact, and may mislead the reader.

Human remnants

The remnant is the nonlinear part of the man's response. It does not correlate with the track, and so is not represented in the transfer function or describing function. The remnant has 3 rather different sources: the man's variability in phase, his nonlinear strategies, and his muscle tremor.

Variations in phase

Variations in phase get into the remnant in the following way. In computing the transfer function at each frequency, the response is cross-correlated with the track (see Chapter 3). Since the response tends to lag behind the track, the crosscorrelation is greatest when the response is advanced in phase by an amount which corresponds to the average phase lag. If the man maintains a constant phase lag, the amplitude of his response when the crosscorrelation is greatest will represent all the energy in his response at the frequency.

In practice the man's phase lag varies. Sometimes he is not quite so far as average behind the track. Sometimes he is rather further than average behind the track. This produces a crosscorrelation which has a less definite maximum value as the response is advanced in phase through the phase angle which represents the average phase lag. The amplitude of the response at the average phase lag appears in the transfer function. The remaining energy in the response, which represents the transient phase lags on either side of the average, is one component of the remnant.

Discrete corrections

The other major component of the remnant is produced by the man's nonlinear strategies. The functions in Figure 8.10 are entirely remnant, except at the frequencies of the single sine wave tracks. We saw that the additional frequencies result from discrete corrections of position and changes in rate. Discrete corrections of phase also produce frequencies in the remnant.

Onoff control

Onoff or bangbang control is a nonlinear strategy which is sometimes used with control systems of high order. The man holds his control always either at its center where its output is zero, or in one of its 2 extreme positions. Onoff control may be quite a good strategy with an acceleration or higher order control system, provided the man is able to time his control movements correctly. With an acceleration control system, onoff control is the quickest way of correcting an error in position (see Figure 16.1).

In the man's response function, onoff control produces frequencies which correspond to twice the average time intervals between the control movements. It also produces odd numbered harmonics like those illustrated in Figure 11.8. The harmonics appear in the remnant. The fundamental frequencies of the onoff movements also appear in the remnant if they do not correspond to a frequency in the track, or if they vary in phase.

Dither

Dither is another nonlinear strategy which is sometimes used. The man oscillates his control at a fairly high frequency but low amplitude. The frequency of the dither is unrelated to the track frequencies, and so appears in the remnant. With a position control system and a compensatory display, the dither appears in the display superimposed upon the error (Poulton, 1967, Table 4). It may help the man to feel that he is in control of the error marker. But this is achieved at the cost of an increase in RMS error.

With an acceleration or higher order control system, the man may dither symmetrically about the central zero of the control. It does not affect the display marker very much, provided the dither is of high frequency. This is because high response frequencies are attenuated in the output of a high order control system. However if the man dithers for a single cycle more to one side than to the other with an acceleration control, he changes the rate of the display marker by a corresponding amount. A single out and back movement of an acceleration control has a similar effect when the man is not dithering.

Symmetrical dither about the central zero may mask the quick out and back movements which are often used with an acceleration control. But the dither does not change the behavior of the acceleration control system. It is stated (Briggs, 1966, page 419) that dither can make a higher order control system behave like a simple first order system. This is not so.

Suppose a person dithers with an acceleration control system, maintaining the average position of the control a little to one side of its central zero. Each cycle of dither puts on a small positive acceleration, which is followed by a smaller negative acceleration. The difference is a smaller positive acceleration. The resultant smaller positive acceleration increases the average rate of the display marker by a small amount.

The small increases in the average rate produced by each cycle of the asymmetrical dither gradually accumulate. With an acceleration control system, asymmetrical dither therefore produces a gradually increasing average rate. It does not reduce the effective order of the acceleration control system by producing a constant rate. As we have just seen, a constant rate is produced by a single out and back movement of an accceleration control, or by a single asymmetrical cycle of dither, not by continuous symmetrical or asymmetrical dither.

Discrete corrections, onoff control, and dither, are 3 nonlinear strategies. If the man uses other nonlinear strategies, they also will be reflected in the remnant.

Muscle tremor

Muscle tremor is a third source of the remnant. Sutton (1957) studies muscle tremor by asking people to maintain a constant force of 5 lb for 30 sec. The man is shown on a CRT display the difference between the force which he is exerting and the required force. In a task of this kind, all the frequencies in the man's response represent remnant. When the response is analyzed by frequency, the amplitude is found to decrease with increases in frequency, like the function in Figure 8.10 for a sine wave track of 6 cpm. However there is a small peak at frequencies between 7 and 9 Hz (420 and 540 cpm). The peak is just visible in the bottom right hand corner of Figure 8.12.

The peak is more marked for people who can be described as slightly shaky. Of Sutton's (1957, Figure 5) 4 experienced trackers, the man with the largest peak has about 3% of his total response energy in this frequency band. Two men hardly show peaks.

The remnant at frequencies of 7 to 9 Hz is too small to make much difference in ordinary tracking. But its size can be greatly amplified in aiming at a distant object. In using a camera with a telescopic lens, small rotary movements produce relatively large movements of the distant object in the visual field of the camera. If the camera has a control mechanism which amplifies frequencies of between 7 and 9 Hz, muscle tremor could be a major source of tracking error.

The size of the remnant

The remnant is large when the man adopts a nonlinear strategy in an attempt to keep down his tracking error. This happens with tracks of high frequency, like the track of Figure 8.12 with the top frequency of 144 cpm. Here the remnant represents over 70% of the man's total mean square output. This part of the man's response is not fitted by the describing function.

Another cxample is in tracking with a high order control system like the control system of an aircraft. Here 65% or more of the man's mean square output may be in the remnant (McRuer & Krendel, 1957, Table 15).

It is possible to reduce the apparent size of a remnant by using a linear measure of correlation. Suppose the transfer function accounts for about .64 of the man's total mean square output, as the open loop transfer function does with the compensatory task of Figures 3.3 and 3.4. Taking the square root, the average linear correlation becomes .8 (Elkind, personal communication). McRuer and Krendel (1957, Table 15) quote a figure of .92, because they omit the part of the remnant which lies above the top track frequency. The reader may not realize that about 35% of the man's mean square output is not fitted by the describing function.

The remnant is small when the man can successfully predict the track and preprogram his responses. This is the case with a track of low frequency and a position control system, like the track represented by squares in Figure 8.12 with the top frequency of 38 cpm. Here the remnant represents only about 5% of the man's total mean square output. The man preprograms his responses so successfully that he behaves much like a linear servomechanism.

The remnant and tracking error

In order to determine the sources of error from a frequency analysis, it is necessary to study both the closed loop transfer function and the remnant. When a man is tracking reasonably well, most of his mean square error is represented by the remnant. A closed loop transfer function like that illustrated by the squares in Figure 8.11 for the track with the top frequency of 38 cpm, accounts for only about 30% of the mean square error (Elkind, 1956, Figure 4-9d an Table 4-VI).

Closed loop transfer functions account for more than half of the mean square error only when the man ceases to track adequately. Figure 8.7 shows that for the track with a top frequency of 144 cpm, the man produces a RMS error larger than the error which the track produces when the man does nothing. The track is represented in Figure 8.11 by the diamonds. Here the reduced response amplitude contributes about 60% of the total mean square error. The .18 sec time lag contributes another 5% of the error. (In calculating the power contributed by the .18 sec time lag, it is necessary to take account of the reduced response amplitude.) The remnant contributes the remaining third of the mean square error (Elkind, 1956, Figure 4-10d and Table 4-VI).

At first sight it may seem curious that increasing the top frequency of an irregular track increases the proportion of the total response represented by the remnant, yet reduces the proportion of the total error contributed by the remnant. As we have just seen, for the track with a top frequency of 144 cpm in Figure 8.11, more than 70% of the response output is in the remnant. Yet the remnant is responsible for only about one third of the mean square error.

This is due largely to the reduced amplitude and increased time lag of the closed loop transfer function. The reduced amplitude leaves the remnant a greater proportion of the total response output. Yet the reduced amplitude and the increased time lag leave uncorrected much of the error produced by the track. This uncorrected error swells the man's total error, and so reduces the proportion of the total error for which the remnant is responsible.

Chapter

9

Pursuit and compensatory displays

Summary

A conventional pursuit display has 3 major advantages over a conventional compensatory display. With the pursuit display the man can predict the future movement of the track more accurately, and so reduce his time lag. He can learn the control system more easily, and monitor its output. Also the status information in the pursuit display helps the man to avoid and detect mistakes. A conventional pursuit display has always been found to give at least as accurate tracking as a conventional compensatory display, except when the results are biased by the transfer of inappropriate phase relationships from the compensatory to the pursuit condition.

Tracking with pursuit and compensatory displays

So far most of the book has been concerned with pursuit or true motion displays. Figure 1.1 shows how a pursuit display differs from a compensatory or relative motion display. A pursuit display benefits from the capacity of the eyes for spatial vision. The eyes can appreciate the true motion of 2 markers against a structured background, and also their relative motion when they are close together. A pursuit display makes use of both capacities simultaneously, while a compensatory display uses only the capacity of the eyes to appreciate relative motion.

In order to obtain the greatest benefit from a pursuit display, the 2 markers must be fairly close to each other and have a well structured background. The structure can be provided by the texture or calibrations against which the markers move. Or it can be provided by the texture of the fixed edges of the display, if they are close enough. A textured background is probably more efficient than textured edges, but the point has still to be investigated by experiment.

True motion and relative motion in the air

Figure 9.1 illustrates a relative motion or zero reader display of the kind used in aircraft. A flight director of this kind shows the pilot the extent to which he is off his flight path. It is used for descent and landing, especially in poor visibility. In **A** the aircraft is a little low, and to the right of the prescribed flight path.

Figure 9.2 illustrates a true motion display for directing the pilot. The hollow circle with the 2 small wings represents the aircraft. It indicates where the aircraft is going to. The spot beyond the parallel lines indicates where the aircraft should be going to. The parallel lines represent a runway in the sky. The display incorporates also a gyro horizon, which shows the direction and tilt of the horizon relative to the attitude of the aircraft. It is represented by the lines on either side of the aircraft symbol.

True motion and relative motion at sea

The top part of Figure 9.3 illustrates a compensatory radar display. Relative motion displays of this kind are responsible for numerous so-called radar assisted collisions between ships at sea (Calvet, 1960). The ship carrying the radar is represented by the center of the display. The display shows the motion of other ships relative to the motion of the ship carrying the radar. The display predicts collisions very clearly, as the figure shows. But it does not give the captain a clear indication of how to avoid a collision.

The bottom part of the figure represents the corresponding pursuit radar display at one minute intervals. It is not so easy to detect collisions with this true motion display. It helps to have a transparent movable overlay with parallel lines engraved upon it, like the broken lines in the figure. This makes it easier to detect a ship approaching on a constant

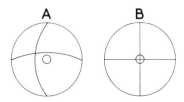

Figure 9.1. A zero reader display.
This compensatory display is used to give the pilot directions while he is flying.
The aircraft is represented by the fixed circle in the center. When the aircraft
is on the flight path, the 2 crosswires pass through the center of the fixed circle
as in **B**.

bearing, which indicates a future collision. The figure shows that the
true motion display presents the captain with sufficient information to
enable him to avoid a collision.

Aiming with a sight

A newsman may have to report a race meeting using a movie or
television camera. To show the racehorse or automobile in the lead,
he has to track it with a moving sight. This is a pursuit or true motion
task. The newsman can see the horse or automobile racing along the
track. He can also see the crosswire in his sight sweeping along the
track. The display thus corresponds to the pursuit display of Figure
1.1A.

But suppose the newsman has to report an aeroclub meeting when
the sky is clear and blue. To show a flying aircraft he again has to
track it with a moving sight. But now there is no structured background
for the aircraft and crosswire to move across. When the newsman is
tracking well, the aircraft appears almost stationary on the crosswire
in the center of the sight. The display corresponds to the compensatory
display of Figure 1.1B. As soon as the aircraft flies low enough to be
silhouetted against distant mountains like the headup display of Figure
9.2, the display changes to true motion or pursuit (Hammerton & Tickner,
1970).

It is possible to convert the compensatory display to a pursuit display,
using a beam splitting prism. Part of the light to the eye comes directly
from the sight which tracks the aircraft. The remainder of the light
comes from a miniature sight. The miniature sight looks at a miniature
cylindrical grid which does not move. As the first sight tracks the aircraft,
the miniature sight sweeps over the stationary grid. When the 2 pictures
are superimposed, the aircraft and crosswire both appear to move across
the stationary grid. The grid has the same effect as distant mountains.
It converts the compensatory display to pursuit.

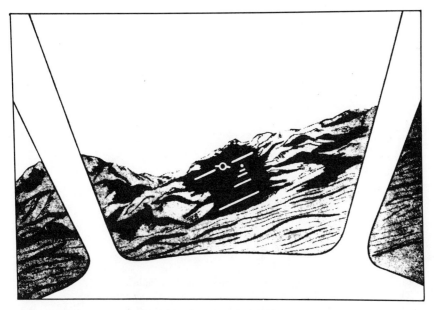

Figure 9.2.   A headup display.

Naish's (1964, 1970) true motion headup display is reflected off the windscreen of the aircraft into the pilot's eyes. It is collimated at infinity to ensure that it is always in focus. The display is being used to give the pilot directions while he is flying low. The pilot has been instructed by the spot and parallel lines of the flight director to change course to the right, in order to avoid the hill on the left. The pilot has therefore banked to the right. The outside world, the runway in the sky, and the gyro horizon have rotated through the corresponding angle to the left.

When the aircraft has finished banking, the gyro horizon and the parallel lines representing the runway in the sky will be horizontal. When the pilot has satisfied the demand of the flight director, the aircraft symbol will be over the spot. The spot will need to rise as the aircraft approaches the range of hills, to carry it safely over the top. (Courtesy of Specto Avionics Ltd. and Computing Devices of Canada Ltd.)

When the gyro horizon is reflected off the windscreen, it is not as difficult to interpret as it is when it is mounted in the cockpit. Most of the instruments in the cockpit tell the pilot what the aircraft is doing, its speed, its height, and so on. In contrast, the gyro horizon shows what the outside world is doing. This can be confusing when the gyro horizon is placed among the other instruments. The pilot may in error take the attitude of the gyro horizon to be the attitude of the aircraft (Fitts and Jones, 1961b, page 362). This causes crashes, because the gyro horizon tilts the opposite way to the way the aircraft tilts. When the gyro horizon is reflected from the windscreen, it loses its ambiguity. It moves as the world outside the aircraft appears to move when viewed through the windscreen.

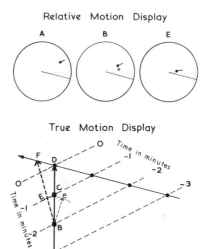

Figure 9.3. A radar assisted collision

The true motion display at the bottom shows what actually happens. The thick vertical arrow represents the course of the ship carrying the radar display. It will collide with any ship which remains on a constant bearing. A ship which crosses each broken sloping line at the same time as the main ship, will be on a constant bearing. The course of such a ship is shown by the thin unbroken line on the right. It will collide with the main ship at **D** on the broken sloping line labeled 0 min, unless avoiding action is taken.

At point **B** the captain of the main ship slows speed a little, and alters course away from the ship which is on a constant bearing. The new course is indicated by the thick broken arrow. If the captain is unlucky, he may still collide with the ship he is trying to avoid. The collision will occur a little later, at **F** instead of at **D**. The captain may reach point **E** at the same time as he would otherwise have reached point **C**. The other ship is then still on a constant bearing. The captain would be better advised to slow speed and alter course by steering **toward** the threat. The course is indicated by the thin broken arrow ending at **e**. He would then pass well behind the other ship.

A at the top of the figure illustrates what the captain sees on his relative motion display 3 min before the expected collision. At **B** the captain has just slowed speed, and altered course away from the other ship. The new bearing is indicated by the unfilled circle. At **E** the captain can see that the other ship is still on a collision course. It appears to be coming straight at his ship. Yet it is clear from the true motion display at the bottom, that the captain's ship could hit the side of the other ship and cut it into two. This has happened a number of times.

Display mode with step tracks

With a step track there may be little difference between the accuracy of tracking with a pursuit display and with a compensatory display. With a pursuit display the track marker jumps to a new position. The man has to move the response marker across to this position. With a compensatory display the error marker jumps to a new position. The man has to move the error marker back again to the fixed reference point from which it came.

The 2 tasks are probably about equally difficult, although they do not appear to have been compared by experiment. The principal difference between the 2 displays is that the pursuit or true motion display shows the man what is really happening, while the relative motion compensatory display does not. This point is discussed later in the chapter.

Display mode with ramp tracks of constant velocity

With a ramp track of constant velocity, a compensatory display presents a slightly easier visual task than a pursuit display. But the advantage is probably too small to produce a measurable difference in performance. With a pursuit display the track marker and the response marker both move together. Detecting small gaps between the moving display markers involves what has been called dynamic visual acuity (Ludvigh & Miller, 1958). As the man's eyes follow the display markers, they do not do so perfectly. There is a certain amount of blurring of the images of the 2 markers on the retinas of the man's eyes. This must increase slightly the man's difficulty in detecting small differences in position and rate between the 2 markers.

However Ludvigh and Miller (1958) report little or no measurable effect upon dynamic visual acuity at rates below 10° per sec. At a distance of 18 in from the man's eyes, this corresponds to a track rate of 3 in per sec. It is near the upper limit of the rates normally used in tracking tasks. Thus the effect of blurring is not likely to upset pursuit tracking very much.

When a man is tracking reasonably accurately with a compensatory display, the error marker remains close to the fixed reference marker. The task of detecting small misalignments and rates of change of misalignment then resembles more closely what can be called static visual acuity, to distinguish it from the dynamic visual acuity of the moving display. Thus, provided the man tracks reasonably accurately, the visual task should be slightly easier with the compensatory display.

There may be no major source of error to counteract the effect of the slightly easier visual task. With the compensatory or relative motion display, the man cannot see the rate of the track. But this may not matter very much with a ramp track of constant velocity, because the rate does not change. In this a ramp track of constant velocity differs from a sine wave track. With a ramp track of constant velocity, probably the only serious disadvantage of the compensatory display is that it does not show the man what is really happening.

Pursuit and compensatory displays have not been compared using a ramp track of constant velocity, because a target of constant velocity disappears off the edge of a pursuit display. A mechanism is required to switch the target and response markers to the opposite edge of the display just before they disappear.

This can be done. For example, when the marker representing an aircraft reaches the edge of a map display, winding on the map can be made to move the aircraft marker a corresponding distance in the same direction. This arrangement may or may not be preferable to the alternative of a fixed aircraft marker and a moving map display. Controlled experiments comparing the 2 kinds of display have still to be carried out.

Display mode in predicting and learning single sine wave tracks

With a sine wave track, a pursuit display is easier to use than a compensatory display. The track marker of the pursuit display shows the man what the track is doing. His response marker shows him the output of his control or control system. The gap between the 2 markers indicates the direction and size of the error. Whereas a compensatory display shows the man only the direction and size of the error. If he succeeds in tracking really accurately, all he can see is a stationary error marker. This gives him no visible indication of the output of his control system, nor of what response to make next.

With a pursuit display the man can see the movements of the track marker. From the visible position and rate of the track marker, he can predict where it will be a short time ahead and the rate at which it will be moving. In the experiment illustrated in Figure 9.4, 3 of the young enlisted men track at the very start with the pursuit display and the single sine wave track of 32 cpm. The times at which the response marker reverses direction can be compared with the times at which the track marker reverses direction. For the very first 10 reversals, the response lag averages only .04 sec.

If the man always waits until the track starts to reverse direction before reversing the direction of his response, his average time lag will be at least as long as a visual reaction time, or about .18 sec. Instead, the man starts to initiate his reversal almost a reaction time before the track reverses direction. His average time lag is therefore small.

With a compensatory display, the man cannot see the track while

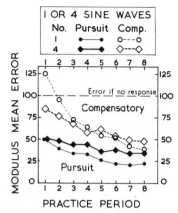

Figure 9.4.   Learning curves for pursuit and compensatory displays

The experimental arrangement is illustrated in Figure 8.4. The compensatory display has half the amplitude of the pursuit display, but requires control movements of the same size as the pursuit display. Halving the amplitude of the display does not alter the modulus mean error appreciably (Poulton, 1952a, Table 1).

The circles represent performance with a single sine wave of 32.5 cpm. The diamonds represent performance with a track comprising 4 sine waves of equal amplitude. The frequencies are 32.5, 25, 22.5 and 14 cpm. With both tracks the modulus mean error on the ordinate is adjusted to make 100 the level if the man does not respond at all. Each of the 12 young enlisted men practices twice daily for 4 min under each of the 4 experimental conditions illustrated in the figure. This probably produces transfer effects which favor the compensatory display. To be reliable statistically, differences in height have to be at least 12 for practice period 1 and at least 5 for practice period 8. (After Poulton, 1952a, Figure 3.)

he is attempting to reproduce it. In the experiment of Figure 9.4, another 3 of the young enlisted men start with the compensatory display and the single sine wave track. For the very first 10 reversals of the track, their average time lag is .30 sec. This is because while the man is tracking with the compensatory display, he cannot see that the track has reversed direction. He has to infer the reversal by relating the movement of the error marker to his own control movements. This takes time. It leads to a very much larger modulus mean error with the compensatory display during the first practice period. This is illustrated by the unfilled circle in Figure 9.4 at the top on the left.

The figure shows that the difference between the 2 display modes is considerably reduced by practicing alternately with the 2 displays. The 12 men have trials each morning and afternoon with both displays. They soon learn the single sine wave track. The knowledge is particularly advantageous in tracking with the compensatory display. On the extreme right of the figure the unfilled circles of the compensatory display are still approaching the filled circles of the pursuit display. Pew and colleagues (1967a) report that after sufficient practice alternately with the 2 displays, performance with the 2 displays can be indistinguishable when the man is tracking a single sine wave.

A strategy with compensatory displays and single sine wave tracks

In tracking a single sine wave of fairly high frequency with a compensatory display, the man has to get the amplitude of his response right. He has also to time his response correctly without being able to see the track. Figure 4.1A illustrates the error if the man's response amplitude is too small. When the man reverses the direction of movement of his position control, he still leaves some uncorrected error.

Figure 4.1C illustrates the error if the man's response amplitude is too large. The error changes sign before the man reverses the direction of his control movement. In order to respond with about the correct amplitude, the man has to increase or decrease the amplitude of his control movements until the error changes sign at about the time that he reverses the direction of his control movements.

His response then has a phase difference of about 90° with the error. Figure 4.1B shows that if his response lags a little behind the track, his response lags rather more than 90° behind the error. Similarly, if his response leads the track a little, his response leads the error by rather more than 90°. Thus the phase of the error tells the man whether to advance or retard the phase of his response. He has simply to follow the phase of the error until the error has no lag or lead.

A highly practiced man can make the response movements which are appropriate for tracking the single sine wave, and use the error simply to indicate how to adjust his response movements. He performs as illustrated in Figure 8.8, although here the display is in fact pursuit. If an error develops with a phase advance ahead of the man's response, it indicates that the response is a little behind the track in phase. If an error develops with a phase lag behind the man's response, it indicates that the response is a little ahead of the track in phase. The practiced man adjusts the phase of his response accordingly.

An error with a phase which either synchronizes with the man's response or has a phase difference of 180°, indicates that his amplitude is too large or too small. The sign of the error tells him which. If the error is in the same direction as the man's position control, it indicates that his response amplitude is too large. A small constant error in position indicates that his response has wandered off center. Again the sign of the error tells the man which way to make his adjustment.

Display mode in predicting and learning
irregular sine wave tracks

Tracking is more difficult with an irregular track containing fairly high frequencies, because the man cannot predict the track very well. In the experiment of Figure 9.4, 6 young enlisted men track at the very start a mixture of 4 sine waves with a top frequency of 32 cpm. Three men start with the pursuit display, the other 3 men start with the compensatory display. For the first 10 reversals of the track, the average time lags are .08 and .40 sec respectively. These time lags are rather longer than the time lags of .04 and .30 sec for the first 10 reversals with the single sine wave track. They reflect the greater difficulty of predicting the track.

With practice the man can learn the statistical characteristics of an irregular track. When he has a compensatory display, he can then predict the average behavior of the track. But usually the track does not behave quite like its average. Prediction can never be very accurate when the track contains fairly high frequencies.

Prediction is not as difficult with a pursuit display, because the man can see the movement of the track marker. Figure 8.9 shows that with a pursuit display the man can predict ahead fairly accurately about .25 cycle of the top track frequency.

The lower part of Figure 3.4 shows that the greater difficulty of predicting with a compensatory display is still present after practice. The results are from 3 practiced people using a quasirandom track with a top frequency of 58 cpm. The time lag averages about .14 sec with the compensatory display, compared with an average of only .04 sec with the pursuit display.

The diamonds in Figure 9.4 are for the irregular track composed of 4 sine waves with a top frequency of 32 cpm. The functions representing the pursuit and compensatory displays appear to be running more or less parallel over the last 3 practice periods. It seems unlikely that the modulus mean error with the compensatory display will ever reach the level with the pursuit display.

A strategy with compensatory displays
and irregular sine wave tracks

In tracking an irregular sine wave of fairly high frequency with a compensatory display, the man cannot use the strategies which have been described for a single sine wave. This is because he cannot predict the irregular track well enough when he cannot see it. His best strategy is to predict the track as well as he can, and to time his response so that it lags in phase about 90° behind the error.

The reason for the phase lag is illustrated in Figure 4.1. The man cannot predict an irregular track very well, and so tends to lag behind it. The error produced by a lag in phase is advanced in phase. When the response is of about the correct amplitude, Figure 4.1B shows that the advance in phase of the error is 90° minus $\frac{1}{2}$ the phase lag of the response. If the man responds with a phase lag of about 90° behind the error, his response will more or less synchronize with the track.

Figure 4.1A shows that if his response has too small an amplitude, the optimal phase lag behind the error is less than 90°. Figure 4.1C shows that if the amplitude of the response is too large, the optimal phase lag behind the error is more than 90°. But if on average the amplitude of the man's response more or less matches the amplitude of the track, the average optimal phase lag behind the error is about 90°.

With tracks composed of a number of sine waves of different frequency, the duration of the optimal phase lag will be different for each frequency. The man has to assess the average time lag which represents the resultant of the optimal phase lags.

Display mode in learning and monitoring the control system

With a pursuit display the man can see the results of his response movements independently of the track movements. If the output of his control is transformed by the dynamics of a control system before it affects the display, he can learn what effect a particular control movement or pattern of movements has. And he can discover what movement or pattern of movements is required to produce a particular effect. With a compensatory display the man cannot see the output of the control system uncomplicated by the track movements. Thus it takes him a good deal longer to learn the control system.

Chapter 17 describes a number of control system variations in which it is particularly useful to have a pursuit display, because the display shows the man directly the output of the control system. This is the case in learning to track with a crosscoupled control system, and with a control system which produces low frequency oscillations. Also a sudden unexpected change in a control system is identified more easily with a pursuit display than with a compensatory display.

Errors due to misunderstanding compensatory displays

Perhaps the greatest disadvantage of a compensatory display is that it can produce stupid errors, due to the man misunderstanding the status information. In the experimental laboratory stupid errors occur when the man first starts to track with an unfamiliar track and control system. In one experiment each of 8 men sits in turn in front of the apparatus illustrated in Figure 8.4. The pursuit display is screened from him. He is told to keep the error marker of the compensatory display on the fixed line. The control is a wheel. He is given no indication of which way to turn it, nor how far. The track generator is started just before he starts to move the control.

When the man starts to track, he has no way of telling whether the movements of the error marker are being produced by the track or by his own control movements. The control movements of 2 men out of the group of 8 make the error marker wander gradually in one direction until it disappears off the display. For each of the 2 men the experiment is stopped, and the man is asked what he thinks he is doing. From his reply it is clear that he thinks the amplitude of the track is too large for the display. He does not realize that he has himself made the error marker disappear (Poulton, 1950b, page 12).

Misunderstandings of this kind are not very common with a simple position control system. The man may stop moving his control before the error marker disappears off the edge of the display. He can then see the effect of the track uncomplicated by his control actions, and so deduce the effect of his past control actions.

More sophisticated trackers start by responding with a quick step. This is reflected at once in the movement of the error marker. Doing this a few times enables the man to learn the relationship between his control movements and the display movements which they produce. After this he can more easily deduce the disturbances fed in by the track.

Misunderstandings are more likely to occur with an unfamiliar acceleration control system. While the error marker is following the track, it does not respond immediately in the appropriate direction when the man makes a control movement. The track may even make the error marker start to accelerate in the wrong direction. The man may then think that it is his own control actions which have started the acceleration.

When the man centers his control, he may leave the acceleration control system putting out a considerable rate without realizing it. He may think that the increasing error is being produced by the track. He may not realize that it is his past control actions which are responsible for the increasing error.

In most everyday tracking tasks the man knows his control system, and knows the kind of track he has to deal with. Stupid errors are likely to be made with a compensatory display only when the man perceives the situation incorrectly. The absence of status information in the compensatory display may then prevent the man from spotting his misapprehension. Figure 9.3 shows how in a socalled radar assisted collision the captain may see the other ship coming straight at him, and feel unable to avoid a collision (Calvert, 1960).

Another example occurs in flying an aircraft using an instrument with a gyro horizon like that illustrated in Figure 9.2. The pilot may in error mistake the movement of the gyro horizon for the movement of the aircraft (Fitts & Jones, 1961b, page 362). He may then make the corresponding inappropriate control actions. They will increase the error which he is attempting to reduce. The gyro horizon does not show the pilot that he has made inappropriate control actions. He may assume that his previous control actions are insufficient, and make still larger control movements in the wrong direction.

An old example comes from World War II. After changing to a new type of aircraft, the pilot may mistake the direction in which to move a control, without being aware of his error (Fitts & Jones, 1961a, page 335). If he is flying by a compensatory display, he may interpret the resulting increase in error as an effect of turbulence, or in some other way. The display does not show him that he has moved his control in the wrong direction.

The principal advantage of a pursuit display over a compensatory display is that it shows the man the cause of an error. Substituting a pursuit display for a compensatory display should therefore reduce the number of accidents.

Tables 9.2 and 9.3 show that a pursuit display also allows more accurate tracking than a compensatory display. It could be argued that the differences in accuracy are relatively small with low frequency tracks, which are representative of many of the tracks met in everyday life. The gain in accuracy may no more than balance the reduced cost and greater convenience to the design engineer of using a compensatory display. This reasoning does not take account of the reduced risk of accidents with a pursuit display. In most practical situations it should be the overriding consideration.

Displays intermediate between pursuit and compensatory

The results in Table 9.1 show that the advantage of a pursuit display is not simply that the man can see directly what the track is doing, and what the output of his control is doing. The pursuit display has the added advantage that the man can see how the error arises from

Table 9.1
Performance with displays intermediate between
pursuit and compensatory

Visible markers	Relative modulus mean error
Error (pure compensatory)	45
Response + Error	43
Error + Track	41
Response + Error + Track	38
Response + Track (pure pursuit)	33

If the man does not respond, the modulus mean error is 100. To be reliable, differences must be at least 4. (Results from Poulton, 1950c, 1952b.)

the difference between the track movements and the output of his control.

The compensatory display listed in the top row of the table is illustrated at the bottom of Figure 8.4. The display is supplemented by placing a track marker just to the right of the error marker, and a response marker just to the left of the error marker. When the man does not respond, the amplitudes of movement of the track and error markers are the same. When the man responds without a track movement, the amplitudes of movement of the response and error markers are the same.

In the experimental conditions listed in the table, 2, 1 or none of the 3 markers are covered. The man has to track using whichever markers he can see. The 2 low frequency tracks of the experiment of Figure 8.3 are used. Six of the 12 young enlisted men who serve in the experiment receive first all the conditions with the single sine wave. The other 6 men receive first all the conditions with the track consisting of 2 sine waves. The results for the 2 tracks are combined in the table.

The top row of the table represents the standard compensatory display. The bottom row of the table represents a pursuit display. The compensatory display gives an average modulus mean error about one third larger than the pursuit display.

The second row of the table shows that adding a response marker to the single error marker does not reduce the average modulus mean error very much. The man cannot easily compute the track movement from the movements of the 2 markers. Whereas he can tell directly what effect his control movements are having from the movements which his arm is making, because he has a position control system. He does not need an extra marker to tell him this. Thus the response marker is little help.

If the man tracks with a rate or acceleration control system, he may benefit more from a response marker which shows him directly the output of his control system. This point has still to be checked.

The third row of the table shows that adding a track marker to the single error marker reliably reduces the average modulus mean error. The man can then see the track movements which he has to copy. But the error marker is not a very satisfactory indicator of his success in copying the track movements. The average modulus mean error is reliably smaller still when the error marker is replaced by a response marker, as in the bottom row of the table. The man can then compare the effects of his control movements directly with the track, and see in what ways they fail to match the track. This is clearly the optimal display.

The fourth row of the table shows that adding an error marker between the track and response markers produces a reliable increase in the average modulus mean error. The error marker supplies no information which cannot already be obtained from the track and response markers. It simply makes it more difficult for the man to compare the movements of the response marker directly with the movements of the track marker.

Mixed pursuit and compensatory displays

Senders (1953, Senders & Cruzen, 1952) describes experiments with mixed pursuit and compensatory displays related to the display listed in row 3 of Table 9.1. Figure 9.5 shows that there is a pursuit display in which the 2 display markers move together like the track when the error between them is zero. There is a compensatory display in which the same 2 display markers remain stationary together when the error between them is zero.

Between these 2 extremes Senders introduces displays in which the 2 display markers move together with 75%, 50% and 25% of the amplitude of the track when the error between them is zero. He calls these intermediate displays 75%, 50% and 25% pursuit. Unfortunately Senders uses time on target as his measure of performance. This measure is not related linearly to tracking error (see Figure 4.2).

The left of Figure 9.6 (Briggs & Rockway, 1966) illustrates the results of a repeat experiment using modulus mean error. The pure compensatory display gives an average modulus mean error which is almost twice as large as with the pure pursuit display. The display with only a 25% pursuit component gives an average modulus mean error which lies about half way between the errors for the pure compensatory and the pure pursuit displays. Thus being able to see even an attenuated version of the track, is a great help to the man when he is tracking reasonably accurately.

It would be possible to carry out the corresponding experiment using mixed pursuit and compensatory displays related to the display listed in row 2 of Table 9.1. When the tracking error is zero, the 2 display markers move together like the response, only with a reduced amplitude. The results in Table 9.1 suggest that this may not be much help to the man unless he has a rate or acceleration control system. But the comparison has still to be made.

Asymmetrical transfer between pursuit and compensatory displays

The right side of Figure 9.6 (Briggs & Rockway, 1966) illustrates asymmetrical transfer between pursuit and compensatory displays, just as Figure 2.1 does (Gordon, 1959). In Figure 9.6, the group represented by the unfilled circles at the top on the right, practices for 8 blocks of trials with the pursuit display. The group then has 4 blocks of trials with the compensatory display. On the last 3 blocks the average error is almost identical with the average error of the group represented by the unfilled squares, which tracks throughout the 12 blocks of trials with the compensatory display. Thus except on the first block trials after transfer, there is 100% transfer from the pursuit display to the compensatory display.

However transfer is not so complete in the opposite direction. The group represented by the filled squares at the bottom on the right practices for 8 blocks of trials with the compensatory display before being transferred to the pursuit display. On the last 3 blocks of trials after transfer, the average error is about 13% larger than the average error of the group represented by the filled circles, which tracks throughout the full 12 blocks of trials with the pursuit display.

As in the experiment of Figure 2.1, transfer between the 2 display modes is positive in both directions, because all the other engineering variables remain the same. But transfer is larger from pursuit to compensatory than in the reverse direction. Unfortunately Briggs and Rockway (1966) are not on the lookout for the asymmetrical transfer, and do not test it for statistical reliability.

Most probably it is the difference in the phase relationships which

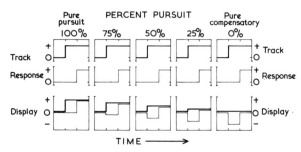

Figure 9.5. Mixed pursuit and compensatory displays.

The 5 displays are used by Senders (1953; Senders & Cruzen, 1952) and by Briggs and Rockway (1966). The track has an upward step. After a reaction time, the man moves his control the corresponding distance. The 100% pursuit display at the bottom on the left exactly reflects the movements. In the 75% pursuit display, the track marker moves upward only 75% of the distance. The man's response marker simultaneously moves downward the remaining 25% of the distance. Thus the size of the error still corresponds to the full size of the step in the track. As before, the man's response superimposes the response marker on the track marker again.

In the 50% and 25% pursuit displays, the movements of the track marker are reduced still further, and more of the track movement is reflected in the movement of the man's response marker. The pure compensatory, or 0% pursuit, display is illustrated on the right. Here the track marker becomes the stationary reference marker. The response marker becomes the error marker. The upward step in the track moves the error marker downward. The man's response moves it up again to the stationary reference marker.

reduces the size of the transfer from the compensatory display to the pursuit display. We have just seen that with a compensatory display the practiced man reproduces the track with a lag in phase of about 90° behind the error marker. When he changes to the pursuit display, he still tends to lag, now behind the movements of the track marker. Unfortunately the man's time lags are not· reported in either of the experiments. Thus it is not possible to check on this point.

Experimental comparisons between pursuit and compensatory displays

Table 9.2 lists experiments which compare pursuit and compensatory displays using a position control system. The right hand column of the table shows that usually the pursuit display gives reliably more accurate tracking than the compensatory display. In no experiment is a compensatory display reliably better than a pursuit display.

Table 9.3 lists the corresponding experiments using higher order con-

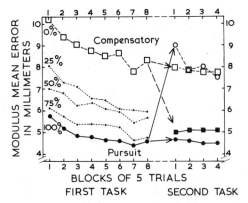

Figure 9.6.   Performance with pursuit, compensatory, and mixed displays.
The filled points represent performance with a pure pursuit display. The unfilled points are for a pure compensatory display. The small points and dotted lines are for mixed displays. The proportion of pursuit in the display is printed against each function. All the functions on the left are for separate groups of 24 undergraduates. The functions on the right represent subgroups of 12 undergraduates.

The track comprises 3 sine waves of 14.8, 9.2 and 5.5 cpm. The man has a simple position control. There are 6 blocks of 5 trials per day for 2 days. Trials last 35 sec. All the functions on the left of the figure are reliably different from each other. (After Briggs & Rockway, 1966, Figure 2.)

Briggs (1969, page 215) states that the group represented by the filled squares shows 100% positive transfer. This is clearly not true. Briggs' conclusion is based upon the pooled results of the 4 groups on the left of the figure which train with the 0%, 25%, 50% and 75% pursuit tasks. But only the group with the 0% pursuit task receives no pursuit training. In measuring the effect of transfer from a compensatory task to a pursuit task, groups pretrained on a partly pursuit task need to be excluded.

trol systems. The experiments with separate group designs have 2 entries in the column headed **N** for the number of people used. The results of these experiments cannot be biased by transfer from the other conditions in the experiment, because each person performs only one condition. There are 2 of these experiments which show a pursuit display to give reliably more accurate tracking than a compensatory display. One is the experiment by Bauerschmidt and Roscoe (1960) with the control system of an aircraft (Roscoe, Personal Communication). The other is the experiment by Hammerton and Tickner (1970) with a rate control system. No experiment with a separate group design shows a compensatory display to be reliably better than a pursuit display.

The remaining experiments in the table use balanced treatment designs. We have seen that these designs can bias the results in favor of compensatory displays. The majority of the experiments confirm the

Table 9.2
Experiments comparing pursuit and compensatory displays using
a position control system

Author(s)	Year	N	Highest frequency in track (cpm)	Other variables	Difference reliably in favor of:
Briggs and Rockway (see Figure 9.6)	1966	24 + 24	14.8		Pursuit
Chernikoff, Birmingham and Taylor	1955	6	15	Control system	Pursuit
Chernikoff and Taylor (see Figure 8.6)	1957	6	6.7		Pursuit
		6	16.7	Control system	Pursuit
		6	26.7		Pursuit
Christ and Newton	1970	24 + 24	Steps		Pursuit
		24 + 24	Ramps		Pursuit
Conklin (see Figure 17.5)	1957	3	30	Lags. Practice favors compensatory	—
Elkind (see Figure 8.7)	1956	3	9.6 to 144 in different trials	Practice favors compensatory	—
Gordon (see Figure 2.1)	1959	40 + 40	7.5‡		Pursuit
Hartman	1957a 1957b	8	10 to 60 in different trials	Practice favors compensatory	—
Hartman and Fitts	1955	8	30		—
Heinemann	1961	3 + 3	4‡ Ramps		—
		3 + 3	9‡ Ramps		—
		3 + 3	2‡		—
		3 + 3	4‡		—
Howell and Briggs (see Figure 11.12)	1959	24	10	Noise masking	—
			30		—
Obermayer and colleagues	1961	9† (some pilots)	2.2	Control system	—
Obermayer and colleagues (see Figure 8.6)	1962	6† (some pilots)	3.3		—
			6.7	Control system	Pursuit
			16.7		Pursuit
Pew, Duffendack and Fensch	1967a	3	6 to 300 in different trials		—
Poulton (see Figure 8.3)	1952a	16 (3 pilots)	15		Pursuit
			20		Pursuit
			30		Pursuit
			40		Pursuit

Table 9.2 (cont.)

Author(s)	Year	N	Highest frequency in track (cpm)	Other variables	Difference reliably in favor of:
Poulton (See			45		Pursuit
Figure 8.3)			60		Pursuit
			80		Pursuit
(see Figure 9.4)		12	32		Pursuit
		12	20		Pursuit
Poulton (see					
Table 9.1)	1952b	12	20		Pursuit
Poulton (see	1967	6 + 6	40		Pursuit
Figure 13.4)		6 + 5	40	Matching rates	Pursuit
Regan (see	1960	24 + 24	7.5‡	Displays and	Pursuit
Table 11.3)				controls	
Senders and Cruzen	1952	5	18‡		Pursuit
Senders	1953	10	10‡	Room light or	Pursuit
		10	36‡	dark	Pursuit
Walston and Warren	1954	3	30		—
		3	45§		—
Wargo	1967	5 + 5	17‡	Transmission	Pursuit
				lags	
Wortz, McTee,	1965	24	12.5‡ Ramps ⎫	⎧ Lags.	—
Swartz, Rhein-			6.7‡ Ramps ⎬	⎨ Nonlinear	Pursuit
lander, and			Steps ⎭	⎩ controls	Pursuit
Dalhamer					

† Six of the same people serve in both experiments.
‡ Half the number of reversals per minute.
§ Excludes high frequencies of small amplitude.

conclusion that a pursuit display is at least as good as a compensatory display. The 3 experiments with exceptions are listed in part **A** of the table. It is important to deal with the exceptions in detail, to see why they can be disregarded. For they are sometimes quoted as evidence in favor of compensatory displays.

In all the 3 experiments with exceptions, the same men use both pursuit and compensatory displays with various orders of control system. The experiments by Oberymayer and colleagues (1961, 1962) are really 2 parts of a single experiment, with 6 of the same people performing in both. Both experiments can be regarded as partly repeats of the Chernikoff and Taylor (1957) experiment. The designs of 2 of the experiments are outlined in the caption to Figure 8.6.

Table 9.3

Experiments comparing pursuit and compensatory displays using higher order control systems

Author(s)	Year	N	Highest frequency in track (cpm)	Control system	Other variables	Difference reliably in favor of:
A. Tracking with a compensatory display reliably more accurate than tracking with a pursuit display, probably due to bias.						
Chernikoff and Taylor* (see Figure 8.6)	1957	6	6.7	Rate aided	Control system	Compensatory
			6.7	Rate		Compensatory
Obermayer and colleagues*	1961	9† (some pilots)	2.2	Acceleration	Control system	Compensatory
Obermayer and colleagues* (see Figure 8.6)	1962	6† (some pilots)	3.3	Rate		Compensatory
			3.3	Acceleration	Control system	Compensatory
			6.7	Acceleration		Compensatory
			16.7	Acceleration		Compensatory
B. Tracking with a pursuit display reliable more accurate than tracking with a compensatory display, or not reliably different.						
Allen and Jex (see Figure 16.8)	1968	4 pilots	31§	Rate	Combined pursuit and compensatory	—
			31§	Acceleration		—
Bauerschmidt and Roscoe	1960	7 + 7 pilots	5° Step	Aircraft simulator	Only pursuit display shows pitch	Pursuit
Chernikoff and colleagues	1955	6	15	Aided 1:2:3	Control system	—
Chernikoff and colleagues	1956	5	3.3			—
		5	10	Acceleration (simulated aircraft)		Pursuit
			10			Pursuit
			20			Pursuit
			30			Pursuit

Study	Year	No. of subjects		Aided/Rate	Situation	Comparison	
Chernikoff and Taylor* (see Figure 8.6)	1957	6	16.7	Aided		Control system	Pursuit
			16.7	Rate			Pursuit
		6	26.7	Aided			Pursuit
			26.7	Rate			Pursuit
			2.5 (Irregular ramp)	Rate			Pursuit
Hammerton and Tickner	1970	11 + 11		Rate			—
Heinemann	1961	3 + 3	4‡ Ramps	Rate			—
		3 + 3	9‡ Ramps	Rate			—
		3 + 3	2‡	Rate			—
		3 + 3	4‡	Rate			—
Jacobs, Williges and Roscoe	1972	8 pilots	3	Aircraft simulator		Flight director displays	Pursuit
Johnson and colleagues	1971	8 pilots	3	Aircraft simulator (moving base)		Flight director displays	Pursuit
Obermayer and colleagues*	1961	9† (some pilots)	2.2	Rate	Control system		—
Obermayer and colleagues*	1962	6† (some pilots)	6.7	Rate	Control system		Pursuit
Poulton (see Figure 13.4)	1967	6 + 5	16.7	Rate			—
		6 + 6	40	Rate		Matching rates	—
Regan (see Table 11.3)	1960	24 + 24	40	Rate		Displays and controls	—
			7.5‡	Rate			—
Roscoe and Williges	1972	16 (nonpilots)	3	Aircraft in flight		Flight director displays	Pursuit

* Included in both parts of the table.
† Six of the same people serve in both experiments.
‡ Half the number of reversals per minute.
§ Excludes high frequencies of small amplitude.

Table 9.4 lists the phase relationships between control and display movements which produce the smallest average errors in tracking with various orders of control system. The optimal phase relationship for the compensatory display in the top row of the table is discussed earlier in the chapter. The optimal phase relationships for control systems of higher order are discussed in Chapter 16.

Chernikoff and Taylor (1957) use the 6 experimental conditions listed in the top 3 rows of the table. The experiment is designed so that the man receives the 6 experimental conditions in different random orders each day. He is simply allowed a 1 min practice trial on each experimental condition before his 3 test trials. This kind of experimental design encourages asymmetrical transfer and range effects (see Chapter 2).

With the pursuit display the man's control movements have to lead the movements of the track marker by 0°, about 45°, or 90°. With the compensatory display his control movements have to lag behind the movements of the error marker by 0°, about 45°, or 90°. It seems likely that as the man is switched between the 2 display modes, there is transfer of response lag from the compensatory conditions to the pursuit conditions. This increases the average error in the pursuit conditions.

The top entry of Table 9.3 shows that in the Chernikoff and Taylor

Table 9.4
Optimal phase relationships between control and display

	Display mode and marker	
Order of control system	Pursuit track marker	Compensatory error marker
Position	0°	90° lag
Rate aided (aiding ratio 1:2, response frequency 20 cpm)	about 45°* lead	about 45° lag
Rate	90° lead	0°
Acceleration	180° lead	90° lead

With the pursuit display the man can see the track which he has to copy. He has simply to maintain the correct phase relationship. With the compensatory display the man needs to be able to predict the track, as well as to maintain the correct phase relationship.

* With a pursuit display and rate aided control system, the optimum phase lead varies between 0° and 90°. For an aiding ratio of 1:2, the optimum lead is 10° at a response frequency of 120 cpm. The optimum lead is 80° at a frequency of 4 cpm. With an aiding ratio of 1:4 the optimum phase lead at each response frequency is larger.

(1957) experiment only rate and rate aided control systems are reliably worse with the pursuit display. Table 9.4 shows that these are the 2 conditions which require phase leads. They are therefore the most likely to suffer from a transfer of response lag from the compensatory conditions. Unfortunately it is not possible to check on the phase or time relationships, because they are not reported.

In both their experiments, Obermayer and his colleagues (1961, 1962) use the 2 experimental conditions in the top row of Table 9.4, and the 4 conditions in the bottom 2 rows. With the pursuit display the optimal phase relationships are leads of 0°, 90° or 180°. With the compensatory display the optimal phase relationships are a lag of 90°, no lag or lead, and a lead of 90°.

The second and third entries of Table 9.3 show that in the Obermayer experiments it is again the pursuit conditions requiring leads which are reliably worse than the corresponding compensatory conditions. The rate control system requires a lead of 90° when it is used with the pursuit display. It produces reliably more error with the pursuit display than with the compensatory display on the track with a top frequency of 3.3 cpm.

The acceleration control system requires leads of 180° and 90° respectively with the pursuit and compensatory displays. It always produces very much the worst performance. With all 4 tracks reliably the worst performance results from the acceleration control system combined with the pursuit display. This requires the largest phase lead of all, 180°. The phase angle has to be 270° ahead of the optimal phase lag of 90° when the position control system is used with the compensatory display.

Most probably the pursuit conditions requiring leads do badly because of transfer of response lags or smaller leads from the compensatory conditions. The lower right part of Figure 16.8 (Allen & Jex, 1968) illustrates the greater phase lag with a pursuit display than with a compensatory display when tracking with an acceleration control system. The experiment is listed as the first entry in part B of Table 9.3. Only rate and acceleration control systems are used. The phase lag with the acceleration control system and the pursuit display is probably smaller than it would be if a position control system were also included in the experimental design, as it is in the Obermayer experiments.

The results in part A of Table 9.3 thus appear to be biased by transfer of inappropriate phase relationships, produced by the balanced treatment designs used. As long as the control system is not changed during the experiment, pursuit displays are always found to be at least as good as compensatory displays. This is shown in part B of the table by the

2 experiments of Chernikoff, Birmingham and Taylor (1956), and by the experiments of Jacobs, Williges and Roscoe (1972), of Johnson, Williges and Roscoe (1971), and of Roscoe and Williges (1972). In these 5 experiments performance is reliably better with the pursuit display than with the compensatory display, even with the high order control system of an aircraft, because no other order of control system is included in the experimental design.

Compensatory displays, high order control systems, and low frequency tracks

A rate control system reduces the disadvantage of a compensatory display. The top row of Table 9.4 shows that when a man has a compensatory display, he needs to reproduce the track with a lag of about 90° behind the movements of the error marker. A rate control system automatically inserts a phase lag of 90° between the man's response movement and the movement of the marker. Thus a rate control system matches a compensatory display in phase.

A rate control system is difficult to use because the man has to reproduce the track with a phase lead of 90°. It means predicting the track well ahead. A compensatory display is also difficult to use, because the man has to reproduce the track without seeing it. But when a rate control system is paired with a compensatory display, at least there need not be a discrepancy in phase between control and display.

An acceleration control system reduces the disadvantages of a compensatory display for a similar reason. The bottom row of Table 9.4 shows that an acceleration control system matches a compensatory display in phase better than it matches a pursuit display, because the optimal phase lead is smaller. The only control systems in Table 9.4 which do not match a compensatory display in phase better than they match a pursuit display, are position and rate aided control systems. A position control system definitely favors a pursuit display. A rate aided control system probably favors neither display. But it matches a compensatory display better than a position control system does.

Tracks of low frequency also reduce the disadvantage of a compensatory display. This is because reducing the frequencies in the track reduces the amount of change which the track introduces during the man's reaction time. The man can predict a low frequency track more accurately a reaction time ahead. This is more helpful with a compensatory display than with a pursuit display, because predicting the track ahead is more difficult with a compensatory display. It follows that reducing the frequencies in the track reduces both the tracking error and also the difference in error between compensatory and pursuit displays. Figures 8.3, 8.6 and 8.7 illustrate this.

When the error in tracking is small, a small variable error in the electronic device which computes the tracking error may appreciably favor a compensatory display. Figure 1.1B shows that with a compensatory display the man can see a displacement which is directly proportional to the recorded error voltage. An error in the electronic device which subtracts the response from the track, is shown in the displayed error. The man sees it and can compensate for it.

Figure 1.1A shows that with a pursuit display the man sees only the track and his response before they have been operated on by the electronic scoring device. He does not see the error computed by the device which subtracts the response from the track. Thus he cannot compensate for an error in the scoring device.

All the exceptions in part **A** of Table 9.3 involve rate aided or higher order control systems, and fairly low frequency tracks. We have just seen that the advantage of a pursuit display is likely to be smaller under these conditions. When this is so, experimental biases which favor the compensatory display may produce a reliably smaller error with the compensatory display than with a pursuit display. One such bias can be introduced by a balanced treatment design. Another source of bias may be an error in the electronic device which computes the tracking error. The atypical results listed in part **A** of Table 9.3 are almost certainly produced in this way.

Magnifying pursuit and compensatory displays

It has been stated as a general rule (Morgan, Cook, Chapanis, & Lund, 1963, p. 220) that in tracking, a compensatory display allows greater magnification than a pursuit display. This is because a pursuit display has to show the full range of possible values of the track. While a compensatory display need show only a range of values sufficient to include all sizes of error which are likely to occur. The implicit assumption is that with the compensatory display the output of the control system will always have the opposite sign to the sign of the track. The amplitude of the error is then smaller than the amplitude of the track.

This is true of automatic servosystems. But Figure 11.1 shows that it is not true of manual compensatory tracking, especially early in training. The man himself generates error which sometimes adds to the error generated by the track. If the display is magnified, the error marker may then need to go beyond the edge. The marker either disappears, or rests against a stop at the edge of the display.

Even after practice magnification of a compensatory display is no advantage in tracking, although it loses much of its disadvantage. Chapter 11 discusses the bias introduced by transfer, which often makes it appear that tracking is more accurate with a greatly magnified compensatory display.

Recommended display mode

Whenever there is a choice between a conventional pursuit or true motion display and a conventional compensatory or relative motion display, the true motion display should be used. The only proved exception with conventional displays is when 2 tracking tasks are carried out simultaneously using circular displays and crank controls (see Table 11.3). The recommendation does not apply to unconventional displays without moving markers, nor to nonvisual displays (see Chapters 13 and 14).

Chapter

10

Augmented displays

Summary

Augmented displays are used with control systems of high order. Tracking improves when the 2 components of a rate augmented display are skillfully integrated in a single instrument. A velocity vector display is a rudimentary predictor display. A phase plane display is suited only to compensatory tracking. With an acceleration control system, the switching line should be shown.

A quickened display is not suitable for tracking ramps or sine waves. With a step track, a balanced treatment design exaggerates the value of quickening. The danger of a quickened display is that the man may think that it represents the output of his control system. A predictor display is better than a simple rate augmented display. It is better than a quickened display when dealing with an unprogramed event.

In pursuit tracking, a preview of the track ahead reduces the man's time lag, and improves his copying of the track.

The need for augmented displays

Augmented displays are designed for use with control systems of high order. Steering an automobile is the example given in Chapter 1 of tracking with an acceleration or second order control system. The control system is illustrated at the top on the right of Figure 10.1. It is represented by 2 integrators and an amplifier.

In tracking with an acceleration control system, the man can tell the size of the control signal which he is feeding into the system. He has simply to note the position of his control. Also he can see the position output of the control system. In steering an automobile the 2 pieces of information are given by the position of the steering wheel, and by the side to side position of the automobile on the road. But the man does not always appreciate the rate of the control system, or the size of the signal between the 2 integrators in the figure. In steering an automobile, this corresponds to the exact direction in which the automobile is pointing.

When the man knows the rate of the control system, he can tell how

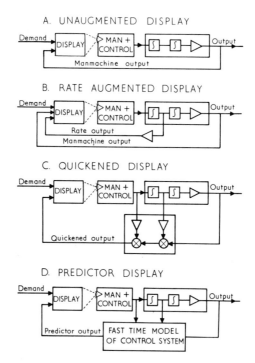

Figure 10.1. Augmented displays.

Each small square marked ∫ represents an integrator. Each small triangle represents an amplifier. In the block diagram of the quickened display (after Birmingham & Taylor, 1961) each circle marked with a cross represents an electronic differential. It sums the 2 signals which it receives. (The block diagram of the predictor display is after Kelley, 1962.)

the position output of the control system is going to change. If he does not wish it to change in this way, he can alter the rate by an appropriate control movement. When the man does not know the rate of the control system, he cannot predict changes in the position output so easily. He may have to wait until they occur, and then correct them as best he can. As a result, his position error is likely to be larger and more variable.

Steering a large ship along a river or canal involves a third order control system (see Chapter 16). If the rudder is too heavy for the man to turn directly, he may have to operate it through a rate control system. Steering the ship then involves a fourth order control system. It can be represented by 4 integrators and an amplifier. Again the man may be clearly aware only of the input to, and the position output of, the control system. There are now 3 unknown sizes of signal within the control system, one between each integrator and the next integrator in the series. Accurate steering is exceedingly difficult even if the man has the values of the intermediate signals displayed to him. Without them accurate steering is virtually impossible.

Augmented track displays are not yet exploited commercially. They would be useful when driving an automobile in fog. Driving in fog with only the edges of the road visible on either side, corresponds to conventional pursuit tracking. An augmented track display is a substitute for the usual preview of the road ahead.

Kinds of augmented display

Figure 10.1 illustrates 3 different ways of helping a man who has a control system of high order. Figure 10.1B gives the block diagram of a rate augmented display. The display shows the man the rate output of his control system as well as the position output. An example of rate augmentation is the rate of climb indicator used in aircraft. The pilot uses this information, together with the height shown on his altimeter and the position of his control stick, in order to level off at the correct height.

Figure 10.1C gives the block diagram of a quickened display. The display combines the position output of the control system, the rate output, and the position of the man's control, in a single value. The left column of Figure 10.4 shows how this is done for a step. If the man keeps the error in the quickened display as small as possible, the output of his acceleration control system will quickly step to the required value. During the movement the quickened display does not tell the pilot his true height. It simply tells him how to move his control in order to level out at the required height.

The block diagram of a predictor display is given in Figure 10.1D. The display itself is illustrated in Figure 10.7. A predictor display combines the same 3 sources of information as a quickened display. But it does not tell the pilot what to do. Instead it shows him his present height, and the predicted height profile of his aircraft over the next few seconds. The pilot can alter the profile to suit himself by adjusting his control stick.

An augmented track display can be designed to correspond to each of the 3 kinds of augmented display in Figure 10.1. In driving an automobile a rate augmented track display would show the driver the present direction of the road, and also its present degree of curvature. The experiment which comes closest to investigating this, is the experiment by Obermayer, Webster and Muckler (1967, Experiment 3) which is listed in Table 10.1C. Obermayer and his colleagues display error and error rate side by side. The error rate is the difference between the rate output of the control system and the rate of the track.

A quickened track display would use a combination of the direction and degree of curvature of the road in a single indication of the present demand. A predictor track display would show the driver the predicted road ahead. An accurate prediction corresponds to the preview of the road ahead which the automobile driver receives in good visibility. Tracking with preview is discussed at the end of the chapter.

Rate augmented displays

The simplest form of rate augmentation is an additional instrument showing rate, like the speedometer of an automobile. Tracking can be reliably more accurate still if the display markers showing position and rate are skillfully integrated in a single instrument (Bailey, 1958).

Pew's (1966) velocity vector display is an integrated display. The position output of the control system is represented by the position of a dot. The rate output of the control system is represented by a line ahead of the dot. The far end of the line indicates where the dot will be in .5 sec if its rate does not change. This is probably the most compatible rate augmented display which has yet been devised. It is a rudimentary predictor display, because it predicts roughly the position of the dot .5 sec ahead in time.

Phase plane displays

Figure 10.2 illustrates a phase plane display (Platzer, 1955). Position is represented in the side to side dimension, while rate is represented vertically. The display is suited to compensatory tracking. Zero position error and zero rate error are shown at the center of the cross wires. A sine wave track produces movement always in a clockwise direction. In Figure 10.2 it is assumed that there is no track and that the acceleration control system is always either in full acceleration or full deceleration.

When the marker which represents the output of the control system is in the upper right quadrant, it is moving toward the right. Its accelerating path from the origin is represented by the rising broken arrow. To bring the marker to rest on the cross wires in the center of the display as quickly as possible, the man has to move his acceleration control as far as possible over to the left. He does this at **a** in the figure. The output of the control system gradually stops, leaving a position error. This is indicated at **b** in the figure, where the path of the marker is vertical.

From now on the position output of the control system is reduced at an increasing rate. The phase plane display shows this by the continued movement of the marker down the broken arrow in the lower right quadrant. At **c** the man has to move his acceleration control as far as possible over to the original right side again, or he will overshoot the center of the display and bring the marker to rest too far over to the left. If the man times his control movement correctly, the marker will move toward the center along the unbroken inverted **S** shaped line. As the marker reaches the cross wires in the center, the man has to return his control to the central position.

The dotted lines and the points **a′**, **b′** and **c′** represent the same strategy as that already described. The only difference is that all the signs are reversed. The response marker starts by moving down to the left instead of up to the right. If the display is rotated through 180°, the points **a′**, **b′**, and **c′** are superimposed respectively upon the points **a**, **b**, and **c**.

The unbroken inverted **S** shaped line is called the switching line. If the man moves his acceleration control fully over in the other direction as the marker reaches the line, the marker will travel down the line towards the center. With a rate control system, the switching line becomes the vertical line passing through the center of the display. With a delta acceleration or third order control system, there is no fixed switching line. The momentary position and shape of the switching line depend upon the present acceleration output of the control system (Yasui and Young, 1967).

When a phase plane display is used for compensatory tracking, the switching line helps the man to reverse the direction of his control movement at the correct time (Miller, 1969). The optimal strategy is to hold the control always full over one way or the other, except when

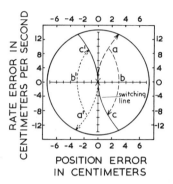

Figure 10.2. A phase plane display.
The fixed switching line is for an acceleration control system. For control systems of higher order, the optimal switching times cannot be represented by a fixed switching line.

the error marker is at rest in the center of the display. The strategy is called onoff or bangbang control. The task is easier if the man is supplied simply with 2 switches. Pressing the left switch produces the full output of the control system to the left. Pressing the right switch produces the full output to the right.

A phase plane display does not appear to have been used for pursuit tracking. The switching line is not relevant to the pursuit task because the response marker does not usually have to be centered over the cross wire.

An experiment comparing rate augmented displays
for compensatory tracking

Figure 10.3 (Pew, 1966) shows that a phase plane display without a switching line is not as easy to use as a velocity vector display. Each function represents the performance of a separate group of 6 undergraduates. A trial starts with the error marker jumping to the right from the cross wire in the center of the CRT. The man has to return the marker to the center as quickly as possible. He has 2 switches, one for each hand. Pressing a switch produces an acceleration in the corresponding direction.

During the first 6 sessions, the average modulus mean error is considerably larger with the unaugmented display than with either of the 2 rate augmented displays. The difference between the unaugmented display and the velocity vector display is reliable statistically. During the first session, the velocity vector display gives a reliably smaller average modulus mean error than the phase plane display without a switching

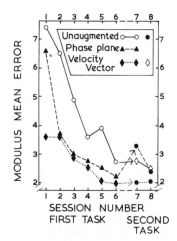

Figure 10.3 Compensatory tracking with velocity vector and phase plane displays.
The unaugmented reference display has a spot which moves from side to side.
In the velocity vector display a horizontal line extends from the spot in its direction
of movement, to show its rate of movement. A line 1 cm long represents a rate
of 2 cm per sec. The phase plane display is illustrated in Figure 10.2, but the
switching line is not present.

The man has 2 switches, one for each hand. Pressing the right switch accelerates
the spot to the right. Pressing the left switch accelerates the spot to the left.
When neither switch is pressed, or both switches are pressed at once, the spot
continues to move at its existing rate. Three accelerations are used in different
blocks of trials, 2, 10 and 30 cm per sec². The figure gives the results only for
the largest acceleration, where the differences are largest.

Trials last 6.6 sec. At the start of a trial the spot jumps from its central position
to a position which depends upon the track. One track is a single step 5 cm
to the right. Another track combines a 5 cm step to the right with a 2 cm per
sec rate to the left. The third track combines a 3 cm step to the right with
a 2 cm per sec rate to the right. The man has to restore the error marker to
the central position as quickly as possible, and hold it there for the rest of the
trial. A separate group of 6 undergraduates tracks with each display for 6 daily
sessions. They then have 2 sessions with one of the other displays. A session consists
of 5 consecutive trials with each of the 9 combinations of 3 tracks and 3 accelerations.
(Results from Pew, 1966).

line. After session 1 there is little to choose between the 2 rate augmented
displays.

The initial advantage of the velocity vector display reflects the compatible integration of the position and rate information. The phase plane
display is less well integrated, and so takes longer to learn to use effectively. Learning is probably a good deal quicker if the switching line
is shown.

The right side of Figure 10.3 illustrates the effect of changing displays in sessions 7 and 8. Changing between the unaugmented display and the velocity vector display has little effect upon performance. The students continue to track much as they have previously learned to do.

Changing from the phase plane display to the unaugmented display increases the average modulus mean error at first by 50%. This is due almost entirely to 1 of the 6 students. Presumably the student comes to depend too much upon position in the 2 dimension phase plane display for deciding on his switching times. In the conditions illustrated in the figure, he has simply to switch just before or just after the spot reaches the edge of the display. When this information is first removed, he is less likely to switch at exactly the correct time.

A disadvantage of a phase plane display is that the rate information uses a separate dimension. A tracking task in 2 dimensions requires a display with 4 dimensions, if both dimensions of the tracking task use phase plane displays. This arrangement does not appear to have been investigated by experiment. But the results of the multiple tracking tasks described in Chapter 12 suggest that using 4 dimensions would considerably reduce the accuracy of tracking. Whereas a velocity vector is as compatible with a 2 dimension tracking display as with a single dimension display.

Quickened displays

Quickened displays and step tracks

The left hand column of Figure 10.4 illustrates the components of a quickened display in tracking a step with an acceleration control system. The top cell shows the direct output of the man's control. The cell below shows the output of the control system after the first integrator illustrated in Figure 10.1C. The third cell shows the true output of the acceleration control system after the second integrator. Figure 10.1C shows that the 3 outputs are summed, taking account of the signs. The sum is shown in the bottom cell on the left of Figure 10.4. It represents the movements of the quickened display marker.

The advantage of using a quickened display can be seen by considering the movements of the unaugmented display on the left of Figure 10.4. With the acceleration control system, the man has to move his control in the direction of the 8 in step in order to produce a rate which will move his response marker. Before the response marker has moved the full 8 in, he has to move his control in the opposite direction in order

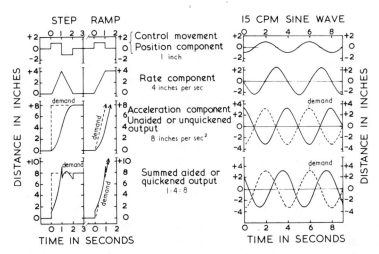

Figure 10.4.   Acceleration aiding or quickening.
With each kind of track the top function shows the theoretical movements of
the control, and the corresponding component of the movement of the response
marker. The second function shows the effect of the rate component on the movement
of the response marker. The third function shows the effect of the acceleration
component. This is how an unquickened or unaided response marker moves. The
bottom function shows the sum of the effects of these 3 components when the
aiding ratios are 1:4:8. This is how a quickened or aided response marker moves
when the control is moved as in the top function.

to remove the rate again. The control movement is illustrated at the
top on the left of the figure.

The displayed output of the acceleration control system is illustrated
by the third function down on the left. This unaugmented display does
not tell the man when to move his control in the opposite direction.
If he is not used to an acceleration control system, he may not move
his control in the opposite direction until the response marker has moved
the full 8 in. By then the response marker will be moving so fast that
it cannot be stopped until it has gone another 8 in.

The movements of a quickened response marker tell the man when
to reverse the direction of movement of his control. They are illustrated
at the bottom on the left. As soon as the man moves his control, the
quickened response marker moves 1 in. After 1 sec the man should
be moving his control in the opposite direction. By then the quickened
response marker has reached the 8 in demand mark and has started
to overshoot. This tells the man that he should move his control in
the opposite direction.

A quickened display works with an acceleration control system and a step track, because the quickened response marker and the output of the acceleration control system always came to rest in the same position. The extra displacements of the quickened response marker, produced by adding the direct output of the control stick and the rate component of the control system, are taken off as the marker comes to rest.

While the step movement is being made, the position of the quickened response marker and the output of the acceleration control system do not correspond. But when the quickened response marker comes to rest again, the 2 outputs are exactly the same.

The left column of Figure 10.4 illustrates the strategy which will get the quickened response marker to the required position as quickly as possible and leave it there without any further control movements. Most people are probably not sufficiently sophisticated to do this. They are more likely to move the control less far in the opposite direction. This strategy results in a rather larger second overshoot, and calls for additional small control movements.

For tracking steps, a quickened display can be said to be more compatible with an acceleration control system than is an unquickened display. The top and third functions in the left hand column of the figure show that with an acceleration control system the man has to make relatively high frequency responses in order to produce a relatively low frequency output. The low frequency movements of the response marker in the unaugmented display are not directly compatible with the higher frequency movements of the control. Whereas the movements of the response marker of the quickened display contain the frequencies of the movements of the control. The frequencies are simply mixed with the lower frequency output of the control system, and with the intermediate frequencies after the first integrator.

Part A of Table 10.1 lists 3 experiments, all of which report a quickened display to be reliably better than a conventional display with step tracks. There are no contradictory results. The first 2 experiments by Bailey (1958) and by Goldstein (1961) involve tracking. The third experiment by Runner and Sweeney (1961) involves monitoring the autopilot of a simulated submarine. Here the quickened display produces reliably quicker reports from the man that the autopilot has started to misbehave.

However in all 3 experiments the third or fourth order control system is difficult to use without some form of augmented display. The experiments show only that with step tracks a quickened display is better than a conventional or unaugmented display. We shall see that there are better augmented displays.

Table 10.1

Experiments comparing quickened and unquickened displays

Author(s)	Year	N	Order of control system	Track	Displays compared	Special experimental conditions	Reliably better
A. Step tracks							
Bailey (Sweeny, Bailey & Dowd)	1958 (1957)	6	Simulated helicopter	Steps	Quickened Conventional	Separate and integrated conventional displays	Quickened
Goldstein (see Figure 10.5)	1961	10 + 10	Slow 3rd order	Steps	Quickened Unaugmented	Transfer	Quickened
Runner and Sweeney	1961	8	4th order (submarine)	Steps	Quickened Unaugmented	Monitoring for malfunctions	Quickened
B. Sine wave tracks							
Dooley and Newton	1965	6 + 6	2nd order	3 cpm	Quickened Unaugmented	Transfer	—
Verdi and colleagues	1965	10	2nd order	Irregular up to 10 cpm§	Quickened Unaugmented	Additional partly quickened display	Unaugmented
C. Confounded variables favoring the quickened display							
Obermayer and colleagues	1967	6 + 6	2nd order	Irregular up to 15 cpm	Quickened Rate augmented	Instructions favor quickening	Quickened
Ritchie and Bamford	1957	9 pilots	Simulated aircraft	Irregular sine waves (rough air)	Quickened Unaugmented	Damping added to quickening	Quickened and damped

§ Excludes high frequencies of small amplitude.

Asymmetrical transfer between quickened and unquickened displays

Figure 10.5 (Goldstein, 1961) illustrates asymmetrical transfer between a quickened and an unquickened display. Separate groups of men perform each condition. The man has to move a response marker down a distance of between .5 and 1.5 in, using a slow third order control system. The response marker has then to be held in a target

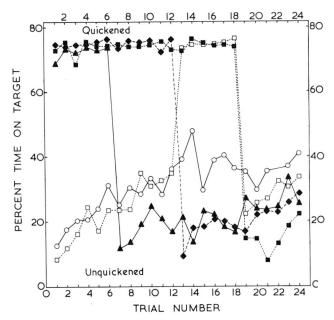

Figure 10.5 Asymmetrical transfer between quickened and unquickened displays.
It takes 10 sec with the control full on for the slow third order control system to move the response marker .25 in. The marker has then acquired a rate of .75 in per sec, and an acceleration of 1.5 in per sec². For the first 18 trials the response marker starts alternately .5 and 1.5 in above the center of the target zone. The last 6 trials cannot be compared directly with the first 18 trials, because in the last 6 trials the response marker always starts 1.0 in above the center of the target zone.

The results are from 5 separate groups, each of 10 men undergraduates. The points at the top for the quickened display lie reliably above the points below for the unquickened display. None of the 3 groups which start with the quickened display perform as well subsequently with the unquickened display as the group which practices throughout on the unquickened display. The differences are reliable statistically when averaged over the last 6 trials. (After Goldstein, 1961, Figure 4.)

zone of .25 in for the remainder of the 2.5 min trial. The ordinate shows
the proportion of the trial time for which the response marker is held
on target. In the quickened condition the man has an additional quickened marker. Moving the quickened marker down and holding it over
the center of the target brings the response marker into the target zone
and keeps it there.

The figure shows that the trials with the quickened display result
in over twice as long on target as the trials with the unquickened display.
The group represented by the unfilled squares has 12 trials with the
unquickened display before transferring to the quickened display. On
the first trial with the quickened display the group performs as well
as the group which practices all the time with the quickened display.

The filled triangles represent a group which practices with the quickened display for 6 trials before transferring to the unquickened display.
The group's first trial with the unquickened display is about as successful
as the first trials of the 2 groups which start with the unquickened
display. But the group does not learn as rapidly as the 2 groups which
start with the unquickened display. The group's second 6 unquickened
trials are numbers 13 through 18 in the figure. The average time on
target is 19% of the 2.5 min trials. This value can be compared with
the average of 30% for the second 6 unquickened trials of the 2 groups
which start with the unquickened display. The difference is not tested
for statistical reliability, but it is almost certainly reliable. The 2 other
groups which start with the quickened display also show a tendency
to learn more slowly when transferred to the unquickened display.

Goldstein (1961) includes a group (not shown in the figure) which
always practices alternately one trial with the quickened display, and
2 trials with the unquickened display. Times on target with the quickened display are very nearly as long as the times of the groups which
practice only with the quickened display. With the unquickened display
the times on target are about as short as the shortest times at the bottom
of the figure. Thus transfer is almost 100% from the unquickened display
to the quickened display. But practice with the quickened display retards
subsequent learning with the unquickened display.

Asymmetrical transfer in favor of the quickened display is reported
also in the experiment by Dooley and Newton (1965), which is listed
in part **B** of Table 10.1. The 4 experiments shown in the table as having
only one group of people, all use some kind of balanced treatment
design. The same people work alternately with the quickened and unquickened displays. The bias introduced by the experimental design
almost certainly favors the quickened displays.

Disadvantages of quickened displays

Quickened displays produce slow acquisition

One disadvantage of a quickened display is that targets are not acquired by the control system as quickly as they can be. The optimal strategy in step tracking with an acceleration control system is to alternate between full acceleration and full deceleration. Whereas with a quickened display the man tends to make control movements which are proportional to the sizes of the displayed errors. Alternating between full acceleration and full deceleration makes the quickened marker jump over and back in a jerky fashion. This is illustrated at the bottom of Figure 10.4 on the left. The man does not usually adopt this optimal strategy. As a result his average tracking errors are larger with the quickened display than they need be.

In compensatory tracking with an acceleration control system, a phase plane display with a switching line like that illustrated in Figure 10.2 helps the man to alternate between full acceleration and full deceleration. It enables him to acquire a target more rapidly than he does with a quickened display. Unfortunately quickened displays and phase plane displays do not appear to have been compared experimentally.

Quickened displays are no help in unforeseen circumstances

A more serious disadvantage of a quickened display is that it is suited only to procedures which are programed into the quickening circuits. It may be of no help with procedures which are not considered by the designer. Usually the man also has status displays, which we can use when he finds that the quickened display is no longer a help. However Figure 10.5 shows that if he is accustomed to tracking with the quickened display, he will be less skilled when he comes to use an unquickened display than a man who has always used an unquickened display.

In an experiment by McLane and Wolf (1966), the helmsman of a simulated submarine has to avoid a homing torpedo. Three quickened displays all tell the man how to steer toward his target position. They also enable him to predict that the torpedo will hit his ship, because they show him the position of the torpedo and the position of the ship. But they do not tell the helmsman how to avoid the torpedo. The man avoids the torpedo reliably more often with a predictor display, which is discussed later in the chapter.

Quickened displays can be mistaken for status displays

The greatest disadvantage of a quickened display is that the man may think that he has got a quickened control system. This can happen because the quickened display gives the correct status information whenever it is at rest. It is only when the quickened display is moving that it is misleading. Yet the display responds to the man's control movements, just as status displays do. It is easy to think that a quickened display is a status display.

The pilot of an aircraft may find that he has suddenly to avoid an obstacle such as the top of a mountain or another aircraft. If he uses a quickened display, he may for an instant feel that he has done all that is necessary to avoid the obstacle as soon as the quickened display marker has moved to the desired position.

The left of Figure 10.4 shows that the quickened display marker can have reached the desired position well before the output of the high order control system has done so. This can give the pilot a false sense of security. It is not known how many collisions have been produced in this way.

As we shall see, confusions between quickened displays and quickened control systems are not restricted to people tracking with quickened displays. Taylor and Birmingham (1956) who advocate quickened displays, use an experiment with a quickened control system to illustrate the advantage of quickened displays.

Quickened displays are misleading
with velocity ramp tracks

The column labeled ramp on the left of Figure 10.4 shows that a quickened display is a handicap when tracking a constant velocity ramp, because it produces an invisible lag in position. The man has to put on an acceleration in order to give the display marker a rate. The acceleration is then taken off again. With the quickened display at the bottom of the column, position and rate components are also put on and taken off again.

But while the rate component is on, it produces an extra forward displacement of the quickened display marker, which is not removed. The displacement is illustrated by the second function. The quickened display at the bottom tells the man that he is fully satisfying the demand signal. Whereas the output of his acceleration control system just above has the correct rate, but is lagging in position behind the demand signal. The quickened display only catches up with the unquickened display when the ramp track comes to rest.

In directing a rocket toward a moving target, a constant lag produced in this way is likely to be a more serious handicap than a variable error. There appear to be no experiments comparing quickened and unquickened displays using constant velocity ramps. This is presumably because an experiment would almost certainly show the quickened display to be the worse.

Quickened displays are misleading with sine wave tracks

A quickened display is also a handicap in tracking sine waves. Here the invisible lag in position becomes an invisible lag in phase. This is illustrated on the right of Figure 10.4 for a sine wave of 15 cpm. The figure shows the control being moved in phase with the demand signal. The acceleration output of the control system is 180° behind in phase. This is illustrated by the third function from the top.

The quickened display at the bottom is only about 130° behind in phase. This is because the acceleration output of the control system is mixed with the direct output of the control which is in phase with the demand signal, and also with the rate component of the control system which is only 90° behind in phase.

With the quickened display, the man does not realize the full size of the phase lag of the acceleration output of his control system. In the experiment by Verdi, Ornstein, Heydorn and Frost (1965, Table 3) which is listed in part **B** of Table 10.1, the track has a nominal cutoff at 10 cpm. The fully quickened display is found to give a reliably larger system error than the unaugmented display.

At a track frequency of 30 cpm, the amplitude of the acceleration output of the control system is only one quarter as large as it is at 15 cpm. The movements of the quickened display marker are dominated largely by the rate component of the control system. The apparent lag in phase with the quickened display is less than half the 180° lag in phase of the acceleration output of the control system.

With a sine wave of 3 cpm, the lag in phase of the quickened display is dominated by the acceleration output of the control system. The difference in phase between the quickened display and the output of the acceleration control system is only about 10°. A single sine wave of this frequency is used by Dooley and Newton (1965) in the other experiment listed in part **B** of Table 10.1. Dooley and Newton report that the quickened display is actually an advantage early in practice. After practice there is little to choose between the 2 displays. With additional practice the unquickened display would presumably give the more accurate tracking. This is because it does not have the hidden 10° lag in phase, which represents a time lag of about .5 sec.

The 2 experiments in part C of Table 10.1 are not valid comparisons of quickened with unquickened displays, because in both cases an experimental variable favors the quickened display. In the experiment by Obermayer and colleagues (1967, Experiment 3) the students who track with the rate augmented display are told to keep both the position and rate errors as small as possible all the time, as if their error score is to be the sum of the position and rate errors. This is not the best strategy for minimizing position error. A large position error can be corrected quickly only by making a large rate error (Poulton, 1967, Table 1, Pursuit position normal tracking with a rate control). The instruction to minimize both position and rate errors prevents the students from doing this.

With the quickened display the students necessarily minimize the displayed sum of the 2 errors. Telling the students with the rate augmented display to do the same, means that they suffer the disadvantage of having to look at 2 displays, without the corresponding advantage of the improved strategy which the 2 displays can give them. The experiment needs to be repeated with instructions to minimize only the position error, which is the error in the output of the control system.

Quickened displays and quickened control systems

It is important to distinguish between experiments evaluating quickened displays, and experiments evaluating quickened control systems which necessarily produce quickened displays. The distinction can be made by checking the measure of performance used for the evaluation (Dooley & Newton, 1965). The measure of performance may use the output of the control system, which is shown on the right of Figure 10.1C. If so, the experiment is evaluating a quickened display. But the measure of performance may use the error displayed to the man, which is shown on the left of the figure. This is equivalent to the error of a quickened control system like that illustrated in Figure 16.2. The distinction between the 2 measures is illustrated in Figure 10.6.

In this chapter we are concerned only with quickened displays, which are used for tracking with a high order control system. The effects of quickening or aiding the control system are discussed in Chapter 16. Unfortunately authors do not always distinguish clearly between the 2 kinds of quickening.

Perhaps the most misleading confusion is made in the journal report by Taylor and Birmingham (1956) entitled "Simplifying the pilot's task through display quickening." Aircraft have control systems of high order. The control systems cannot be aided by adding rate and position com-

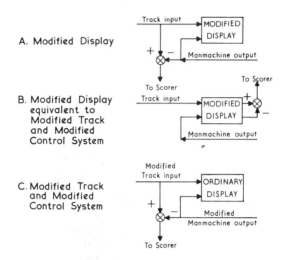

Figure 10.6.   A modified display and a modified control system.

The distinction is based upon what is scored as the tracking error. The modified display might be a quickened display. It might be a magnified, a nonlinear, a delayed, a noisy, or a filtered display, all of which are discussed in Chapter 11. The modified display might be one of the stepped displays discussed in Chapter 12. The figure does not show the boxes which represent the man, the control, and the control system on the right of Figure 10.1.

With the modified display in **A,** the experimenter measures the difference between the track and the output of the control system. The man does not see this error value directly. He sees only a modified version.

In **C** the man again sees a modified track and a modified control system output. But here it is the modified functions which are used to compute the error. The display does not change the function. The man sees a representation of the error which is scored against him.

The arrangement shown at **B** can cause confusion. The display is modified, but it is the error seen by the man which is scored against him. From the point of view of the man, the arrangement is equivalent to the arrangement shown at **C.** The only difference is that the track and control system output are shown as being modified in the box labeled display, instead of being modified before reaching the display. This is a confusing description. It is less confusing to use the block diagram of **C.**

ponents, because they depend upon aerodynamics. But the displays used in the aircraft can be quickened.

Taylor and Birmingham start by discussing the preliminary experiment on display quickening which is described by Bailey (1958) in the report listed at the top of Table 10.1. They continue without further explanation to describe the experiment by Birmingham, Kahn and Taylor (1954) which is illustrated in Figure 16.3. The experiment uses the error displayed to the man as the measure of performance, as illustrated in Figure

10.6B. The man has to keep either the quickened or the unquickened marker from leaving the display.

The quickened response marker is of course far easier to control, because the man is in effect tracking with an aided or quickened control system. In controlling the unquickened response marker, the man uses a third order control system. The experiment is therefore on control system aiding or quickening, not on display quickening. The point is not mentioned in the report by Taylor and Birmingham.

The experiment has since been presented as an illustration of display quickening in the first NASA Bioastronautics Data Book (Webb, 1964, page 358). To discover the confusion it is necessary to refer to the report of the original experiment of Birmingham and colleagues (1954), which is not generally available.

Predictor displays

A compensatory predictor display is illustrated in Figure 10.7 (Kelley, 1962). It shows the man the predicted output of his control system over the next few seconds. In normal circumstances the behavior of the control system can be predicted with reasonable certainty. But the predicted output of the control system some time ahead depends upon what the man does with his control during this time. An assumption about the man's future control movements has to be built into the fast time model. The usual assumption is that the man gradually returns his control to the neutral position.

The compensatory predictor display of Figure 10.7 has future time on the abscissa as one of its 2 dimensions. More sophisticated predictor displays are 3 dimensional and pursuit, with time shown in the distance dimension. The required path of a vehicle is shown as a runway in the sky, as in Figure 9.2, or as a runway in the water. The vehicle is shown in its present position and attitude relative to the runway, and also in its predicted position and attitude perhaps 10 and 20 sec ahead (Kelley, 1968, Figure 10.3).

When the task is difficult, a predictor display is reported to give reliably more accurate tracking than 3 different simple rate augmented displays (Kelley, Mitchell, & Strudwick, 1964). Four experienced pilots were used in this experiment. Unfortunately a predictor display has not yet been compared experimentally with a velocity vector display, which is a rudimentary predictor display.

In compensatory tracking with an onoff acceleration control system, a predictor phase plane display is no better than a phase plane display with a fixed switching line. With both displays the error in switching

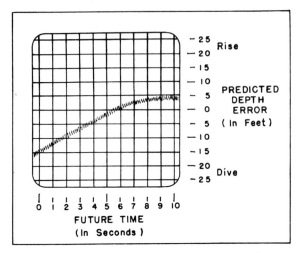

Figure 10.7. A compensatory predictor display.

The display shows the predicted error in the depth of a submarine over the next 10 sec, on the assumption that the man gradually returns his control to the neutral position. (After Kelley, 1962.) If the man controls the depth so that the predicted path always ends at the target depth, the rate of approach to the target depth becomes slower and slower as the submarine approaches it. This is not the quickest way of reaching the required depth. The man reaches the target depth more quickly if he first selects a path which soon reaches the target depth and then overshoots, as in the figure. When the target depth is approached, he cancels the predicted overshoot. If he is skillful, he ends with the predicted path running horizontally at the target depth.

time is only about one third the error with 2 simpler displays, a phase plane display without a switching line, and an unaugmented display (Miller, 1969). As we have seen, a fixed switching line is only appropriate to compensatory tracking with an acceleration control system. A compensatory predictor display has not yet been compared with a phase plane display having the varying switching line which is required for higher order control systems.

A predictor display is reported to be reliably better than 3 different quickened displays at helping the helmsman of a simulated submarine to avoid a homing torpedo (McLane & Wolf, 1966).

The concepts of predictor and quickened displays can be compared with the concepts of pursuit and compensatory displays. Both compensatory and quickened displays tell the man simply what to do. They may be adequate for certain kinds of tracking as long as fairly large errors can be tolerated, and an unusual event does not occur.

Pursuit and predictor displays give the man the opportunity to track more accurately than with compensatory and quickened displays, respectively. They also help the man with an unusual event. The pursuit display tells the man whether the unusual event is occurring in the outside world or in his control system. The predictor display helps the man to determine the correct action to take when the unusual event is in the outside world, though not when it is in his control system. The ideal combination is a pursuit predictor display.

Unfortunately a predictor display can be misleading if the fast time model ceases to mimic the control system. This can happen if a sudden change occurs in either the computer which generates the fast time model, or in the control system. There are dangers of this kind with any sophisticated display system.

Preview of track ahead

In tracking along a contour, the effect of preview depends upon whether the task is unpaced or paced. When contour tracking is unpaced, the man increases his speed as the preview ahead is increased. He also tracks more accurately (Poulton, 1957a).

When contour tracking is paced, the man cannot increase his speed as the preview ahead is increased. But the top part of Figure 10.8 shows that he considerably reduces his average error. The reduction is reliable with all 4 tracks. The experimental arrangement is illustrated in Figure 1.2. The approaching track is covered by a horizontal screen. In different conditions the man is allowed to see the track for the last few seconds, or only for a fraction of a second.

The middle part of Figure 10.8 shows that increasing the duration of the preview also reduces the average time lag. Similar findings are reported by Drewell (1972) and by Welford (1958, Figure 4.13b). Figure 3.5 shows the different average time lags before and after a reversal in the track, when the preview is 2.5 sec.

More detailed measures than those illustrated in Figure 10.8 indicate that there can be reliable changes in performance when the preview is increased beyond .5 sec. The man needs to be able to see at least as far as the next track reversal in order to perform at his best (Poulton, 1964). The movement between one reversal and the next can then be made as a single response.

In the top part of Figure 10.8, the modulus mean error is given in seconds. By comparing the top and middle parts of the figure, it is possible to determine how much of the modulus mean error is produced by the man's time lag. When there is a preview of only .1 sec, 85% of the modulus mean error with the high frequency track represents

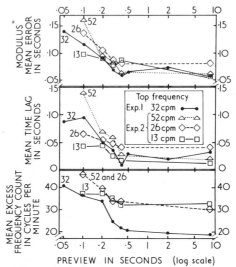

Figure 10.8. Performance with preview.

The track is drawn on a paper tape which moves 1 in per sec. The filled circles of Experiment 1 represent the performance of 12 young enlisted men. The track comprises 4 sine waves with frequencies of 32.5, 25, 21.5 and 14 cpm. The low frequency sine wave has half the amplitude of the other 3 sine waves. Before the experiment there is a practice trial with each of the 8 previews.

The unfilled points of Experiment 2 represent the performance of another group of 15 young enlisted men. The 3 tracks each consist of 3 sine waves. The high frequency track has equal amplitude sine waves of 52 and 42 cpm, and a sine wave of 21 cpm with twice the amplitude. The 2 lower frequency tracks are obtained respectively by halving all the frequencies, and by halving them again. There are 3 practice trials before the experiment in order to introduce the 3 tracks and the range of previews. In the balanced design of Experiment 2, the track is not changed until it has been presented with all 5 sizes of preview. (Some of the results are from Poulton, 1954, Table 3.)

The difference between the 2 experiments in the excess frequency count must be due to transfer between trials with the 3 tracks used in Experiment 2. The transfer occurs during the 3 practice trials, one with each track, because at the start of the experiment there is already no reliable difference in the excess frequency count between the 3 tracks. Other range effects are mentioned in the text.

time lag. When the preview is increased to 8 sec, only 30% of the modulus mean error represents time lag. For the track with a top frequency of 13 cpm, the mean time lag represents only 40% of the modulus mean error with a preview of .1 sec, and only 15% with a preview of 8 sec. The remainder of the modulus mean error represents variation around the average time lag.

The bottom part of the figure illustrates a measure of the man's variability. This is the number of times that he changes the rate of movement of his ball point pen when the track does not call for a change. With short previews it probably represents incorrect predictions about the track. Increasing the preview to 8 sec reliably reduces the average excess frequency count with all 4 tracks.

With a very short preview, the man faces much the same problem as in tracking with a conventional pursuit display. If he copies the track which he can see, he will lag a reaction time behind. He can reduce his time lag only by responding according to his predictions of what the track is about to do next. The left side of the middle part of Figure 10.8 shows that with the 2 low frequency tracks the man does respond with an average time lag of less than a reaction time.

However for the track with a top frequency of 52 cpm, the man's performance shows no evidence of prediction. Adding the preview of .1 sec to the mean time lag of .14 sec gives a total mean time of .24 sec. This is longer than a simple visual reaction time of about .18 sec.

The man's performance can be compared to the performance illustrated in Figure 3.4 (Elkind, 1956) for pursuit tracking with a top frequency of 58 cpm. Elkind's 3 people have an average time lag of only about .04 sec. The larger time lags in the experiments of Figure 10.8 with short previews must be due to a range effect produced by the balanced experimental designs. The man tends always to predict the track only a moderate time ahead, as if he has a moderate preview.

With a preview of reasonable duration, the man can see ahead what he will be required to do. His problem is simply to match the track as accurately as he can. The figure shows that the man does not track particularly well with a preview of 8 sec. He tends to lag in time behind the track. And he changes his rate of movement more often than he need do. These 2 results must also be due to range effects produced by the balanced experimental designs. With all durations of preview, the man's performance tends to be somewhat like his performance with a preview of moderate duration.

Recommended augmented displays

A predictor display should be used whenever an augmented display is required for a control system of high order.

If a phase plane display is used for compensatory tracking, the switching line should be shown. A compensatory velocity vector display is preferable to a phase plane display without a switching line.

A quickened display is not recommended.

With a sine wave track, preview ahead should extend as least as far as the next reversal.

Chapter

11

More display variations

Summary

The relationship between the magnification of a compensatory display and the error in tracking is **U** shaped. The increased accuracy found with a large magnification is an artifact of transfer.

Delaying, filtering, and adding visual noise to a display, all degrade tracking. Complete transfer from a simulated display to the real display on the first trial occurs only when the 2 displays are almost identical.

Two tracking tasks are easier to perform simultaneously when the displays are compatible. A well designed integrated display can give more accurate tracking than 2 separate displays.

Kinds of display variation

Linear and nonlinear display magnification

Aircraft cockpits have only a limited amount of space available for instruments. When large display movements have to be shown, it is necessary to use a circular instrument. Clocks show a large range of movement by employing 2 hands. The early altimeters had 3 hands.

Unfortunately it is possible to confuse the hands. Aircraft have crashed into the ground because pilots misread their 3 handed altimeters.

Nonlinear display magnification can be used to avoid the difficulty of an excessively large range of movement. Distances are magnified in the center of the display where the markers spend most of the time. Distances toward the edge are reduced in size, so that the markers never disappear off the edge.

Delayed, filtered and noisy visual displays

A man on the ground may wish to control the movements of an unmanned vehicle over the surface of the moon. A transmission delay of a second or two occurs before the effect of the change can be seen by the controller. There is not much point in making a second adjustment until the effect of the first adjustment has been seen. Thus tracking is a slow and laborious business.

Electrical circuits carry noise of low amplitude. If the tracking signal is also of low amplitude, its amplitude may not be very much larger than the amplitude of the noise. The man may not be able to distinguish between the signal and the noise, and may track them both.

Noise of high frequency can be attenuated by passing the combined tracking signal plus noise through a lowpass filter. Unfortunately the filter both delays the tracking signal and distorts it. This may be worse than tracking the unfiltered signal.

Simulated displays

An imperfectly simulated display can be regarded as a distorted version of the true display. Simulators are used to train pilots, and controllers of rockets. Aircraft simulators are used also to practice emergency procedures, and to present tests of proficiency (Adams, 1961). This is because the cost of running the simulator is less than the cost of carrying out the real job. Also training on a simulator may be safer than training on the job.

A simulated visual display of the airfield and its approaches is required to teach a trainee pilot to land. A realistic visual background is required to train the controller of a rocket. The cost of exact simulation of the display may be so great that training organizations are tempted to buy cheaper visual simulators which are not so perfect. The reduced cost of the simulator has to be set against the reduced efficiency of the training obtained on the simulator when first carrying out the real task.

Multiple and integrated displays

Conventional aircraft present the pilot with a large number of instruments, which he has to look at in turn. A device may be invented to measure some new aspect of the behavior of the aircraft. The usual outcome is yet another instrument crowded somewhere into the instrument panel. The pilot then has one more instrument to look at. The new instrument clutters his field of view when he wishes to look at one of the other instruments.

This piecemeal approach to the design of instrument panels is challenged by designers who take an overall view of the pilot's task in flying. Groups of instruments should be designed to be compatible, and should be located appropriately. It may be possible to combine the information from several instruments into a single display, like the headup display illustrated in Figure 9.2. If the integrated display is skillfully designed, it should make the pilot's task easier.

Magnified displays

Magnifying a display increases the sizes of the movements of the display markers, and so makes the errors look larger. Experiments on display magnification are listed in Table 11.1.

Part **A** of the table gives the experiments using pursuit displays. The experiments by Fitts and colleagues (1953) have 2 entries in the column headed **N** for the number of people. The results cannot be biased by asymmetrical transfer, because each person has only one magnification. The experiments show that increasing the magnification of a single sine wave track of 60 cpm from an amplitude of 1 in to an amplitude of 4 in reliably reduces the RMS error. The advantage of magnification is not reliable with single sine waves of only 30 and 15 cpm.

The experiments by Hartman and Fitts (1955) also favor a magnified pursuit display. Clearly the track marker should move across practically the whole face of a CRT with the usual diameter of 5 in.

Asymmetrical transfer with magnified compensatory displays

The experiments in part **B** of Table 11.1 are for compensatory displays. Only the experiment by Battig, Nagel and Brogden (1955) at the top uses separate groups, and so cannot be biased by asymmetrical transfer. Moderate magnification is found to be reliably better than too much magnification or too little magnification. The **U** shaped relationship between magnification and the average tracking error is illustrated by the top function in Figure 11.1 (Battig and others, 1955).

Both the functions in the figure must turn up sharply on the extreme left. This is because as the error magnification approaches 0, it becomes impossible for the man to see the error which he is supposed to correct. The point is illustrated in Figure 13.2 by the unbroken function.

On the extreme right of Figure 11.1 the magnification is too high. This is because the error marker tends to disappear off the edge of the CRT. Yet the greatest magnification of the displayed track movement produces a maximum movement of only 2.4 in, compared with the 5.0 in diameter of the CRT. Thus the marker will not disappear off the edge of the CRT by itself. An inappropriate control movement is required to make the marker disappear.

The adverse effect of the largest display magnification is reduced by trials 13 to 15, because the man is more practiced. But the adverse effect of magnification is still statistically reliable.

In the remaining experiments listed in part **B** of Table 11.1, everybody tracks with all the display magnifications. Owing to asymmetrical transfer, the largest magnification almost always gives the smallest error. The only exception is in the 1958 Bowen and Chernikoff experiment, which includes a magnified track with a display movement of 12.5 yd.

Performance with the largest magnification is almost always best, because it is followed by a degradation of performance with the smaller magnifications. When tracking with the smaller magnifications, the displayed errors look small compared with the displayed errors when tracking with the largest magnification. The man's main effort is devoted to reducing what he sees to be the large errors. He does not worry too much about the apparently small errors of the displays with the smaller magnifications (Helson, 1949 page 492).

The results of the 1958 Bowen and Chernikoff experiment are illustrated in Figure 11.2. The numbers printed against the filled points represent the amplitude in inches of the unmagnified tracks. The effect of the 10 times display magnification is indicated by the corresponding unfilled points. Here the displayed errors are 10 times the plotted errors.

With the sine wave of 2 cpm, magnifying the amplitude of the display from 15 to 150 in reliably reduces the average modulus mean error by about 10%. This is the largest amplitude sine wave to give an improvement in performance after magnification. Magnifying the display amplitude from 45 to 450 in reliably increases the error by 45%. The experimental results follow the U shaped relationship for compensatory displays illustrated in Figure 11.1. But owing to the asymmetrical transfer, the magnified track amplitude required to reach the right hand side of the U is very much larger than in Figure 11.1.

The very large magnification is possible because Bowen and Chernikoff (1958) use practiced people, a predictable single sine wave of low frequency, and a special procedure for switching in the magnification. With

Table 11.1
Experiments on display magnification

A. Pursuit displays

Author(s)	Year	N	Track frequencies (cpm)	Largest magnification	Largest magnified amplitude of track (in)	Other variables	Reliably better
Fitts and colleagues	1953	9 + 9	15	4	4	Control gain	—
		9 + 9	30	4	4		—
		9 + 8	60	4	4		—
Hartman and Fitts	1955		15	16	4	Control gains. Four people also practiced with a compensatory display	Magnified
			30				Magnified
			60				Magnified
			30 + 20				Magnified
			30 + 20 + 10				Magnified
							Magnified
Poulton*	1952a	12	15	2	3		—
			20 + 15	2	3		—
(see Figure 8.3)*		16 (3 pilots)	15	2	3	Control gain. Compensatory display	—
			30				—
			45				—
			60				—
			20 + 15				—
			40 + 30				—
			60 + 45				—
			80 + 60				—

B. Compensatory displays

Author(s)	Year	N	Track frequencies (cpm)	Largest magnification	Largest magnified amplitude of track (in)	Other variables	Reliably better
Battig, Nagel, and Brogden (see Figure 11.1)	1955	20 + 20	Irregular up to 5 or 10	6	2.4	Size of error marker	Intermediate
Bowen and Chernikoff	1957	6	$6.7 + 4.4 + 2.7$	10	40	Nonlinear display	Magnified
			$16.7 + 11.1 + 6.7$				Magnified
			$26.7 + 17.8 + 10.7$				Magnified

Study	Date	N	Track			Amplitude of track	Depends on amplitude of track
Bowen and Chernikoff (see Figure 11.2)	1958	6	2 8 30 }	10	450 112 30 }		
Chase, Cullen, Openshaw, and Sullivan	1965	24	No track	40	—	Task stress	Magnified
Garvey and Henson	1959	5	11 + 7 + 3	6.7	13.4	Aiding ratios	Magnified
Helson	1949	6	Low	4	?	Rate and acceleration control.	Magnified
Hershberger	1967	4	?	200	?	Computer aiding. Control gain.	Magnified
Noble, Fitts, and Marlowe	1953	7	15 60	4	2	Control gain	—
North and Lomnicki	1961	6	12 + 6 + 2	8	180		Magnified
Poulton*	1952a	12	15 20 + 15	2 2	1.5 1.5 }		—
(see Figure 8.3)*		16 (3 pilots)	15 30 45 60 20 + 15 40 + 30 60 + 45 80 + 60	2	1.5	Control gain. Pursuit display	—
Seidenstein, Chernikoff and Taylor	1960	5	10 + 6.7 + 3.2	32	32	Distance from display. Position and aided control systems	Magnified Magnified
Smith, Garfinkle, Groth and Lyman	1966a	6	Irregular up to 15‡	5	?	Aiding ratio. Cues of motion.	Magnified
Smith, Garfinkle and Lyman	1966	4	Irregular up to 15‡	4	?	Size of field of view	—

* Included in both parts of the table.
‡ Half the number of reversals per minute.

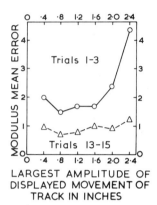

LARGEST AMPLITUDE OF
DISPLAYED MOVEMENT OF
TRACK IN INCHES

Figure 11.1. Performance with a magnified compensatory display.
The points in each verticle column are from a separate group of 20 undergraduates.
The CRT has a diameter of 5 in. The 2 dimensional track is produced by an
irregular cam with a top frequency of perhaps 5 or 10 cpm. The man has a
lightly loaded joystick 7 in long.
The ordinate gives the average of the modulus mean errors in the 2 dimensions.
With the larger magnifications, the errors of course look larger than they do with
the smaller magnifications. An average error equal to the largest amplitude of
the displayed track movement would be 5. This value probably corresponds to
a relative modulus mean error of about 300%. In each dimension the function (not
shown) fitted to the corresponding 6 points have reliable quadratic terms. This
means that they are reliably curved. (Results from Battig and colleagues, 1955.)

a high frequency unpredictable track, the man is likely to lose the error
marker from his CRT if the display magnification is large. He may
then be unable to retrieve it again.

The experiment by Battig and his colleagues (1955) is the only experiment in part **B** of Table 11.1 which excludes the possibility of asymmetrical transfer. Thus it is the only experiment from which a valid conclusion
can be drawn about the optimum magnification for a compensatory
display. The conclusion is that the magnification should be sufficiently
small to keep the error marker away from the edge. Figure 11.1 shows
that early in training the maximum movement of the magnified track
should not take the error marker outside the central part of the display.

Even after a good deal of training, there appears to be no advantage
in increasing the magnification any further. The extra magnification
simply increases the chance of the error marker reaching the edge of
the display, and either disappearing from view, or else resting against
the stop at the edge of the instrument. When this happens, it conceals
from the man the size of his error. If he is not attending and the error
marker disappears, he may not know the direction in which the marker

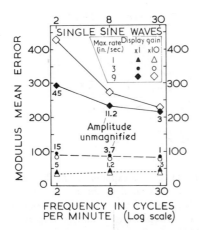

Figure 11.2.   Asymmetrical transfer with 10 times magnification.
The display is compensatory. The tracks are single sine waves of the 3 frequencies indicated on the abscissa. The amplitudes of the tracks in inches are printed against the filled points. Within each of the 3 functions, the amplitudes are inversely proportional to the frequencies. This holds constant the maximum rates of the tracks. It produces average errors of about the same size with each track. The CRT has a diameter of 5 in.

The 9 combinations of 3 frequencies and 3 maximum velocities are presented in random order. Each combination is tracked 4 times in succession, twice with and twice without magnification. The order is either $\times$ 1, $\times$ 10, $\times$ 10, $\times$ 1, or $\times$ 10, $\times$ 1, $\times$ 1, $\times$ 10. In the trials with the magnified displays, the man tracks for 5 sec with the unmagnified display before the magnification is automatically switched in. He then has 10 sec to adjust himself before scoring starts. (Results from Bowen & Chernikoff, 1958.)

has gone. He may attempt to retrieve it from the incorrect direction. If the pilot of an aircraft were to do this, it could be dangerous.

Nonlinear displays

An exponential nonlinearity like that illustrated in Figure 11.3 can be used to prevent markers from disappearing off the face of a CRT. As long as the man needs to use only the central part of the CRT, he has the benefit of reasonable magnification. When a marker happens to reach the edge of the CRT, it comes almost to a stop. It never wanders off the edge and gets lost. This might be thought to be an advantage.

However in practice an exponential nonlinearity does not help. When the track or error marker is toward the edge of the CRT, the reduced scale here conceals the true size of the error. Thus the man does not make as accurate a control movement to correct the error as he does when he sees its true size. When the track or error marker spends a

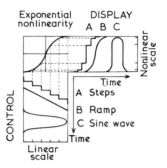

Figure 11.3. An exponential nonlinearity.
The exponential function is illustrated at the top on the left. Below it are some control movements in the horizontal dimension. For the movements, time runs vertically down the page. The corresponding nonlinear display movements are shown at the top on the right in the vertical dimension. For them time runs horizontally toward the right. The points on the linear functions below can be related to the corresponding points on the nonlinear functions at the top on the right. Vertical lines are drawn up to the exponental function and then horizontal lines are drawn across to the right. This has been done for a series of steps. The time relationships remain unchanged.

good deal of the time toward the edge of the display, the reduced magnification here offsets the advantage of the larger magnification in the center.

A major disadvantage of a nonlinear display is that the movements of the nonlinear display markers do not correspond to the real movements in the outside world. In this a nonlinear display resembles a compensatory display (see Chapter 9) and a quickened display (see Chapter 10). It can mislead the man and result in a stupid error, or perhaps a fatal accident.

Prediction with nonlinear and linear pursuit displays

There is no experiment comparing the accuracy of tracking with nonlinear and linear pursuit displays. Garvey, Knowles and Newlin (1957) compare the accuracy of prediction with the 2 kinds of display. They use separate groups of 8 sailors for each display. In the linear display the targets move at constant speeds in straight lines. Garvey and his colleagues report that future positions can be predicted much more accurately with the linear display.

It is pointed out in Chapter 9 that one of the advantages of tracking with a pursuit display over tracking with a compensatory display, is that the man can make more accurate predictions of the future track movements with a pursuit display. Making the pursuit display nonlinear reduces the man's ability to do this, and so must reduce the accuracy of his tracking. But the point has still to be investigated.

Nonlinear and linear compensatory displays

The only experiment comparing tracking with nonlinear and linear compensatory displays is the 1957 experiment by Bowen and Chernikoff, which is listed in part **B** of Table 11.1. Tracking is in 1 dimension with a rate aided control system. Unfortunately the balanced treatment design biases the results in favor of magnification. The nonlinear display illustrated in Figure 11.3 is reported to be no advantage over a display with linear magnification. The nonlinear display gives a reliably smaller modulus mean error than an unmagnified linear display. But this is only when the errors are small, as with the easy low frequency track listed in Table 11.1, and with the track of intermediate frequency after sufficient practice.

When the errors are large, there is little difference between the nonlinear display and the unmagnified linear display. Large errors occur with the difficult high frequency track listed in the table, and also with the track of intermediate frequency before the man has had sufficient practice. The reduced magnification of the large errors toward the edge of the nonlinear display makes a large error of one size look much the same as a large error of another size. The man cannot tell very easily the size of control movement which is required to correct the error. This offsets the advantage of the larger magnification in the center of the display.

The experiment needs to be repeated with a separate group design to prevent the asymmetrical transfer which favors magnification. Probably both nonlinear and linear magnification will be found to be worse than no magnification.

Delayed displays

The effect of a simple time delay is illustrated in Figure 11.4. The man does not see the track for the duration of the delay. If he responds as soon as he sees the track, his response will lag behind the track by the duration of the delay. The figure shows that the effect of a simple time lag of constant duration becomes more damaging as the frequency of a sine wave track is increased.

It is not possible for a man to compensate for a simple time lag unless he knows what the track will be doing at the corresponding time ahead. If the man does have this information, he should be able to advance his control movements in time so that they match the track movements after the time lag.

A delayed display can be distinguished from a time lag in a control system. In part **A** of Figure 10.6, a display time lag goes in the box labeled modified display. Both the track input and the manmachine output are delayed before the man sees them. Whereas a control system time lag goes in the box (not shown) which represents the control system. It delays only the manmachine output.

However as far as the man is concerned, the effects of the 2 kinds of transmission time lag are identical. This is illustrated on the left of Figure 11.5. The only difference between display and control transmission time lags is that events appear later in the display with the display time lag. What the man sees is indicated by the unbroken functions in the figure. The error introduced by the step in the track appears 1 sec late in the delayed display. The man therefore responds 1 sec

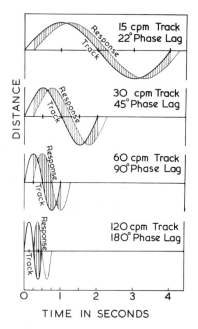

Figure 11.4.   Phase lags and errors in position.
    A simple time lag of .25 sec separates the response from the track. The vertical lines between the response and the track indicate the sizes of the errors. With the track of 60 cpm, the lag in phase produces errors which are larger than the errors produced by the track alone. With the track of 120 cpm, the errors are double the errors produced by the track alone. With phase lags greater than 180°, the errors get smaller again.

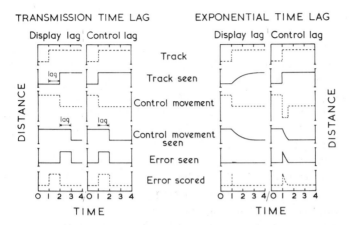

Figure 11.5.   Delayed and filtered displays and control systems.

The theoretical relationships are shown for a track with a single step. Filtering with an exponential control lag is illustrated on the extreme right. In attempting to correct for the step in the track the man makes a large control movement, because he has learned that a small control movement does not have enough effect. In this way he corrects the error more quickly than he would if he responded with a step of the same size as the step in the track. Once the error has been corrected, he has to move his control back to the position corresponding to the step in the track, or his response will overshoot.

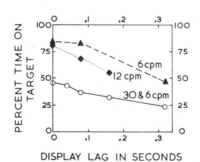

DISPLAY LAG IN SECONDS

Figure 11.6.   Performance with simple time lags.

The unfilled circles are for a track comprising 2 sine waves. The sine wave of 30 cpm has about twice the amplitude of the sine wave of 6 cpm. All the differences in height between the circles are reliable. The filled triangles and diamonds are for single sine waves of 6 and 12 cpm respectively. To be reliable, differences in height between the filled points must be at least about 7.

The relative heights of the 3 functions are arbitrary. The amplitudes of the tracks are selected to give about 50% or 80% time on target when there is no time lag. Ten or more laboratory staff perform with each track. They use a compensatory display and a position control system. (Results from Warrick, 1949).

later than with the control lag. The error remains for 1 sec in both conditions.

Warrick (1949) describes his experiments illustrated in Figure 11.6 as on transmission type control lags. He is in fact investigating display lags, not control lags. The man has to track with a compensatory display. The unfilled circles represent a track comprising sine waves of 30 and 6 cpm. The percent time on target is reliably reduced with a time lag as short as .04 sec. Warrick (1949, page 1) states that many people cannot appreciate time lags as short as this.

The 2 top functions in the figure are for single sine waves of 6 and 12 cpm respectively. With a time lag of .08 sec there is a reliable reduction in the percent time on target when tracking the faster sine wave, but not when tracking the slower sine wave. With the slower sine wave the man is able to predict the track position .08 sec ahead sufficiently accurately to stay within the target area for almost as great a proportion of the time as he can without a time lag.

Figure 11.7 (Henry, Junas & Smith, 1967) illustrates the effect of delay when the man has to hold constant the pressure of suction in his mouth. The left part of the figure shows the effect of training. The filled circles represent the performance of a group which practices with a 3.2 sec delay between making control adjustments and seeing their effects in the display. The unfilled circles represent the performance

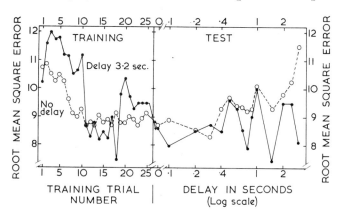

Figure 11.7. Performance during and after training with a single 3.2 sec time lag.
A constant negative pressure of suction in the mouth has to be maintained at 2 cm of water. The left part of the figure illustrates the results of 25 training trials of 60 sec each. The delay (filled points) and no delay (unfilled points) groups each contain 4 people. The right part of the figure illustrates the results of 18 test trials carried out subsequently with delays of various lengths. In the test trials the interaction between the 2 groups and the delays is reliable statistically. (After Henry and colleagues, 1967, Figures 4 and 7.)

of a group which practices without delay. The difference in RMS error between the 2 groups is not reliable. This may be because there are only 4 people in each group. Both groups reduce their average RMS error by about 20%. The reduction reflects mainly learning how to suck at a constant pressure.

The right part of the figure illustrates the results of subsequent test trials at each of 15 delays ranging from 0 to 3.2 sec. The group which practices with the 3.2 sec delay performs about equally well on average at all delays. The group which practices without delay shows an increase in RMS error of about 20% with increasing delay. The increase is almost certainly reliable statistically, although it is not tested directly. It reflects lack of practice with the technique of tracking with a delayed display.

Response frequencies with delayed displays

Tracking usually involves trial and check. The man adjusts his response, sees how he has done, and then adjusts his response again. In tracking with a delayed display, the man cannot see the effect of an adjustment until after the delay. While he is waiting, there is little point in making a second adjustment. The man therefore learns to adjust his response at intervals of time which are a little longer than the duration of the delay. This is illustrated in Figure 11.8 (Pew, Duffendack & Fensch, 1967b). The track is a single slow sine wave. The figure shows the relative RMS amplitude of all the frequencies in the man's response except the track frequency.

The bottom function in the figure is for a time lag of 1.44 sec. The greatest RMS amplitude of the error lies at about 18 cpm, or 1 cycle about every 3.3 sec. An error cycle represents 2 corrections of the rate of the response, 1 correction about every 1.65 sec. The man corrects the rate, and then waits until he sees the correction 1.44 sec later. He then corrects the rate again. Adding a visual reaction time of about .2 sec to the transmission lag of 1.44 sec gives an interval of about 1.65 sec between corrections. This produces the peak amplitude at about 18 cpm. A response with intermittent corrections of rate is illustrated on the right side of Figure 7.2.

The smaller peaks in the bottom function of Figure 11.8 at the higher frequencies represent the odd numbered harmonics of the fundamental frequency of 18 cpm. The peaks are centered at about 54, 90, 126, and 162 cpm. Odd numbered harmonics are produced by symmetrical distortions of a sine wave.

The peaks of the other error functions of Figure 11.8 are produced in exactly the same way. For the transmission lag of .18 sec the tallest peak comes at about 80 cpm, or 1 cycle about every .75 sec. It suggests

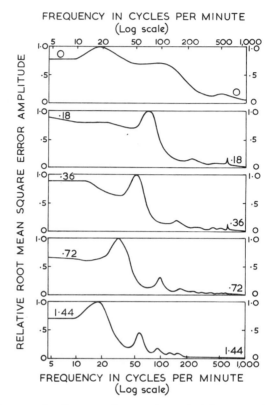

FREQUENCY IN CYCLES PER MINUTE
(Log scale)

RELATIVE ROOT MEAN SQUARE ERROR AMPLITUDE

FREQUENCY IN CYCLES PER MINUTE
(Log scale)

Figure 11.8.   Response frequencies with delayed displays.
The duration of the time lag in seconds is printed against the ends of each function. The RMS amplitude of each function is expressed relative to its maximum RMS amplitude, which is called 1. The display is compensatory. The track is a single sine wave of either 3 or 5.5 cpm. These 2 frequencies are excluded from the functions. The time lags are always presented in the order: 0, .18, .36, .72 and 1.44 sec. The results are for 3 people using both tracks. Unfortunately with only 3 people it is not possible to tell how representative the results are likely to be. (From Pew and colleagues, 1967b.)

that the man corrects the rate once about every .38 sec. This time interval represents the transmission lag of .18 sec added to a reaction time of about .2 sec. The odd numbered harmonics of the fundamental frequency of about 80 cpm are centered at about 240 and 400 cpm.

It is pointed out in Chapter 7 that 3 responses per sec is probably the upper limit to the rate at which people can respond. Usually people settle for a rate nearer to 2 responses per sec. The rather high rate of responding with the transmission lag of .18 sec is presumably caused by transfer from the conditions with the longer transmission lags. The man learns to let the longer lags determine his rate of response. When he changes to the lag of .18 sec, he continues to use the same strategy.

The function at the top of Figure 11.8 is for tracking without a transmission lag. The RMS error amplitude is greatest at about 18 cpm. This is about the same frequency as the maximum RMS amplitude with the transmission lag of 1.44 sec. It suggests that the strategy of the last trial with the first track, where the transmission lag is 1.44 sec, carries over to the first trial of the second track where there is no transmission lag. At frequencies above 20 cpm, the shape of the top function corresponds reasonably well to the error frequency function of Figure 8.10 for tracking a sine wave of 6 cpm without a delayed display. The peak at 500 cpm represents muscle tremor (see the last part of Chapter 8).

Filtered displays

Simple lowpass filters produce exponential or sigmoid lags like those illustrated in Figure 11.9. An exponential lag is produced by a single lowpass filter. Two or more lowpass filters connected in series produce a sigmoid lag.

The behavior of a single lowpass filter with a time constant of .6 sec is illustrated in Figure 11.10. The filter introduces a time lag which varies with frequency. This is indicated by the broken function labeled lag and the right hand ordinate. At frequencies of 16 cpm and below, the time lag is 80% or more of the time constant of the filter. At higher frequencies the time lag is a lot less, because the phase lag never quite reaches 90°.

A lowpass filter also attenuates the higher frequencies. This is indicated by the unbroken function labeled relative amplitude, and the left hand ordinate. Calling a single lowpass filter an exponential time lag can be misleading, because it does not draw attention to the attenuation of the higher frequencies. Increasing the time constant of a lowpass filter increases the time lag which it introduces at the lower frequencies. It also increases the attenuation of the higher frequencies.

Filtered displays and filtered control systems

Figure 10.6 can be used to illustrate the difference between a filtered display and a filtered control system. The block diagram of a filtered display corresponds to the diagram at the top of the figure. The error which is scored against the man is the difference between the unfiltered track and the unfiltered output of the control system.

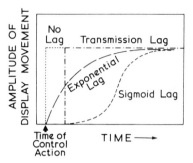

Figure 11.9.   Common kinds of lag following a step.
The dotted line represents the output when there is no lag. Turning on a switch produces a theoretical step of this kind. If the switch is turned on by a pulse reflected from a telecommunications satellite, there will be a transmission time lag while the pulse is traveling to and from the satellite.

An exponential lag is produced by a lowpass filter like that illustrated in Figure 11.10. The display marker has a large velocity at first, but slows down as it approaches its final position. It moves 63% $(1-1/e)$ of the distance during a time equal to the time constant of the exponential filter. A sigmoid lag is produced by 2 or more lowpass filters connected in series. The display marker first accelerates and then decelerates.

The man does not see this. He sees only a filtered version of the track and the filtered output of the control system. He does not see the full amplitude of the high frequencies in the track which he is supposed to copy. And he sees a delayed version of his control movements with the high frequencies attenuated.

The danger with a filtered display corresponds to the danger with a nonlinear display, and with a quickened display (see Chapter 10). The error which the man sees is not the true error of the system which is scored against him.

The block diagram of a filtered control system corresponds to Figure 10.6C, except that the track is unmodified, not modified as indicated in the figure. The man sees the track without a delay, and with the high frequencies unattenuated. Also the man sees the error which is scored against him. He does not see a filtered version of the error, as he does with a filtered display.

The first column on the right of Figure 11.5 illustrates the optimal strategy with a filtered display. If the man has a position control system, he should try to make control movements which correspond to the movements of the unfiltered track. When he cannot predict the track, his responses are bound to lag behind. But he should avoid attempting to compensate for this by making large amplitude responses of high frequency which are not called for by the track. If he can predict the

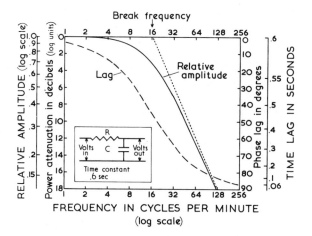

Figure 11.10. The behavior of a lowpass filter.

The filter attenuates high frequencies. This is indicated by the unbroken function labeled relative amplitude and the left hand ordinate. The attenuation of the power is shown in decibels (dB), the usual logarithmic units. The relative amplitude is shown on a separate logarithmic scale. The dotted line is the asymptote of the unbroken function. It meets the line indicating zero attenuation at the break or turnover frequency. The break frequency at 16 cpm indicates that the time constant of the filter is about .6 sec $[(60/16) \times (1/2\pi)]$. Halving the time constant to .3 sec doubles the break frequency to 32 cpm. It shifts the functions 1 octave to the right. At the break frequency the filter attenuates the power 3 dB. This gives a relative amplitude of .7. At frequencies well above the break frequency the power is attenuated 6 dB per octave. Doubling the frequency then halves the amplitude.

The filter also produces a phase lag which increases with frequency. This is indicated by the broken function and the right hand ordinate. The time lag which corresponds to the phase lag at each frequency is shown on a separate scale. The phase lag is 45° at the break frequency. At high frequencies the phase lag approaches 90°. At low frequencies it approaches zero. The phase lag corresponds to a time lag which is smaller at high frequencies. At very low frequencies the time lag is almost as large as the .6 sec time constant of the filter. At the break frequency the time lag is .47 sec, or about 80% ($\pi/4$) of the time constant. Four octaves higher it is only .06 sec, or about 10% of the time constant.

A **highpass** filter is produced by reversing the positions of the resistance and condenser illustrated at the bottom on the left. It behaves in the opposite way to a lowpass filter. The high frequencies are amplified and advanced in phase. This is illustrated at the bottom of Figure 8.17.

track successfully, the figure shows that his average error can be small. This is because Figure 10.6A shows that there is not a filter between the output of his control and the scoring device.

The last column on the right of Figure 11.5 illustrates the quite different optimal strategy with a filtered control system. The man should try to compensate for the filter which comes between the output of his control and the scoring device. To overcome the delay introduced by the filter, he has to respond with higher frequencies than the frequencies in the track. To overcome the attenuation of the high frequencies, his high frequencies have to have a relatively large amplitude.

The figure shows that in tracking a step of known size, the man is bound to have a larger average error with a filtered control system than he need have with a filtered display. But at least he can see the system error which is being scored against him. Exponential and sigmoid control system lags are discussed in Chapter 17.

Asymmetrical transfer between filtered displays and filtered control systems

Figure 11.11 (Garvey, Sweeny & Birmingham, 1958) illustrates the only experiment comparing filtered displays and filtered control systems. Two lowpass filters are connected in series, to produce a sigmoid lag. Unfortunately the display is compensatory, and a balanced treatment design is used.

Both filtering the display and filtering the control system increase the average error reliably. The effect of filtering the display is reliably greater than the effect of filtering the control system. The difference in favor of the filtered control system is a good deal larger than would be predicted from the discussion in the last section. This is because

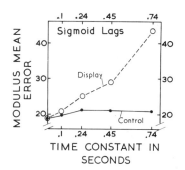

Figure 11.11. Asymmetrical transfer between filtered displays and control systems.
The display is compensatory. The track consists of 3 sine waves with frequencies of 11, 5, and 3 cpm. The amplitudes are inversely proportional to the frequencies. The man has a position control system. A balanced treatment design is used with 8 men. (After Garvey and colleagues, 1958, Figure 2.)

With the largest time constant of .74 sec, the sigmoid lag reduces the amplitude of the sine wave with a frequency of 11 cpm to about half, as well as producing a time lag of about 1.2 sec. Curiously enough Garvey and colleagues (1958, page 8) describe the attenuation as negligible. The sine wave of 3 cpm is attenuated by only about 5%.

the experiment uses a balanced treatment design and a compensatory display.

When tracking with a filtered control system, the man responds with high frequencies of large amplitude, in order to overcome the effect of the delay and attenuation produced by the control system. On the next trial the man may be switched to a filtered display. Figure 10.6A shows that now the man does not have to overcome the effects of a filtered control system. With his position control system he has simply to make control movements which correspond to the unfiltered track. If he does so, no error is scored against him.

The delay introduced by the filtered display makes accurate tracking impossible. But the filtered display does attenuate the high frequencies in the track. It therefore calls for high response frequencies of smaller amplitude than are required in the previous condition with the filtered control system. The man does not realize this, because he has a compensatory display which does not show him the smaller amplitude of the high frequencies in the filtered track. He continues to use the strategy which he has been using with the filtered control system.

Garvey and his colleagues (1958, page 10) report that the displayed error looks much the same as in the previous trial. It is therefore larger than it need be. Worse still, Figure 10.6A shows that the displayed error is not now the error which is being scored. In scoring, the man's unfiltered control output with its high frequencies of large amplitude, is compared with the unfiltered track with its lower frequencies of smaller amplitude. The man does not see the scored error, only the filtered error. This is the major danger of a display which does not present the man with the status information to tell him what is really happening.

The error with the filtered display will probably be found to be a good deal smaller if the man learns to use the filtered display exclusively, as in a separate group experimental design. The point needs to be checked by an experiment on transfer between filtered displays and control systems, using both pursuit and compensatory display modes.

Noisy visual displays

A noisy visual display increases the error in tracking. The size of the increase depends upon which marker is perturbed by the noise. This is illustrated in Figure 11.12 for visual noise of low amplitude. Howell and Briggs (1959) instruct their 24 men undergraduates to ignore the visual noise. But the instruction is probably impossible to follow when the noise perturbs the track or error marker, because the noise and track have common frequencies.

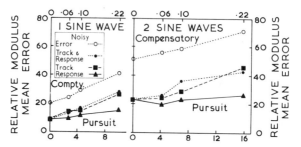

Figure 11.12. Performance with noisy visual display markers.
The single sine wave track on the left has a frequency of 10 cpm. It produces a modulus mean error of about 1.1 in when not tracked. The 2 equal amplitude sine waves on the right have frequencies of 30 and 10 cpm. They produce a modulus mean error of .7 in. On the ordinate of the figure the 2 modulus mean errors both represent 100. The scale of the error on the right side of the figure is thus 1.6 times as large as the scale of the error on the left side. The added visual noise is given on the abscissa in the same units, but the scale is 5 times as large as on the ordinate. The absolute amplitude of the added visual noise is shown at the top of the figure.

The unfilled points represent a compensatory display with the visual noise added to the movements of the error marker. The filled points represent a pursuit display with the visual noise added to the movements of one or both markers. The visual noise is peaked at 30 cpm. It has a bandwidth of 15 to 60 cpm with an attenuation of 24 dB per octave. By itself it produces a modulus mean error of half the size of its average amplitude. (After Howell & Briggs, 1959, Figures 1 and 2.)

The figure shows that the average modulus mean error increases as the amplitude of the visual noise increases. The filled triangles represent visual noise masking only the movements of the response marker of the pursuit display. The increase in tracking error is not large enough to be reliable statistically. This is presumably because the man can tell what response he is making from his control movements. He does not need to see the results of his control movements accurately displayed.

The slopes of all the other functions in the figure are larger and reliable statistically. The filled squares represent visual noise masking the movements of the track marker. This considerably increases the tracking error, because the man cannot see exactly what size of control movements to make.

The filled circles represent uncorrelated visual noise masking the movements both of the track marker and of the response marker. The slightly greater average height of the filled circles than of the squares, represents the effect of adding visual noise to the response marker. It is not much of an extra handicap. These results are rather similar to the results illustrated on the left of Figure 12.2, where one or both display markers are blanked out intermittently for short periods of time.

The unfilled circles in Figure 11.12 represent visual noise masking the error marker of the compensatory display. The slopes are about the same as the slopes for the filled circles and squares.

If the man ignores the visual noise as he is told to, the functions in Figure 11.12 will all be horizontal. If the man tracks the visual noise added to the track or error marker, his relative modulus mean error will be increased by the relative modulus mean noise amplitude. This is because in scoring, the man's copy of the noisy track is compared with the noise free track. The copied noise counts as error.

With the single sine wave, the largest visual noise amplitude is equivalent to a relative modulus mean error of about 10. Whereas the increase in the man's relative modulus mean error is about 20 when the visual noise is added to the track or error markers. With the 2 sine waves the corresponding values are about 16 and 20. Thus only part of the increase in error can be due to tracking the visual noise.

The remainder of the increase in error is probably caused by the high frequencies of small amplitude in the noise. Figures 8.13, 8.14 and 8.15 show that high frequencies of small amplitude degrade tracking at lower frequencies.

Robinson (1967) shows that it is easier to neglect visual noise added to the track marker of a pursuit display when the frequency of the visual noise is a good deal higher than the frequency of the track. Unfortunately Robinson's results do not appear to have been tested for statistical reliability. Also with only 4 people it is not possible to tell how repeatable the results are likely to be.

Rate of learning with noisy visual displays

Adding visual noise of low frequency to the error marker of a compensatory display does not slow down the rate of learning. It simply depresses the measured level of performance. This is illustrated in Figure 11.13 (Briggs, Fitts & Bahrick, 1957a). The task simulates flying an aircraft to intercept an enemy aircraft using a radar fire control system.

Undergraduates are first trained on the task for 20 trials without added visual noise. They are then split into 4 equal groups for the next 60 trials. One group continues to practice without visual noise. Two other groups practice with visual noise added to the error marker of the compensatory display. The fourth group practices each day for 1 block of 5 trials without visual noise, and for 3 blocks with various levels of visual noise. On the last day all 4 groups are transferred to this last

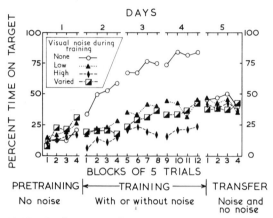

Figure 11.13. Performance after training on a noisy visual display.

The figure shows the proportion of the time for which a simulated aircraft is on target with a noisy or noise free compensatory visual display during the last 3 sec of an interception. The task is described in the caption to Figure 17.8. Each function represents the performance of a separate group of 12 undergraduates. The visual noise has a normal amplitude distribution with a peak at about 10 cpm. Only 5% of the power is above 40 cpm.

For the group represented by the triangles, the visual noise during training has a RMS amplitude of .06 in and a range of about .4 in. For the group represented by the diamonds the values are, respectively, .09 and .6 in. The group represented by the half filled squares alternates between blocks of 5 training trials with 4 different levels of visual noise: no visual noise, the 2 visual noise levels just specified, and visual noise with an RMS amplitude of .16 in and a range of about 1 in. The 4 groups are not reliably different during pretraining, nor during transfer. (After Briggs and colleagues, 1957a, Figure 3.)

condition. The undergraduates are told not to track the visual noise, but it is probably impossible to avoid tracking the low frequency visual noise used.

In Figure 11.13 the group which trains without visual noise is represented by the unfilled circles. During training the group has a reliably longer average time on target than the groups which track with added visual noise. However on the final 20 trials there is no reliable difference between the 4 groups, even during the first block of 5 trials.

The group which practices throughout without visual noise performs as well with the visual noise as the groups which practice throughout with visual noise. The groups which do not achieve very good time on target scores during practice with visual noise, improve to the standard of the no noise group as soon as the visual noise is removed from the error marker.

Presumably the undergraduates do not distinguish between the relatively low frequency visual noise added to the display, and the effects of their control movements. They track as accurately as they can, tracking out all the error which they see. During training all 4 groups learn to fly the aircraft and to perform the interception task. The learning is fully reflected in the performance of the group which tracks without visual noise. The learning is probably reflected also in the displayed errors of the groups which track with visual noise.

Unfortunately the displayed errors are not measured. The measure of performance illustrated in Figure 11.13 represents the displayed errors with the visual noise subtracted. If the undergraduates are tracking the visual noise, they are in effect subtracting it from the displayed error. The measure of performance then subtracts the visual noise a second time. This is equivalent to adding the visual noise to the man's tracking error before scoring. The group which tracks with the greater level of visual noise added to the target marker, corresponds to a group which tracks with more noise added to the error before scoring is carried out. The average recorded scores are therefore worse during training.

On transfer all groups are treated like the group which trains with various levels of visual noise. Their measured performances therefore correspond to the measured performance of the group with various levels of visual noise. This is what one would expect. There is no need to introduce a 2 stage theory of training to account for the results, as Briggs and his colleagues (1957a) do.

Simulated displays

After training on a simulated display, a change to the real display upsets the man's performance on the first trial. This happens even when exactly the same control movements are required with the 2 displays. Table 11.2 lists the results of a series of experiments which illustrate this (Hammerton, 1963, 1966; Hammerton & Tickner, 1967). The displays are ordered according to the degree of similarity between the simulated display and the real display, from an identical display at the top to a very simple representation at the bottom. Figure 11.14 illustrates the results of the 2 extreme conditions.

After 10 training trials daily for 3 days on the simulated display, the man is transferred on day 4 to the real display. The simulated displays are all driven from the real display. The angles subtended at the man's eyes are identical in all cases. The only differences between the displays are in the display markers, and in the 2 dimensional or 3 dimensional structure of the displays.

The unfilled squares in the figure represent the performance of a

Table 11.2
Performance after training on a simulated display

N	Training condition	Average acquisition time in seconds on trial number:			
		Simulation		Transfer	
		1	30	31	33
12	Real display (reference condition)	6.6	3.5	3.3	3.5
12	Televised display	12.8	3.7	4.1	4.1
12	Televised display with target and response markers	8.4	4.1	4.8	3.8
12	Televised model with target and response markers	9.8	4.4	5.5	4.1
12	CRT with correctly scaled transparency and target and response markers	10.6	4.4	6.2	4.1
12	CRT with transparency double the correct scale and target and response markers	11.0	4.0	8.3*	4.5
11	Plain CRT with target and response markers (the simple simulated display of Figure 11.14)	12.0	3.1	8.2*	4.3

* Trial 31 reliably worse than trial 30. Also reliably worse than the reference condition in the top row on trial 31. (Results from Hammerton, 1963, 1966 and Hammerton & Tickner, 1967.)

group which tracks throughout with the real display. The 12 men have to move a trolley a distance of 6 ft to the left and to line it up with a target. The average times taken to do this on trials 1, 30, 31 and 33 are listed in the top row of the table. At first the man requires an average of 6.6 sec. After practice the average time is reduced to 3.5 sec.

The filled circles in the figure represent tracking with the simplest simulated display, a plain CRT. The average acquisition times are listed in the bottom row of the table. At first the 11 men require an average of 12 sec. After 30 trials the average has fallen to 3.1 sec. On trial 31 the men are transferred to the real display. They take an average of 8.2 sec to acquire the target on this trial. The time is reliably longer than the average time on the previous trial. It is also reliably longer than the average of 3.3 sec taken on trial 31 by the group which practices throughout with the real display.

Two trials later the average time has fallen to 4.3 sec. This is still about 1.0 sec too long, but the differences are no longer reliable. On trial 35 the figure shows that the group which trains on the simple

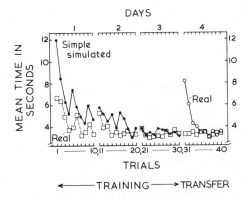

Figure 11.14. Performance after training on a simulated display.
The squares represent the average acquisition times of a group of 12 enlisted men who practice for 40 trials with the real display. The circles represent the performance of a group of 11 enlisted men who practice for 30 trials with a simple simulated display on a 5 in CRT at a distance of 50 cms. For trials 31 to 40 the CRT is removed, and the man sees the real display. When the tip of the man's thumb joystick is moved sideways 1 cm, the trolley rapidly acquires a rate of about 10 ft per sec. (After Hammerton, 1963, Figure 1.)

A similar pattern of results is obtained when the target moves from side to side at a constant speed of 5 ft per sec. This represents 2° per sec at the man's eyes. The average times taken to acquire the target are about 3 times as long when the target moves. There is also more variability from trial to trial.

simulated display reaches the level of performance of the control group which practices throughout with the real display.

A televised display like that in the second row of Table 11.2 can be used in controlling from an unmanned vehicle. The television camera is mounted in the position which the man's eyes occupy when the vehicle carries a man. A televised display with target and response markers corresponds to a portable field simulator. The markers simulate real objects which are not present in the field of view.

The televised model with target and response markers corresponds to a simulator in a training establishment. The CRT with a correctly scaled transparency represents a cheaper kind of simulator. The scale of the transparency may not necessarily correspond to the scale of the background met in the field where the real task is performed. The table shows that for simulated displays which resemble the real display more closely, the disturbance caused by transfer on trial 31 is smaller.

Clearly the degree of simulation necessary depends upon how important performance is on the first transfer trial. The pilot of a high performance aircraft may not survive if he does not land his aircraft correctly on his first trial. Elaborate expensive simulation is required (Adams,

1961). In guiding rockets the man may be given several opportunities to do the real job before success is essential. If so, elaborate expensive simulation is less necessary.

Compatible displays

The information which the man needs in tracking can often be combined in a compatible way. This makes the man's task easier, and improves the accuracy of his tracking. Figure 11.15 (Fitts & Simon, 1952) illustrates good and less good combinations of the positions of target zones on pairs of instruments used in compensatory tracking. The number printed beneath each pair of instruments represents the average time in seconds for which both needles remain within their target zones.

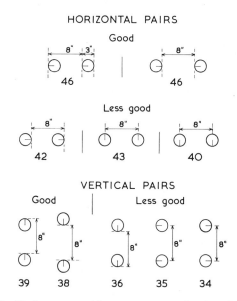

Figure 11.15.   Performance with arrangements of pairs of instruments.

The pairs of instruments are used for compensatory tracking. The needles are drawn in their positions on target. The average time in seconds for which both needles are simultaneously on target is printed beneath each pair. The maximum possible time on target is 165 sec. The pairs of instruments are all mounted so that when the 2 needles are both on target, their tips are 8 in apart.

The needles follow an unspecified irregular track. The man has a separate control knob for each instrument. A clockwise rotation of the knob rotates the needle in a clockwise direction. One group of 20 undergraduates has the 5 horizontal arrangements illustrated in the upper part of the figure. Another group of 20 undergraduates track with the corresponding 5 vertical arrangements illustrated in the lower part of the figure. (After Fitts & Simon, 1952, Figure 2.)

The horizontal pairs of instruments illustrated in the upper part of the figure give reliably longer times on target than the vertical pairs illustrated in the lower part. Reliably the 2 best horizontal arrangements are illustrated at the top. Both targets should be at 9 o'clock, or a target at 9 o'clock should face a target at 3 o'clock.

Reliably the 2 best vertical arrangements are illustrated at the bottom on the left. Both targets should be at 12 o'clock, or a target at 12 o'clock should face a target at 6 o'clock. The figure shows that with all these 4 good arrangements the 2 needles lie on a single straight line when they are both on target. An error shown by either needle is therefore relatively easy to spot.

When the 2 targets face each other, the man has an added advantage. The moving ends of the 2 needles, which show when errors are increasing in size, are separated only by blank panel when they are on target. The eyes have nothing to distract them as their point of fixation jumps from one moving end to the other and back again.

The man has a different added advantage when the 2 targets are both at 9 o'clock or at 12 o'clock. The moving ends of the 2 needles are then both in the upper left quadrant when they are on target. In reading or scanning a book or newspaper, a person's eyes usually start in the top left quadrant. When the fixation point of the man's eyes jumps from one instrument to the other, it will be more likely to alight on the moving ends of the needles when the targets are both at 9 or 12 o'clock.

With the pairs of targets at 3 o'clock and at 6 o'clock, the moving ends of the needles lie in the lower right hand quadrant when the needles are more or less on target. The fixation point of the man's eyes is less likely to alight here. Thus errors which are increasing in size take longer to spot, even though the 2 needles lie on a single straight line when they are both on target. This is probably why pairs of targets at 3 o'clock and 6 o'clock give smaller times on target than the other pairs illustrated in the figure with the 2 needles in a straight line.

The combinations of target positions labeled less good in Figure 11.15 are better than combinations which are not shown. Examples of less compatible combinations are one target at 9 or 3 o'clock, and the other target at 12 or 6 o'clock. This is because when one needle is near its target at 9 or 3 o'clock, it has to be aligned in the vertical dimension. Whereas when the other needle is near its target at 12 or 6 o'clock, it has to be aligned in the horizontal dimension. The next experiment shows that having separate dimensions for the 2 alignments adds to the man's difficulty.

The left side of Figure 11.16 (Regan, 1959) illustrates 2 targets at

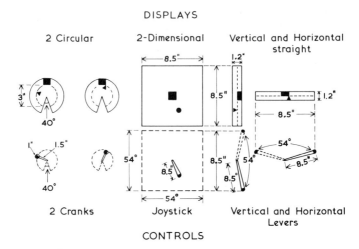

Figure 11.16. Displays and compatible controls.
The filled squares and rectangles are 1 in across. They represent the targets
of the compensatory displays. In the pursuit mode the filled squares and rectangles
represent the track markers. The man controls the filled triangles or circle, which
are .5 in across. The markers of the circular displays move the same distances
as the markers on the straight displays, but in an arc. All the controls are spring
centered. With the position control system and the pursuit display mode, the handles
of all the controls move exactly the same distances in exactly the same directions
as the circular and triangular response markers of the displays directly above them.
With the rate control system and the pursuit display mode, the response markers
all move at rates which are proportional to the distances of the controls from
their centers. The maximum rate is about 4 in per sec. The track is irregular
with an average of 15 reversals of direction per min. Movements in the 2 dimensions
are identical, but the track in the horizontal dimension lags 45 sec behind the
track in the vertical dimension. Separate groups of 8 undergraduates perform each
of the 12 conditions listed in Table 11.3, 4 with the position control system and
4 with the rate control system. (After Regan, 1959, Appendix A.)

12 o'clock. The vertical and horizontal straight scales on the right of
the figure are somewhat comparable to circular scales with targets at
3 o'clock and 12 o'clock respectively. The man has to align one error
marker in the vertical dimension and the other error marker in the
horizontal dimension.

Table 11.3 (Regan, 1959, 1960) shows that in compensatory tracking
the pair of circular scales and cranks on the left of the figure gives
a reliably longer average time on target than the pair of straight scales
on the right side of the figure. It does not matter whether levers or
cranks are used with the straight scales. Both combinations are equally
ineffective in compensatory tracking. Clearly it is not easy to track simultaneously in the vertical and horizontal dimension using separate displays.

Table 11.3
Performance with the displays and controls of Figure 11.16

Kind of:		Average percent time on target with display mode:	
Display	Control	Pursuit	Compen-satory
2 Dimensional	{ Joystick	76	81
	{ 2 Cranks	62	50
Straight vertical + straight horizontal	{ Vertical and horizontal levers	61	55
	{ 2 cranks	63	55
2 Circular with midpoints at 12 o'clock	{ Vertical and horizontal levers	55	52
	{ 2 Cranks	56	66

To be reliable, differences must be at least 9. (After Regan, 1959, 1960).

Display mode and display design

The most compatible combination of displays is different when the task is pursuit. In pursuit tracking, the square targets of the 2 circular scales on the left of Figure 11.16 move around the scales independently. When the triangular response markers are more or less on target, the man no longer has to align both markers in the horizontal dimension. Alignment may be in any dimension, different for the 2 markers, and varying all the time.

The task is more difficult than pursuit tracking with the 2 straight scales on the right of the figure, where the dimensions of alignment are fixed. Table 11.3 shows that the 2 straight scales give a reliably longer average time on target in pursuit tracking than the 2 circular scales. It does not matter whether levers or cranks are used with either pair of scales.

Pursuit tracking is so difficult with the 2 circular scales on the left of Figure 11.16 that compensatory tracking actually results in a reliably longer average time on target when using the 2 cranks. The times are listed in the bottom row of Table 11.3. The result cannot be due to transfer, because Regan (1959, 1960) uses separate groups of undergraduates for each of his experimental conditions.

Tables 9.2 and 9.3 show that with a separate group design and a conventional visual display, a single pursuit tracking task is never performed reliably worse than the corresponding compensatory task. So it must be the incompatibility of the 2 circular scales when they are used in the pursuit mode, which makes them reliably worse than when they are used in the compensatory mode.

Integrated displays

Instead of providing the man with 2 separate instruments to look at, it may be possible to combine the information in a single integrated display like the headup display of Figure 9.2. An integrated display can be difficult to use if too much information is crowded into it. The man may not be able to find the marker which he is looking for. He may confuse 2 markers, and look at the wrong marker in error. The instrument designer needs to use his ingenuity to combine the information in the most appropriate way. If this is done, tracking can be easier with the integrated display (Bailey, 1958).

The display in the center of Figure 11.16 illustrates how two 1 dimension tracking tasks can be integrated into a single 2 dimension task. It is not necessary for the 2 tasks to have the same markers, as they do in Figure 11.16. There can be separate markers.

Chernikoff and Le May (1963) compare compensatory tracking with 2 separate error markers and with a single error marker. The upper part of Table 11.4 shows that a single error marker is a reliable advantage when the control system is the same in the 2 dimensions, either position

Table 11.4
Performance with 1 or 2 error markers and control sticks

Number of:		Average modulus mean error with control system:	
Error markers	Control sticks	Position	Acceleration
Same dynamics			
1	1	42	42
1	2	48	58
2	1	56	73
2	2	57	87
Different dynamics			
2	2	60	78
1	2	60	85
2	1	70	110
1	1	73	97

(Results from Chernikoff & Le May, 1963.)

or acceleration. When the control system is position in both dimensions, and the control is a single joystick, the advantage of the single error marker has been confirmed by Sampson and Elkin (1965). But there were only 4 people in the experiment.

The lower part of the table shows that when a position control system in one dimension is paired with an acceleration control system in the other dimension, there is little difference between 1 and 2 error markers. Perhaps having 2 separate error markers for the 2 control systems helps the man to keep separate the 2 control systems which he is using. This may just about compensate for the disadvantage of having 2 error markers to look at.

Unfortunatly Chernikoff and Le May (1963) use a balanced treatment design. The same 6 enlisted men are switched from condition to condition in an irregular order. An experiment with separate groups of people for each condition may possibly show an advantage for 1 display marker. This has still to be investigated. Aircraft have different dynamics in the vertical and in the side to side dimension. Yet they can be flown using the headup display illustrated in Figure 9.2, which has a single aircraft marker.

Tracking in 1 dimension and in 2 dimensions

Even when two 1 dimension tracking tasks are compatible with each other and fully integrated, tracking in 2 dimensions is less accurate than tracking in a single dimension. This is because with 2 dimensions the man has to decide the angular direction in which to move his joystick, as well as the distance. Whereas when tracking in a single dimension, the man has only to decide on the distance. The extra dimension increases the complexity of the task.

In their experiment on display magnification listed in Table 11.1B, Garvey and Henson (1959) present the same compensatory tracking task either in a single dimension or in 2 dimensions. For the standard task in 1 dimension, the track moves the error marker only from side to side. The man has a position control lever which also moves from side to side.

For the modified task in 2 dimensions, the track is connected to both the x and y plates of the CRT. The track moves the error marker up and to the right along a slope at 45°. The man has a joystick which can move the error marker both horizontally and vertically. Thus although the track is still in 1 dimension, the error marker can move in 2 dimensions.

To null the error, the man has unfortunately to move the joystick at an angle of 45° forward and to the right or backward and to the left. It is pointed out toward the end of Chapter 7 that this is the least accurate direction of aim for movements of the right hand (Corrigan & Borgden, 1948). Garvey and Henson measure the tracking error only in the horizontal dimension. The error becomes reliably larger in this dimension when the man has to control the error marker in both dimensions.

An identical result is reported by Garvey and Taylor (1959, Experiment 3) in the experiment discussed at the end of Chapter 2. The second dimension produces a reliable deterioration both with the position control system and with the acceleration control system. The deterioration is reliably larger with the acceleration control system.

Ziegler (1968) subsequently uses separate tracks for the 2 dimensions. He also reports that the difference in error between compensatory tracking in 1 and in 2 dimensions is smallest with a position control system. In Ziegler's experiment the difference is not reliable statistically, although it favors the single dimension.

When Ziegler changes the dynamics to rate and then to acceleration, the difference between tracking in 1 and 2 dimensions becomes larger and reliable statistically. When a delta acceleration aided control system is used, the difference is larger still. With the higher order control systems the man has a task which is difficult enough when tracking in a single dimension. Adding the second dimension increases the difficulty of the task still more.

Recommended display variations

The magnification of a pursuit display should be set up so that the movements of the track marker cover most of the display area without quite reaching the edge. The magnification of a compensatory display should be rather smaller than the magnification of a pursuit display. Nonlinear display magnification is not recommended.

A display should not be delayed, filtered or noisy. The display used in training should be an exact copy of the real display if first trial transfer is to be complete.

When 2 or more compensatory displays have circular scales, the directions of zero error should be aligned. Figure 11.15 shows the most compatible pairs. A pair of circular scales should not be used for pursuit tracking.

A single integrated display is preferable to 2 or more separate displays, provided the information is suited to integration, and provided the integration is skillfully executed. It may be an advantage to reduce the total number of markers on the integrated display, provided it can be done without loss of information.

Chapter

12

Display sampling

Summary

When a single display is sampled automatically, tracking is improved by reducing the time between samples, by increasing the duration of the glimpses, and by increasing the rate of sampling. The effect of sampling depends upon which marker is sampled. In displays which are stepped by amplitude, tracking is more accurate with small sizes of step.

When a man has more than one tracking task to perform simultaneously, the durations of his looks at each display depend upon how long he can afford not to look at the other displays. As the number of tasks increases, performance deteriorates. Competition between tracking and an additional task may be visual, motor, or more central. The priorities given to the tasks determine which task is the more affected.

A man seldom blinks during a difficult visual tracking task. Voluntary blinking is distracting.

Kinds of display sampling

Automatic display sampling

Automatic display sampling occurs when a target disappears behind a cloud or behind smoke. A certain number of experiments have studied single blackouts of this kind. But most experiments on automatic display sampling have been concerned with repeated blackouts.

When a radar aerial rotates, echoes from the objects in the path of the radar beam are received once per rotation. On a plan position indicator display like that illustrated at the top of Figure 9.3, the spots of light which represent objects remain stationary from one sweep to the next. They then jump to their next position.

The man sees a succession of stationary spots of light which represent the track of the ship or aircraft, perhaps 1 spot every 5 or 15 sec. He may track the succession of stationary spots with a response marker which can be seen to move all the time. This may be an advantage over having a response marker which moves only intermittently like the target spot.

A faster frequency of sampling is used by a predictor display (see Chapter 10). The frequency depends upon the time taken by the fast time model of the control system. The computer has to calculate the future state of the system at the end of the prediction span of perhaps 10 sec. This may take .01 sec. Until the calculation is finished, the computer is not ready to calculate the next prediction.

The first experiments on automatic display sampling use methods adapted from tachistoscopes. The man's view of the display markers is blanked out intermittently by a rotating wheel with a clear sector. Or a light flashes on and off at a constant rate to illuminate the markers intermittently. During the glimpses the man can usually see the movement of the markers. The only exception is when the glimpses are very brief (Poulton, 1952b, Figure 1). The display corresponds to what a man sees when he takes a quick glance at an instrument. The experiments are listed in part **A** of Table 12.1, according to which display markers can be seen only intermittently.

More sophisticated experiments use electronic devices to sample the track, the output of the man's control system, or the displayed error. Between sampling times the marker remains visible but stationary. At the sampling time the marker suddenly steps to its new position. The sampling can occur at a constant rate, like the sampling of the early tachistoscopic displays. The electronically sampled displays then correspond to displays linked to rotating radar aerials, and to other electronic displays which sample on a time basis. The experiments are listed in section **B** of Table 12.1.

The sampling can be made to depend upon the amplitude of the sampled voltage. The display marker remains stationary until the voltage changes to a specified amplitude. The marker then jumps to the position corresponding to the new voltage. This is equivalent to a row of warning

Table 12.1
Experiments on automatic sampling of a single display

Kind of sampling	Author(s)	Year	N	Cycle time in seconds
A. Intermittent displays				
Intermittent track marker	Poulton (see Figure 12.2)	1957b	12	60 to .6, continuous
Intermittent response marker	Poulton (see Figure 12.2)	1957b		
Intermittent track and response markers	Battig, Gregg, Nagel, Small and Brogden	1954	16	2.5 to .06 (fused)
	Battig, Voss and Brogden	1955	16 / 10 + 10	.5 to .06 (fused)
	Katz and Spragg	1955	18	2 to .25
	Poulton (see Figure 12.1)	1952b	12	1.7 to .5, continuous
	Poulton (see Figure 12.2)	1957b	12	60 to .6, continuous
	Poulton (see Figure 12.1)	*	12	1 to .1, continuous
	Poulton (see Figure 12.1)	*	12	5.5 to 1, continuous
	Poulton (see Table 12.2)	*	12	1 to .5, continuous
	Poulton and Gregory (see Figure 12.4)	1952	12	1.2, continuous
Intermittent error marker	Senders	1955	8	.25 to .05, continuous
B. Displays stepped intermittently				
Stepped track marker†	Tipton	1965	3	7.5 to 1
Stepped error marker	Humphrey, Thompson, and Versace	1953	3	.2 to .02, continuous
	Platzer	1955	2	2 to .33
C. Displays stepped by amplitude				
				Number of positions
Stepped track marker†	McConnell and Shelly	1960	5	2 to 12, continuous
Stepped error marker	Hunt	1961	8 + 8	2, 7, 13, continuous
	Hunt	1964	7 + 7	3, 7, 11
	Micheli	1966	3 + 3 / 10 + 10	3, 7, 13, continuous / 1, 13, continuous
	Rund and colleagues	1957	6	2, continuous
	Schoeffler	1955	15 + 15	1 to 7
D. Digital displays				
				Comparisons
Stepped error	Allnutt and colleagues	1966	8	Digital, continuous
	Rolfe and Clifford	1964	12	Digital, continuous

† Can be distinguished from a stepped track by the method indicated in the text, and illustrated in Figure 10.6.

* Not previously published.

lamps, which come on one at a time as the voltage exceeds the limit set for each particular lamp. Experiments on displays stepped by amplitude are listed in section C of the table. The digital displays in section D are a special case of this.

An experiment on a stepped display needs to be distinguished from an experiment on a stepped track, and from an experiment on a stepped input to a control system. Possible confusions are indicated in a footnote to the table. The distinction is illustrated in Fig. 10.6.

The kind of experiment is distinguished by the measure of tracking error which is used. The error may be summed before steps are introduced. If so, the experimenter is measuring the effect upon performance of a stepped display. In another experiment the scoring device may measure only the error which the man can see in the display. In this case the experimenter is measuring the man's performance with a stepped track (Chapter 6) or with a stepped input to a control system (Chapter 17).

Display sampling by the man

The frequency of sampling may be determined by the man instead of by the display. When the pilot of an aircraft is flying by his instruments, he has to keep track of the readings on a number of instruments. He may have additional visual tasks to perform as well, such as map reading or checking on warning lights.

The sampling of more than one visual display by the man differs in several respects from the electronic sampling of a single display. One difference relates to the amount which the man has to do. To ensure that the man does sample all the displays, he is usually given a separate task to perform with each display. Whereas in an experiment on automatic sampling, the man usually has only one display to watch. Thus an experiment on display sampling by the man tends to involve the man in more work than does an experiment on automatic display sampling.

Other differences relate to what the man sees. When the man samples a number of displays in turn, he sees the movement of the moving markers while he looks at a display, and very little of the display while he looks at the other displays. Whereas in electronic sampling of a single display, the man sees the markers all the time, but in a series of stationary positions.

The sampling which results from blinking is also determined by the man. A man who blinks frequently has only the intermittent views of the display between his blinks. However a person blinks mostly when he does not need to look. Blinks occur as the eyes move from one display to another. The driver of an automobile blinks more on a road between fields without much traffic, than in a congested city center (Drew, 1951).

Intermittent displays

Figure 12.1 shows that tracking is less accurate when a display is blanked out for a longer time, and when the glimpses between the blackouts are briefer. In the experiment the man looks through a transparent rotating wheel at 2 white display markers. The markers move against a matt black background. Vision is interrupted intermittently by an opaque black sector of the rotating wheel.

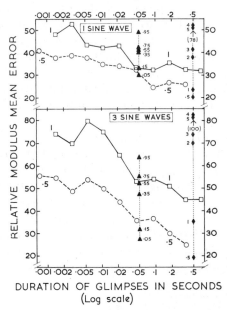

DURATION OF GLIMPSES IN SECONDS
(Log scale)

Figure 12.1.   Performance with intermittent views of a pursuit display.
The duration in seconds of the blackouts between glimpses is printed against the functions or points. Thus the unfilled squares are for blackouts of 1 sec, while the unfilled circles from the same experiment are for blackouts of .5 sec. The relative modulus mean error on the ordinate reaches 100 if the man does not respond at all. The upper part of the figure represents a single sine wave track with a frequency of 10 cpm. The lower part of the figure represents a track consisting of 3 equal amplitude sine waves with frequencies of 10, 7 and 5 cpm.

The unfilled points are from a group of 12 young enlisted men. The filled triangles and diamonds are from 2 other groups of 12 young enlisted men. To be reliable, differences in height between the unfilled points must be at least 6. Differences in height between the filled triangles and diamonds must be respectively at least 9, and at least 16. (Partly after Poulton, 1952b, Figure 2.)

The durations of the glimpses are given on the abscissa. The durations of the blackouts in seconds are printed against the functions. The unfilled points on the extreme left of the figure correspond to an electronic display painting once or twice per second. The filled diamonds on the extreme right correspond to a man glancing at an instrument for .5 sec once every few seconds.

The average tracking error increases reliably as the duration of the blackouts increases. This is because the man has to track for longer without seeing what is happening.

The average tracking error also increases reliably as the duration of the glimpses decreases. For reductions in the duration of glimpses down to about .05 sec, the increase in tracking error occurs because the blackouts occupy a greater proportion of the time. For reductions in the duration of glimpses below .05 sec, an additional difficulty is that the brightness of the display markers decreases. People track less accurately when the display markers are less bright (Voss, 1955). With very short glimpses, the rates of movement of the display markers are hard to see (Poulton, 1952b, Figure 1). The greater difficulty in seeing probably accounts for most of the reliable increase in tracking error as the glimpses are reduced below about .05 sec.

The changes in relative modulus mean error are reliably larger for the irregular track of the lower part of Figure 12.1, than for the single sine wave track of the upper part of the figure. This is because the man can generate a single sine wave of about the right amplitude and frequency. He has only to ensure that the sine wave which he is generating matches the track in phase, in amplitude, and in position on the display. It is pointed out in Chapter 8 that a man can do this reasonably well without seeing the display all the time. The irregular track is more difficult to predict during the blackouts.

Frequency of intermittence

Increasing the frequency of intermittence reduces the duration of both the blackouts and the glimpses. It improves the accuracy of tracking, even though the glimpses become shorter. The increased frequency of the glimpses more than compensates for their reduced duration. Many of the experiments listed in part **A** of Table 12.1 show this.

The advantage gained by increasing the frequency of intermittence is greater when the blackouts are long than when the blackouts are shorter. In the top 2 rows of Table 12.2 the frequencies of intermittence are 1 and 2 glimpses per sec, respectively. Doubling the frequency reduces the duration of the blackouts from .6 to .3 sec. For 12 naval

Table 12.2
Performance with double the frequency of intermittence

Percent of time display visible	Duration in seconds		Relative modulus mean error when track:	
	Glimpses	Blackouts	1 Sine wave	3 Sine waves
40	.4	.6	41	44
	.2	.3	38	32
70	.7	.3	32	27
	.35	.15	31	24
100	60	0	25	19
	(no blackouts)			

When the man does not respond, the modulus mean error is 100. To be reliable, differences must be at least 4. The track frequencies are twice the frequencies of the tracks of Figure 12.1. (Results not published previously.)

ratings, it reduces the average tracking error with the 2 tracks by 3 and 12, respectively.

In the next 2 rows of the table the frequencies of intermittence are still 1 and 2 glimpses per sec. Doubling the frequency reduces the duration of the blackouts from .3 to .15 sec. This reduces the average tracking error by only 1 and 3 respectively for the 2 tracks. Prediction is less of a problem with short blackouts. The error can be kept reasonably small during a short blackout simply by continuing to respond in much the same way as during the previous glimpse. Thus doubling the frequency of intermittence does not help so much.

Strategies during blackouts

During blackouts which last less than 1 sec the practiced man tracks much as he does when there are no blackouts. His response continues to match the track during the blackouts, although Table 12.2 shows that his errors tend to be larger when there are blackouts.

When the display is blanked for 2 or 3 sec, the practiced man adopts different strategies according to the frequencies in the track. With a sine wave of a single frequency, the man continues to respond at about the correct frequency and amplitude (see Chapter 8). With a track comprising a number of sine waves all of low frequency and a pursuit display, the man tends to respond during the blackouts with an average rate which is rather less than the previous average rate of the track (Gottsdanker, 1952a, b, 1955, 1956a; McLeod, 1972).

With an irregular track of frequencies mainly between 20 and 60 cpm, the recent average track rate is not a good predictor of the future average track rate in 2 or 3 sec. The man therefore tends almost to stop responding until he can see the track again (Gottsdanker, 1956a). These strategies are probably as good as any which the man is capable of using to minimize his tracking error.

Partly intermittent displays

Figure 12.2 shows that the effect of intermittent blanking depends upon which display marker is blanked out. The man is instructed to continue to respond whether he can see the markers or not. The tracks are the same as those of Figure 12.1. The relative modulus mean errors are larger in Figure 12.2 because the display markers are less easy to see during the glimpses. The man looks at the display with 1 eye through the eyepiece of a tachistoscope. The markers and background are both

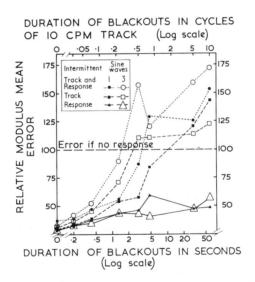

Figure 12.2. Performance with intermittent views of one or both markers.
The tracks are the same as the tracks of Figure 12.1, with a top frequency of 10 cpm. The glimpses last about .4 sec. Trials usually last 60 sec. But the control trials without blackouts are followed without a break by trials of 60 sec during which the intermittent pointer or pointers cannot be seen at all. These latter trials give the relative modulus mean errors for blackouts of 30 and 60 sec.
Before the experiment, each of the 12 young enlisted men tracks for 40 trials with intermittent views. To be reliable, the differences in height in the center and on the right of the figure must be at least 20. The differences on the left of the figure need not be as large as this, because the differences between individuals are smaller. (After Poulton, 1957c, Figure 1.)

black. The light is not very bright. The changes are necessary to prevent the display markers from being seen when they have to be invisible.

The triangles in Figure 12.2 indicate the error when the track marker can be seen all the time, but the response marker can be seen only during the glimpses. Even when the man cannot see the response marker for 30 or 60 sec, he is able to copy the movements of the track marker reasonably accurately. This is because the track marker tells him what movements to make. From his previous practice he knows the sizes of control movement which are required for various sizes of display movement.

The principal source of error is that the invisible response marker gradually wanders up or down the display. The track marker of course maintains its average position in the center of the display. Another common source of error is that the amplitude of the response gradually changes. The amplitude generally becomes too large.

The squares represent the error when the response marker can be seen all the time, but the track marker can be seen only during the glimpses. The average error is a good deal larger in this condition than in the condition with the track marker visible all the time. The filled squares represent the single sine wave track. From previous practice the man knows and can predict the track. His principal source of error is in the timing of his responses. When he cannot see the track marker for 30 or 60 sec, his response marker gradually gets out of phase with the invisible track marker.

The unfilled squares represent the track composed of 3 sine waves. The calibrations at the top of the figure show the duration of the blackouts in cycles of the top track frequency. When the blackouts last .5 cycle of the top track frequency, the unfilled squares reach the horizontal broken line, which represents the error if no response. The value of .5 cycle agrees reasonably well with the maximum useful span of prediction for the track, which is illustrated in Figure 8.9 by the unfilled points. During the course of blackouts longer than .5 cycle of the top track frequency, the man's response movements become unrelated to the movements of the track marker.

In Figure 12.2 the circles represent the condition in which both markers are invisible during the blackouts. The average error is larger in this condition than in the condition which allows the man to see his response marker all the time. This is because when the man cannot see either marker, he combines the kind of errors which he produces when he cannot see the track marker, with the kind of errors which he produces when he cannot see his response marker.

Blanking out a marker intermittently for short periods of time has a rather similar effect to masking the movements of the marker with visual noise of low amplitude. Compare the left side of Figure 12.2 with Figure 11.12.

Stepped displays

Displays stepped intermittently

Section **B** of Table 12.1 lists experiments on displays stepped intermittently. Unfortunately none of the experiments uses more than 2 or 3 people. The experiments cover a wide range of time intervals, from about 7.5 sec. to .02 sec. Over this range tracking deteriorates with longer sampling intervals.

Displays stepped by amplitude

Section **C** of Table 12.1 lists experiments on displays stepped by amplitude. The number of positions on the display varies between 1 and 13. Tracking is not very accurate with only 1 or 2 possible positions. Accuracy increases as the number of steps is increased, provided this means that the steps are smaller.

In most of the experiments, the full range of movement of the markers on the CRT is divided into a number of equal sized sections, each of which represents a step. More steps mean smaller steps. Smaller steps give the man a more precise indication of what he has to do in order to minimize his tracking error. The man therefore tracks more accurately with more steps. He tracks most accurately in the continuous condition with an infinite number of steps, because he can see exactly what he has to do.

In the original experiment by Schoeffler (1955), the steps are arranged differently. There is a central red lamp which comes on when the man is on target. Three white lamps are mounted on each side of the red lamp. When they are in use, they indicate the direction of error voltages greater than certain fixed sizes. When only the red lamp and one white lamp on either side are in use, the man knows only whether he is on target, and the direction of his error if he is off target.

When 2 white lamps on either side are in use, the man has some indication also of the size of his error. The white lamp next to the red lamp indicates an error of 19° or less in the angular position of the man's crank control. The white lamp further away indicates an error in the same direction greater than 19°. When all 3 white lamps on either side of the red lamp are in use, the man knows the direction of his error, and whether it is less than 19°, between 19° and 42°, or greater than 42°.

Schoeffler (1955) uses separate groups of 15 army recruits for each condition. After practice, the group with the 2 white lamps on each side of the red target lamp achieves reliably the longest average time on target. One white lamp on each side gives reliably less time on target, because the man knows only the direction of his error, not its size.

Three white lamps on each side give reliably less time on target than 2 white lamps on each side. The information on very large errors provided by the extra lamp on each side is not a help. It must mislead the man into thinking that the errors indicated by the more central lamps do not matter very much.

Three white lamps on each side should be an advantage if they are used to indicate the sizes of the smaller errors. For example, the 3 white lamps could indicate errors of less than 9°, errors between 9° and 19°, and errors greater than 19°. The change from 2 white lamps on each side to 3 white lamps would then correspond to the change from 5 to 7 positions on the CRTs used in the other experiments listed in section **C** of Table 12.1. It can be predicted from the results of these other experiments that the change would increase the accuracy of tracking.

Displays with nonlinear sizes of step

In tracking with these compensatory displays, a nonlinear arrangement of step sizes increases the error just as a nonlinear continuous display does (see Chapter 11). In Hunt's 1964 experiment he includes 2 nonlinear arrangements of sizes of step, as well as the usual linear arrangement. In the magnification conditions a change of error of a fixed size produces a large jump of the error marker when the error is small. When the error is large a change of error of the same size produces only a small jump. The display is rather like the nonlinear display magnification of Bowen and Chernikoff (1957) illustrated in Figure 11.3. However, Hunt uses a logarithmic nonlinearity, while Bowen and Chernikoff use an exponential nonlinearity.

In Hunt's minification conditions the jumps are small when the error is small. The jumps are larger when the error is larger. There are always 3, 7 or 11 positions. Separate groups of 7 men undergraduates track with each of the 9 combinations of 3 numbers of steps and 3 kinds of linearity or nonlinearity. The man has a spring centered acceleration control.

Hunt (1964) reports that the linear display produces a smaller average

modulus mean error than either of the nonlinear displays. The effect
of changes in linearity is reliable statistically. Unfortunately the differences between the individual conditions are not tested separately.

Displays with only 2 states

Special strategies are required in order to track adequately with displays which have only 2 states. The 1 position displays used by Schoeffler
(1955) and by Micheli (1966, main experiment) indicate only when
the man is on target. A light comes on when the man is on target,
and goes off when he is off target. The man is not shown the direction
of his error when he is off target.

The best strategy is probably to keep the light on as much of the
time as possible by making dithering movements of the control. The
output of the control system should dither with an amplitude rather
smaller than the size of the target area. When the light goes off, the
man notes the direction of the output of the control system at this
time, and adjusts the average position of his control in the other direction.
In this way he should be able to keep track of the direction of his
error.

Unfortunately neither Schoeffler nor Micheli give the man any indication of how he is to stay on target. He is simply instructed to do the
best he can. From the average number of times that the target light
goes on and off in Schoeffler's experiment, it is clear that the man does
not use the dither strategy. His performance hardly improves during
the course of 10 trials of 2 min each.

The 2 position display used by Rund, Birmingham, Tipton and Garvey
(1957) shows the man the direction of his error, but not when he is
on target. There are 2 lamps, 1 or other of which is on all the time.
The error is zero only as 1 lamp goes off and the other lamp comes
on. When the lamps are not flickering, the man does not know how
large his error is.

The best strategy is to bracket the zero by small amplitude dithering
movements of the high order control, so that the 2 lamps are always
flickering. The man is instructed to do this with the minimum of control
movement. Even with this strategy, the binary display gives a reliably
larger average tracking error than a conventional CRT display.

Digital displays

Part D of Table 12.1 lists 2 experiments comparing a digital display
of error with a continuous display. The digits are presented by the
counter of a counter pointer altimeter used in aircraft. The counter
is compared with the circular scale and needle which is mounted directly

below it in the altimeter. When the man is tracking with one display, the other display is covered up. The man has to maintain the height of the simulated aircraft at perhaps 20,000 ft.

The counter shows height to the nearest 50 ft. In this it resembles the displays stepped by amplitude listed in section C of the table. The needle of the circular scale rotates once every 1000 ft. With large errors in height the man has to remember whether he is too high or too low. The needle can be pointing to the zero position when the man is in error by 1000 ft.

The experimenter measures the time during which the man is within 50 ft of the target height of 20,000 ft. In both experiments the counter is found to give less time on target than the continuous display of height. In the experiment of Allnutt, Clifford, and Rolfe (1966) the difference is reliable. The result is in keeping with the results of the other experiments on displays stepped by amplitude.

When using the counter, the best strategy is probably to keep the counter moving all the time between 19,950 ft and 20,000 ft by dithering movements of the control. Unfortunately people are not told this, and no indication is given of how many people use the strategy.

Sampling 2 displays

When a man is given 2 tracking tasks to perform simultaneously, he can look directly at only one display at a time. The other display is seen in peripheral vision. Small errors and rates of change are probably not detected in peripheral vision. But the man does use the peripheral display. This is indicated by the experiment of Table 12.3 (Levison and Elkind, 1967a).

Tracking using peripheral vision

In the experiment each CRT display has a spot of light with a diameter of about 1 mm which moves up and down. The 4 pilots have to try to hold the spot inside a stationary reference circle with a diameter of about 5 mm and a thickness of about 1 mm. Before performing the 2 conditions in the upper part of the table with visual angles of 30° and 56°, each pilot receives the 4 other conditions in the table. When tracking with 2 displays, he has a separate spring centered rate control stick for each hand. He is instructed to minimize the sum of the 2 mean squared errors.

When tracking with the single display in peripheral vision, the pilot has to look all the time at an identical spot resting in the center of

Table 12.3
Performance and visual angle

Number of tasks	Visual angle (deg)	Relative RMS error (track = 100)		Seconds per look	
		Mean	SE*	Mean	SE*
1	0	22(23)	5.2		
1	30	−(60)	(1.9)		
1	56	−(89)	(6.4)		
2	.8	27(27)	6.4		
2	30	43(43)	1.8	1.2	.13
2	56	65(64)	9.1	1.3	.10

The top unattenuated frequency of the track is 20 cpm. Its RMS amplitude is 2 cm. The values in brackets are computed from the results of only 3 of the pilots. The remaining values represent all 4 pilots. (From Levison and Elkind, 1967a, Experiment 1.)

* The standard error represents the differences between the pilots.

an identical circle. The plane of the 2 displays in 28 in from the eyes. At this distance an angle of 56° represents a horizontal separation of 30 in.

Table 12.3 shows that the error in tracking increases with increases in the angle of the display from the man's line of sight. Figure 13.5 (Moss, 1964b) illustrates increases in error for a single tracking task, which correspond to the increases in the upper part of the table. Other experimenters (Adams & Xhignesse, 1960; Briggs & Howell, 1959; Fitts & Simon, 1952) report increases in error for 2 simultaneous tracking tasks, which correspond to the increases in the lower part of the table.

The upper part of the table shows that with a single display at an angle of 56° to the man's line of sight, the relative RMS error is 89. It is hardly less than the value of 100 when the man does not track at all. This is partly because the display is not designed for use in peripheral vision. The display is reliably less easy to use in peripheral vision than is the display illustrated in Figure 12.3 (Levison, Elkind, & Ward, 1971, Table B-1).

Sampling strategy with 2 displays

The lower right part of Table 12.3 shows that the average duration of the looks at the 2 displays does not change very much when the angular separation increases from 30° to 56°. This may be because both in the practices and in the experiment, the man changes from one condition to another a number of times in an irregular order. It encourages him to adopt a common sampling strategy for all conditions.

The strategy involves obtaining information from both displays, although only one display is fixated. This is indicated by the report of Levison and Elkind (1967b, page 206) that if the error spot of light which is not being looked at is blanked out, the pilot is unable to hold the markers on the tube faces. Thus the pilot must use some information from the peripheral display, even when it is at an angle of 56° to his line of sight.

It is not clear what determines when the pilot switches his eyes from one display to the other. One possibility is that he changes to the second display when he has got the error in the first display more or less under control. Another possibility is that the pilot looks always at the display with the larger error, changing to the second display as its error becomes the larger. In order to discover which possibility is correct, it is necessary to make simultaneous records of eye position and of tracking performance. This has not yet been done.

Sampling strategy with 2 displays
of different track frequencies

In the experimental condition shown in rows 3 and 4 of Table 12.4 (Levison & Elkind, 1967a), the top unattenuated frequencies of the tracks on the 2 displays are 5 cpm and 20 cpm respectively. The man can look away from the display with the low frequency track for longer before the error marker wanders too far from the target, than he can look away from the display with the high frequency track. This means that looks at the display with the high frequency track can last longer than looks at the display with the low frequency track. The right hand ends of rows 3 and 4 of the table show that this does happen when the man is instructed to minimize the sum of his 2 mean squared errors. Looks at the 2 displays average 2.0 and 1.2 sec, respectively.

Column 3 of the table shows that the unequal time spent looking at the 2 displays changes the sizes of the average RMS errors. For the display with the high frequency track, the relative RMS error is 36. It is smaller than the relative RMS error of 42 in the bottom 2 rows of the table, where both displays have high frequency tracks.

The reduction in the error is achieved at the cost of an increase in error on the display with the low frequency track. The relative RMS error here of 29 is larger than the relative RMS error of 15 in the top 2 rows of the table, where both displays have low frequency tracks. By spending more time on the display with the difficult high frequency

Table 12.4
Simultaneous performance with 2 different tracks

Top unattenuated frequencies (cpm)	RMS amplitudes (cm)	Relative RMS error (track = 100)		Seconds per look	
		Mean	SE*	Mean	SE*
5	5.7				
5	5.7	15	.2	1.4	.05
5	2	29	1.7	1.2	.10
20	2	36	.4	2.0	.33
5	4	18(× 2 = 36)	.2	1.3	.04
20	2	39	1.5	1.7	.29
20	2				
20	2	42	.9	1.4	.06

The 2 displays are separated by a visual angle of 30°. (From Levison and Elkind, 1967a, Experiment 3.)

* The standard error represents the differences between the 3 pilots.

track, the man makes the average RMS errors on the 2 displays more nearly the same size.

Sampling strategy with 2 displays of different track frequencies and amplitudes

In the experimental condition shown in rows 5 and 6 of Table 12.4, the RMS amplitude of the track with a top unattenuated frequency of 5 cpm is increased from 2 to 4 cm. This halves the average time which the error marker takes to wander away from the target. The man cannot look away from the display for as long as he can when the amplitude is smaller. The right hand ends of rows 4 and 6 of the table show that it reduces the duration of looks at the display with the high frequency track from an average of 2.0 to 1.7 sec. The average duration of the looks at the magnified display increases slightly, from 1.2 to 1.3 sec.

The 3 pilots are instructed always to minimize the sum of the 2 mean squared errors. What they do is to keep the 2 mean squared (or RMS) errors more or less the same size. In comparing the errors in rows 5 and 6, it is necessary to double the relative error of the track with a top unattenuated frequency of 5 cpm, because the track has twice the amplitude of the track with the top unattenuated frequency of

20 cpm. The RMS error values for the 2 tracks are then 36 and 39 respectively.

Sampling 4 displays

When a man is given 4 comparable tracking displays, he does not necessarily look at each display for one quarter of the time. The 4 compensatory displays used by Levison and colleagues (1971) are illustrated in Figure 12.3. The large numbers printed beside each display indicate the average percent of the time which the 4 pilots spend looking at the display. The upper right display receives 3.5 times as much observation time as the lower left display.

The displays are oriented so that when looking at one display, the pilot knows more or less the position of the fixed target line of the next display in a clockwise direction. When he looks at the upper right display, he can at the same time appreciate the direction and size of the error in the lower right display. Since both display markers are controlled by the right hand, he can decide how best to respond with his right hand. Similarly looking at the lower left display is the best strategy when responding with the left hand.

The lower part of Table 12.5 shows that the favored upper right display receives more looks and longer looks than the other displays. The lower left display receives the fewest looks and the shortest looks. However the second column of the table shows that the RMS error is hardly affected by the proportion of time spent looking.

The sampling pattern is pretty stable. In a subsequent experiment with the same 4 pilots, Levison and his colleagues (1971, Table B-14) double the RMS amplitude of the track of the lower left display. This increases the proportion of time spent looking at the lower left display only from 12% to 15%. The sampling pattern is probably specific to the particular display configuration. Usually the upper left part of a display receives the most attention.

Moving the fixation point of the eyes from one display to another is a considerable help. The upper part of the table lists the results of an earlier experiment in which the same 4 pilots have to look always at the upper left display (Levison and colleagues 1971, Table D-12). The experimental conditions are otherwise identical with the conditions of the experiment of the lower part of the table. The relative RMS error is smaller on the fixated upper left display, 55 compared with 78.

But the relative RMS error is greater than 100 on the nonfixated displays. Averaged over all 4 displays, the man's relative RMS error is over 100. It means that the man has a lower average score if he

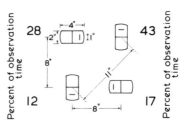

Figure 12.3.   A display to present 4 compensatory tracking tasks.
At the viewing distance of 28 in, the separation of 8 in between the displays
represents a visual angle of 16°. The brightness of the lines is not stated. The
average percent of the time spent by the man looking at each display is printed
against the display. The quasirandom tracks are similar for all 4 displays. They
resemble white noise with a top frequency of about 300 cpm. The high frequencies
are attenuated by a lowpass filter with a break frequency of 20 cpm. Each track
is mixed with the output of the man's control. The combined signal is then fed
into the rate control system. This is a different configuration to that illustrated
in the block diagram of Figure 1.1B. The tracks have a RMS amplitude of .7
in per sec.
The pilot has 2 rate control pressure joysticks, 1 for each hand. Sideways movements of the left stick alter the position of the error marker in the upper left
display. Vertical movements control the error marker of the lower left display.
Vertical and sideways movements of the right stick control respectively the error
markers of the upper right and lower right displays. In order to cancel out the
disturbance fed in by the track, the man has to change the force on his control
with a RMS amplitude of about 2.7 oz per sec. Of the 4 pilots who serve in
the experiment, 2 served previously in the experiments of Tables 12.3 and 12.4.
(After Levison and colleagues, 1971, Figure A-2a.)

stops tracking and holds his controls still in the center. Whereas when
he is free to look at any display, his relative RMS error averages 81.
This shows that it pays to move the eyes from one display to another.

The number of tracking tasks

The average duration of looks is a good deal shorter in Table 12.5
than it is in Tables 12.3 and 12.4. The relative RMS error is a good
deal larger in Table 12.5. There are a number of differences between
the experiments of Table 12.5 and the experiments of Tables 12.3 and
12.4, but the most important difference is that the man has 4 tracking
tasks instead of only 2. It means shorter looks and larger errors.

In the experiment of the upper part of Table 12.5, Levison and his
colleagues (1971, Table B-10C) compare the man's performance under
2 conditions which are not shown in the table. In one condition the
pilot tracks with only the upper left display, looking directly at it. The
average modulus mean error is 33. It is a good deal smaller than the
average error of 55 in the upper part of Table 12.5, where the man

Table 12.5
Simultaneous performance with the 4 displays of Figure 12.3

Display	Relative RMS error (track = 100)		Seconds per look		Looks per minute	
	Mean	SE*	Mean	SE*	Mean	SE*
Upper left (fixated)	55	4				
Lower left	125	13				
Upper right	102	11				
Lower right	147	8				
Average	107					
Upper left	78	2	.68	.08	25	2
Lower left	83	2	.50	.06	15	3
Upper right	84	8	.89	.08	30	3
Lower right	77	4	.61	.13	19	5
Average	81		.67		22	

(From Levison and colleagues, 1971, Appendix B.)
* The standard error represents the differences between the 4 pilots.

looks at the upper left display but has to track also with the other 3 displays in peripheral vision.

In a second condition the pilot has to fixate the stationary upper left display, and track with all the other 3 displays in peripheral vision. The average relative modulus mean errors for the 3 displays are 110, 92 and 139. These values are smaller than the average errors of 125, 102 and 147 respectively for the same 3 displays in the upper part of Table 12.5, where the man looks at the upper left display but has to track with all 4 displays. It follows from these results that increasing the number of tracking tasks from 1 to 4, and from 3 to 4, increases the tracking error.

In an earlier experiment Hoffeld, Seidenstein and Brogden (1961) compare 1, 2 and 4 tracking tasks, using separate groups of 15 students for each task. They do not control where the student looks. Increasing the number of tasks from 1 to 2 and from 2 to 4 reliably lowers the standard of performance on the tasks. Some additional experiments comparing performance with 1 and 2 tracking tasks are listed in Table 12.7, and discussed later in the chapter.

When a man has a number of independent tracking tasks, his looks must be related to his responses. Unfortunately no experimenter has yet examined the relationships. The relationships have been investigated only in flying a simulated aircraft. They are discussed in the next section. This is probably because the experiment requires fairly elaborate recording. Jackson (1958) sidesteps the difficulty by making the man respond to one tracking task at a time in a fixed order. But the results probably apply only to tasks in which the man works in a fixed order.

Sampling many displays while flying

Table 12.6 (Milton, 1952) gives the results of experiments in which 40 pilots have their eyes filmed while they are carrying out standard maneuvers in the air using instruments. The view of the outside world through the windscreen is blanked out. The table lists the main results for 2 kinds of approach before landing.

In the instrument approach (Instrument Low Approach System, or ILAS) a zero reader display, somewhat like that illustrated in Figure 9.1, shows the pilot the size of his error from the correct flight path. The fifth column of the table indicates that the pilot spends on average about 40% of the time looking at this instrument. On average, another 25% of the time is spent looking at the direction gyro. This tells the pilot the side to side direction in which his aircraft is pointing. Changes in the side to side direction of the aircraft change the rate of the side to side error of the zero reader.

The table shows that on average another 25% of the time is spent looking at either the gyro horizon or the airspeed indicator. The gyro horizon shows the pilot whether his aircraft is flying level, diving, or

Table 12.6
A pilot's eye movements while approaching to land

Information obtained	Instrument	Instrument approach			Talk down		
		Mean seconds per look	Mean looks per minute	Per- cent of total time	Mean seconds per look	Mean looks per minute	Per- cent of total time
Tracking error	Zero reader	.86	30	41			
Side to side error rate	Direction gyro	.56	28	25	.90	33	49
Rate of descent	Gyro horizon	.52	17	15	.56	21	19
	Airspeed indicator	.38	16	10	.57	18	17

Unfortunately measures of variability are not given.
(From Milton, 1952.)

climbing. A gyro horizon is illustrated in Figure 9.2 on each side of the aircraft symbol. The gyro horizon and airspeed indicator together tell the pilot how quickly he is descending. Changes in the rate of descent change the rate of the vertical error of the zero reader. The table indicates that the pilot spends on average 90% of his time looking at these 4 instruments during an instrument approach. No other instrument takes on average more than 2% of his time.

On average about 30% of the pilot's eye movements are between the zero reader and the direction gyro. These are the 2 instruments most frequently looked at. Eye movements between each of these 2 instruments and each of the other 2 instruments listed in the table range between 10% and 15% of all eye movements. Curiously enough only about 5% of eye movements are between the gyro horizon and the airspeed indicator. The pilot looks at one or other of these 2 instruments which together indicate the rate of descent. He does not often look at one after the other.

The right side of the table shows the results for a talk down, or Ground Control Approach (GCA). Here a controller on the ground watches the aircraft on a radar display. He tells the pilot over the radio his errors from the correct flight path. The pilot does not have to look at his zero reader. He therefore has more time for his other instruments.

The time which a pilot takes to look at an instrument depends upon the information which he wants. It takes longer to assess the rate at which a marker is moving, than to note its position (Poulton, 1952b, Figure 1).

The time taken to look at an instrument depends also upon the amount of time which the pilot can spare from looking at his other instruments. If he does not look at an instrument very often, he may fail to notice a large error sufficiently soon to be able to correct it before his aircraft deviates from its prescribed path. The slowest safe rate of scanning depends upon the frequencies of the signals displayed by the instruments, and upon the importance of the instruments. Curiously enough, a skilled pilot's control movements are not related in a detectable way to his looks at the instruments (Senders, Carbonell & Ward, 1969).

The results in Table 12.6 on 40 pilots do not agree very well with results obtained more recently on 2 small groups each of 3 pilots, using simulated aircraft (Senders and colleagues, 1969; Weir and Klein, 1970). This could be simply because the performances of the 2 small groups of pilots are not representative. Milton (1952) notes that pilots vary a good deal among themselves in their eye movements while flying standard maneuvers in the same aircraft. This may be due partly to differences in training, and partly to individual styles of flying. When people vary a good deal, quite large numbers of people are required in order to obtain a representative sample. The 2 recent experiments do not use an adequate number of pilots (see Chapter 2). There are other possible reasons for the discrepancies between the results in Table 12.6 and the recent results. The pilot's strategies could be affected by the changes in the design of the instruments, and in the layout of the instrument panels. Also the changes in the cockpit may be accompanied by changes in the scanning procedures which pilots are taught to use.

Tracking with an additional task

Table 12.7 lists experiments in which a person tracks while he is carrying out another task at the same time. As is to be predicted from the experiments on sampling 2 or more tracking displays, performance on one or both tasks usually suffers. The 2 right hand columns of the table indicate which task suffers reliably, where the information is available.

The priority given to the additional task

The table is divided into 4 sections, according to which task is to have priority when both tasks cannot be performed together as well as each is performed alone. Part **A** of the table lists experiments in which the additional task is given priority by the experimenter. Here it is the tracking which suffers most. In parts **B** and **C** of the table neither task is given priority by the experimenter. If 1 of the 2 tasks receives priority, the decision rests with the man, not with the experimenter.

In the experiments listed in part **D** of the table, the experimenter gives priority to the tracking. Here the additional task should suffer most. This is not so in the experiments by Trumbo and Milone (1971) on tracking while memorizing light sequences or lists of numbers, nor in the experiments by Trumbo and Noble (1972) on tracking while responding to clicks or tones. The probable reason is that the tracking is being used as a measure of the spare capacity not required for the additional task. The undergraduates presumably realize this, and give priority to the additional task.

Where the tracking task takes priority, it need not suffer provided 2 requirements are met. One requirement is that the man does not have to look in 2 different directions in order to perform the 2 tasks. If the tracking display is visual, the additional task can be auditory. If both displays are visual, they must be properly combined. The second requirement is that the responses to the additional task are spoken, not made with the other hand or with the foot.

These requirements are met in the experiment by Huddleston and Wilson (1971) on flying a simulated aircraft while reading digits. The tracking task uses the headup display of Figure 9.2. For the additional task, large digits are projected one at a time just above and to the right of the headup display. The distance between the target spot and the center of the digits presents an angle at the man's eyes of only about 3°. Thus the man can read the digits while he is looking directly at the tracking display.

Table 12.7 shows that the additional visual task is carried out reliably less well than when it is performed alone. But the tracking task does not suffer. This is because the man can keep his eyes on the tracking display while he is performing the additional task. Increases in the rate of the error in the tracking display can capture his attention away from the additional task, before they produce appreciable increases in the size of the error. Also the man's spoken responses to the digits do not interfere much with his tracking movements.

Visual competition between tracking and an additional task

Garvey (1960) and Fuchs (1962) report that with an additional task the practiced man tracks much like an unpracticed person. This is sometimes called the progression regression hypothesis. Progression occurs during the original learning of the task. Regression occurs when the additional task is performed as well as the tracking task. The regression is probably caused largely by the visual competition between the tracking and the additional task.

Both experimenters use a compensatory visual tracking display. Table 12.7B shows that Fuch's (1962) additional task is a second visual tracking task. It is performed with the left hand. The additional display is located to the left of and below the main display, at a visual angle of about 45°.

Table 12.7A shows that the 2 additional tasks which Garvey (1960) finds to degrade tracking are also visual. For reporting the range and bearing of targets, the synthetic radar dispay is placed directly above the tracking display. For the 5 choice task, 5 lamps are placed in a row above the tracking display. The man has to press 1 of 5 keys with his left hand.

With the compensatory displays which Garvey (1960) and Fuchs (1962) use, the novice corrects for errors in position. With practice, the man learns to detect small changes in error rate. He corrects for these small changes in rate before they produce large errors in position.

When the practiced man is given an additional visual task, he cannot

Table 12.7

Experiments on tracking with an additional task

Author(s)	Year	N	Tracking task	Additional task	Reliable deterioration in	
					Tracking task	Additional task
A. Priority to additional task						
Garvey (see Figure 7.6)	1960	6	Compensatory rate control	Subtract heard digit	No	No
				Report range and bearing of visual targets	Yes	No
Garvey and Henson	1959	5	Compensatory position control	5 Choice response to lights	Yes	No
				Subtract heard digit	Yes	No
				Second identical compensatory position control	Yes	No
				Report range and bearing of visual targets	Yes	No
Garvey and Taylor	1959	24	Compensatory acceleration control	Subtract heard digit	Yes	No
				Second identical compensatory acceleration control	Yes	No
				Report range and bearing of visual targets	Yes	No
		16	Compensatory acceleration aided control	Subtract heard digit	Yes	No
				Second identical compensatory acceleration aided control	Yes	No
				Report range and bearing of visual targets	Yes	No
		8	Compensatory position control	Subtract heard digit	No	No
				Second identical compensatory position control	Yes	No

Study	Year	N	Control type	Additional task		
Johnston and colleagues	1970	12	Compensatory position control	Report range and bearing of visual targets	Yes	No
				Memory storage of heard words	Yes	
Martin	1970	14	Compensatory position control	Retention of heard words	Yes	
				Recall of heard words	Yes	
				Memory storage of heard words	Yes	
		14	Compensatory position control	Recall of heard words	Yes	
				Memory storage of heard words	Yes	
McLeod	1973a	11	Pursuit lagged rate control	Recall of heard words	Yes	
				Add heard digits aloud	Yes	No
				Add heard digits silently	Yes	Yes
				Repeat back heard digits	No	No
Poulton (see Table 12.9)	*	12	Pursuit position control	Blink 40 times per min	Yes	
				Blink in time to metronome	Yes	
		12	Pursuit position control	Speak in time to metronome	Yes	
				Blink in time to metronome	Yes	
Poulton and Gregory (see Figure 12.4)	1952	12	Pursuit position control	Blink about 50 times per min	Yes	

B. Priority to neither task

Study	Year	N	Control type	Additional task		
Adams and Chambers	1962	16 + 16	Pursuit position control with steps	Pursuit position control to auditory steps synchronous with visual steps		
				Independent of visual and unpredictable	Yes	Yes
		+ 16		Correlated with visual and predictable	No	No

Table 12.7 (cont.)

Author(s)	Year	N	Tracking task	Additional task	Reliable deterioration in Tracking task	Reliable deterioration in Additional task
Adams and Creamer	1962b	15 + 15	Pursuit position control with steps	Pursuit position control to uncorrelated auditory steps synchronous with visual steps		Yes
		+ 15		Unpredictable auditory steps	Yes	
				Predictable auditory steps	Yes	
Brown and colleagues	1961	92	Compensatory position control	Simple reaction to lights	Yes	
Day	1955	30	Compensatory position control	2 Choice response to lights	Yes	
Fuchs	1962	5	Compensatory acceleration control	Compensatory position control	Yes	
Mirabella	1969	4	Steering simulated submarine	Depth keeping with quickened visual display	Yes	
Smith	1963	90 + 60 (some pilots)	Pursuit position control	Recenter dial pointer	Yes	
C. No instruction on priority						
Broadbent	1956	6	Pursuit position control	Repeat distorted words	Yes	
Griew	1959	20	Pursuit position control with preview	Simple reaction to buzzer	Yes	Yes
Katz, Emery, Gabriel, and Burrows	1966	24	Simulated aircraft	Search for visual targets	Yes	

Author	Year	N	Tracking task	Additional task		
Monty and Ruby	1965	24 pilots	Simulated aircraft	Recenter 4 dial pointers	Yes	Yes
D. Priority to tracking						
Allnutt and colleagues	1966	8	Compensatory acceleration control	2 Choice response to peripheral lights	Yes	Yes
Benson and colleagues	1965	16 (8 pilots)	Compensatory rate control	2 Choice response to lights	Yes	Yes
Huddleston and Wilson	1971	8	Simulated aircraft	Classify seen digits as odd or even	No	Yes
				Add 2 successive seen digits	No	Yes
				Search for 2 identical successive seen digits	No	Yes
				Search for 2 identical seen digits separated in time by 1 digit	No	Yes
Knowles and Rose	1962	2 pilots	Simulated lunar landing	12 Choice response to lights	Yes	Yes
Noble, Trumbo, and Fowler	1967	16 + 8	Pursuit position control with steps	Predict heard digits	Yes	Yes
		12 + 12		Predict heard digits	Yes	
		+12	Pursuit position control with steps	Randomly generate digits	No	
		+12		Learn heard digits	No	
		+12		Repeat back digits	No	Yes
Rolfe	1966	16 (6 pilots)	Compensatory rate control	2 Choice response to lights	Yes	Yes
Rolfe	1967	6	Compensatory rate control	2 Choice response to lights	Yes	No
Trumbo and Milone	1971	16	Pursuit position control with steps	Memory storage of light sequence	Yes	No
				Retention of light sequence	Yes	No
				Recall of light sequence	Yes	No

Table 12.7 (cont.)

Author(s)	Year	N	Tracking task	Additional task	Reliable deterioration in Tracking task	Additional task
Trumbo and Milone (cont.)	1971	10 + 10	Pursuit position control with steps	Memory storage of heard number sequence	Yes	No
		+ 10		Retention of heard number sequence	No	No
		+ 10		Recall of heard number sequence	Yes	No
Trumbo and Noble	1972	8 + 32		Simple response to clicks	Yes	
		+ 32		5 Choice random generation of responses to clicks	Yes	
		8 + 6	Pursuit position control with steps	Simple response to tones	Yes	
		+ 6		2 Choice random genera-	Yes	
		+ 6		3 Choice tion of re-	Yes	
		+ 6		5 Choice sponses to tones	Yes	
		16 + 16		Simple response to tones	Yes	
		+ 16		2 Choice random genera-	Yes	
		+ 16		3 Choice tion of re-	Yes	
		+ 16		5 Choice sponses to tones	Yes	
Trumbo, Noble, and Swink	1967	18 + 36	Pursuit position control with steps	Predict heard digits	Yes	
		12 + 12		Predict heard digits	Yes	
		+ 12		Randomly generate digits	Yes	
		16 + 8		Predict heard digits	Yes	

A blank in one of the 2 right hand columns indicates that the information is not available.
* Not previously published.

detect the small changes in error rate while he is looking at the additional display. By the time his eyes return to the tracking display, the changes in error rate have produced errors in position. The practiced man therefore finds himself correcting errors in position like the novice, instead of preventing the errors from arising.

Visual competition probably occurs whenever the man has to track while he is making choice responses to lights. It may help to account for some of the reliable deteriorations in tracking listed in Table 12.7D where the tracking is supposed to take priority (Allnutt and colleagues 1966; Benson, Huddleston & Rolfe, 1965; Rolfe, 1966, 1967).

Motor competition between tracking and an additional task

An additional task can interfere with tracking if the same hand is used to respond to both tasks. Here the interference occurs at the hand, or in the part of the brain which is concerned with the execution of hand movements.

Motor competition probably occurs in the experiments by Benson and colleagues (1965) and by Rolfe (1966, 1967), which are listed in Table 12.7D. In these experiments the man has to press the correct 1 of 2 buttons in response to 1 of 2 lights. The buttons are mounted on the control stick. Pressing a button probably interferes to some extent with tracking.

Tracking can also be degraded by an additional task which involves the use of the other hand. The movement of the other hand may be minimal, like simply releasing the pressure on a button. This additional response is used by Elkind and Miller (1966) in the experiment of Figure 17.11. It produces a reliable deterioration in the tracking of at least 1 of their 3 students (Elkind & Miller, 1966, Table 6).

Here the interference must lie principally within the part of the brain which is concerned with the execution of hand movements. Competition between the responses made by the 2 hands may be partly responsible for the degradation of tracking produced by any additional task in Table 12.7 which requires responses with the hand not used for tracking.

It is possible to assess the extent of motor competition by using an additional task which requires either a hand movement or a spoken response. There is considerably less competition between tracking and spoken responses than between tracking and movements of the other hand. If performance improves when the responses of the additional task are changed from manual to verbal, then there must be motor competition in the part of the brain which is concerned with the execution of the hand movements.

Central competition between tracking and an additional task

In the experiment by Johnston, Greenberg, Fisher and Martin (1970) in Table 12.7A, tracking is reliably degraded by the retention of heard words. In the first experiment by Trumbo and Milone (1971), tracking is reliably degraded by the retention of light sequences. In these experiments there is no obvious visual or motor competition. The competition may occur more centrally in the brain. Perhaps some of the man's limited brain capacity is being used to rehearse the words or light sequences which will soon have to be recalled. Less central capacity is therefore available for the tracking.

The competition produced by the rehearsal may possibly affect the man's tracking in one or more different ways. The rehearsal may raise the man's threshold for small changes in the display. If so, the man may respond only to larger errors or rates of change of error. The rehearsal may reduce the output capacity of the part of the man's brain which is concerned with the execution of responses. If so, the man's responses may be made more slowly or less accurately.

The rehearsal may affect only the man's central computing capacity. If so, the man's reaction time may be increased, and he may occasionally respond in the wrong direction. More detailed information about the man's tracking performance is required in order to discover which are the more important effects of interference.

Order of control in tracking with an additional task

In the experiments listed in Table 12.7A, Garvey and Taylor (1959) use both a position control system and an acceleration control system. With all the additional tasks, there is reliably more deterioration with the acceleration control system than with the position control system. This holds when the main competition is visual, between tracking and reporting the range and bearing of visual targets. It holds when the main competition is motor, between tracking with both hands simultaneously. And it holds when there is no obvious visual or motor competition, between tracking and subtracting heard digits. Here the competition may be more central.

An increase in central competition with the acceleration control system, may be due to the more complex computations which the man has to carry out with the higher order control system. The increased motor competition with the acceleration control system, is due to the greater number of control movements which the man has to make with the high order control system in correcting errors in position (see Figure

16.1). The increased visual competition with the acceleration control system, indicates that the man has to watch the display more continuously with the higher order control system.

Blinking

In blinking, the upper eyelid blanks out vision for about .2 sec. The full duration of a blink is rather longer than this. The upper eyelid takes time to come down and to return again. A blink may also be accompanied by an upward rotation of the eyeball. The eyeball has to rotate down again after the blink. The full cycle may take about .55 sec (Lawson, 1948). It could interfere considerably with visual tracking.

Fortunately Table 12.8 shows that people blink mostly when they have nothing important to look at. They blink least when the track contains high frequencies of large amplitude. They blink most immediately after the period of tracking. The average resting rate corresponds to Lawson's (1948) estimate of about 1 blink every 3 sec for the average person.

The man's response during the blink blackout and immediately afterwards is usually indistinguishable from his response at other times. The man does not stop responding, or respond at a constant rate, simply because he cannot see what he is doing.

In the experiment of Table 12.8, blinking produces a reliable increase in tracking error only when the track comprises 3 sine waves with a top frequency of 25 cpm, and the man does not have a preview. When

Table 12.8

Unintentional blinking during an experiment

Stage of experiment	Average number of blinks per minute
Resting with electrodes in place	18
Immediately before tracking	24
Tracking:	
Track of 2 cpm. with an amplitude of 7.5 mm.	9
Track with a top frequency of 25 cpm and an	
amplitude of 15 or 30 mm	3
Immediately after tracking	42
Resting with electrodes still in place	22

Each of the 15 young enlisted men tracked continuously for 20 min without a break. All the differences are reliable. (From Poulton and Gregory, 1952.)

the man has a preview of the track, he programs his response before he blinks. When the man does not have a preview but the track is a single sine wave of 25 cpm, the man still programs his response reasonably accurately before he blinks, because he can predict the track. Blinking degrades tracking only when the man cannot program his response very accurately before blinking. These are conditions which give rise to few blinks.

Intentional blinking as an additional task

With most people intentional blinks obscure vision for about .2 sec, just like the more usual unintentional blinks. However, intentional blinks probably degrade tracking more than unintentional blinks, for 2 reasons. First, blinking as instructed is an additional task which has to be carried out while tracking, whereas unintentional blinking occurs spontaneously. And secondly, the man may be instructed to blink at a critical point in the track, where he would not blink spontaneously.

Figure 12.4 illustrates the detrimental effect of intentional blinking as an additional task. Tracking while blinking 50 times per min is compared with tracking while the display is blanked out an equal number

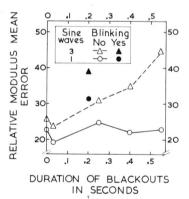

DURATION OF BLACKOUTS
IN SECONDS

Figure 12.4. Performance with intentional blinks and intermittent blackouts.
The circles are for a single sine wave of 25 cpm. The triangles are for a track composed of 3 equal amplitude sine waves of 25, 22.5 and 14 cpm. The 12 men have a pursuit display and a position control system. The relative modulus mean error on the ordinate reaches 100 if the man does not respond at all.

A balanced experimental design is used. The man is told to blink about 50 times per min. The frequency of the mechanical blackouts is chosen to match the frequency with which the man blinks intentionally in preliminary practice trials. Frequencies of between 48 and 52 blackouts per min are avoided because they are too close to double the top track frequency of 25 cpm. For the group of 12 men the average frequencies of blinks and mechanical blackouts match almost exactly. (Results from Poulton and Gregory, 1952, Table 1.)

of times. In this experiment the man knows how often he has to blink, but he can choose his own times for blinking. He may be able to avoid critical points in the track when he blinks. Whereas the mechanical blanking samples the track independently of the critical points. In this respect intentional blinking may be an advantage. Yet the figure shows that the average error in tracking is larger when the man blinks than when the display is blanked out for a comparable period of time.

The triangles represent a track composed of 3 sine waves. The filled triangle for intentional blinks lies reliably above the unfilled triangle for mechanical blackouts lasting .25 sec. The circles represent a single sine wave track. Here the filled circle for intentional blinks lies reliably above all the unfilled circles for mechanical blackouts. Thus intentional blinking is an additional task which interferes with tracking more than by simply blanking vision. With the single sine wave track, the intentional blinks probably interfere with the rhythm of the man's response.

Experiment 2 of Table 12.9 compares intentional blinking as an additional task with saying "now." When blinking and speaking have to synchronize with the beat of a metronome 40 times per min, both tasks reliably increase the error in tracking. However the intentional blinking is reliably the more detrimental additional task. This is partly because it blanks vision, and partly because it is a less familiar task than speaking. It probably produces more interference with the tracking in the part of the brain which is concerned with the execution of responses, than saying "now" does.

Table 12.9
Performance with intentional blinks or speech

	Relative modulus mean error	
	Experiment 1	Experiment 2
No blinking, no metronome	33	31
No blinking, metronome		32
Blinking in own time	45	
Blinking between metronome beats	53	
Blinking on metronome beats	54	47
Blinking when truck marker at rest		34
Speaking on metronome beats		40
Speaking when track marker at rest		33

Each experiment uses a separate group of 12 young enlisted men. When the man does not respond, the modulus mean error is 100. To be reliable, differences must be at least 6. The results from 2 tracks like those of Figure 12.4 are combined. (Results not published previously).

It is pointed out in Chapter 5 that having to close the eyes at the start of an aiming movement is an additional task. It probably degrades performance both by blanking vision and by distracting the man, just as intentional blinking does.

Intentional blinking at selected times

Experiment 2 of Table 12.9 shows that intentional blinks 40 times per min do not appreciably affect the error in tracking when they are timed to occur as the track marker is more or less at rest. In this they resemble unintentional blinks.

Curiously enough Experiment 1 shows that intentional blinks 40 times per min do reliably increase the error when the man can choose the times of his blinks. Thus he does not choose his times very wisely. However the error is reliably larger still when the times of the blinks have to conform to the beat of a metronome. It makes little difference whether the man blinks on the beats or between the beats. Both are about equally detrimental.

Recommendations for display sampling

Machine sampling rates should be as fast as possible. A function which is not sampled should be displayed as a continuous variable.

In a display which is stepped by amplitude, the sizes of the gaps between steps should be as small as possible. Digital displays are not recommended for tracking.

If a man has to use 2 or more visual tracking displays, they should be placed as close together as possible. In flying, instruments which are often looked at in turn should be placed together. The arrangement selected may have to be a compromise between the ideal arrangements for different maneuvers.

If a man has to perform an additional task while using direct vision for tracking, the task should be designed so that it does not require direct vision.

Conditions which increase blinking should be avoided.

Chapter

13

Displays using alternative visual dimensions

Summary

People track most accurately with a display in central vision which shows position. In peripheral vision, the combination of direction and rate of flash gives more accurate tracking than the combination of direction and rate of movement. The combination of direction and brightness can also be used in peripheral vision. When a man has to track using 2 conventional displays at different distances, a supplementing display designed for use in peripheral vision can improve his performance.

The need for alternative sensory dimensions

In flying an aircraft down a glidepath when coming in to land, the pilot needs to look ahead for the runway as well as to watch his flight instruments. While he is looking directly at either the runway or his instruments, the other display is out of focus. In order to look at the 2 displays in turn, he has to change the accommodation and convergence of his eyes from distant vision to close vision and back again. The return journey out and back takes an average of about 2 sec (Ellis & Allan, 1954). It means that the pilot can look at each display only about 30 times per min.

The design engineer can help the pilot to sample more frequently. He can present the pilot with the important information from the flight instruments on an additional display, which is reflected off the windscreen and focused at infinity, as in Figure 9.2.

An alternative is to use peripheral vision for the additional display. The pilot can then keep his eyes directed forward at the runway, while he is checking on and adjusting the performance of his aircraft. The peripheral display can use changes in the direction and rate of flash, of movement, or brightness. Another alternative is to use a nonvisual display like those discussed in the next chapter.

The displays designed for peripheral vision are compensatory. There is no advantage in using a pursuit display. Pursuit displays are suited only to position and rate of movement in central vision, where the capacity for spatial perception is most fully developed. With moving displays in central vision, the man can appreciate the true motion of both the pursuit display markers, as well as their relative motion with respect to each other. True motion or pursuit displays are therefore preferable (see Chapter 9).

Neither rate of flash nor brightness involves spatial perception. A pursuit display which employs either of these 2 sensory dimensions is used by the man as if it is a compensatory display. The man responds only to the difference between the 2 displayed values. He is not able to use the changes in the absolute values. With both rate of flash and brightness, a compensatory display is therefore likely to be as efficient as a pursuit display.

Direction and rate of flash

The filled circles in Figure 13.1 (Brown and colleagues, 1961) show that direction and rate of flash is a fairly good combination for indicating the direction and size of the error in compensatory tracking. The display uses four lamps, which are mounted about 30° out from the man's line of sight at 3, 6, 9 and 12 o'clock. When a lamp flashes, the man has to move his joystick control toward it. The rate of flash indicates the size of the error. To ensure that the 4 lamps are not looked at directly, the man is given a central display of 3 lamps to look at. He has to press a switch with his left hand as quickly as possible whenever 1 of the 3 central lamps is switched on or off.

The unfilled circles in the figure represent performance with a con-

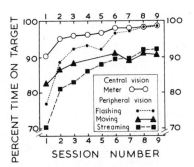

Figure 13.1. Performance with displays in peripheral vision.

The reference display is a rather poor zero reader meter, which is looked at directly. The displays used in peripheral vision subtend angles of about 30° to the line of sight. The moving display is produced by 2 rotating white cylinders, each of which has a black helix painted on it. The direction and rate of rotation of a cylinder determines the apparent direction and rate of movement of the helix. Side to side errors are indicated by side to side movements of a horizontal helix mounted below the central display of 3 lamps. Vertical errors call for forward and backward movements of the control stick. They are indicated by forward and backward movements of a horizontal helix mounted at the side.

The streaming display is produced by horizontal and vertical rows of 48 lamps. In each row every sixth lamp is on at the same time. When a control movement to the right is required, 8 points of light stream toward the right. Vertical errors are indicated by streaming up or down. The irregular sine wave track has 4 reversals in 5 min. The joystick position control is not spring centered. Each display is used by a separate group of between 5 and 12 naval enlisted men. (Results from Brown and colleagues, 1961.)

ventional compensatory display. The display is a rather poor version of the zero reader illustrated in Figure 9.1. The meter is mounted beside the 3 lamps, so that it can be looked at directly. Figure 13.1 shows that in the early sessions the flashing display gives a considerably smaller percent time on target than the conventional compensatory display. But after practice both displays are equally good. The increase in reaction time to the 3 central lamps is about the same size, whichever tracking task is added to the central lamps task.

The advantage of the flashing display is the clear indication it gives the man of the general direction in which to move his control. A disadvantage is the difficulty of telling from the rates of flash the exact direction and distance to move. By session number 9 the man is always so close to the center of the target that he probably needs to know only the general direction of his error. The task can be made more difficult by reducing the size of the target. The man would then need to know the exact direction and size of his error. This could make the flashing display reliably worse than the zero reader.

A related disadvantage of the flashing display is that the 2 dimensions are not integrated. The man's errors in the vertical and in the horizontal dimensions are shown by separate parts of the display. The man has to obtain information from 2 different directions. Whereas with the zero reader the 2 dimensions are integrated. All the information is presented in one place. The man can tell the direction and distance to move his joystick from the position at which the 2 moving needles cross.

Results similar to those illustrated in Figure 13.1 are reported by Brown and his colleagues (1961) in a subsequent experiment using as the track a series of randomly timed steps. If anything the flashing display gives the quickest acquisition times. The display tells the man as soon as the track has stepped, wherever he happens to be looking at the time. With the zero reader the man has to be watching the display in order to see the time at which a step is introduced.

The best combination of displays is the flashing display paired with the zero reader. The flashing display tells the man the general direction in which to move his control as soon as there is a step. While the man is responding, he can look at the zero reader to determine the exact direction and distance to move the control (Brown and others, 1961, Table 3).

Rate and brightness of flash

Ziegler, Reilly, and Chernikoff (1966) use rate of flash to signal the direction of the error when tracking in the vertical dimension. A rate of 1 flash per sec indicates that the error marker is too high and should be lowered. A rate of 2 flashes per sec indicates that the error marker should be raised. The error marker does not flash when it is more or less on target. The code is reasonably easy to learn. But rate of flash is not very compatible with up and down directions of movement.

Rate of flash is used to supplement a conventional compensatory display when the display is so distant that the direction of the error up or down is hard to see. Figure 13.2 illustrates the modulus mean error as the CRT display is moved further from the man, and the amplitude of the track therefore subtends a smaller angle at the man's eyes.

The figure shows that the flashing display is only a slight advantage as long as it is possible to track at above the level of chance with the conventional unsupplemented display. The level of chance is represented by the broken horizontal line at a relative modulus mean error of 100. The supplemented flashing display is a reliable advantage only when the error with the unsupplemented display is 100 or greater.

A difficulty with the flashing code is that it does not indicate the

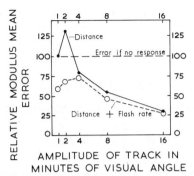

Figure 13.2.   Performance with a supplementing flashing display.
The display is illustrated in Figure 1.1B. The track is a sine wave of 6 cpm
with an amplitude of ~.5 in. At a distance of about 5 ft this represents a visual
angle of 16 min. The 7 naval enlisted men have a spring centered control and
an acceleration aided control system. With the supplementing display, flashing starts
as soon as the spot is .12 in above or below the fixed line.
The experiment is conducted in a dark room. The man tracks with the largest
visual angle first, and then in turn with smaller visual angles. As the room is
only 20 ft long, the 2 smallest visual angles are obtained by placing a concave
lens in front of the display. This is unfortunate because the 2 smallest visual
angles are the only conditions to show a reliable difference between the 2 displays.
It is possible that looking through the lens can have some other effect as well
as reducing the apparent size of the movement. (After Ziegler and colleagues,
1966, Figure 2.)

size of the error. The size of the error is indicated by the distance
of the flashing error marker above or below the horizontal target line.
As long as the size of the error is visible, the direction of the error
is also visible. Using flashing to indicate the direction of the error
is hardly necessary. Supplementary flashing is a major advantage only when
the amplitude of the track presents such a small visual angle that the
track movement cannot be seen.

Ziegler and his colleagues (1966, Experiment 2) subsequently vary
the brightness or amplitude (depth) of the flash in order to indicate
the size of the error. The extra information reliably reduces the average
modulus mean error. Unfortunately it is not possible to tell how much
better the man would track with a conventional compensatory display
at the conventional distance of about 2 ft.

Rate of flash is probably not the most appropriate dimension to indicate the direction of the error. Visual direction is the dimension which
is most compatible with the direction of control movements. This is
the dimension used by the flashing display of Figure 13.1, and by Vallerie
(1966) for the peripheral lights display of Figure 13.6. However bright-

ness of flash may be as good a dimension as rate of flash or simple brightness for representing the size of the error. These points have still to be investigated.

Rate of movement

Size can be displayed as a rate of movement, instead of as a distance. It is simply necessary to integrate the continuous function before displaying it. For example, the speed of an automobile can be displayed on the instrument panel as a rate of rotation, instead of as a displacement of the speedometer needle. This corresponds to using the conventional display on the left side of Figure 13.3, instead of the speedometer display on the right side.

The left side of Figure 13.4 shows that the modulus mean error in pursuit tracking increases when size is displayed as a rate of movement. In the later sessions both sets of triangles for matching rates lie reliably above the corresponding circles for matching positions. This shows that

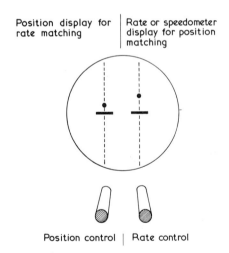

Position display for | Rate or speedometer
rate matching | display for position
  | matching

Position control | Rate control

Figure 13.3.   Displays and controls for rate matching and position matching.
The movements of the position display on the left are obtained by integrating the movements of the speedometer display on the right. The control system on the left is one order lower than the control system on the right. The movements of each control are directly compatible with the movements of the corresponding display marker immediately above it. For convenience the display and control on the left are called position, and the display and control on the right are called rate. But position matching using the rate display and rate control on the right, is in fact direct tracking with a zero order control system. This is because the order of the display is the same as the order of the control system.

people are better at estimating positions than at estimating rates. Exactly the same control movements are required with both kinds of display. The only difference between the 2 tasks of a pair is in the nature of the display.

The filled triangles on the left side of Figure 13.4 are for rate matching with a position control. The man uses the display and control on the left side of Figure 13.3. He has to move his control at a rate which corresponds to the rate of the track marker. This is a response which is directly compatible with the movement of the display.

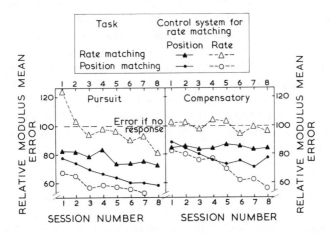

Figure 13.4. Performance in rate matching and position matching.

The displays and controls are illustrated in Figure 13.3. The track consists of white noise with an upper cutoff at 40 cpm of 20 dB per octave. It is fed directly into the speedometer display which is used in position matching. For rate matching the track is integrated. The gain of the display is adjusted so that the movement of the display markers always covers most of the face of the 6 in CRT. Each function represents the performance of a separate group of 5 or 6 naval enlisted men. (After Poulton, 1967, Figure 1.)

The relative modulus mean error given on the ordinate represents the position error seen by the man with the compensatory speedometer display. In the other conditions the man does not see directly the error which is scored against him. Thus he is unable to compensate for transient small mismatches in the device which subtracts the output of his control system from the track input. With the pursuit speedometer display the man sees only the positions of the track and response markers before the distance between them has been computed by the scoring device. This is indicated by the block diagram of Figure 1.1A.

In the rate matching conditions the man sees only either the difference in rate between the track and the response, or the 2 actual rates. The rates are integrated to voltages which represent positions on the speedometer display, before they are passed to the scoring device which computes the error. However the errors produced by the equipment are likely to be small compared with the errors produced by the man. They can probably be neglected.

The filled circles represent a task which requires the same movements of the position control. The only difference is that the man uses the speedometer display on the right of Figure 13.3, and so has to match position. After practice the filled triangles for rate matching lie reliably above the filled circles for position matching. Rate matching is the more difficult task in spite of the compatible relationship between display movements and control movements.

The unfilled triangles on the left of Figure 13.4 represent rate matching with a rate control. Here the man uses the display on the left side of Figure 13.3, and the control on the right side. He has to make control movements whose sizes are proportional to the rate of the track marker. The figure shows that this is in fact the worst pursuit condition. The error is reliably greater than in any other pursuit condition.

The man has 2 difficulties. First, rate of movement is not an easy sensory dimension to use in tracking. And secondly, the size of a control movement is not very compatible with a rate of movement of a display marker. The man tracks better with a position control which he can move at a rate corresponding to the rate of the display marker. This is represented by the filled triangles. Rate controls and position controls are discussed in greater detail in Chapter 16.

The tasks represented by the unfilled circles and by the unfilled triangles of Figure 13.4 require the same movements of the rate control on the right of Figure 13.3. For the unfilled circles the man uses the speedometer display, which is also on the right of Figure 13.3. This is the best combination of control and display, because a displacement of the response marker of any desired size is directly proportional to the size of the control movement. The condition produces the smallest average tracking error.

The right side of Figure 13.4 illustrates the corresponding results for compensatory tracking. Instead of matching the rate of the track marker with the rate of a response marker, the man has simply to hold the error marker at rest anywhere on the display. This is comparable to the task with the moving and streaming displays of Figure 13.1. It is an easy task to describe, but a difficult task to carry out.

The difficulty is that when the error marker is at rest, the man cannot see the movement of the track which he is nulling (see Chapter 9). After practice the average error in tracking with the compensatory display is always greater than the average error of the corresponding condition with the pursuit display. For the filled points the differences are reliable.

After practice the rank order of the conditions for the compensatory display is identical with the rank order for the pursuit display. Both sets of triangles for nulling a rate lie reliably above the corresponding circles for nulling an error in position. Clearly rate of movement makes a less good tracking display than distance.

Figure 10.3 (Pew, 1966) shows that a man's tracking performance can be improved reliably when the rate of a spot of light is represented by a velocity vector. The velocity vector shows the rate as a distance, and so enables the man to assess the rate more accurately. It corresponds to the speedometer display on the right of Figure 13.3. The results in Figures 10.3 and 13.4 are therefore in line with each other.

Movement versus flash in peripheral vision

In peripheral vision, direction and rate of movement is not as good a combination as direction and rate of flash. This is illustrated in Figure 13.1 (Brown and others, 1961). The filled triangles and squares represent respectively performance with moving and streaming displays in peripheral vision. Separate displays are used for errors in the vertical and in the side to side dimension. The direction and rate of the movement or streaming indicates the direction and distance to move the control. At the end of training both designs of display give reliably less time on target than the flashing display represented by the filled circles.

The periphery of the retina of the eye is sensitive to movement. To primitive man movement at the side is a danger signal. Those who are not sensitive to it do not survive. But the direction and rate of the movement cannot be assessed easily in peripheral vision, whereas rate of flash can be assessed almost anywhere on the retina. This may be why the moving and streaming displays do not give such long times on target as the flashing display.

The moving display can be improved by integrating the 2 dimensions of movement into a single display. Vallerie (1968) compares the integrated 2 dimension display (Fenwick, 1963) with the 2 piece separated display, when the displays are placed at an angle to the line of sight. The integrated display gives reliably better tracking performance than the 2 piece separated display.

Unfortunately the part of the separated display which shows the error in the vertical dimension is mounted at about 30° to the line of sight, as it is mounted in the cockpit. Whereas the other displays are mounted at angles of only 15° to the line of sight. The 2 piece separated display thus has this additional disadvantage. It is not possible to tell how much the additional disadvantage affects the size of the difference found.

Brightness

The left of Figure 13.5 (Moss 1964b) shows that in central vision a display which codes the error as a difference in brightness gives a reliably larger tracking error than a conventional compensatory display (Moss, 1964a). The brightness display comprises 2 adjacent electroluminescent lamps. The lower lamp has a constant brightness of 1 ft lambert. The man has to try to keep the brightness of the upper lamp matched to the brightness of the lower lamp.

However the top of Figure 13.5 on the right shows that in peripheral vision, the brightness display gives a reliably smaller tracking error than the conventional display. The interaction between the kind of display and the angle subtended at the man's eyes is reliable.

When the man tracks with the displays in peripheral vision, he has to look at a red jeweled lamp directly in front of him. The experimenter records the number and duration of his looks away from the red lamp.

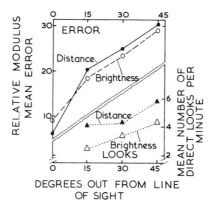

Figure 13.5. Performance in brightness matching and position matching.
In different trials the display is looked at directly, and viewed at angles of up to 45° from the line of sight. The relative modulus mean error on the left hand ordinate will be 100 if the man does not track at all. The average number of times per minute that the man looks at the display directly, instead of looking straight ahead, is shown by the 2 lower functions and the right hand ordinate.

The conventional display comprises a split horizontal line on a CRT. The 2 half lines are about .6 in long and .066 in wide. One part of the line remains stationary, while the other part moves up and down. The brightness of the lines is not stated. The track is a sine wave with a frequency of 12 cpm. The amplitude on the face of the CRT is 3 in. The track varies the brightness display between 0 and 5 ft lamberts. The 6 highly practiced men undergraduates have a position control stick. Forward rotation of the stick raises the error marker, but reduces the brightness of the variable upper lamp. (After Moss, 1964b, Figures 1 and 2.)

The 2 bottom functions in the figure and the right hand ordinate indicate the average number of direct looks per min. at the 2 displays when the displays are not supposed to be looked at directly.

Since looks average about 1 sec, the 2 bottom functions also indicate the approximate number of seconds per minute spent looking directly at the displays. The conventional display is looked at reliably more often than the brightness display. This reflects the greater difficulty of using the conventional display in peripheral vision.

The conventional display is not designed for use in peripheral vision. A well designed display like that of Figure 12.3 might not give such large increases in tracking error when used in peripheral vision. An improved brightness display, like that at the top on the right of Figure 13.6, could also be used. It is not known whether an improved brightness display would be better or worse in peripheral vision than an improved conventional display.

Direction and brightness

The top part of Figure 13.6 (Vallerie, 1966) shows that the conventional compensatory display on the left produces a smaller average modulus mean error in tracking than the display using the combination of direction and brightness on the right. The 4 lamps on the right are mounted 30° out from the line of sight at 3, 6, 9 and 12 o'clock, as in the flashing display of the experiment of Figure 13.1. The position and brightness of the 2 lamps which are on indicate the direction and size of the error. The average modulus mean error of 34 with this display is almost 3 times the error of 12 with the conventional display.

The difference between the 2 displays corresponds to the difference on the left of Figure 13.1 between the filled circles of the flashing display, and the unfilled circles of the conventional display. Presumably the difference in Figure 13.6 can be reduced by practice, like the difference in Figure 13.1. It is not known which is the better alternative visual display, the 4 lamps which vary in brightness, or the 4 lamps which vary in rate of flash.

A supplementing display when 2 conventional displays are at different distances

The middle part of Figure 13.6 shows that when the 2 parts of the conventional display are at different distances from the man, a supplementing display of direction and brightness reduces the average tracking error. In the display on the left, the horizontal line is projected to a

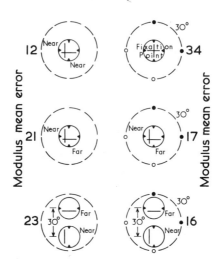

Figure 13.6.   Performance with a peripheral brightness display.

The reference display is shown at the top on the left. It is 2.5 ft from the man's eyes. The horizontal and vertical moving lines are about 3 in long and .1 in wide. They are dark, against a background with a brightness of 1 ft lambert. The display in the middle on the left has the same dimensions, but the horizontal line is 12 ft from the man's eyes. It is superimposed by means of a beam splitting mirror upon the display with the vertical line.

The middle right display is identical, but has in addition 4 lamps fixed at angles of 30° to the man's line of sight. As the figure shows, when the vertical line of the central display is to the left of its center, the left peripheral lamp is on. When the horizontal line is below its center, the lower peripheral lamp is on. The brightness of the peripheral lamps can vary between 0 and 250 ft lamberts, according to the size of the error. The top right display uses only the peripheral lamps. The stationary central display provides a fixation point.

In the displays at the bottom, the 2 parts of the central display are separated by a visual angle of 30°. The upper display is 12 ft away, the lower display is only 2.5 ft away. There are 5 additional experimental conditions which are not shown in the figure.

The tracks for the 2 dimensions comprise 3 sine waves of 60, 21 and 4 cpm. The amplitude of the 4 cpm sine wave is 3 or 4 times larger than the amplitude of the other 2 sine waves. The output of the man's pressure stick in each dimension is mixed with the corresponding track output. The combined signal is passed through a second order control system which represents an aircraft or spacecraft. Thus the disturbances introduced by the track and by the man's control actions are both shaped by the dynamics of the control system. This is rather different from the conventional configuration illustrated in Figure 1.1B. One pilot and 7 nonpilots serve in the experiment. (After Vallerie, 1966, Figure 2.)

distance of 12 ft from the man. The distant line is increased in size so that it presents the same visual angle as the near line. There is no apparent change in display gain.

When the man looks at one line, the other line is out of focus and may look like 2 lines. As a result, the average modulus mean error in tracking is 21. It is reliably greater than the average error of 12 when the 2 parts of the display are at the same distance.

The middle of the figure on the right shows that adding the 4 peripheral lamps reliably reduces the error from 21 to 17. This is because the man can look at 1 of the 2 lines, and track in the other dimension using the peripheral lamps. The bottom part of the figure shows that the 4 peripheral lamps help just as much when the 2 parts of the conventional display are separated by a visual angle of 30°, as well as being at different distances.

Vallerie (1966) watches the man's eyes while he performs the experimental condition illustrated at the bottom on the right. Most of the time the man looks at only 1 of the 2 conventional displays. He tracks in the second dimension using peripheral vision. He apparently uses only 1 conventional and 1 brightness display.

A check is made on this in a condition not illustrated in the figure. Here the man has only the part of the conventional display which shows the error in the vertical dimension. He has only the 2 peripheral lamps which show the error in the side to side dimension. His average tracking error is 18. It is not reliably greater than the averages of 17 and 16 for the 2 conditions illustrated on the right of the figure, where the man has a choice between a conventional display and a brightness display for both dimensions. Thus the man needs only 1 conventional display and 1 brightness display.

Recommended alternative visual dimensions

A visual display which shows position in central vision should always be used except in special circumstances.

An exception is when a man has to look at 2 different distances at once. Here 1 of the 2 displays should use direction and rate of flash, or direction and brightness, instead of position. But an integrated display like the headup display of Figure 9.2 is probably preferable.

A display using rate of movement is not recommended.

Chapter

14

Nonvisual displays

Summary

Tracking with a compensatory 3 state auditory or cutaneous display is almost as accurate after practice as tracking with the comparable 3 state visual display. But a conventional visual display of position in central vision is far better than any auditory or cutaneous display.

In tracking loudness and pitch, a compensatory display is at least as good as a pursuit display. Integrated auditory displays have been used to fly simulated aircraft without vision, but tracking is at least as accurate with conventional aircraft instruments.

A skilled pilot usually controls a simulated unstable aircraft or helicopter more accurately when he can feel it moving.

Available nonvisual sensory dimensions

Tracking by ear

After the eyes, the ears are the best sense organs to use in tracking. A man has 2 ways of locating the side to side direction of a sound. If a sound is more intense in one ear than in the other, the sound appears to come from the direction of the ear with the more intense sound. The side to side direction of a sound can also be determined by a difference in timing or phase between the 2 ears. If a sound reaches one ear a few milliseconds before it reaches the other ear, the sound appears to come from the direction of the ear with the leading sound.

In tracking, only intensity has been used to indicate the side to side direction of the error. The display is nonlinear. A small mismatch in intensity produces a relatively large shift in the apparent localization of the composite sound. A large mismatch in intensity does not shift the apparent localization much further to the side (Stevens and Davis, 1938, Figure 71). In this, the display is rather like the nonlinear display used by Bowen and Chernikoff (1957), which is illustrated in Figure 11.3.

Unfortunately the ears do not locate sounds well in the vertical dimension. The dimension of frequency has been used as a substitute for the vertical dimension of the eyes. But up and down hand movements are not as compatible with changes in frequency, as they are with up and down seen movements.

The ears have less capacity than the eyes for spatial perception. In this respect auditory dimensions suffer a similar disadvantage to the visual dimensions of rate of flash and brightness. Sizes of error cannot be appreciated as readily in an auditory code like intensity, frequency, or rate of interruption, as in a spatial visual code.

An auditory pursuit display is used like a compensatory display. The man responds only to the difference between the 2 displayed values. He is not helped by the changes in the absolute values. As we saw in Chapter 13, full visual spatial perception is required in order to use a pursuit display properly.

Tracking on the skin

Curiously enough, spatial perception is not well developed on the skin. People do not rely on being touched in order to identify things. They do the touching themselves. In the dark they actively explore objects with their hands. A person can identify an object more accurately if he manipulates it with his hands, than he can if it is pressed against the palm of his inactive hand (Gibson, 1962).

When used as an input channel for tracking, the skin suffers the same kinds of disadvantage as the ears. Exact sizes of error are difficult to appreciate. A pursuit display cannot be used at all.

In order to obtain good passive localization on the skin, it is necessary to use much of the skin surface of the body. Suppose that a series of stimulators is fixed from the right hip, up the right side of the body, across the shoulders, and down the left side of the body to the left hip. Compensatory tracking should be feasible using a display of this kind. Control movements to the right and to the left would be signaled by stimulating the right or left side of the body. The extent of the control movement would be indicated by the distance of the stimulator on the shoulder or side of the body from the neck.

This is probably one of the best cutaneous display systems which could be devised for tracking. Unfortunately it does not appear to have been tried out, perhaps because it would be too cumbersome to use in any practical application. The cutaneous displays which have been tried out use compatible indications for the direction of the required control movement. But the size of the required control movement is coded by intensity, frequency, or rate of repetition. These dimensions are not very compatible with sizes of movement.

A practical difficulty in using areas of skin to give an input for tracking is that a stimulator has to be attached to each area. The stimulator may get in the way. When fixed under the clothes, it increases their bulk. But if neither the eyes nor the ears are available for tracking, the skin senses offer a possible alternative input.

A difficulty with both auditory and cutaneous displays is that people are not used to tracking with them. Almost all everyday tracking tasks use the eyes. People take longer to learn to track when using the ears and the skin senses. This could mean that performance deteriorates more when tracking under difficult conditions, although the point has not yet been checked. Garvey and Taylor (1959) show that a tracking task which takes longer to learn deteriorates more under difficulties. The experiment is described at the end of Chapter 2.

Vestibular and proprioceptive senses

The vestibular sense organs in the head are sensitive to acceleration. They enable a person to keep his balance when his eyes are shut. As soon as the person's head and body start to tilt, signals indicating the acceleration are sent to his brain. He is therefore able to correct his posture before he leans over so far that he falls.

When a person is sitting down, he can tell that his seat is tilted by the parts of his body which press against the seat. Sensations of acceleration and tilt may enable a pilot to fly his aircraft more effectively. If this is so, it may be desirable for aircraft simulators on the ground to move so that they present similar sensations.

There are sense organs in the arms and legs which tell a person the approximate position of his limbs. The same sense organs are stimulated both when a person moves his arm, and when he allows his arm to be moved or guided. If a man can learn to track while his arm is being guided, guidance might be used during automatic landings to help the pilot to keep in practice.

A 3 state display of the direction of sound

For a simple 3 state indication of side to side direction, an auditory display is almost as effective as a visual display (Mowbray & Gebhard, 1961, pages 123, 124). With the auditory display, an error to the right is signaled by a tone in the right ear. An error to the left is signaled by a tone in the left ear. When the man is on target he hears nothing. Moving the position control to the right increases the error to the right.

The corresponding visual signals are right lamp on, left lamp on, and no lamp on. When the track is a slow sine wave of 2 cpm, tracking is about equally accurate with both sensory dimensions (Humphrey & Thompson, 1952a). If anything, the 4 men perform at first rather less well with the auditory display, because auditory tracking is new to them.

The track is then changed to a combination of 3 sine waves with a top frequency of 15 cpm. Here the auditory display is always tracked less accurately than the visual display, although the difference is reliable only on the second day of practice (Humphrey & Thompson, 1952b). Thus after practice, a well designed 3 state auditory display is almost as effective as the comparable 3 state visual display.

Direction and rate of interruption of sound

For indicating the size of an error, an auditory display is not as good as a display of position in central vision. In this an auditory display corresponds to a visual display using rate of flash or brightness. In their third experiment, Humphrey and Thompson (1953) use the rate of interruption of a tone to indicate the size of the error. A faster rate of interruption means a larger error. Zero error is indicated by a constant tone presented to both ears.

The visual display is a conventional CRT. The size of the error is indicated by the distance of the error marker from a fixed vertical line. With 10 new people, the conventional visual display gives much more accurate tracking than the auditory display. A similar result is reported subsequently by Micheli (1966), who uses separate groups of 10 undergraduates for the 2 displays.

People are used to making movements proportional to distances. They are not used to making movements proportional to rates of interruption. The visual display which corresponds to the rate of interruption of a sound, codes the size of the error as a rate of flash. Figure 13.1 shows that the combination of direction and rate of flash is not as good for tracking as a rather poor display of position in central vision, except after a good deal of practice. So it is not surprising that the combination of direction and rate of interruption of a sound is not as good as position in central vision.

Direction and intensity of sound

An auditory display can code the size of an error to the right or left by the apparent localization of a sound to the right or left. Wargo (1967) reports that the display gives less accurate tracking than a conventional visual display. He uses both pursuit and compensatory displays. For the pursuit display, a pure track tone of 2000 Hz is presented to the right ear through a headphone. The tone varies in intensity. The man is instructed to control the intensity of an independent response tone of 2000 Hz presented to the left ear, to make it match in loudness.

When 2 tones of the same pitch are presented simultaneously to the 2 ears, the man hears a single composite tone. The cue which tells him when the 2 tones are matched in loudness, is that the composite tone is centered in his head. Thus the man has a compensatory task to perform, although the concurrent changes in loudness indicate the disturbance fed in by the track.

For the compensatory display, the reference tone presented to the right ear has a fixed intensity. The error tone presented to the left ear varies in intensity. Again the man has to control the intensity of the tone in the left ear so that the composite tone is centered in his head. The man has a position control stick which increases the loudness of the tone in the left ear when it is moved to the left.

The track is produced by an irregular cam which gives an average of 34 reversals per min. On the CRT of the visual display, the maximum amplitude of movement is about 3 in. With the auditory display, the maximum amplitude covers the range of subjectively comfortable loudnesses, from well above threshold to not uncomfortably loud. In the compensatory task, zero error is at about the subjective center of the range of loudnesses. Unfortunately the sound pressure levels are not stated.

The position control system has a transmission time lag (see Chapter 17) of 0, .21, .42 or .84 sec. There are 4 separate groups, each of 5 men undergraduates. They track respectively with the auditory pursuit display, the auditory compensatory display, a conventional visual pursuit display, and a visual compensatory display.

The auditory tasks give reliably less time on target than the visual tasks. The average difference in time on target beween the auditory and visual tasks is about 3 times as large as the reliable difference between the pursuit and compensatory modes of the visual task. The results indicate that the side to side direction of a sound is not as easily matched by sizes of control movement, as is distance in central vision.

Pursuit and compensatory displays of direction and intensity of sound

With Wargo's (1967) auditory task there is little difference between the pursuit and the compensatory displays. This indicates that the man is unable to improve the accuracy of his tracking with the pursuit display, by using the changes in loudness which occur as the intensity of the track increases and decreases. Presumably the man cannot very easily attend to the changes in loudness while he is attempting to keep the composite tone centered in his head. The difficulty of using 2 dimensions of an auditory display simultaneously are discussed later in the chapter.

The poor performance with the auditory pursuit display is in line with results reported by Pikler and Harris (1960). The interpretation of Pikler and Harris' results is complicated by their use of 2 tones of 500 and 1000 Hz, instead of 2 tones of the same frequency. It makes tracking with the pursuit display reliably less accurate than tracking with the compensatory display.

With the pursuit display the 5 practiced people have to match the loudness of 2 tones of different pitch. This is a difficult task even with unlimited time. Whereas with the compensatory display the man can neglect the reference tone. He has simply to hold constant the loudness of the error tone of varying intensity.

In an earlier experiment using 3 of the same 5 people, Harris and Pikler (1960) report that their 5 people can do this equally well for 2 minutes without a reference tone at all. Hattler (1968) confirms this. Thus the advantage of the compensatory display over the pursuit display in Pickler and Harris' experiment, is that with the compensatory display the man does not have to match loudness across a difference in pitch.

Pitch of sound

Tracking by auditory pitch is not as accurate as tracking with a conventional visual display. Goldman (1959) gives 16 soldiers a compensatory auditory pitch display for the vertical dimension of a 2 dimensional compensatory tracking task. A tone centered on 1000 Hz is reduced in intensity when the man is on target, to call attention to the target pitch. The tone ranges between 1500 Hz and 500 Hz. The horizontal dimension of the compensatory tracking task is presented visually on a CRT. Another 16 soldiers track with the corresponding 2 dimensional visual display.

The audiovisual display gives less than half the time on target given by the 2 dimensional visual display. Unfortunately the visual display has an added advantage in that the 2 dimensions are better integrated than are the 2 dimensions of the audiovisual display.

Pitch and beating of 2 tones

Instead of tracking by pitch alone, it is easier to track using also the clearly audible beats which occur when 2 tones of slightly different pitch are presented simultaneously to the same ear. A beating sound is rather like an interrupted sound. Unfortunately the audible beats do not indicate the direction of the error.

The difficulty of direction is similar to the difficulty of direction in tracking a single sine wave of high frequency using a visual display, which is discussed in Chapter 8. The man can tell that his response does not synchronize with the track, but he cannot tell whether his response frequency is too high or too low. With the auditory display, the direction of the error can be determined from the direction of the difference in pitch. But this is not an easy discrimination to make.

Milnes-Walker (1971) uses both pursuit and compensatory displays. Two tones are centered on 900 Hz, and range between 750 and 1050 Hz. The target zone extends 15 Hz on either side of 900 Hz. With the pursuit display, the varying pitch of the track tone has to be matched by the pitch of the response tone. With the compensatory display, the pitch of a reference tone remains constant. The pitch of the error tone has to be kept matched to it, by nulling the disturbances of pitch fed in by the track. The 8 men use a rotary position control. With both displays the 2 tones are fed either to both ears or 1 tone to each ear.

The average times on target are reliably longer when both tones are presented to both ears, than when the 2 tones are presented to separate ears. This is because clearly audible beats occur only when both tones are presented to the same ear or ears. It is easier to match the pitches of the 2 tones using beats, than it is to match the pitches of a tone in each ear without the aid of beats.

Pursuit and compensatory displays of auditory pitch

Milnes-Walker (1971) also reports that the pursuit display gives reliably less time on target than the compensatory display, both with and without the aid of beats. This is because with the pursuit display the man has to match a varying pitch. It is a relatively difficult task. Whereas with the compensatory display the man has simply to hold constant the pitch of the error tone.

Many people can maintain a constant pitch without a reference tone. It is done when singing in tune unaccompanied, and when playing a solo in tune on a reed instrument like an oboe. Harris, Pikler and Murphy (1963, Experiment 1) report that all their 5 practiced people can compensate pretty well for changes in pitch for up to 6 min without a reference tone.

Maintaining a constant musical interval

In the same paper Harris, Pikler, and Murphy (1963, Experiment 2) describe an experiment with tones centered on 256 and 323 Hz (middle C and middle E). Their 5 practiced people have to try to maintain the constant musical interval, against slow variations introduced by a track containing intermittent slow ramps. The task is almost impossible for 3 of the 5 people when using the pursuit display, with the track tone varying in pitch. It is possible for all 5 people when using the compensatory display. But all 5 people perform better in Experiment 1, where there is no reference tone.

Pitch and rate of interruption of sound

Figure 14.1 (Ellis, Burrows, & Jackson, 1953) illustrates what is probably one of the best auditory displays for indicating error in the vertical dimension. The direction of the error, up or down, is indicated respectively by frequencies of 2300 and 170 Hz. The size of the error is indicated by the rate of interruption of the sound. This is probably more effective than using a continuous change in pitch to indicate both the direction and size of the error, as Goldman (1959) does.

Rises and falls in pitch are not very compatible with up and down control movements. A display which uses changes in the direction of a sound between right and left, paired with right and left control movements, is a more compatible arrangement. But Ellis and his colleagues (1953) wanted an auditory display to indicate airspeed. An increase in pitch is fairly easily related to an increase in airspeed, while a change in the direction of a sound from left to right is not.

The display of Figure 14.1 bears a resemblence to the visual display of rate and brightness of flash, which is used subsequently by Ziegler and colleagues (1966) and is discussed in Chapter 13. It has a similar weakness in the method of indicating the direction of the error.

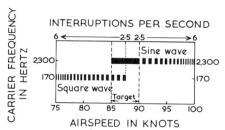

Figure 14.1. An audio airspeed indicator.

The target airspeed of between 85 and 90 knots is shown on the lower abscissa. The conventional airspeed indicator has a needle moving over a circular dial. There are no target markings. It is placed 28 in from the pilot's eyes at a visual angle of about 30° below and to the left of the distant display. The airspeed is perturbed irregularly at a top frequency of about 4 cpm. The task which represents maintaining the correct approach angle, has a top track frequency of about 2 cpm. The man has separate position controls for the 2 tasks, which he operates with separate hands. (After W. H. B. Ellis and colleagues, 1953, Figure 2.)

Ellis and his colleagues (1953) use the display of Figure 14.1 in a simple simulation of the pilot's task in approaching to land on the deck of an aircraft carrier without an automatic throttle control. Aircraft cannot be flown very slowly without stalling. Yet too fast a speed on landing may damage the aircraft. So the pilot has to watch his airspeed, as well as looking to see that he is on the correct approach path. To represent staying at the correct approach angle, the pilot has to track in the vertical dimension using a compensatory visual display placed 9 ft away. He has also to maintain his simulated airspeed within a target region of 5 knots.

In the reference condition the pilot has a conventional airspeed instrument. The instrument is mounted in the same relative position as it is in the cockpit of aircraft operating from carriers. In an experimental condition the pilot uses the audio airspeed indication illustrated in the figure. When the airspeed is within the correct range, between 85 and 90 knots, the pure high pitched tone is continuous. Between 85 and 87.5 knots the pilot hears also the interrupted rough low pitched tone. It tells him that his airspeed is a little below the center of the correct range.

Both 24 pilots and 24 nonpilots carry out the combined tracking task reliably more accurately with the audio airspeed indicator. With the conventional airspeed instrument mounted in the cockpit, the man has to look alternately at the distant display and at the near display. Each time he looks at the other display, he has to change the accommodation of his eyes. He cannot look at the 2 displays in turn more often than about once every 2 sec (Ellis & Allen, 1954). With the auditory display the man can sample the 2 displays more often than this. As a result, he is able to track more accurately on the combined task.

There are a number of visual methods which can be used to display airspeed, without requiring the pilot to change the accommodation of his eyes. They are discussed in Chapter 13. Unfortunately there have been no experimental comparisons between the display of Figure 14.1 and the best visual displays. Ellis and his colleagues (1953) include a 5 state visual display in their experiment. But the display presents less information on the size of errors than does the display of Figure 14.1 (see Chapter 12). As a result, it is reliably less good.

Integrated auditory displays

A man does not sample a number of auditory displays in turn as adequately as he samples the corresponding number of visual displays. In his first investigation of the possible use of auditory displays in flying, Forbes (1946) has 3 separate auditory signals. The most successful combination of signals is as follows (Forbes, personal communication). A turn of the aircraft to the right is indicated by a tone in the right ear. A turn to the left is indicated by a tone in the left ear. Rate of turn is indicated by the rate of interruption of the tone.

A roll to the right is indicated by the pitch of a second tone. The pitch in the left ear is high, to indicate that the left wing is raised. The tone falls in pitch as it moves to the right ear, to indicate that the right wing is lowered. The size of the change in pitch indicates the steepness of the roll.

The airspeed is indicated by the rate of interruption of a third tone. The 3 tones are mixed and presented to the man.

In tracking with the 3 auditory displays, the man tends to respond to only 1 display, and to neglect the others. This can happen even when the man has only 2 of the auditory displays to respond to, instead of all 3. Probably the man finds so much difficulty in tracking with 1 of the auditory displays, that little or no time is available for tracking with the others.

The difficulty can be reduced by using an integrated auditory display. In Forbes' (1946) integrated auditory display, an apparent sweeping motion of a tone from the left ear to the right ear indicates a turn to the right. The apparent motion is produced by starting with the tone loud in the left ear, and ending with it loud in the right ear. The apparent motion from left to right is then repeated. The rate of repetition is faster when the angle of turn is greater.

The angle of roll of the simulated aircraft is indicated by variations in pitch. The tone which produces the apparent sweeping motion changes in pitch as it changes ears. A lower pitch in the right ear indicates that the simulated aircraft is rolling to the right. The difference in pitch is greater when the angle of roll is greater.

The airspeed of the simulated aircraft is indicated by the rate of interruption of the signal. It produces a low pitch "putt" sound, something like the sound of a piston engine. When the airspeed is too great, the rate of interruption is faster. A standard comparison rate is alternated with the rate which indicates the airspeed. The standard rate lasts about .5 sec. The rate which indicates the airspeed lasts about 1 sec. All 3 indications, of heading, of angle of roll, and of airspeed, are produced by changes in the same single tone signal.

The experiment uses 10 young men who are unfamiliar with aircraft and simulators. They first learn to fly the simulated aircraft using the 3 conventional visual instruments showing heading, roll angle, and air speed. They then learn to fly a respectably straight course in rough air using the integrated auditory display. This takes a couple of hours of practice. Performance with the auditory and with the visual displays is said to correspond quite well.

However Forbes (1946, Figures 2 and 3) shows records from a person whom he selects as representative of the better performers. All 8 records of courses flown with the auditory display vary in height during the first 10 min more than any of the 7 records of courses flown with the conventional visual instruments. Thus for the man whose records are shown, performance with the 3 conventional instruments is reliably better than performance with the integrated auditory display.

Unfortunately it is not possible to tell how much of the advantage of the integrated auditory display over 3 separate auditory displays is due to greater practice with the integrated auditory display, and perhaps to practice with some of the prototype auditory displays. The unpracticed man is likely to find a single auditory display so difficult that he has little time available for tracking with more than one of them. This is probably true also of a single dimension of the integrated auditory display. Final performance with the integrated auditory display may be better partly because the man has had more practice. He can therefore deal more adequately with 2, or perhaps all 3, dimensions. No mention is made of the amount of practice devoted to the separate auditory displays.

Forbes' (1946) comparison between the integrated auditory display and the 3 visual displays is not fair to visual methods of presentation. The auditory display uses a single integrated representation of 3 dimensions of variation of the aircraft. The corresponding visual display uses

3 separate instruments. Performance might be a good deal better with an integrated visual display like the headup display of Figure 9.2, with an airspeed indicator shown directly above it. However Forbes does not intend to make a comparative evaluation of auditory and visual methods of displaying information. He is concerned only to show that flying with an integrated auditory display is feasible.

The integrated auditory display of Figure 14.2

About 20 years later Katz and his colleagues (1966, Experiment 2) test another integrated auditory display. The display again uses changes in side to side localization, in pitch, and in the rate of repetition, but in a different way from Forbes' (1946) display. This time a louder sound in the right ear than in the left ear tells the pilot to roll his aircraft to the right. The difference in loudness between the 2 ears indicates the size of the error in roll.

Figure 14.2 shows how the 2 remaining auditory dimensions are integrated. A rapid fall in pitch of the carrier frequency of 2000 Hz tells the pilot to reduce the normal acceleration. A larger fall in pitch calls for a larger change in normal acceleration. The swoop in pitch is illus-

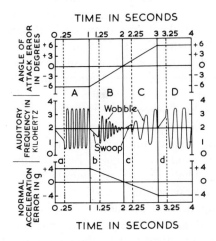

Figure 14.2. An integrated auditory display.
The swoop and wobble signals are modifications of an earlier auditory display used by Abbott and Woodbury (1965, Figure 8). For all 8 pilots used in the experiment, side to side auditory localization indicates the correct angle of roll. For 4 pilots wobble and swoop are related respectively to the correct angle of attack and to the correct normal acceleration, as illustrated in the figure. For the remaining 4 pilots swoop indicates the correct angle of attack while wobble indicates the correct normal acceleration. (Modified from Katz and colleagues, 1966, Figure B3.)

trated in the middle row of the figure at **a, b, c** and **d**. It lasts .25 sec each time. The error in the normal acceleration is illustrated at the bottom of the figure.

Swoop alternates with a sine wave modulation of the carrier frequency which lasts .75 sec. A modulation at 11 Hz tells the pilot to raise the nose of his aircraft. A modulation at 4 Hz tells the pilot to lower the nose. A modulation of larger amplitude calls for a larger change in the angle of attack of the aircraft. The modulation or wobble signal is illustrated in the middle row of the figure at **A, B, C** and **D**. The error in the attitude of the aircraft is illustrated at the top of the figure. The wobble signal is more or less an auditory analog of the brightness of flash signal used by Ziegler and colleagues (1966), which is described in Chapter 13.

Katz and his colleagues (1966) compare control of the simulated aircraft using the 3 auditory dimensions with control using 3 separate visual pursuit displays. The 3 visual pursuit displays show respectively the roll angle and the required roll angle, the normal acceleration and the required acceleration, the angle of attack and the required angle of attack. In addition to controlling the simulated aircraft, the pilot has to respond to the digits 1, 2, 3 and 4 when he hears them, by moving a switch to 1 of 4 corresponding positions with his left hand.

Tracking with the full integrated auditory display is reliably less accurate than tracking with the 3 visual displays, both in roll error and in angle of attack. The only reliable advantage of the integrated auditory display is on the auditory messages. Unfortunately the criterion of performance on the messages is not described.

The experiments by Forbes (1946), and by Katz and his colleagues (1966), show that after practice people can fly a simulator using an integrated auditory display for certain flight parameters, provided the auditory display is carefully designed. But tracking with an integrated auditory display is likely to be less accurate than tracking with a well designed integrated visual display.

The principal application of auditory displays is when a man needs to be able to monitor 2 displays simultaneously which are at different distances. An auditory display may then be a practical alternative to a supplementing visual display, although suitable auditory and visual displays have not yet been compared.

Correlated audiovisual tracks

When tracking with a conventional visual display, an auditory signal which is perfectly correlated with the track may improve the timing of the man's response. This is suggested by some results of Benepe, Narasimhan and Ellson (1954, Experiment 4).

The experimenters use a conventional pursuit display. The track is a sine wave of 20 cpm. The man has a position control system. The auditory signal varies in frequency between 900 and 1100 Hz. A group of 22 undergraduates have the synchronized audiovisual track. A control group of 22 undergraduates have the visual track and an auditory distraction. They hear a similar tone to the experimental group, but modulated at a frequency of 15 cpm.

The synchronized audiovisual track gives a reliably smaller mean square error than the visual track with the auditory distraction. The tracking error on the last day is analyzed by frequency. The amplitudes of the error in the control condition are similar to the amplitudes which are reported in comparable experiments in the same paper (Benepe and others, 1954, Experiments 1, 2 and 3) when there is no auditory signal. The amplitudes resemble fairly closely the error amplitudes in Figure 8.10 for a frequency of 30 cpm. In contrast, with the synchronized audiovisual track the error amplitudes are so small that they can hardly be detected. The undergraduates are able to program their movements so accurately that they do not need to make the usual corrections.

More recently Pitkin and Vinje (1973) report that with a compensatory display, audiovisual tracking is more successful than visual tracking. They use an unstable control system which gradually becomes more and more unstable. Their 4 men can all maintain control with a more unstable control system when they use the synchronized audiovisual display of error, than when they use the visual display alone.

Correlated audiovisual step tracks

Step tracking also can benefit from an auditory signal correlated with the track. McGee and Christ (1971) use a repeating sequence of 8 steps between 4 positions on a CRT. Each position appears twice in the repeating sequence. Steps in the track occur regularly every .8 sec. The experimental apparatus is that used by Noble and Trumbo (1967) and described in the caption of Figure 6.4.

In the tone condition, the auditory signals are perfectly correlated with the visual steps. The 4 positions from left to right on the CRT are represented by tones of 300, 690, 1590 and 3650 Hz respectively. A step by the track to 1 of the 4 positions on the CRT is accompanied by a .04 sec burst of the tone of the corresponding frequency.

In a noise condition the auditory and visual track signals are correlated only in timing. A burst of white noise is substituted for the tones. It is of equal loudness to the tones, but does not vary with the position on the CRT. There is a reference condition with the visual display only. A separate group of 12 people serve in each condition.

Both the audiovisual conditions give reliably smaller modulus mean errors than the reference visual condition. They do so by improving the timing of the man's responses. The man tends to initiate his response before the step in the track appears, so that the start of his response more or less coincides with the appearance of the step. If anything, the tone condition gives the smallest modulus mean error.

The noise condition produces first responses with reliably less accurate amplitudes than do the other 2 conditions. This is because the noise burst is the same for all step positions. It produces a kind of inappropriate generalization. If the man concentrates too hard on the noise which tells him when to respond, he can forget which part of the sequence he is in, and move to the wrong position by mistake.

This is less likely to happen in the other 2 conditions. In the tone condition, the tones provide the man with a running auditory memory of where he is in the sequence. In the reference visual condition, there is no auditory signal to distract him.

Adams and Chambers (1962) report a rather similar finding in 2 handed step tracking. Their 16 men respond to a 3 state visual signal with 1 hand, and to a 3 state auditory signal with the other hand. The 3 state controls have to be moved only 1 step at a time. When a control is in the central position, the next signal is uncertain. It may call for a movement in either direction. But when the control is in either extreme position, the next signal is certain. It calls always for a return to the central position. Visual and auditory signals occur simultaneously every 2 sec. The certain visual and auditory signals always occur together. So do the uncertain visual and auditory signals.

Usually the average response time to a visual signal is reliably longer than the average response time to an auditory signal. But when a certain visual signal calling for a return to the center synchronizes with a certain auditory signal, the man tends to respond with both hands simultaneously. This reliably reduces the response time to the visual signal. The average response time to the certain visual signal is .1 sec. It is almost as short as the average response time of .09 sec to a certain auditory signal when performing only the auditory task. Both values are about half the average response time to a visual or auditory signal when the man waits for the signal before he responds.

The 4 experiments indicate that in certain circumstances a man's timing can be improved by using as a track a perfectly correlated audiovisual signal. This is a promising line for future research.

There is of course no advantage in using auditory and visual signals which are not perfectly correlated. The man then has 2 different tracking tasks to perform simultaneously. The top 2 entries in part B of Table 12.7 show that the additional task reliably degrades the man's tracking performance, unless it is perfectly correlated with the main task.

Vibration on the skin

Success in tracking with cutaneous displays is probably about as great as success in tracking with the corresponding auditory displays. Both cutaneous and auditory displays have been compared with the impoverished but directly comparable visual displays. After practice with the less familiar cutaneous or auditory display, tracking may be almost as accurate as with the visual display. But visual tracking with a conventional CRT is far more accurate.

Apparent movement over the skin

Geldard (1960, page 1586) describes an experiment by R. C. Bice which uses directly comparable cutaneous and visual displays. Three vibrators are strapped in a horizontal line to the chest of each of 10 men. The direction in which to turn a steering wheel is signaled by the order in which the vibrators are activated. When the order of activation is from left to right, the man has to steer to the right. The apparent movement across the skin corresponds to the apparent movement between the 2 ears which is used by Forbes (1946) in his integrated auditory display.

The distance to turn the steering wheel is signaled by the rate of repetition of the apparent movement between 30 and 60 repetitions per min. The fastest repetition rate calls for a turn of the steering wheel of 90°. When the man is on target there is no signal. The relationship between the rate of repetition and the size of the error is not a very compatible one. Distance on the skin might be a better dimension for the size of the error.

A separate group of 10 men tracks with the corresponding visual display. It comprises 3 lamps in a row. The direction of the required control movement is signaled by the direction of streaming of the 3 lamps, as with the streaming display which yields the results in Figure 13.1. The size of the required control movement is signaled by the rate of repetition of the streaming. This is by no means the optimal visual display for tracking, but it is directly comparable to the cutaneous display.

After 80 min of practice, tracking is about as accurate with the display of 3 vibrators as it is with the display of 3 lamps. The experiment suggests that there need not be much difference between visual and cutaneous displays after practice, provided both displays are simple and directly comparable.

Direction and amplitude of vibration on the skin

Hahn (1965) describes a different method of indicating the direction and size of the error. To signal the direction of the error he straps on 2 vibrators, 1 to each side of the man's chest. The size of the error is indicated by the amplitude of the vibration. A CRT provides the conventional compensatory visual display which Hahn uses for comparison. Separate groups of 5 men undergraduates track with each display.

The average modulus mean error with the vibrators is 2.5 times larger than the average error with the CRT. This is to be expected. The CRT shows the size of the error coded as a distance. The man can see at once how far he is off target, and make a control movement of the appropriate size.

The cutaneous display is a good deal less compatible with the size of the control movement. The man has to assess the amplitude of the vibration, and recode it as a size of movement. The visual display which is directly comparable to Hahn's 2 vibrators comprises 2 lamps, with the size of the error coded by brightness of flash. Unfortunately Hahn does not compare this flashing display with his vibrating display.

Tracking in 2 dimensions on the skin

Simultaneous tracking in 2 spatial dimensions at right angles to each other has not yet been achieved on the skin, despite the skin's extension in 2 dimensions. Hahn (1965) describes a 2 dimensional compensatory display used by L. B. Durr. It is constructed by attaching 5 vibrators to the man's chest. This time the size of the error is indicated by the rate of vibration, not by the amplitude of vibration.

It is necessary to present the error information in 1 dimension at a time, because 2 vibrators which start to vibrate simultaneously feel no different to a single vibrator (Hahn, 1965). If 1 vibrator comes on just before the other, apparent movement is felt from the position of the first vibrator to the position of the second vibrator (Geldard, 1960, page 1584).

Hahn (1965) reports that the error with the 2 dimension vibratory display is about 4 times as large as the error with a conventional compensatory display on a CRT. It makes little difference whether the vibrators indicate only the direction of the error, or indicate also its size by the rate of vibration. A 2 dimension cutaneous display of direction is as much as a man can manage. Adding rate of vibration to indicate the size of the error overloads his cutaneous sensory capacity.

Electric shock on the skin

The direction and intensity of electric shock on the skin is probably about as effective as the direction and amplitude of vibration, although no tracking experiments have been published comparing the 2 sensory dimensions. Hofmann and Heimstra (1972) compare the direction and intensity of electric shock with analogous auditory and visual displays. As in an experiment by Schori (1970), the mild electric shocks are presented through 2 electrodes, 1 on each side of the neck. The positions of the electrodes are adjusted until the man can feel shocks of about equal magnitude on both sides, without them being painful. Stimulation is by .5 millisec square wave DC pulses at a rate of 20 per sec. The intensity varies between 2.2 and 3.4 milliamp. when the man is off target. There is no stimulation when the man is in a target area of a size 10% of the maximum track amplitude.

In the analogous auditory display, white noise is presented to one ear or the other by earphones. The intensity varies between about 54 and 103 dB.

For the visual display, direction is indicated by the eye stimulated. This is not a good indicator of direction, because both eyes normally accept information from both sides of the visual field. The intensity of the light varies from about 10 microlamberts to 1.0 lambert, or from about 50 to 100 dB re the threshold of seeing at 10^{-10} lambert (Hofmann, Personal Communication).

The track is irregular, with 4 reversals per min. The position control is a steering wheel. A separate group of 10 undergraduates tracks with each display. Four measures of performance are used: the standard deviation of the error (see Figure 3.6) which Hofmann and Heimstra call RMS error, the modulus mean error which they call average error, the constant position error, and time on target.

On 3 of the 4 measures the electrocutaneous display is worse than the auditory display. Of the 2 reliable differences, time on target favors the electrocutaneous display, while constant position error favors the auditory display. On this evidence, there is little to choose between the electrocutaneous and auditory displays. But the authors note that responses are more rapid with the auditory display.

The visual display is the worst on 3 of the 4 measures of performance. This is because there is no adequate indication of the direction of the error. With proper information on direction, the visual display would

presumably be at least as good as both the electrocutaneous display
and the auditory display.

Felt acceleration and tilt

When a man rides in the vehicle which he controls, he can feel its
accelerations and its tilts. Provided the movement is not excessive, the
man can use the cues which the movement provides to track more efficiently. He may even be able to track without vision, using only the
changes in acceleration and tilt which he feels.

Figure 14.3 (Meiry, 1965) illustrates an experiment in which 3 experienced trackers have to control the roll of a simulated aircraft cockpit.

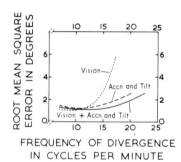

FREQUENCY OF DIVERGENCE
IN CYCLES PER MINUTE

Figure 14.3.   Performance with felt acceleration and tilt.

The frequency of divergence on the abscissa indicates the instability of the aircraft,
as in Figure 4.3. The control system is of the form $2\omega^2/(S^2 - \omega^2)$, where ω is
the frequency of divergence, and S^2 in the denominator indicates that the control
system is of second order. Undamped divergent frequencies of 7, 10, 14, 17, 20
and 23 cpm are used in different trials.

For the condition with only cues of felt acceleration and tilt, the man sits in
the dark. He is strapped to his seat. His head is fixed so that he cannot move
it. For the condition which combines movement and vision, the man is again strapped
in the cockpit. But he is in the light, and can see the walls of the laboratory
through the windscreen. Crossed horizontal and vertical reference lines are fixed
to the wall of the laboratory directly in front of him at a distance of 10 ft.
When the control is visual, the man sits behind the simulated cockpit at a distance
of 10 ft. A horizontal line on the back of the cockpit helps him to judge the
tilt.

The man uses a light spring centered control stick. There is no track. The more
stable control systems are presented before the less stable. The figure shows the
curves fitted to the average points by the method of least squares. With vision
alone, control is not possible when the frequency of divergence is 20 cpm or
greater. Unfortunately with only 3 people in the experiment, it is not possible
to tell how representative the results are likely to be. (After Meiry, 1965, Figure
7.7.)

In a blind condition represented by the broken line, the man has only the cues of acceleration and tilt felt while sitting in the cockpit. In the condition represented by the unbroken line, the man can both feel and see the roll of the cockpit. The dotted line represents a condition in which the roll can only be seen. The simulator has the characteristics of an undamped inverted pendulum.

The more stable control systems are represented by the low frequencies of divergence on the left of the figure. Here there is little difference between the 3 conditions. Probably with these low frequencies of divergence the cockpit rolls sufficiently slowly for the man to be able to see the movement at about the time that the acceleration is large enough to feel.

The less stable control systems are represented by the higher frequencies of divergence on the right of the figure. Here the pure visual condition is by far the worst. The man is unable to control the simulator with frequencies of divergence of 20 cpm and above.

The condition which combines visual cues with feelings of acceleration and tilt gives the smallest average error. In order to control the unstable system, the man needs to know the direction in which it is accelerating. When he is strapped in the cockpit, the vestibular senses in his head tell him this. He has, as it were, an acceleration augmented display (see Chapter 10). Thus he is able to control the accelerations before they become too large.

The broken line indicates that the man can control the attitude of the simulator using the felt acceleration and tilt alone. An acceleration stimulates the vestibular sense organs in his head. A tilt changes the distribution of pressure on him from his seat, and from the harness which straps him to the seat. He can correct for this at the same time as he is controlling the acceleration of the cockpit.

However the unbroken line indicates that tracking is carried out more accurately when the man can use his eyes as well as the feelings of acceleration and tilt. Feelings of acceleration and tilt alone do not give the most accurate tracking at any frequency of divergence.

Meiry (1965, Chapter 6) describes 2 experiments in which the man is not able to control the movement of a simulator without vision. In one experiment a simulator rotates about a vertical axis running through the man's head. This corresponds to an aircraft turning in yaw.

In the other experiment the man has to control a simulator which moves forward and backward along a horizontal track. Without vision, the man can control the accelerations of the simulator in both experiments. But the simulator tends to drift off target at a more or less constant rate.

The difference between these 2 experiments and the experiment of Figure 14.3 is in the plane of motion. In the experiment of Figure 14.3 movements of the simulator change the direction of gravity acting on the man. The man can feel the tilt, and so is able to keep the simulator more or less vertical all the time without vision.

The other 2 experiments involve respectively horizontal rotation and translation. The movements of the simulator do not change the direction of gravity acting on the man. Thus the man cannot hold the simulator more or less stationary without vision. A similar problem faces the astronaut in a space vehicle when he is not subjected to gravity. He cannot maintain a constant orientation in any plane without the help of vision.

A number of other experiments compare control of a simulated unstable aircraft or helicopter with and without cues of acceleration and tilt. Skilled pilots are used to the additional cues. They track more accurately with them, provided the cues are congruent (Guercio and Wall, 1972). Perhaps this is because they do not get sufficient practice at tracking without cues of acceleration and tilt. Nonpilots often track better without the additional cues (L. R. Young, 1967), perhaps because they do not get sufficient practice at tracking with them. The effect of practice with cues of acceleration and tilt needs to be investigated.

The cues of motion obtained from a moving simulator are rather different from the cues obtained in flight. When an aircraft starts to roll, the pilot feels the rotary acceleration. But with a constant roll, the pilot does not always feel the tilt. The angular acceleration of the aircraft may produce a force on the pilot which makes him feel that he is sitting upright in a vertical cockpit. He may be aware of the roll of the aircraft only when he sees that the horizon is not horizontal, as in Figure 9.2. The disappearance of the feeling of tilt can be simulated by a cockpit which gradually returns to the horizontal when the simulated aircraft has a constant acceleration. The effects of this washout motion have yet to be compared with the effects of conventional simulator movement, using similar groups of people for the 2 conditions (Ince, Williges and Roscoe, 1973).

Cues of acceleration and tilt can be a help in aiming a sight at a weaving aircraft. Smith, Garfinkle, Groth and Lyman (1966a) provide cues of acceleration by letting each of the 6 undergraduates ride on the mount as the sight rotates in a horizontal plane. The man tilts his head as he aims the sight in the vertical dimension.

In the reference condition without cues of acceleration and tilt, the man sits in an isolation booth and uses a television monitor. Table 11.2 suggests that use of a television monitor need not degrade tracking performance very much. Thus most of the advantage of riding on the mount is probably due to the cues of acceleration and tilt.

Th acceleration of the man must not be too large, because a large acceleration adversely affects human performance (Poulton, 1970). Sadoff (1962) presents 2 pilots with sudden failures of the stability augmentation system of a simulated aircraft. The nose of the simulated aircraft suddenly starts to oscillate up and down at a frequency of 75 cpm.

When the pilot tracks with cues of acceleration, he is suddenly vibrated at this frequency. The vibration indicates to the pilot that there has been a failure. But it hinders him in his efforts to adapt to the failure. The advantage of the sensory cues is counterbalanced by the disadvantage of the buffeting. The experiment is discussed at the end of Chapter 17.

Forced response guidance

In learning to track with a pursuit display, a few guided trials early in training sometimes produce as good a final performance as an equal number of practice trials (Holding, 1959; Macrae & Holding, 1966). But forced response guidance is never better than active practice. In these experiments the man holds lightly a rotary position control. The control carries out the movements which are required to keep a response marker in line with a track marker.

In one experiment (Holding, 1959) the tracks comprise 21 short constant velocity ramps separated by stationary periods of about .6 sec. In the other experiment (Macrae & Holding, 1966) the tracks consist of one or more sine waves with top frequencies of 40 or 60 cpm. In the guided trials the man both feels the control movements and sees their outcome, without actually initiating the movements himself.

Guidance is less effective if the man watches the display without holding the control. It is less effective still if the man holds the control without looking at the display (Holding, 1959). This last condition is probably equivalent to tracking with a stationary error marker on a compensatory display. To benefit most from guidance, the man has to be able to see and to feel at the same time, so that he can learn to relate what he sees to what he feels. It is not yet known whether forced response guidance is effective with rate or acceleration control systems.

Recommended nonvisual displays

An auditory or cutaneous display should not be used for tracking if it is possible to use a conventional visual display in central vision.

When an auditory display is required, changes in side to side direction should be used to indicate the direction of the error. Changes in rate of interruption or intensity should be used to indicate the size of the error. These combinations are probably preferable to changes in pitch.

Auditory and cutaneous tracking displays should be compensatory.

Pilots learning to control a simulated unstable vehicle should be given cues of acceleration and tilt, although large accelerations should be avoided.

Forced response guidance should not be used as a substitute for active practice until more research has been carried out on it.

Chapter

15

Controls

Summary

A stylus is quicker to use than a joystick. A joystick is quicker than a joyball, and better than 2 separate controls when the tasks in the 2 dimensions are similar.

Controls are easier to use when their movements are compatible with the corresponding display movements. A hand operated joystick is better than a thumb joystick, which is better than a joystick operated by the forearm. The eye acquires targets more quickly than the hand, but there are disadvantages in control by eye.

The best control loading is spring centering. A pressure control has no travel time, but fine adjustments are less accurate than with a moving control. Friction, inertia, backlash, and appreciable deadspace, all reduce the accuracy of tracking. The man tracks better when he can feel the resistance in the control system which has to be overcome.

Kinds of control variation

Available controls

In drawing on a computer display, a person may use a stylus or light pen which he holds like a pencil. A light pen is also used in tracking targets on a radar screen. A joystick or joyball may be used instead of a light pen. A joystick is used to control the attitude of an aircraft. Some of the early rockets were controlled by a thumb joystick. Now a hand joystick is becoming more common. For tracking in one dimension, a joystick becomes a lever. Automobiles and ships have a wheel for steering.

Cranks and handwheels were commonly used at the start of World War II. In aiming a searchlight using a crank, the man himself supplies the power. Gearwheels are placed between the man's control and the searchlight to reduce the amount of force which is needed to move the searchlight. The man rotates the crank or handwheel a number of times in order to turn the searchlight through a few degrees. Power controls are now often used instead of cranks and handwheels.

Compatible controls

When a control is moved, it may produce a compatible movement of the corresponding display marker, as if there is a simple mechanical link between them. Examples are given in Figure 11.16. An example of a less compatible relationship between control and display is depressing the gas pedal of an automobile in order to move the needle of the speedometer round its circular scale.

An astronaut may have to steer his space vehicle while he is being subjected to a large acceleration. He can do this more easily if he has a portable control resting in his lap than if he has to reach for a control fixed to the equipment. A portable control can be held in a compatible or incompatible position. There is no fixed relationship between the direction of control movement and display movement.

Control by muscle action potentials

Electrical potentials can be picked up from the muscles and used to operate a control system directly. Most of the experimental work using muscle action potentials is carried out for the designers of artificial limbs. The aim is to enable a disabled person to control his artificial limb. He either contracts the remnants of his limb muscles, or he contracts muscles which he does not normally make much use of, such as the muscles of his neck or back.

Control by eye

The eye can be used to provide electrical inputs to a control system. The methods are used to study people's eye movements while looking at moving scenes and pictures. The methods do not appear to be used much to compare the efficiency of tracking by eye with manual tracking.

It is surprisingly difficult to obtain an invariant linear relationship between the angle moved by the eye and the output obtained from the eye. There are 2 other disadvantages of control by eye. One disadvantage is that the man's head has to be held still if the output from the eye is to be used directly. Otherwise the movements of the eye are not proportional to the movements of the target which the eye is tracking. To equate eye movements with target movements, it is necessary to correct for head movements. There are ways of doing this, but they complicate the equipment.

The other disadvantage of control by eye is that it is not feasible in an unsteady vehicle, whether on land, at sea, or in the air. This is because the accelerations of the vehicle stimulate the vestibular sense organs in the man's head. This produces eye movements which the man is unable to prevent (Poulton, 1970, Chapter 16). It is probable that these disadvantages are responsible for the small amount of experimental work which has been carried out on control by eye.

Control loading

Every control offers some resistance to being moved. A pressure control is a spring centered control which hardly moves. Friction in a control delays its movement when a man first exerts force upon the control. Friction also introduces a delay when a man reverses the direction of the force which he exerts upon the control. The delays introduced by friction resemble the delays introduced by backlash and by deadspace in a control.

In a tracking task like aiming a long telescope, some viscous damping and inertia necessarily result from the physical characteristics of the telescope and its mount. In controlling a light aircraft, the rudder and flaps resist movement. So do the front wheels in steering an automobile. Where the forces involved are not too great, the design engineer has 2 possible courses of action. He can let the man exert the forces which are necessary, or he can introduce a power operated control system.

In tracking with the power operated control system, the man does not himself feel the resistances which have to be overcome. Whereas when the man has to provide the power, he can feel the resistances. Engineering practice is moving in the direction of power operated control systems and power steering, which take away the man's feel.

Stylus versus joystick

A stylus or light pen is held and used like a pencil. The person puts the tip of the stylus on top of the marker which he is tracking, and moves it as he would a pencil. This gives the stylus a considerable advantage over a joystick when it is used as a position control with a pursuit display.

A joystick may be located close to the display, but it does not touch a display marker. Also a joystick several inches long calls for different control movements from the movements which are used in drawing and writing. It seems likely from results which are available that changing from a hand joystick to a stylus would about halve the error in tracking irregular sine waves of fairly high frequency with a position control system. But a direct experimental comparison has still to be made.

Hick and Fraser (1948) compare a kind of stylus with a kind of joystick in step tracking. Unfortunately neither control is used in the conventional way. Both controls remain vertical; they cannot be tilted. The controls have to be moved over a sheet of paper which lies on a table to the right of the display. The lower ends of the controls are connected mechanically to a device which moves the response marker.

The stylus is held between the fingers like a pencil. The joystick is grasped in the closed fist. Its lower end is not anchored as it is with a conventional joystick. With both controls the ratio of control movement to display movement is about 1 to 1. Five enlisted men have to track with the stylus, 4 with the joystick.

After practice the men average 1.3 sec per plot with the stylus, 1.7 sec with the joystick. The difference is reliable statistically. If anything positioning is slightly more accurate when using the stylus, but the difference is small and unreliable.

The advantage of the stylus should be greater if it is moved directly over the display like a light pen. For its tip then remains in contact with the response marker. This is not possible when the relationship between the display and control is less compatible, for example when the display is compensatory, or the control system is of high order. Here the tip of the stylus does not remain superimposed upon the marker which it controls.

The stylus or the man's hand may then obscure his vision of the marker. To prevent this, the stylus can be made to move over a separate response area at the side, as in Hick and Fraser's (1948) experiment. A stylus and joystick have not yet been compared using control systems other than position.

Joystick versus joyball

Figure 15.1 (Thornton, 1954) shows that a joystick is quicker to use than a joyball in step tracking with a position control system. A joyball has a diameter of 4 or 5 in. It is usually mounted in a horizontal control panel. Rather less than half the surface area of the ball projects above the surface of the panel through a circular hole.

A joyball rotates in any direction practically without friction. A good push will start it rolling reasonably quickly. It continues to roll until it is stopped. In step tracking it requires 2 responses, 1 to start it rolling and 1 to stop it. Whereas a joystick requires only a single response.

In the experiment of Figure 15.1 the control sensitivities are about optimal both for the joyball (Ellis, 1967) and for the joystick. The unbroken lines for the joystick lie reliably below the broken lines for the joyball. The differences are smaller when the target is not so far off, but they always favor the joystick. This is because the joystick requires only a single response, instead of 2 responses. Thus for acquisition with a position control system, a joystick is quicker than a joyball, although it is slower than a stylus.

Joystick versus 2 controls

When tracking in 2 dimensions it is possible to use a single joystick, or 2 separate controls for the 2 dimensions. Which arrangement to use

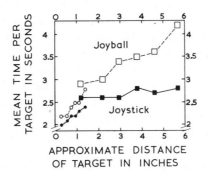

Figure 15.1. Performance with joystick and joyball.
To move the response marker 1 in, the joystick has to be rotated through an angle of 10°. The surface of the joyball has to be moved 6.5 in. A target can occupy any 1 of 49 locations in a 7 × 7 matrix in the center of a 12 in CRT. The small matrix represented by the circles in the figure fits into a square with a side of 1.1 in. The large matrix represented by the squares has a side of 4.4 in. The target spots have a diameter of 1 mm. The response marker is a ring with a diameter of about 3 mm.

The man works his way through a series of 25 targets selected irregularly from the matrix of 49 locations. Each time he rings a target, he presses a switch and the next target appears. If the ring does not contain the target spot, an error is recorded automatically. Two people who average more than 10% of errors are excluded. For the remaining 24 enlisted men and women, the errors average 2.6% with the joystick and 2.7% with the joyball. (After Thornton, 1954, Figure 2.)

depends upon whether the 2 dimensions of the task are better kept separate or not. This is illustrated by the results in Table 11.4 (Chernikoff & Le May, 1963).

The upper half of the table represents conditions in which the control system is the same in the 2 dimensions, either position or acceleration. Rows 1 and 3 of the table are for a single joystick. The modulus mean error averages 53 for the 4 conditions. Rows 2 and 4 of the table are for 2 levers. Here the modulus mean error averages 63. The difference of 10 is not large enough to be reliable, but it favors the single joystick.

The result agrees with previous reliable results in favor of a single joystick when used with 2 identical control systems (Clutton-Baker, 1950; Regan, 1959). Clutton-Baker (1950) uses an integrated display with a single error marker, and 2 rate control systems with exponential time lags of .08 sec. Regan's (1959) results are listed at the top of Table 11.3. He also uses an integrated display, and either 2 position control systems or 2 rate control systems.

The lower half of Table 11.4 represents conditions in which a position control system in one dimension is combined with an acceleration control system in the other dimension. Rows 7 and 8 are for the single joystick. The modulus mean error averages 87 for the 4 conditions. Rows 5 and 6 of the table are for the 2 levers. Here the modulus mean error averages 71, a difference of 16. Again the difference is not large enough to be reliable. But this time it favors the 2 levers.

In the analysis of variance the interaction between same or different dynamics, and 1 joystick or 2 levers, is reliable. The difficulty with the single joystick is that there is a certain amount of crosscoupling (see Chapter 17) between the 2 dimensions. The man makes responses in each dimension which are partly appropriate to the other control system.

Separate controls are also preferable when 2 compensatory displays are well separated, and the amplitudes of the tracks are very different. In the experiment which demonstrates this, Levison and his colleagues (1971, Table D-11) use 2 of the compensatory displays illustrated in Figure 12.3. The pilot looks all the time at one display. The second tracking display is at an angle of 16° to his line of sight. The RMS amplitude of the track of the peripheral display is rather less than half the amplitude of the track of the fixated display. The rate control system is the same for both displays.

When the 4 pilots have a separate control for each display, the RMS errors average .67 for the central display and .65 for the peripheral display. When a single joystick is used, the average errors increase reliably to .75 and .70 respectively. Presumably with the 2 controls the pilot makes response movements of sizes appropriate to the 2 different track amplitudes. Whereas with the single control he tends to make movements of intermediate size to both tracks.

It follows that for tracking in 2 dimensions, a single joystick is likely to be an advantage over separate controls only when the tasks in the 2 dimensions are similar. If the control systems are different, separate controls are preferable to a single control. Separate controls are also preferable when 2 compensatory displays are far apart, and the tracks of the 2 displays have different amplitudes.

Lever versus crank

Figure 11.16 (Regan, 1959) illustrates circular and straight instruments. Below each instrument is shown a compatible control. The bottom 2 rows of Table 11.3 list the average times on target with the circular instruments on the left of the figure. For the compensatory display mode, 2 cranks give a reliably longer average time on target than 2 levers. This suggests that it is probably better to stick to circular controls if circular scales are used. The same presumably applies to levers and straight scales.

Compatibility of control with display

The perfectly compatible control is the display marker itself. When the man wants to move the marker, he simply takes hold of it and moves it directly. The nearer a control can approach to this ideal, the simpler the coding problem becomes for the man. In order to minimize the coding problem, the control should be mounted as close as possible to the display. The control should move in the same direction as the display marker. And there should be the minimum of control system dynamics to upset the direct relationship between control and display movements.

One of the advantages of a stylus over a joystick is that the stylus can link the man's hand directly to the response marker. This happens when the display is pursuit and the control system is position. One of the advantages of a joystick over 2 levers is that it is the more compatible control when there is a single error marker, and the tasks in the 2 dimensions are similar.

The joystick of Figure 11.16 projects forward toward the man more or less in the horizontal plane. An upward movement of the handle of the joystick should clearly move the response marker upward.

The most compatible directional linkage between the display and the joystick is less clear when the joystick stands up vertically from the floor, as it can do in aircraft. Most people who know nothing about flying push the joystick forward to raise the response marker. The pilot has to learn to pull the joystick backward to raise the nose of his aircraft. The very first aircraft happened to use this relationship, and it has not been changed since. It is not known how many trainee pilots have been killed by moving the joystick in the wrong but expected direction (Fitts & Jones, 1961a, page 346). Mounting the joystick horizontally like the one in Figure 11.16 removes the ambiguity.

One of the advantages of quickening a display with a high order control system is that it increases the compatibility between control movements and display movements. The left side of Figure 10.4 shows that a quickened display has a position element. As soon as the man starts to move his control, the display marker moves a little in the same direction.

Compensatory displays reduce the compatibility between control movements and display movements. So do nonlinear, filtered, and noisy displays and control systems, and also stepped inputs to displays and control systems.

One of the principal disadvantages of the alternative displays discussed in Chapters 13 and 14 is that there is no very compatible indication of the size of the required control movement. With simple displays of auditory pitch, even the direction of the control movement may not be obvious. With the digital displays of Chapter 12, both the direction and size of the control movement have to be deduced by reading the digits and recoding them as a direction and size. This is not a very compatible relationship

Incompatible arm oriented and space oriented controls

A portable control which is not fixed to the equipment can be held in any position. It can give any directional relationship between control and display movements. Three possible arrangements are illustrated in Figure 15.2 (Hammerton and Tickner, 1964).

Early in training a portable control should be held so that it moves in the same direction as the display marker. This is indicated by training trial number 1 with the incompatible, but correctly arm oriented, arrangement in the center of the figure. A movement of the thumb joystick away from the wrist moves the display marker away from the man, just as it does in the compatible arrangement on the left.

But because the arm is bent across the body at a right angle, the thumb and joystick actually move toward the man's left. Acquisition takes an average of 39 sec with this arrangement, compared with aver-

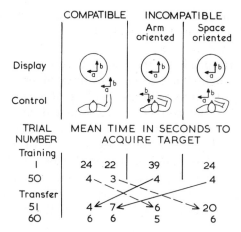

Figure 15.2. Performance with incompatible arm oriented and space oriented controls.

In the compatible arrangement, a movement of the thumb control to the left moves the response marker to the left. A forward movement of the thumb control moves the response marker away from the man. In the incompatible, but correctly arm oriented, arrangement the same thumb movements are required. But since the arm is bent at a right angle, the direction in which the thumb moves does not correspond to the direction in which the response marker moves.

In the incompatible, but correctly space oriented, arrangement the direction in which the thumb moves corresponds to the direction in which the response marker moves. But a movement of the thumb to the right with respect to the wrist moves the response marker away from the man. A movement of the tip of the thumb away from the wrist moves the response marker to the left. The average acquisition times are from 4 separate groups, each of 6 enlisted men.

After an auditory warning, a vertical target line about 7 mm tall suddenly jumps 3 cm up and to the left. The man has to move a spot with a diameter of about 1 mm after it. He has to hold the spot within 1.5 mm of the center of the line for 2 sec. The average times in the figure have the 2 sec holding time deducted. The man uses the thumb joystick illustrated in Figure 15.3A, and a rate control system. (Results from Hammerton & Tickner, 1964.)

In a subsequent experiment the target marker jumps down and to the right on trial 51, instead of up and to the left as it has always done on the 50 training trials. The difference between the incompatible, but correctly arm oriented, arrangement and the incompatible, but correctly space oriented, arrangement is just as large (Hammerton & Tickner, 1969, Experiment 2).

ages of 22 to 24 sec with the 2 arrangements in which the control and display move in the same direction. The differences are reliable.

Once the man has learned to use the thumb control, he does not need to hold his arm in the compatible position. He moves the response marker around the display without looking at his thumb. This is illustrated by the group which transfers to the incompatible, but correctly arm oriented, arrangement on trial 51 from the compatible arrangement on the left of the figure. The average time taken to acquire the target increases only from 4 to 6 sec.

The result corresponds to the use of a screwdriver. Once the man has learned thoroughly that screws are inserted by a clockwise movement, he can insert screws with his arm held at almost any angle.

An incompatible, but correctly space oriented, arrangement between control and display is illustrated on the right of the figure. Here a movement of the thumb joystick away from the wrist moves the display marker to the left. The thumb and joystick move in the same direction as the display marker. But because the arm is bent across the body at a right angle, the control movement is different from the control movement which moves the display marker to the left in the compatible arrangement.

The incompatible relationship takes no longer to learn than the compatible relationship. After learning, transfer to the compatible arrangement on trial 51 increases acquisition time only from 4 to 7 sec. This is because the new but compatible control movements are easy to learn. Most of the increase in acquisition time on trial 51 is probably taken in discovering what the new movements are.

However transfer from the compatible arrangement to the incompatible, but correctly space oriented, arrangement is not so simple. This is shown toward the bottom of the figure on the right. On transfer acquisition takes 20 sec, compared with times ranging from 4 to 7 sec for the other groups on trial 51. The differences are reliable. It is not until trial 60 that acquisition time becomes as short again as it is in the other conditions. This is because the man has to learn new and incompatible control movements. The increase in time reflects an increase both in travel time and in adjustment time (Hammerton and Tickner, 1969, Experiment 1).

Thumb, hand, and forearm controls

Tracking with a well designed hand control is more accurate than tracking with a thumb or forearm control. This is indicated in Table 15.1 (Hammerton & Tickner, 1966). The 3 controls are illustrated in Figure 15.3. Each man uses only one kind of control, and performs only the 2 conditions listed in the same column of the table.

The most difficult tracking conditions are with the high gain and the 2 sec exponential lag. They are listed in the lower right quadrant of the table. Here the hand control gives reliably the shortest acquisition time. The forearm control gives reliably the longest acquisition time.

The easiest tracking conditions are with the low gain and no lag. They are listed in the upper left quadrant of the table. Here there is virtually no difference between the 3 controls.

The other 2 quadrants of the table represent tasks of intermediate difficulty. Here the hand is reliably quicker than the forearm, but does not differ reliably from the thumb. This last result is consistent with an earlier finding of Gibbs (1962).

The longer time required with the forearm control is to be predicted. With this control the hand has further to move in order to change the angle of the control by a given number of degrees. The distance can be reduced by increasing the control gain. But the table shows that an increase in control gain results in longer acquisition times. Figure 17.2 suggests that this is because the final adjustment takes longer.

The relatively poor performance of the thumb control, first reported by Gibbs (1962), came as a surprise to some design engineers. Up to this time thumb controls were used instead of hand controls for guiding small rockets, on the assumption that they were better. This is not so. Normally the thumb is used for gripping, not for making precise movements. Whereas the hand makes precise movements in writing and in many other activities. Ever since infancy people have been making precise hand movements. They have become pretty good at it. They are far less practiced at making precise thumb movements.

Control by eye

It is possible to control the position of a response marker using the changes in electrical potential across the eyes which are produced by eye movements (Shackel, 1960). The man has simply to look at a target, and the response marker follows the position of his gaze. A difficulty with this method is that the average level of the potentials across the man's eyes gradually changes. The response marker still follows the movements of the man's eyes, but there is a constant error between the position of the man's gaze and the position of the response marker (Senders and colleagues, 1969).

Constant errors can be prevented by recording eye movements using a beam of light reflected off the eye. The front of the eye is not perfectly circular. As the eye moves, the reflected beam moves in the corresponding direction. By selecting the correct position on the eye, it is sometimes possible to obtain an almost linear relationship between the angle moved by the eye and the angle moved by the reflected beam (Mackworth & Mackworth, 1958).

A related method uses photosensitive transistors to measure the amount of light reflected by the sclera, or white part of the eyeball. As the eye turns to the left, more white shows on the right side of the eye and less white shows on the left side. This increases the amount of light received by the transistor on the right of the eye, and reduces the amount received by the transistor on the left. The method can sometimes produce an almost linear relationship between the direction of the eye and the voltage put out by the electrical circuit (Stark, Vossius & Young, 1962, Figures 2 and 3). Unfortunately it is less easy to record vertical eye movements by this method, because the eyelids cover most of the white part of the eye above and below the pupil.

Experiments on tracking by eye indicate that the eye has a reaction time like the hand. It anticipates when it is presented with a predictable series of steps to follow (Stark & others, 1962, Figure 6). It exhibits refractoriness (Wheeless, Boynton & Cohen, 1966) and range effects (Trumbo, Noble, Fowler, and Porterfield, 1968, Figure 3) just as the hand does. The eye has somewhat similar limitations to the hand in following single sine waves of high frequency, and tracks containing white noise of high frequency (Stark & others, 1962, Figure 10; Michael & Jones, 1966, Figure 6).

All these common characteristics of the eye and the hand indicate that there is a common mechanism in the brain which is used in tracking both by eye and by hand. The principal difference between tracking by eye and by hand is that acquisition movements are made a good deal more quickly by the eye. This is due partly to the smaller mass of the eye and its muscles. The practical disadvantages of control by eye are discussed at the beginning of the chapter.

Table 15.1
Performance with thumb, hand, and forearm controls

| | Average acquisition time in seconds with control gain: | | | | | |
| | Low* | | | High† | | |
Exponential control time lag (sec)	Thumb	Hand	Forearm	Thumb	Hand	Forearm
0	8	8	8	14	12	17
2	15	16	22	32	24	45

Results from Hammerton & Ticker, 1966.
* 2.5 deg per sec of display movement per degree of control movement.
† 12.3 deg per sec of display movement per degree of control movement.

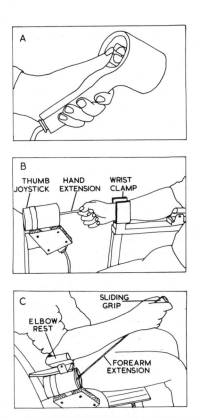

Figure 15.3.   Thumb, hand, and forearm controls.

The spring centered thumb joystick is illustrated in **A**. In **B** the thumb joystick is adapted for use by the hand. A casing is fitted over the end of the joystick. The casing is connected through a pivot to a rod which is held by the man's hand. When the man moves his hand in one direction, the thumb joystick moves in the opposite direction because it is on the other side of the pivot. The electrical polarity of the thumb joystick is reversed to compensate for this. The position of the pivot is selected to make the maximum comfortable hand movement produce the maximum deflection of the modified thumb joystick. The wrist is clamped to prevent arm movements. The hand joystick is clearly not as well spring centered as the thumb joystick. The same principle is used for the forearm joystick illustrated in **C**. The man holds a sliding grip fitted over the joystick, because the pivot of the joystick is below the pivot of his elbow joint.

After an auditory warning, a target circle of 3 mm diameter suddenly jumps a distance of 3.5 cm up and to the left. The man has to place a spot with a diameter of about 1 mm inside the target ring and hold it there for 2 sec continuously. The 12 experimental conditions are listed in Table 15.1. Each column represents the performance of a separate group of 6 enlisted men. Each group first tracks without lag for 3 days, and then tracks with the 2 sec lag for 3 more days. The table lists the average performance on the last day of each condition. (After Hammerton & Tickner, 1966, Figure 1.)

Spring centered controls

Spring centering is the best kind of control loading. One advantage of a spring centered control is that the control returns by itself to its center when the man lets go of it. Automatic centering is particularly advantageous with rate and higher order control systems. It means that when the man lets go of the control, he ceases to feed any disturbance into the control system. The control system operates only with the disturbances which have already been fed in.

A second advantage of a spring centered control is that the man feels a pressure which is proportional to the distance of the control from its center. The pressure cue augments the usual position cue, and helps the man to track more accurately. Pressure cues are particularly advantageous when the man has no way of knowing the exact position of the control except by the feeling which he receives from his controlling hand or arm.

Pressure cues are a help with rate and higher order control systems. The output of the high order control system is not related in a simple way to the man's control movements. He cannot easily tell what he is doing simply by looking at the response marker. He needs to be able to feel where his control is. Spring centering increases the amount of feel, as well as returning the control to its center as soon as the man lets go of it.

Table 15.2 (Briggs, Fitts & Bahrick, 1957b) indicates the advantage of combining pressure cues with position cues when using a high order

Table 15.2
Performance with force and amplitude cues

Relative size of control movement required	Percent time on target when relative force required		
	1	4	Mean
1	51	48	50
4	60	79	69
Mean	56	63	

The simulator normally requires the larger force and larger amplitude of movement. This combination gives reliably the longest average time on target. (Results from Briggs and colleagues, 1957b.)

control system. The compensatory task is intended to represent flying an aircraft to intercept an enemy aircraft, using a radar fire control system. The task is described in the caption to Figure 17.8. Amounts of spring resistance or torque ranging from .09 to 1.4 in lb per deg are combined with 2 levels of control system gain. Separate groups of 17 men undergraduates perform with each of the 4 combinations.

The table lists the average percent of the last 3 sec of the interception for which the men are on target. Here accurate positioning is what matters. The combination of the larger force with the larger amplitude of movement gives reliably the longest average time on target. Reducing either the force or the size of the movements to one quarter, reliably reduces the average time on target. Thus for accurate tracking with a high order control system, both spring centering and adequate movement are important.

There is another condition in which pressure cues can usefully augment position cues. With a compensatory display, the output of the man's control system may be mixed with an irregular track before being fed to the error marker. The man then has no way of telling the exact effect of his control movements, except by using the felt position of his control (see Chapter 9).

Briggs and Wiener (1966) combine these 2 conditions which benefit from adequate spring centering. The man has the high order control system of the experiment of Table 15.2. He also has the compensatory display, and an irregular track comprising 3 sine waves. Briggs and Wiener add to this combination an extra condition which benefits from adequate spring centering. Two of their groups of 12 undergraduates are given an additional simple tracking task to perform, using the left hand, at the same time as the main tracking task. The displays are placed 30 in apart, so that the men can look directly at only one of the 2 displays at a time.

Under these conditions, adequate spring centering is found to be particularly advantageous. The man can keep track more efficiently of what is happening in the main task, when he has an adequate feel of the pressure from the control, as well as of its position.

Pressure controls

A pressure control is a spring centered control which does not move appreciably. The output of the control is usually directly proportional to the force or pressure exerted on it. A pressure control is an advantage when time is short, but a disadvantage when slow accurate positioning is required. The advantage and disadvantage of a pressure control can be related to the 2 aspects of performance which are illustrated in Figure

Table 15.3
Experiments comparing pressure and moving controls

Author(s)	Year	N	Moving control	Display mode
A. Rate or higher order control system and relatively high frequency track				
Birmingham*	1950	7†	Viscous damping	Compensatory
		8†	Viscous damping	Compensatory
Gibbs*	1954	16	Unloaded	Compensatory
North and Lomnicki	1961	3	Unloaded	Compensatory
Notterman and Page*	1962	3	Spring centered	Compensatory
Smith and colleagues*	1966b	8	Weak ⎱ Spring	Compensatory
			Strong ⎰ centered	Compensatory
Ziegler and Chernikoff	1968	5	Spring centered	Compensatory
B. Position control system and slow ramp track				
Burke and Gibbs	1965	5 + 5†	Unloaded	Pursuit
(see Figure 15.4)		9†	Unloaded	Pursuit
Craik and Vince	1943, 1963a	4?	Viscous damping	Compensatory
C. Other combinations of order of control system and track frequency				
Birmingham*	1950	7†	Viscous damping	Compensatory
		8†	Viscous damping	Compensatory
Gibbs*	1954	18 + 18	Unloaded	Compensatory
		24	Unloaded	Compensatory
		14	Unloaded	Compensatory
			Unloaded	Compensatory
Newton	1958	12	Inertia	Compensatory
Notterman and Page*	1962	3	Spring centered	Compensatory
			Unloaded	Compensatory
Russell	1957	36 + 36	Friction	Pursuit
		15 + 16	Friction	Pursuit
R. L. Smith and	1966b	8	Weak ⎱ Spring	Compensatory
colleagues*			Strong ⎰ centered	Compensatory

* Included in two parts of the table.
† All but 1 of the people serve in both experiments.
‡ Half the number of reversals per minute.
§ Excludes high frequencies of small amplitude.

Top track frequency (cpm)	Control system	Complications	Reliably better
"Difficult"	Acceleration aided	Different aiding ratios	Pressure?
"Difficult"	Acceleration aided	Different aiding ratios	Pressure?
Step + slow ramp	Rate with .08 sec exponential lag	Control system output 17 times greater with pressure control	Pressure
12	Rate	Lapse of 1 year between comparisons	Pressure
20§	Acceleration aided	Numerous control loadings and control systems	Pressure
15‡	Rate	Different control shapes and dimensions of movement	Pressure
15‡	Rate		—
7.3	Delta acceleration	Onoff control	Pressure
Slow ramps	Position		Movement?
Slow ramps	Position		Pressure
Slow ramps	Position		—
"Easy"	Acceleration aided	Different aiding ratios	—
"Easy"	Acceleration aided	Different aiding ratios	—
.8	Rate with .08 sec exponential lag	Control system output 17 times greater with pressure control	Pressure
3.5			Pressure
.8			Pressure
3.5			Pressure
18	Position	Cold and warm climates	Pressure
20§	Position	Numerous loadings and control systems	—
20§	Position		—
?	Rate	Cold and hot climates	Movement?
?	Rate	Pressure control moved .2 in.	Movement?
1.5‡	Rate	Different control shapes and dimensions of movement	Pressure
1.5‡	Rate		—

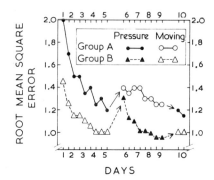

Figure 15.4.   Asymmetrical transfer between pressure and moving controls.

The circles are for a group of 5 people who track for 5 days with the pressure control. They are then switched for 4 days to the moving control, before a final day on the pressure control. The triangles are for another group of 5 people who track with the 2 controls in the reverse order.

The pressure stick is 3.5 in long. It requires pressures of up to 2 lb to follow the track marker. The moving control is 12 in long. It has to be moved about 30° on each side of its central position. Other details of the experiment are listed in part **B** of Table 15.3. (After Burke & Gibbs, 1965, Figure 3.)

5.10. A pressure control has no travel time. But it cannot be adjusted very accurately because it does not provide the man with a cue of distance proportional to its output, as a moving control does.

Table 15.3 lists experiments which compare a pressure control with a moving control. Part **A** lists experiments which should favor a pressure control. With the rate or higher order control system and relatively high frequency track, most of the man's error is likely to be due to time lag. He has little opportunity for accurate positioning. Thus a pressure control should be an advantage over a moving control. All but one comparison greatly favor a pressure control. The single exception (R. L. Smith, Garfinkle, Groth, & Lyman, 1966b) is a comparison of a pressure control with a strongly spring centered control. Here the overall difference is small.

Unfortunately there are complications which reduce the validity of the comparisons. All the experimenters except North and Lomnicki (1961) use a balanced treatment design. Figure 15.4 (Burke & Gibbs, 1965) shows that transfer is likely to favor the pressure control. The experiments need to be repeated with separate groups for each control. In North and Lomnicki's (1961) experiment there is a delay of 1 year after using the moving control, before the pressure control is used. It is difficult to tell what may have changed during this period. Thus none of the experiments provides a really acceptable comparison.

Perhaps an even more serious difficulty is that the maximum output of the control system is not always equated for the 2 controls. Gibbs' (1954) pressure control has a maximum output 17 times greater than the output of his moving control. Ziegler and Chernikoff's (1968) pressure control has 1.5 times the maximum output of the moving control. Only Birmingham (1950) and Smith and his colleagues (1966b) report that they match the maximum outputs. With a high order control system and a relatively high frequency track, a greater maximum control system output is likely to be a major advantage. It alone could account for the better performance with the pressure control in the experiments by Gibbs (1954) and by Ziegler and Chernikoff (1968).

A third difficulty applies to the experiments by Birmingham (1950), by Gibbs (1954), and by North and Lomnicki (1961). These experimenters use moving controls which are not spring centered. So do practically all the experimenters in parts **B** and **C** of the table. Here the advantage of the pressure control could be due to spring centering. It need not be due to the lack of movement. However the results of Notterman and Page (1962) and of Smith and his colleagues (1966b) in the upper part of the table could possibly reflect a genuine advantage for a pressure control over a spring centered control, when used with a high order control system and a relatively high frequency track.

Part **B** of Table 15.3 lists experiments which should not favor a pressure control. With the position control system and slow ramp track, accurate positioning of the control is more important than a reduced travel time. Here there is a reliable difference in the experiments by Burke and Gibbs (1965). It still favors the pressure control. However Figure 15.4 shows that before transfer Burke and Gibbs' pressure control gave a considerably larger RMS error than their unloaded control. This is the only valid comparison between the 2 controls which can be made from the results in the figure (see Chapter 2).

Unfortunately Burke and Gibbs make no mention of statistical tests comparing the 2 controls during the first 5 days before transfer. They report tests only for days 9 and 10. Averaged over these last 2 days, 9 out of their 10 people track more accurately with the pressure control. A subsequent experiment using 9 of the same 10 people also show a reliable advantage for the pressure control after transfer. But again the comparison is not a valid one.

Craik and Vince's (1943, 1963a, Appendix 1) results are similar to the results on the left of Figure 15.4. The average error with the pressure control is a little over double the average error of the moving control with the larger range of movement. Clearly more experiments are required. But it can be concluded provisionally that a spring centered moving control is probably better than a pressure control for a position control system with a slow ramp track.

The experiments listed in part C of Table 15.3 could favor either a pressure control or a moving control. In the experiments by Birmingham (1950), by Gibbs (1954), and by Smith and his colleagues (1966b), a rate or higher order control system which favors a pressure control is paired with a low frequency track which favors a moving control. In the experiments by Newton (1958) and by Notterman and Page (1962), a position control system which favors a moving control is paired with a fairly high frequency track which favors a pressure control. The results can be accounted for in a number of ways.

Taken as a whole, the experiments listed in Table 15.3 suggest provisionally that a pressure control may be an advantage when time has to be saved, as in tracking relatively high frequencies with a high order control system. But a pressure control is not likely to be an advantage when the control has to be positioned accurately, as in tracking slow ramps with a position control system. However a definite conclusion must await more rigorous experiments using separate groups of people for each control.

Friction in a control

Friction produces delays and irregular movements. Lay a rubber pencil eraser on a flat horizontal surface, and press it firmly against the surface with one hand to produce friction. Then try sliding the eraser slowly by pushing it horizontally. Do so by extending a flexed finger of the other hand. This should illustrate the delay introduced by the friction before the movement starts, and the irregularity of the movement.

If a control has friction, a force of a size corresponding to the friction has to be exerted before the control can be moved. This introduces a delay before the movement starts (Hick, 1945). When the control is centered, the delay produced by friction is rather similar to the delay produced by deadspace around the center of a control.

When a control movement has to be reversed, the man has to stop overcoming the friction which resists the movement in one direction, and overcome the friction which resists the movement in the reverse direction. The control does not move while the force of the hand or arm is changing between the 2 values of the friction. At reversals friction thus introduces a delay which is rather similar to the delay produced by backlash. Backlash and deadspace are discussed at the end of the chapter.

Once the friction threshold is exceeded, a little extra force moves the control rapidly, since the only remaining restraints are those built into the man's controlling limb. Thus a control with a good deal of friction as the only form of resistance cannot easily be moved at a constant slow speed. The attempt tends to result in alternate rapid movements and stops, as the force exerted by the man rises above and falls below the threshold required to move the control. This does not produce very accurate tracking.

Part A of Table 15.4 lists experiments on the effects of friction in controls other than cranks. The 2 experiments by Hick (1945) and the 2 by Jenkins and his colleagues all favor small or minimal values of friction. The principal exception is the experiment by Craik and Vince (1963a), in which the man stands without any support for his hand. Here body sway and tremor produce a good deal of oscillation in the absence of some form of control loading. The effect of control loading in preventing accidental movements of this kind is discussed in a later section of the chapter.

Part B of Table 15.4 lists experiments on the effects of friction in cranking. A good deal of friction reduces the maximum rate of winding (Craik & Vince, 1963a). When winding continues for a long time, friction is fatiguing and results in a slower natural rate of winding. Three of the 4 experiments listed favor small or minimal values of friction. It is not clear why Hick's (1945) results are so different.

Viscous damping and inertia in a control

Figure 15.5 illustrates the theoretical effects of viscous damping and inertia when a constant force is exerted on a control of zero mass. Viscous damping feels like moving a spoon through thick syrup. Running through water deep enough to cover the thighs is another example. The rate of movement is directly proportional to the force exerted.

Inertia is met in starting a heavy flywheel. The force exerted has little effect at first, because it produces only an acceleration of the flywheel. The acceleration has to operate for an appreciable time before the flywheel begins to move very much. Inertia opposes quick control movements, and is therefore a disadvantage in tracking. The human arm has enough inertia of its own.

Table 15.5 (Howland & Noble, 1953) shows how time on target with a position control is affected by various combinations of control loading. Separate groups of 10 undergraduates track with each of the 8 combinations. The display is compensatory. The track is a sine wave with a frequency of 15 cpm. The control is a horizontal shaft. The under-

Table 15.4
Friction in a control

Author(s)	Year	N	Control	Track
A. Ordinary control movements				
Craik and Vince	1963a	3	Horizontal lever	Constant velocity ramps
Hick	1945	3	Vertical lever	3 cpm‡ irregular
		?	Vertical lever	Steps
Jenkins, Maas and Olson	1951	4	Knob to rotate	Steps
Jenkins, Maas and Rigler	1950	4	Knob to rotate	Steps
Muckler and Matheny	1954	15 + 15	Vertical lever	4 cpm sine wave
Searle and Taylor	1948	6	Knob to slide	Steps
B. Cranking				
Craik and Vince	1963a	3	Crank, radius 3 cm (1.2 in)	No track
Gerall and Green	1958	13 + 13	2 Cranks, radii 5 cm (2 in)	Constant velocity ramp?
Helson	1949	6	Heavy or light crank radius 5.7 or 11.4 cm (2.25 or 4.5 in)	Constant velocity 2–200 rpm
Hick	1945	3	Crank, radius 9 cm	44 rpm constant velocity, or varied at 7.5 cpm

‡ Half the number of reversals per minute.

graduate grips the handle of the control as he would grip a screwdriver. He rotates the control clockwise and counterclockwise through an angle of 40° to null the error.

The control loadings are all relatively small. The spring resistance or torque of the handle is about .02 in lb per deg (1.2 in lb per rad). It is only one quarter of the smallest value used by Briggs and his colleague (1957b) for the experiment of Table 15.2. Table 15.5 shows

| Friction (gm) | | | Difference | |
Smallest	Greatest	Best	reliable	Measure(s)
$\simeq 0$	1500 (54 oz)	≥ 230 (≥ 8 oz)	?	Modulus mean error
60–80 (2–3 oz)	1800 (4 lb)	60–450 (2–16 oz)	Yes	Modulus mean error
60–80	1800	60–80	Yes	Time to start movement
$\simeq 0$	1000	$\simeq 0$	?	Time to acquire target
100	1300	100	?	Time to acquire target
70 (2.5 oz)	5500 (12 lb)	—	No	Number of trials required to remain always on target
60 (2.2 oz)	620 (22.2 oz)	—	No	Time to complete first movement, Maximum rate of movement, and Modulus mean error of first movement.
.45 kg cm (.37 lb in)	16 kg cm (13.5 lb in)	.45 kg cm (.37 lb in)	?	Maximum rate of winding
900 (2 lb)	6500 (14 lb)	900 (2 lb)	Yes	Average time on target
$\simeq 0$	8.5 kg cm (7 lb in)	$\simeq 0$	Yes	Modulus mean error
≤ 80 (≤ 3 oz)	1800 (4 lb)	1800 (4 lb)	Yes?	Modulus mean error

that this spring centering alone produces the longest average time on target. It is reliably better than virtually no resistance.

The viscous damping is about .02 in lb per deg per sec. If anything the viscous damping appears to increase slightly the proportion of time on target when the control is otherwise unloaded. If anything it also improves performance with a control which is spring centered and has inertia. But adding viscous damping to a spring centered control without inertia, if anything reduces the proportion of time on target.

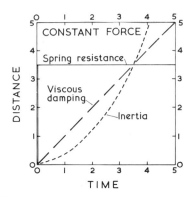

Figure 15.5.   Spring resistance, viscous damping and inertia.

The figure illustrates the theoretical effects of a constant force acting on a control of zero mass with only spring resistance, viscious damping, or inertia. The part of the body which moves the control has some viscous damping and inertia of its own. The effect of this has to be added to the effects illustrated in the figure. A control with only spring resistance moves instantaneously to a distance at which the tension on the spring equals the force exerted on the control. A control with only viscous damping moves at a constant rate. A control with only inertia moves at an accelerating rate. Controls with spring resistance, viscous damping and inertia correspond respectively to position, rate and acceleration control systems.

A control with only friction is not illustrated in the figure. When the constant force is less than the friction, the control does not move. When the constant force is greater than the friction, the control moves instantaneously an infinite distance.

The inertia is about .002 in lb per deg per sec^2. It always reduces the average time on target. The combination of inertia with spring centering is the worst control loading of all. It is reliably worse than no loading. The combination tends to produce oscillation at a frequency of about 30 cpm, compared with the track frequency of 15 cpm. The difference between the 2 frequencies must increase the difficulty of the man's task, although nobody appears to have investigated this.

When the viscous damping is added to the combination of spring resistance and inertia, the damping ratio of the control is about 1.6. The overdamping slows the return of the control to its center when it is released. The table shows that, if anything, the overdamping increases the time on target.

Clearly more experiments of this kind are required, using other values of spring resistance, viscous damping and inertia. A pursuit display should also be tried, and other frequencies of track. For Pew and his colleagues (1967a) report a reliable interaction between track frequency and spring resistance. The interaction is a lot more marked with a compensatory display, like that used by Howland and Noble (1953) in the experiment of Table 15.5, than with a pursuit display.

Inertia in cranking at a fixed speed

Loading a control with inertia almost always degrades tracking. Figure 15.5 shows that inertia in a control corresponds to acceleration in a control system. It is pointed out in Chapter 16 that adding an acceleration component to a control system of lower order also degrades tracking.

The only condition in which loading a control with inertia improves the accuracy of tracking is in cranking at a fixed speed. The hand and arm are not designed for cranking. In attempting to rotate a crank at a fixed speed, the man exerts too much force in one part of the cycle, and too little force in another part of the cycle (Provins, 1956; Glencross, 1973). The rate of rotation of the crank varies accordingly.

Increasing the inertia of the crank reduces the effect of a transient change in the force exerted by the man. The inertia prevents the rate of turn from altering very much, before the force returns again to its optimal value. Inertia can therefore be used to improve the accuracy of cranking at a constant rate. The crank is given a larger radius, and its weight is increased. Both these changes increase inertia, and so reduce the variability in the rate of cranking (Helson, 1949, Table 4).

It is pointed out in Chapter 7 that the rate of cranking is more irregular at slow speeds than at faster speeds. Slow fixed speeds of cranking require more inertia than faster speeds. Extra inertia can be provided by attaching one or more additional flywheels to the crank. This improves

Table 15.5
Performance with small amounts of control loading

Kind of control loading			Percent time on target
Spring	0	0	60
Spring + Viscous damping	0	52
0	Viscous damping	0	44
0	0	0	41
0	0	+ Inertia	35
0	Viscous damping	+ Inertia	35
Spring + Viscous damping	+ Inertia	34
Spring	0	+ Inertia	27

The control with virtually no loading is reliably worse than the spring centered control at the top of the table, but reliably better than the control combining spring centering with inertia at the bottom of the table. (Results from Howland & Noble, 1953.)

the accuracy of cranking at slow fixed speeds, but not at faster speeds (Helson, 1949, Figure 5). The results apply only to cranking at a fixed speed.

Control loading to prevent accidental operation

Control loading can be an advantage for reasons which are unrelated to the results in Table 15.5. A control stick with virtually no resistance does not stay put when the man lets go of it. It falls under the influence of gravity to its lowest limit.

A control is also likely to change position if it is jerked accidentally. This can happen while the man is tracking if his hand and arm are not supported. It can happen even with support, if the man is tracking in a vehicle which jolts or vibrates (Craik & Vince, 1943, 1963a, page 8).

Any form of control loading will help to reduce the effect of jolts. The loading may improve the accuracy of tracking if jolting is a principal source of error. A large amount of friction or inertia may practically eliminate the effect of jolts. Unfortunately it also prevents the man from responding quickly. Clearly the best control loading is the one which reduces the detrimental effect of the jolts, without handicapping the man too much. The optimum should be determined by experiment for each application.

Table 15.5 shows that a spring centered control gives the most accurate tracking in the absence of jolts. It is therefore probably the best control to try when occasional jolts are encountered. Next in order of preference comes viscous damping. It is probably not necessary to follow Craik and Vince's (1943, 1963a, page 10) recommendation and use friction.

Spring centering is not possible with a crank control. If viscous damping is not used, the designer has only inertia and friction to choose between. For cranking at a fixed speed, inertia gives the more accurate tracking in the absence of jolts, and so should be tried first (Helson, 1949, Table 4).

Power operated and hand operated control systems

When the man himself supplies the power for a control system, he can feel the resistances which have to be overcome. Provided the load is not excessive, the man tracks more accurately than when he uses a power operated control system which deprives him of the feel. This is reported by Notterman and Page (1962) for compensatory tracking with a lever control. Notterman and Page use 4 main groups of experimental conditions.

1. To represent the dynamics of various physical control systems, Notterman and Page use 51 combinations of spring resistance, viscous damping and inertia. The values for spring resistance range up to .43 in lb per deg (24 in lb per rad). The values for inertia range up to .035 in lb per deg per sec². These top values are about 20 times the values selected by Howland and Noble for the experiment of Table 15.5. For viscous damping Notterman and Page's (1962) top value is .1 in lb per deg per sec. This is about 5 times greater than the value chosen by Howland and Noble (1953).

2. To represent the corresponding power operated control systems, Notterman and Page use an acceleration aided control system with a pressure control. There are 51 different combinations of values of the gains for position, rate, and acceleration, corresponding to the 51 combinations of spring resistance, viscous damping and inertia. Each acceleration aided control system is the electrical analog of one of the physical control systems.

3. Another representation of the power operated control systems uses a moving spring centered control. It has a spring resistance or torque of .014 in lb per deg, which is not very different from Howland and Noble's (1953) value. This time 16 aiding ratios are selected as representative of the 51 physical control systems.

4. The final group of experimental conditions uses the controls with a position control system. The pressure control has 3 different control gains covering an unspecified range. The moving control is used both with and without its spring centering.

The physical control systems of Condition 1 always produce reliably smaller RMS error scores than the corresponding electrical analogs of Condition 2 with the pressure control. This is so for each of the 3 people, with every one of the 51 physical control systems. Performance with the electrical analogs and the spring centered moving control of Condition 3 is worse still. This last result is indicated in part A of Table 15.3.

The advantage of the physical control systems is particularly marked when they are underdamped, and also when they have a lot of inertia. The man can compensate for these physical characteristics a good deal better when he can feel them. The advantage can be related to the advantage in Meiry's (1965) experiment illustrated in Figure 14.3, when sitting in a simulated rolling cockpit. Sizes of acceleration are not very accurately assessed by eye (Gottsdanker, 1956b). The man tracks better if he can feel the forces which are associated with the accelerations, as well as see the accelerations.

The pressure and spring centered moving controls give smaller average errors with the position control system of Condition 4. The average errors are smaller than, or of the same order of size as, those obtained with the best physical control systems with their viscous damping and inertia. This is in line with the results of Howland and Noble (1953) which are listed in Table 15.5. All Notterman and Page's physical control systems have as much or more inertia than the small amount which Howland and Noble find always to degrade performance.

The order of performance of the 4 groups of experimental conditions is: 4, 1, 2, 3. Notterman and Page (1962) conclude that a pressure or moving spring centered control linked to a position control system produces more accurate tracking than a control with viscous damping and inertia. But if the viscous damping and inertia are characteristics of the equipment which is being controlled, tracking is more accurate if the man can feel them. Power operated control systems degrade tracking because they deprive the man of the feel.

The feel of a power operated control system can be improved by adding extra viscous damping and inertia to the control. But this makes tracking worse still. For the delays while the man is overcoming the control resistances are added to the delays while the power operated control system is overcoming the resistances in the equipment.

Unfortunately Notterman and Page (1962) use a compensatory display, a balanced treatment design, and only 3 graduate students. This important experiment needs to be repeated using both pursuit and compensatory displays, a separate group design, and more people in each group.

Backlash in a control

A joystick or lever can be operated by holding a loose hollow cylinder fitting over it. When the cylinder is moved to the right, the stick touches it on the left. When the cylinder reverses the direction of its movement, the stick does not start to return toward the left until it comes up against the right side of the cylinder. While the cylinder is moving without the stick, the man's control movement has no effect upon the control system. This is called backlash or hysteresis.

Backlash degrades tracking (Helson, 1944, Figure 5). Even .01 in of electrical backlash in a simulated aircraft control system reliably increases the average modulus mean error of a group of 2 pilots and 3 nonpilots (Senders & Bradley, 1956). This is not surprising, because the man cannot feel electrical backlash. Also the dynamics of an aircraft control system are of high order. The effect of a small amount of backlash cannot be detected in the display. Thus the man does not know what he is supposed to compensate for.

A fixed amount of backlash in a control system has a greater effect upon the performance of 6 moderately experienced trackers when the gain of the control system is greater (Rockway and Franks, 1959). This is because the backlash then represents a greater proportion of the total control movement.

Deadspace in a control

Deadspace or deadzone is a kind of backlash around the central position of a control. Rockway (1957) reports that deadspace reliably reduces the average time on target. Even a deadspace which represents only about 6% of the maximum required movement of the control, has a marked effect upon the amount of time on target. The effect of deadspace is particularly detrimental when the gain of the control system is high. A high gain reduces the range of movement required to keep the error marker on target. The deadspace is therefore a larger proportion of the range of movement.

Rockway's (1957) 6 experienced trackers use a compensatory display, an irregular track, a control lever with practically no resistance, and a position control system. This combination is particularly likely to reveal the disadvantages of deadspace, because it deprives the man of any direct way of telling when his control is out of action in the deadspace. A compensatory display does not show the man directly the output of his control system, as a pursuit display does. The output is masked by the track movements. An irregular track is a fairly efficient masker.

Also a compensatory display does not show the man when his position control is at its center, and so must be in its deadspace, as a pursuit display does. If the control is spring centered, the man can feel when the control is at its center. But this cue is not available with an unloaded control. The man can only be sure that the control is in its deadspace when the error suddenly starts to increase rapidly.

With a joyball, deadspace reliably increases the time taken by 12 men to acquire stationary targets (Rogers, 1970). In this experiment a minimum velocity of the surface of the joyball is required to move the response marker. Slower rates of rotation of the joyball have no effect. Faster rates of rotation move the response marker at the corresponding rates. Rogers reports that his 12 men acquire targets most quickly without deadspace.

Both the experiments of Rockway (1957) and of Rogers (1970) use a position control system. With a rate or higher order control system, a small amount of deadspace may be a help when a control stick is spring centered. This is because the control does not spring back to exactly the same position each time it is let go.

Also in electrical equipment zero potential is subject to small fluctuations. Without some deadspace, a spring centered control is likely to produce a small positive or negative voltage when it returns to its center. This can be a disadvantage if the control system is rate or of higher order. An onoff control has a deadspace. Yet the experiment by Hunt (1966) in part **B** of Table 17.1 shows that with an acceleration control system an onoff control is no worse than a conventional continuous control.

Recommended controls

A stylus or light pen should be used with an electronic display. For remote control, a joystick is preferable to a joyball.

A joystick which moves in 2 dimensions is preferable to separate controls for the 2 dimensions, provided the tasks in the 2 dimensions are similar. If the tasks are very different, separate controls should be used.

Controls should be as compatible as possible with their displays. A portable control which is not fixed to the equipment should be placed during training in a compatible position.

For accurate remote control, a small joystick should be provided which can be operated by the hand. It should be spring centered with the minimum of friction, viscous damping and inertia. A pressure control is recommended only when speed of operation is more important than the exact output of the control.

If a control system has to have viscous damping and inertia, the man should be permitted to feel them.

Backlash and deadspace should be minimized.

Chapter

16

Orders of control system

Summary

A position control system is the most compatible control system with step and sine wave tracks. Either a position or a rate aided control system can be used with a constant velocity ramp. Adding an acceleration component to a control system of low order degrades performance. A control system of high order is improved by adding components of lower order. Exceptions to these rules are due to bias introduced by the transfer of inappropriate phase relationships. Transfer favors control systems of intermediate order.

Interference is produced by adaptive training devices which vary the aiding of the control system, and by tracking in 2 dimensions with different orders of control in the 2 dimensions.

Available orders of control system

Most of the book is concerned with position or zero order control systems. The left side of Figure 16.1 shows that with a position control system, there is a direct relationship between a control movement and the display movement which it produces.

ORDER OF CONTROL

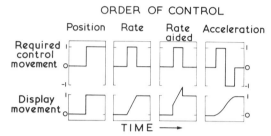

Figure 16.1.   Step tracking with different orders of control system.
The theoretical responses illustrated above produce the display movements illustrated below. The corresponding functions for an acceleration aided control system are illustrated at the top and bottom of the left column of Figure 10.4.

The next column of the figure illustrates a rate or first order control system. Here 2 control movements are necessary to move the display marker a certain distance. The first control movement gives the display marker a rate. The second control movement removes the rate when the marker has reached its target. The gas pedal, engine, and brake pedal of an automobile together comprise a rate control system, but with a time lag.

A rate control system is represented by an integrator. It inserts a phase lag of 90° in the frequencies of the man's response. It also halves the amplitude of the man's response each time he doubles his frequency.

The right side of Figure 16.1 illustrates step tracking with an acceleration or second order control system. Here at least 3 control movements are required. The first control movement puts on an acceleration, which produces a gradual increase in the rate of movement of the display marker. The second control movement puts on a negative acceleration, which gradually brings the display marker to rest. The third control movement returns the control to its central position. It is pointed out in Chapter 1 that in positioning an automobile on the road, the steering wheel is an acceleration control.

An acceleration control system is represented by 2 integrators in series. It inserts a phase lag of 180° in the frequencies of the man's response. It also reduces to one quarter the amplitude of the man's response each time he doubles his frequency.

The control of a chemical plant, or of a nuclear reactor (McLeod & McCallum, 1975), may be of second order. Here the gain of the control system is a good deal smaller. It may take several minutes to change the control system from one steady state to another.

The steering mechanism of a large ship can be represented by a delta acceleration or third order control system. The angular position of the rudder determines the angular acceleration of the ship. Unlike steering an automobile, when the steering wheel of a large ship is returned to center, the ship continues to turn at a more or less constant rate. The rudder has to be rotated in the opposite direction in order to stop the ship from turning. This is because the ship has a large mass or inertia. As with an automobile, the direction of the ship determines the rate at which the ship changes its side to side position as it moves along a river or canal. There are thus 3 integrations between the angle of the steering wheel or rudder, and side to side position in a river or canal.

The rudder of a large ship may be so heavy to turn that power steering is necessary. The man's steering wheel may determine the rate at which the rudder rotates. If so, steering the ship down a canal represents a fourth order control system. If the rudder is operated through an acceleration control system, steering the ship represents fifth order control.

A man tracks most accurately with a position control system. This is because he can change the position of the display marker at once. He does not have to wait while a rate or higher order input to the control system is changing the position of the marker. The difficulty of tracking accurately with control systems of high order is one of the reasons why large ships require tugs to help them to dock.

Aided and quickened control systems

Control systems may combine 2 or more orders of control. A rate aided control system is illustrated in the third column of Figure 16.1. It is sometimes called simply an aided control system. It combines rate control with position control. Rate aiding was introduced during World War II for tracking ships and slow distant aircraft.

Rate aiding should be thought of as aiding performance with a rate control system. It ought to indicate that adding the position component improves the accuracy of tracking with a rate control system. With a position component, a control movement has an immediate effect upon the position of the display marker. This increases the compatibility of the control with the display. The man can see more easily what he is doing, and tracks more accurately.

The name rate aiding does not mean that adding a rate component to a position control system increases the accuracy of tracking. Tracking is usually no more accurate with a rate aided control system than it is with a position control system. This is probably because the size of the rate component in the output of a rate aided control system depends upon the frequency of the man's responses. For responses of very high frequency, the output of a rate aided control system resembles the output of a position control system. For responses of very low frequency, the output of a rate aided control system resembles the output of a rate control system. It is difficult for the man to tell exactly what effect a response is going to have, because it depends upon the frequencies which he uses.

The control movements and display movements of an acceleration aided control system are illustrated respectively at the top and bottom of the left column of Figure 10.4. The control system combines acceleration, rate and position control. Acceleration aiding should be thought of as aiding performance with an acceleration control system. It ought to indicate that adding orders of control lower than acceleration to an acceleration control system makes the man's task easier.

The name acceleration aiding does not mean that adding an acceleration component to a control system of lower order increases the accuracy of tracking. This is not so. An acceleration component probably always degrades performance. The acceleration component of a control system is the electrical analog of inertia, which is illustrated in Figure 15.5. Table 15.5 shows that inertia degrades performance.

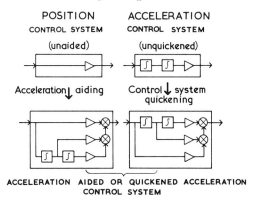

Figure 16.2. Acceleration aiding and quickening.
The unaided position control system above on the left has simply an amplifier. Acceleration aiding is introduced by making the control produce an acceleration component and a rate component, as well as a position component. The two integrators at the bottom on the left do this. The 3 components are then summed to give the output.

The acceleration control system above on the right has 2 integrators and an amplifier. Quickening is introduced by making the control produce a component which bypasses both integrators, and a component which bypasses one integrator. The 3 components are then summed to give the output. The 2 control systems at the bottom are identical, although they are drawn rather differently.

An acceleration aided control system is called by Birmingham and Taylor (1954, 1961) a quickened control system. Figure 16.2 shows that a quickened acceleration control system may be identical with an acceleration aided control system. In order of preference the 3 control systems can be ranked: 1 position, 2 acceleration aided or quickened, and 3 acceleration.

Figure 16.3 (Birmingham and colleagues, 1954) is the classical illustration of the advantage of quickening a control system of high order. The quickened or aided control system has position, rate and acceleration components, as well as a delta acceleration component. In the experiment two 2 × 2 in squares are drawn side by side on the face of a CRT. Each square contains a spot whose position is controlled by a separate joystick, one for each hand. The 6 men have to try and hold each spot within its square.

Trials last 2 min, or until a spot disappears from its square. The

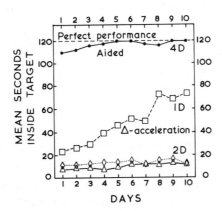

Figure 16.3 Performance with aided and unaided delta acceleration control systems.

The ratios of the amplitudes of the various components of the aided control system are not stated. Without control, a marker takes between 5 and 15 sec to leave its square. This is because the noise in the control system soon simulates a slight displacement of the control. The diamonds represent controlling the left marker in 2 dimensions. The triangles represent controlling the left marker in the leftright dimension, and the right marker in the updown dimension. The 4 experimental conditions are presented each day in a separate random order.

Unfortunately the balanced treatment design probably puts the unaided conditions at a disadvantage as a result of transfer (see Figure 16.5). Also on average the man has 10 times as much practice each day with the aided control system as with either of the 2 conditions with the unaided 2 dimensional task, because a trial finishes as soon as the man loses a marker. (After Birmingham and colleagues, 1954, Figure 6). The experiment is described incorrectly as on display quickening (Webb, 1964, page 358; see Chapter 10).

figure shows the average time for which the spots can be held during the 10 days of the experiment, The squares represent tracking in 1 dimension with the unaided third order control system. Four out of the 6 men learn to control the spot. The other 2 men never learn.

The diamonds and triangles at the bottom are for tracking in 2 dimensions with the unaided control system. The diamonds and triangles lie reliably below the squares. Nobody manages to learn the task.

The filled circles at the top of the figure represent tracking in 4 dimensions with the aided control system. This gives reliably the best performance. Four men never loose a spot. The other 2 men learn respectively rapidly and gradually. Tracking is far easier with the aided control system. With aiding the men can track in 4 dimensions more efficiently than they can track in 1 dimension with the unaided control system.

The aided control system is easy to use because it has a position component. To prevent the spot from leaving the square, the man has simply to move his control in the direction in which he wishes the spot to travel. The spot moves immediately. With the pure third order control system the man can change immediately only the rate of acceleration of the spot. By the time this produces an appreciable change in the position of the spot, the spot may already have left its square. However the figure caption describes 2 procedural biases which favor the aided control system.

Asymmetrical transfer between orders of control system

There is a set of control systems of intermediate order. It includes pure rate control systems, and also aided control systems in which a rate component is combined with other components such as position and acceleration. Tracking with control systems of this intermediate set benefits from training on either a pure position control system or a pure acceleration control system. Whereas tracking with a pure position or a pure acceleration control system does not benefit so much from training on control systems of intermediate order. The training may be a definite disadvantage.

Figure 16.4 and Table 16.1 (Lincoln, 1953) illustrate asymmetrical transfer between a position control system and 2 control systems of intermediate order. Three groups of 18 people each train for 6 days on respectively a position, a rate aided and a rate control system. On day 7 each group of 18 people is divided into 3 subgroups of equal ability. One subgroup of 6 people continues with the same control system. The other 2 subgroups each transfer to one of the other 2 control systems. The figure illustrates the average times on target of the 3 main groups, and of the subgroups which transfer to or from the position control system on day 7. The circles represent the position control system. The unfilled points represent the people who train on the position control system.

The unfilled triangle on the right of the figure represents the average time on target with the rate aided control system, after practice with the position control system. The unfilled triangle lies reliably above the filled triangle on the extreme left of the figure, which represents the average time on target with the rate aided control system before practice. Thus practice with the position control system assists subsequent performance with the rate aided control system. Practice with the position control system may also assist subsequent performance with the rate control system, because the unfilled square on the right of the figure lies a little above the filled square on the extreme left of the figure.

But practice with the rate aided and rate control systems actually hinders performance with the position control system. The 2 filled circles on the right of the figure both lie reliably below the unfilled circle on the extreme left of the figure.

Table 16.1 lists the amount of transfer on day 7 for all the 9 subgroups. The first column is for the 3 subgroups of 6 people who track with the position control system on day 7. The values represent the differences in height between the circles on the extreme right and extreme left of Figure 16.4. The bold 8 printed in the diagonal indicates the amount of transfer for the group which is both trained and tested on the position control system. The 2 remaining numbers in the first column are for transfer to the position control system. As already indicated, both numbers are negative. All the other numbers in the table are positive.

This means that only performance with the position control system is worse after training on a different control system than it is without training. Performances with the rate aided and rate control systems benefit from training on any of the 3 control systems. Thus on transfer, the control systems of intermediate order have an advantage over the position control system. This is indicated by the averages in the bottom row of the table.

The nature of the asymmetrical transfer is suggested by the left column of Table 9.4. With the pursuit display which Lincoln (1953) uses, the rate aided and rate control systems require leads respectively of about 45° and 90°. Whereas the position control system does not require a lead. After training on the rate aided or rate control system, the man may continue to lead when he is transferred to the position control system. This prevents him from remaining on target for as long as he does without previous training. Unfortunately Lincoln (1953) does not

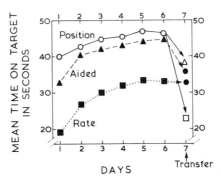

Figure 16.4. Asymmetrical transfer between position, rate aided and rate control systems.

The man sits with his eyes about 6 ft from the display. The track marker or moving target is a white arc 3 cm long and 2 mm wide. It is mounted on the circumference of a rotating wheel with a radius of 23 cm. The response marker is a red line about 3 cm long. It lies along the outer part of the radius of a smaller concentric wheel which rotates in front of the wheel carrying the track marker.

The track reverses direction irregularly 9 times per min. It has a maximum amplitude of about 70 cm. This represents an arc of about 180°. The maximum rate of movement is 14 cm per sec, or 6 rpm. The man has a crank with a radius of 9 cm. For the position control system the gear ratio is 10 to 1. Thus the maximum rate of cranking required is about 60 rpm.

For the rate control system, 1° of rotation of the handwheel gives the response marker a rate of .14 rpm. Thus the maximum track rate of 6 rpm requires a rotation of 43°. The rate aided control system has an aiding ratio of 1:2. The handwheel is rather less sensitive than it is for the position and rate control systems. The gear ratio is 6 to 1 for the position component. For the rate component 1° of rotation gives the response marker a rate of .055 rpm. There are 10 trials daily, each of 60 sec. The longest possible time on target is 54 sec. (Results from Lincoln, 1953.)

report on the phase or time relationships. Thus it is not possible to check on this point.

Asymmetrical transfer between acceleration aided and acceleration control systems

Figure 16.5 (Holland & Henson, 1956) illustrates asymmetrical transfer between an acceleration control system and a control system of intermediate order, in this case an acceleration aided control system. There are 4 separate groups of enlisted men. The 2 groups represented by triangles start with the acceleration control system. The acceleration control system is indicated by the filled points. One group has 14 training sessions on the acceleration control system before transferring to the aided control system.

Table 16.1
Asymmetrical transfer between position, rate aided, and rate control systems

	Increase in time on target after transfer to:		
Training on:	Position	Rate aided	Rate
Position	**8**	5	4*
Rate aided	−4	**12**	9
Rate	−7	6	**16**
Average increase	−1	8	10

The scores represent the average increase in the number of seconds on target per trial on day 7 after transfer, compared with the average on day 1 when using the same control system. (Results from Lincoln, 1953, Figure 3.)

* Not reliably different from zero. The other 8 values in the top 3 rows are all reliably different from zero.

First performance with the aided control system is indicated by the unfilled triangle for session 15. The unfilled triangle lies reliably below the unfilled square and circle on the extreme left. Thus training with the acceleration control system helps performance with the aided control system.

The unfilled triangle lies reliably above the unfilled circle of session 15. So transfer is not perfect on the first transfer session. But in the very next transfer session the unfilled triangle and circle are more or less superimposed. At this stage the group which trains on the acceleration control system is performing as accurately on the aided control system as the group which trains throughout on the aided control system.

The other group represented by triangles trains on the pure acceleration control system for 26 sessions before transferring to the aided control system. In the first transfer session the average error is not reliably less than the average on the very first session of the groups which start with the aided control system. But 4 sessions later the average error has fallen to the level of the groups trained on the aided control system.

Transfer is of considerably less advantage for the 2 groups which train on the aided control system and then transfer to the acceleration control system. The groups are represented by circles and squares. In the first transfer session with the acceleration control system, both groups have reliably smaller average errors than the average errors in the very first session of the groups which start with the acceleration control system.

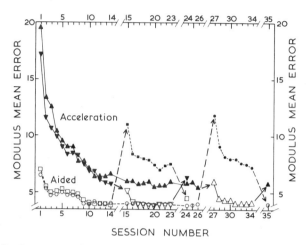

SESSION NUMBER

Figure 16.5   Asymmetrical transfer between acceleration aided and acceleration
control systems.
The aiding ratios are 1:4:8. The 4 functions are for 4 separate groups of 6
enlisted men. The display is compensatory. The track is a sine wave of 3 cpm.
A session comprises 10 trials of 40 sec each. (After Holland & Henson, 1956,
Figure 2.)

But for the remaining transfer sessions with the acceleration control
system, learning is not as rapid as it is for the 2 groups which start
with the acceleration control system. At the end of 8 or 9 transfer sessions, the average errors are still as large as the averages in sessions
9 or 10 of the groups which train initially with the acceleration control
system. And the transfer groups are not improving as rapidly as the
groups which train initially with the acceleration control system.

The asymmetrical transfer is probably due to the different strategies
required with the 2 control systems. The right hand column of Table
9.4 lists the optimal phase relationships for the compensatory display
which Holland and Henson (1956) use. With the acceleration control
system, the man ought to respond with a phase lead of 90° ahead of
the error marker.

With the acceleration aided control system, the optimum phase lead
is not so great. This is because a position component with an optimum
phase lag of 90° is added to the acceleration component. After training
with the smaller optimum phase lead, the man probably takes longer
to achieve the full optimum lead of 90° when he transfers to the acclera-
tion control system. Unfortunately it is not possible to check on the
phase or time relationships, because they are not reported.

The asymmetrical transfer illustrated in Figure 16.5 resembles the asymmetrical transfer illustrated in Figure 10.5 (Goldstein, 1961) for a quickened display. Goldstein uses time on target instead of average error. Thus Goldsteins' figure needs to be turned upsidedown to make it comparable to Figure 16.5. In both figures there is very rapid transfer from the pure high order control system or display to the aided control system or display. But performance with the aided control system or display if anything retards subsequent learning of the pure high order control system or display.

Order of control system with step tracks

Figure 16.1 shows that for step tracks a position control system is the most compatible order of control. To acquire a target, it is necessary only to move the control the corresponding distance in the correct direction.

With a rate control system 2 responses are necessary. Also the man has to wait while the response marker moves over to the target.

The right side of Figure 16.1 shows that with an acceleration control system at least 3 responses are required to acquire a target. Again the man has to wait while his responses are producing their effects. Here nothing much happens when the man first moves the control. In order to bring the display marker to rest on the target, the man has to make his second response well before the target is reached. One of the principal advantages of the augmented displays discussed in Chapter 10 is that they help the man to anticipate correctly, when he has to track steps with an acceleration control system.

As is to be expected from Figure 16.1, a stationary target is acquired more slowly on average with a rate control system than with a position control system. The shortest average times found by Gibbs (1962) are .55 sec for a position control system, and .9 sec for a comparable experiment with a rate control system. Acquisition takes still longer with an acceleration control system. Hammerton's shortest average times are 1.2 sec for a rate control system (see Figure 17.2) and 8.5 sec for a fairly comparable experiment with an acceleration control system (see Table 17.2).

Rate aiding with step tracks

A rate aided control system can be used like a rate control system. The strategy is illustrated in Figure 16.1. If the gain of the position component is sufficiently large, a rate aided control system can also be used like a position control system. The target is reached sooner with this strategy. The man moves his control far enough to acquire the target at once, using the position component of his rate aided control system as he uses a position control system.

When the response marker reaches the target, it will have acquired a rate of movement which will make it tend to overshoot. If the man is skillful, he may be able to move his control back toward its starting point at a rate which is proportional to its distance from the starting point. The rate of return of the control will then cancel the rate component of the control system. This leaves the response marker at rest over the target. Acquiring the target quickly and holding it, is a good deal more difficult with a rate aided control system than it is with a position control system. But in theory acquisition can be just as quick if this strategy is used successfully.

There are a number of compromise strategies which lie between using a rate aided control system like a rate control system and like a position control system. The target takes an intermediate time to reach. Staying on target while backing off the rate is less difficult than it is when the rate aided control system is used like a position control system. It is not known which are the most successful or most popular strategies, because experimenters have not investigated them.

From what has been said, it is clear that acquisition will be quicker when a rate aided control system has a position component with a high gain, and so is more like a position control system. Acquisition will be slower when a rate aided control system has a position component with a low gain, and so is almost a rate control system. This is roughly what S. M. Newhall finds in results reported by Helson (1944, Figure 3). Unfortunately Newhall's results are complicated by a range effect like that illustrated in Figure 16.7.

Acceleration aiding with step tracks

An acceleration aided or quickened control system can be used like an acceleration control system. This is illustrated on the left of Figure 10.4. If the gain of the position component is sufficiently high, an acceleration aided control system can also be used like a position control system. In backing off the acceleration, the control has to be moved back beyond its center before it is left in the center. Again there are a number of intermediate strategies which can be used.

There do not appear to be any published experiments comparing acceleration aided control systems with control systems of lower order using step tracks. This may be because engineers are aware of the incompatibility of acceleration components of control systems with step tracks.

Order of control system with velocity ramp tracks

In tracking a velocity ramp, the man may first have to acquire the target. After this, he has to match the rate of the ramp, and also correct for errors in position. If the velocity of the ramp varies, errors in position have to be corrected fairly frequently. Figure 16.1 shows that a position control system is the most compatible control system both for acquiring a target and for correcting errors in position.

If the velocity of the ramp remains constant, errors in position occur only occasionally once the man has acquired the target and generated the correct velocity. A rate or rate aided control system allows the man to generate the correct constant velocity simply by holding the control in the appropriate position. This is easier to do than generating a constant velocity with a position control system.

However there is no acceptable evidence that a rate or rate aided control system produces reliably more accurate tracking of a single target than does a position control system. It is only in tracking multiple targets moving at constant rates than a position control system is at a disadvantage. Here with a number of rate aided control systems, all the other markers continue to move while the man is adjusting any one marker. Whereas with a number of position control systems, all the other markers are at rest while the man is adjusting any one marker.

Rate aiding with constant velocity ramp tracks

With a constant velocity ramp, a rate aided control system allows a single response to correct both the position error and the rate error at the same time. The center section of Figure 16.6 shows how position and rate change together as the man moves the control. In the left section of the figure the output of the rate aided control system has fallen behind the track. A response which corrects the error in position also increases the rate output. If the man makes his correction at a time after the last response which equals the aiding time constant of the control system, both the position and the rate output of the control system will then match the track. This is shown at **B** for a control system with an aiding time constant of .5 sec.

If the man responds more than .5 sec after the last response when the control system is falling behind, correcting the error in position produces too fast a rate output of the control system. This is illustrated at **C** in the left section of the figure. The man will soon have to make another correction, this time in the opposite direction.

There is also a penalty for responding too soon. Getting the position right too soon does not increase the rate output of the control system

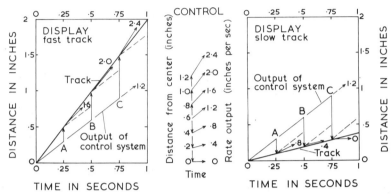

Figure 16.6. Tracking a constant velocity ramp with a rate aided control system.
The center section of the figure shows that the aiding ratio is 1:2. Moving
the control 1 in from its center moves the response marker 1 in and gives the
marker a rate of 2 in per sec. The aiding time constant is therefore ½ or .5 sec.
With a constant velocity ramp it means that if the error in position is corrected
.5 sec after the last correction, the rate output of the control system will match
the rate of the ramp. This is illustrated at **B** on both sides of the figure. In
the left section of the figure the ramp track is a fast one, with a rate of 2 in
per sec. At time O the output of the control system has a rate of 1.2 in per
sec and is falling behind. In the right section of the figure the ramp track is
a slow one with a rate of .4 in per sec. The output of the control system, with
its rate of 1.2 in per sec, is running ahead.

A correction made after .25 sec is illustrated at **A.** In the left section of the
figure the rate output of the control system is increased from 1.2 in per sec to
only 1.6 in per sec, compared with the track rate of 2 in per sec. In the right
section of the figure the rate output is reduced from 1.2 in per sec to only .8
in per sec, compared with the track rate of .4 in per sec. A correction made
after .75 sec is illustrated at **C.** In the left section of the figure the rate output
is increased to 2.4 in per sec, which is .4 in per sec too fast. In the right section
of the figure the rate output is reduced to zero.

sufficiently to prevent the output from falling behind again. This is
illustrated at **A** in the left section of the figure. The corresponding effects
when the output of the control system is running ahead of the track
are illustrated in the right section of the figure.

Figure 16.6 shows that a rate aided control system is ideal for tracking
a constant velocity ramp, provided the man responds always with a
periodicity which corresponds to the aiding time constant of the control
system. This can happen when a rotating radar aerial is linked to a
plan position indicator display like that at the top of Figure 9.3. Each
rotation of the radar beam paints a moving target in a slightly different
position. The man has to keep markers superimposed upon a number
of targets.

The man corrects the positions of the markers as soon as the targets are painted in their new positions. Thus he responds at intervals of time which correspond to the rotation time of the radar aerial. The aiding time constant of the rate aided control system can be equated with the rotation time. Each marker then moves at the average rate of the target, and corrections of position automatically introduce appropriate corrections of rate.

If the man does not correct a marker position for several rotations of the radar aerial, when he does eventually correct the position, the rate aided control system will introduce too large a correction of rate, as illustrated at C in Figure 16.6. But provided the man makes another correction as soon as the target is painted again, the time interval between the 2 corrections will equal the aiding time constant. The second correction will then make the position and rate of the marker match the position and rate of the target.

Range effects with aiding time constants and velocity ramp tracks

Figure 16.7 (Helson, 1944) illustrates the results of a study with 10 different aiding time constants. A pure rate control system with an aiding time constant of zero is shown on the extreme left. A rate aided control system with an aiding time constant of 4.5 sec is shown on the extreme right. This control system is the closest to a pure position control system. The figure shows that the error is smallest with aiding time constants of intermediate size.

Unfortunately the experiment uses a balanced treatment design. With a balanced treatment design, U shaped functions like those in the figure are produced simply by a range effect. People respond always as if they have an aiding time constant of average size. Tracking is therefore most accurate when the aiding time constant happens to be of this size.

A number of other experiments support the result on the left of the figure that rate aiding gives a smaller error than pure rate control. Some of the experiments were performed during World War II at the Franklin Institute. A more recent experiment showing a similar result is reported by R. L. Smith and his colleagues (1966a). However all the experiments use balanced treatment designs. Asymmetrical transfer probably exaggerates the average error shown in the figure with the pure rate control. It is not known how much smaller the error would be in the absence of bias. To find out requires an experiment with separate groups of people for each condition.

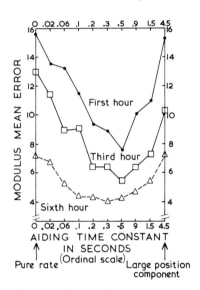

Figure 16.7. A range effect with various aiding time constants.

The aiding time constants on the abscissa are ordered by size, not drawn to scale. An aiding time constant of zero represents a pure rate control. With an aiding time constant of 4.5 sec, a response which moves the display marker 4.5 in gives the marker a rate of 1 in per sec in the same direction.

The display is compensatory. The track represents the angular position of an aircraft which takes between 10 and 60 sec to fly across the sky (see Figure 8.1). The tracks of 4 aircraft are combined to produce a tracking task lasting 4 min with 4 reversals. Between reversals the rate of the track varies at an unspecified frequency about 40% above and below its average value.

The man has a crank with a radius of 5 in. In different trials the pure rate control system is used with 9 different gear ratios. The highest and lowest gear ratios require average rates of cranking of .5 and 117 rpm respectively to compensate for the variations in the rate of the track. The remaining 9 aiding time constants are each paired with 3 of the gear ratios. The longer aiding time constants have lower gear ratios for the rate component than do the shorter aiding time constants. Thus they require faster rates of cranking. But for each aiding time constant, the 3 gear ratios all produce about the same average error (Helson, 1944, Figure 2). Thus the required rate of cranking probably does not affect performance very much. With the tracks used, the size of the position component has little effect upon the required rate of cranking.

The total of 36 experimental conditions are presented in random orders to each of 8 men. Since trials last 4 min, each man does not perform all conditions during any one of the hours illustrated in the figure. Unfortunately statistical tests are not reported, so it is not possible to tell how repeatable the results are likely to be. (From Helson, 1944, Figure 8.)

The increase in the average error with the time constant of 4.5 sec is also due to bias. With a crank control like that used in the experiment of Figure 16.7, Bergum, Klein and Baldwin (1960) report little to choose between a rate aided control system and a pure position control system. This is presumably because they use a separate group experimental design. Rate aiding reduces the high frequencies in the response, and so the number of transitions between being on target and being off target. But both control systems give about the same average time on target, and average distance off target.

To sum up, with a velocity ramp track a position control system is as good as a rate aided control system, and is probably preferable to a rate control system. The only exception is in tracking multiple targets, where rate aided control systems are an obvious choice.

Acceleration control with velocity ramp tracks

An acceleration control system is not very compatible with a constant velocity ramp. The output of an acceleration control system in tracking a constant velocity ramp is illustrated in Figure 10.4 in the third row of the second column. There is always a delay before the appropriate rate can be obtained. During the delay an error in position develops. Correcting the error in position requires a complex 3 movement response, like the one illustrated on the right of Figure 16.1. The error recurs if the rate output of the control system does not quite match the rate of the ramp. Changing rates is achieved by a quick out and back response. Clearly control is more difficult with an acceleration control system than it is with a control system of lower order.

The output of an acceleration aided control system with rate and position components is illustrated in the bottom row of the second column of Figure 10.4. The control system is less well suited to a constant velocity ramp than is a rate aided control system. Suppose the man always corrects errors in position by changing the position of the control, as he does with a rate aided control system. If so, the acceleration component makes the rate output of the control system oscillate around the track rate.

Another strategy is to correct errors in position by making a 3 movement response, like the one illustrated on the right of Figure 16.1 for an acceleration control system. During the correction the position component produces 3 displacements of the ramp output of the control system. Whatever the man does, he is unlikely to track the ramp as accurately as he can track it with a rate aided control system.

Acceleration and acceleration aided control systems do not appear to have been compared with control systems of lower order on constant velocity ramps. This is presumably because they are believed to be less suitable.

Order of control system with sine wave tracks and pursuit displays

For sine wave tracks, a position control system is the most compatible control system. In order to track accurately the man has to move his control in phase with the track at the appropriate amplitude. He has simply to copy the track.

With a rate control system the man's control movements have to lead the track by a phase angle of 90°. It is not possible to achieve such a large lead if the track is irregular and contains high frequencies. If the track is a single sine wave and the display is pursuit, the man may be able to lead the track by 90° after practice. But the control movements which he has to make are not very compatible with the movements of the track marker. In one quarter of a cycle the man moves his control in the same direction as the track marker is moving. In the next quarter cycle the man moves his control in the opposite direction to the direction in which the track marker is moving. In the next quarter cycle the directional relationship between control and display reverses again, and so on.

With an acceleration control system the man's control movements have to lead the track by a phase angle of 180°. If the track is irregular and of high frequency, the man cannot even approach this size of lead. With a single sine wave track and a pursuit display, the man has to copy the movements of the track marker, only always moving his control in the opposite direction to the direction of movement of the track marker. This may give the man the impression that the directional relationship between his control movements and the display movements is the reverse of the actual relationship. It can be confusing if the man gets his amplitude or phase slightly wrong. For his corrective action does not have the immediate effect upon the response marker which it looks as if it should have.

With an aided control system, the man's response again has to lead the track in phase. The right side of Figure 10.4 illustrates what happens if the man simply copies the track as he sees it. The rate component of his control system lags 90° behind the track. If the control system has an acceleration component, it lags 180° behind the track. Summing the components results in a control system output with a phase angle which depends upon the frequency of the track, and upon the aiding ratios. The phase lag of an acceleration aided control system with a 15 cpm track and aiding ratios of $1:4:8$ is illustrated at the bottom of the figure on the right.

Table 16.2 lists experiments which compare position, rate aided, and rate control systems using a pursuit display and a sine wave track. The experiments with separate group designs can be singled out by 2 entries in the column labeled **N** for the number of people used in the experiment. Three of these experiments (Lincoln, 1953; Poulton, 1963b; Regan, 1960) show that tracking with a position control system is reliably more accurate than tracking with a rate control system.

Lincoln's (1953) experiment shows also that tracking with a position control system is reliably more accurate than tracking with a rate aided control system, and that a rate aided control system is reliably better than a rate control system. No experiment with a separate group design shows a higher order control system to be reliably better than a lower order control system. These results are not biased by transfer between conditions, because each condition is performed by a separate group of people.

The remaining experimental comparisons listed in the table are from balanced treatment designs. All but 2 of them confirm the conclusion that a low order control system is at least as good as a higher order control system. The exceptions are listed in part **A** of the table. It is important to consider them in detail, to see why they can be disregarded. For they are sometimes quoted as evidence in favor of aided and rate control systems.

The results of the Chernikoff and Taylor (1957) experiment must be due to bias of the kind illustrated in Table 16.1 (Lincoln, 1953), which penalizes the position control system. The experiment is one of the experiments listed at the top of Table 9.3. These are the unfortunate experiments in which a compensatory display is found to be reliably better than a pursuit display.

Chernikoff and Taylor (1957) pair the position, rate aided and rate control systems with both pursuit and compensatory displays. The 6 men perform all 6 conditions daily for 18 days. The optimum phase relationships between display and control for the 6 conditions are listed in the 3 top rows of Table 9.4. The optimum phase relationships range from a lead of 90° through a lead of about 45° to no lead or lag, and from there through a lag of about 45° to a lag of 90°.

With the pursuit display the aided and rate control systems require phase leads while the position control system does not. It seems likely that there is a carryover to the position control system of some of the

Table 16.2
Pursuit experiments comparing control systems of low order on sine waves

Author(s)	Year	N	Highest frequency in track (cpm)	Other variables	Reliably Better	Reliably Worse

A. Tracking with a higher order control system reliably more accurate than tracking with a lower order control system, probably due to bias

Author(s)	Year	N	Highest frequency in track (cpm)	Other variables	Better	Worse
Chernikoff and Taylor*	1957	6	6.7	Compensatory display	Aided Rate	Position Position
Pearl and colleagues	1955	27	4.5‡	Track amplitude	1:2 (Aiding ratio)	1:1

B. Tracking with a lower order control system reliably more accurate than tracking with a higher order control system, or not reliably different

Author(s)	Year	N	Highest frequency in track (cpm)	Other variables	Better	Worse
Chernikoff and colleagues	1955	6	15	Compensatory display	Position	Aided
Chernikoff and Taylor*	1957	6	6.7	Compensatory display	Aided	Rate
		6	16.7	Compensatory display	Position Aided	Rate Rate
		6	26.7	Compensatory display	Position Position Aided	Aided Rate Rate
Heinemann	1961	3 + 3	2‡		—	—
		3 + 3	4‡		—	—
Lincoln (see Figure 16.4)	1953	18 + 18	4.5‡		Position Position Aided	Aided Rate Rate
Notterman and Page	1962	3	10§		—	—
			20§		—	—
			40§		—	—
Obermayer and colleagues	1961	9† (some pilots)	2.2	Compensatory display	Position	Rate
Obermayer and colleagues	1962	6† (some pilots)	3.3 6.7 16.7	} Compensatory display	— Position Position	— Rate Rate
Poulton	1963b	6 + 6	10		—	—
		6 + 6	40		Position	Rate
Regan	1960	24 + 24	7.5‡		Position	Rate

* Included in both parts of the table.
† Six of the same people serve in both experiments.
‡ Half the number of reversals per minute.
§ Excludes high frequencies of small amplitude.

Table 16.3

Compensatory experiments comparing control systems of low order on sine waves

Author(s)	Year	N	Highest frequency in track (cpm)	Other variables	Reliably Better	Reliably Worse

A. Tracking with a higher order control system reliably more accurate than tracking with a lower order control system, probably due to bias

Author(s)	Year	N	Highest frequency in track (cpm)	Other variables	Better	Worse
Chernikoff and colleagues	1955	6	15	Pursuit display	Aided	Position
Chernikoff and colleagues	1960	6	3.2 or 1.9	Acceleration control	Rate	Position
Chernikoff and Taylor*	1957	6	6.7	Pursuit display	Aided Rate	Position Position
Obermayer and colleagues*	1962	6† (some pilots)	3.3	Pursuit display Acceleration control	Rate	Position

B. Tracking with a lower order control system reliably more accurate than tracking with a higher order control system, or not reliably different

Author(s)	Year	N	Highest frequency in track (cpm)	Other variables	Better	Worse
Chernikoff and Taylor*	1957	6	6.7	} Pursuit display	—	—
		6	16.7		Position Aided	Rate Rate
		6	26.7		Position Position Aided Aided	Aided Rate Rate Rate
Frost	1962	13 + 13	10			
		12 + 11	60		—	—
Heinemann	1961	3 + 3	2‡		—	—
		3 + 3	4‡		—	—
Helson	1949	6	?	Aiding ratios	—	—
Levison and Elkind	1967a	3 pilots	10§	2 Separated displays Acceleration control	—	—
Obermayer and colleagues	1961	9† (some pilots)	2.2	Pursuit display Acceleration control	—	—
Obermayer and colleagues*	1962	6† some pilots)	6.7 16.7	} Pursuit display Acceleration control	— Position	— Rate
Poulton	1963a	6 + 6	40 (filtered)		Position	Rate
		6 + 5	40	.	Position	Rate
Regan	1960	24 + 24	7.5‡		Position	Rate
Smith and colleagues	1966a	6	15	Magnification Cues of motion	Aided	Rate

* Included in both parts of the table.

† Six of the same people serve in both experiments.

‡ Half the number of reversals per minute.

§ Excludes high frequency shelf.

phase lead which is appropriate to the 2 higher order control systems. Unfortunately Chernikoff and Taylor (1957) do not report the phase or time relationships, so it is not possible to check on this point.

The other exception listed in part **A** of Table 16.2 is the experiment by Pearl, Simon, and Smith (1955). Pearl and her colleagues compare 3 rate aided control systems with aiding ratios of 1:4, 1:2 and 1:1 (aiding time constants of .25, .5 and 1.0 sec). The experimental apparatus is described in the caption to Figure 16.4. Pearl uses a latin square design for the 9 combinations of 3 time constants and 3 amplitudes of track. The students practice every combination daily for a total of 4 days. On the last day the aiding time constant of intermediate size is found to give the most accurate tracking.

The results resemble the results illustrated in Figure 16.7 (Helson, 1944). They are presumably due to a range effect. A **U** shaped function would be found if the students tend to respond always as if they have the intermediate aiding ratio of 1:2. The aiding ratio of 1:1 requires the smallest phase lead. With this aiding ratio, a range effect would produce too large a lead. Thus as in the Chernikoff and Taylor (1957) experiment, the discrepant result is probably due to the carryover of a phase lead from the conditions which require greater leads. Unfortunately Pearl and her colleagues (1955) do not report the phase or time relationships.

The results of the 2 experiments listed in part **A** of Table 16.2 are therefore suspect. They could be due to bias introduced by the balanced treatment designs used. All the remaining experiments listed in the table support the conclusion that a control system of lower order is always at least as good as a higher order control system when the display is pursuit.

The left side of Figure 16.8 (Allen & Jex, 1968) illustrates closed loop transfer functions for tracking sine waves with a rate control system. The filled points represent performance with a pursuit display. They are probably fairly comparable to the triangles in Figure 8.13 for a position control system. At a frequency of 5 cpm there is little difference between the position control system of Figure 8.13 and the rate control system of Figure 16.8.

But at the highest unattenuated track frequency of about 30 cpm, the position control system of Figure 8.13 has a relative amplitude of only 1.05, and a phase lag of only 10°. Whereas the rate control system of Figure 16.8 has a relative amplitude of 1.2, and a phase lag of 20°. The greater phase lag at the higher frequencies probably accounts for much of the larger average error found with the higher order control systems in the experiments listed in the lower part of Table 16.2.

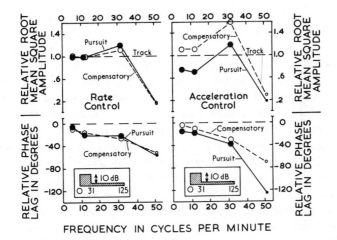

Figure 16.8. Closed loop transfer functions with rate and acceleration control systems.

The frequency spectrum of the track is illustrated at the bottom. It is fairly similar to the track represented by triangles in Figure 8.13. The response above the top unattenuated track frequency of 31 cpm is represented by smaller points. The amplitude at 50 cpm is given as about .2. It is about double the amplitude of the track at this frequency. Unfortunately the amplitudes of the frequencies in the remnant are not reported.

The pursuit display resembles Figure 1.1A, except that the horizontal line is 5 cm long. In the compensatory condition the spot is fixed instead of the line. This is the opposite convention to the one illustrated in Figure 1.1B. The track consists of 9 sine waves which are spaced at equal logarithmic intervals of frequency. Three of the sine waves represent the high frequency shelf. The man has a vertical joystick 5.5 in long. A force of 5.7 lb is required to move the joystick 1 in.

The results from an additional mixed pursuit and compensatory display are not shown. In this mixed display the large sine wave of 5 cpm and the small sine wave of 50 cpm disturb the man's response marker. The remaining 7 sine waves are used as the track. The 4 pilots are always told in advance which display they are to have next. The experimental design is partly balanced. (Results from Allen & Jex, 1968, Figure 16.)

Order of control system with sine wave tracks and compensatory displays

Table 16.3 lists the experiments which compare position, rate aided and rate control systems using a compensatory display and a sine wave track. There are 3 experiments with separate group designs (Poulton, 1963a; Regan, 1960) which show that tracking with a position control system is reliably more accurate than tracking with a rate control system. There is one experiment with a separate group design (Frost, 1962) which shows that tracking with a rate aided control system is reliably more accurate than tracking with a pure rate control system. No experiment with a separate group design shows a higher order control system to be reliably better than a lower order control system. These results are unbiased by transfer between conditions.

The 4 experiments listed in part **A** of the table all have balanced treatment designs. They show reliable results in favor of higher order control systems. The results can all be due to asymmetrical transfer, like the results of the experiments listed in part **A** Table 16.2. Inappropriately small phase lags are presumably carried over from the higher order control systems to the position control system. Again the experiments need to be examined in detail, to see why the results can be disregarded. Like the results listed in part **A** of Table 16.2, they are sometimes quoted as evidence in favor of aided and rate control systems.

The first entry in the part **A** of Table 16.3 is the experiment by Chernikoff, Birmingham, and Taylor (1955). It has the 4 conditions produced by pairing position and rate aided control systems with pursuit and compensatory displays. The 4 optimal phase relationships between display and control are listed in the 2 top rows of Table 9.4. The position control system with the compensatory display has the largest optimal phase lag behind the error marker, a phase lag of 90°. This condition is reliably worse than the 3 remaining conditions, which all have smaller optimal phase lags.

The 6 men perform all 4 conditions daily for 4 days. Presumably they do not lag as far behind the error marker as they should do, when they change to the position control system and compensatory display from one of the other conditions. Figure 4.1A shows that with a compensatory display, a phase lag of less than 90° behind the error marker is produced by reducing the amplitude of the response. This may be what the man does on transfer to the position control system and compensatory display.

A similar criticism can be made of the experiment by Chernikoff, Duey, and Taylor (1960, Table 1), which is the second entry in Table 16.3. The experiment compares position, rate and acceleration control systems, but only with a compensatory display. The optimal phase relationships are listed in the right hand column of Table 9.4. Presumably after performing with the acceleration or the rate control system, the man does not lag as far behind the error marker as he should do when he changes to the position control system.

The third entry in Table 16.3 is the experiment by Chernikoff and Taylor (1957). The experiment appears also in part **A** of Table 16.2. This experiment, and the experiment just below it in Table 16.3 by Obermayer and colleagues (1962), are 2 of the unfortunate experiments which are listed in part **A** of Table 9.3. It has already been explained how the results of both experiments are probably biased by the transfer between conditions. As in the other 2 experiments listed in part **A** of Table 16.3, the man probably does not lag the full 90° behind the error marker when he transfers to the position control system and compensatory display. Unfortunately it is not possible to check on the phase or time relationships, because none of the 4 experimental reports mention them.

The results of all the 4 experiments listed in part **A** of Table 16.3 are therefore suspect. They can all be due to transfer from the other conditions performed by the same people. The remaining experiments listed in the table all support the conclusion that a position and a rate aided control system are always at least as good as a control system of higher order when the display is compensatory.

High order control systems with sine wave tracks and compensatory displays

Table 16.4 lists the experiments which compare acceleration, acceleration aided and higher order control systems with control systems of lower order. There are only 3 experiments which used separate group designs (Garvey & Taylor, 1959; Holland & Henson, 1956). The experiments show that tracking is reliably less accurate with an acceleration control system than with either an acceleration aided control system or a position control system. These results are unbiased by transfer between control systems. All the remaining experiments used balanced treatment designs.

The 3 experiments listed in part **A** of the table show reliable results in favor of higher order control systems. The results must be due to transfer. It is almost inconceivable that a control system with an acceleration component could be better than a control system with only components of lower order. An acceleration component considerably increases the phase lag. It corresponds to inertia, which degrades performance. Like the experiments in parts **A** of Tables 16.2 and 16.3, the 3 experiments need to be considered in detail, to see why their results can be disregarded. This is because acceleration aiding is sometimes added to a control system of lower order, in the belief that it improves the accuracy of tracking.

The experiment by Chernikoff and his colleagues (1960, Table 1) is the second entry in Table 16.4. This experiment appears also in part **A** of Table 16.3. It has just been pointed out how transfer produced by the balanced treatment design probably penalizes performance with

Table 16.4

Compensatory experiments comparing control systems of high order on sine waves

Author(s)	Year	N	Highest frequency in track (cpm)	Other variables	Reliably	
					Better	Worse
A. Tracking with a high order control system reliably more accurate than tracking with a lower order control system, probably due to bias						
Chernikoff and colleagues*	1959	6	2.3 3.8 7.1 12.0		Fourth order aided	Position
Chernikoff and colleagues*	1960	6	3.2 or 1.9		Acceleration	Position
Searle	1951	8	10		Acceleration aided	Rate aided
B. Tracking with a lower order control system reliably more accurate than tracking with a high order control system, or not reliably different						
Allen and Jex (see Figure 16.8)	1968	4 pilots	31§	Pursuit display	Rate	Acceleration
Birmingham and colleagues (see Figure 16.3)	1954	6	No track		Delta acceleration aided	Delta acceleration
Chernikoff and colleagues*	1959	6	20 37.5		— Position	Fourth order aided —
		6	20 37.5 61.8 120 201		— Position	— Fourth order aided

Reference	Year	N	Condition	Control	Display
Chernikoff and colleagues*	1960	6	1 or 2 Controls and error markers	Rate	Acceleration
Chernikoff and Le May (see Table 11.4)	1963	6		Position	Acceleration
Duey and Chernikoff	1959	8	Same or different dynamics in the 2 dimensions	Acceleration aided	Acceleration
Garvey and Taylor	1959	8 + 8	Same or different dynamics in the 2 dimensions	Position	Acceleration
		8 + 8		Acceleration aided	Acceleration
Holland and Henson (see Figure 16.5)	1956	12 + 12		Acceleration aided	Acceleration
Levison and Elkind	1966	3	Same or different dynamics in the 2 dimensions	Position	Acceleration
Levison and Elkind	1967a	3 pilots	2 Separated displays	Position	Acceleration
Notterman and Page	1962	3	Control loading	Position	Acceleration aided
Obermayer and colleagues	1961	9† (some pilots)	Pursuit display	Position / Rate	Acceleration / Acceleration
Obermayer and colleagues	1962	6† (some pilots)	Pursuit display	Position / Rate / Position / Rate / Position / Rate	Acceleration

Values: 3.2 or 1.9; 4.7; 1.9; 3.2; 3.2; 3; 35§; 10§; 20§; 2.2; 3.3; 6.7; 16.7

Table 16.4 (cont.)

Author(s)	Year	N	Highest frequency in track (cpm)	Other variables	Reliably	
					Better	Worse
Rund and colleagues	1957	6	· 3	Binary display	Fully acceleration aided	Acceleration and rate only
Verdi and colleagues	1965	10	10§		Fully acceleration aided	Acceleration
					Acceleration and rate only	Acceleration

* Included in both parts of the table.
† Six of the same people serve in both experiments.
§ Excludes high frequencies of small amplitude.

the position control system, by making the man respond with an insufficient lag in phase behind the movements of the error marker.

The results of the Chernikoff, Bowen, and Birmingham (1959) experiment at the top of Table 16.4 must also be due to transfer. The fourth order aided control system has aiding ratios 1:4:2:.4:.05. The experimental design provides great opportunities for transfer between this control system and the position control system. The right hand column of Table 9.4 shows that with the position control system the man should lag 90° behind the error marker. With the fourth order aided control system, it can be calculated that the man should lead the error marker when he responds at frequencies below about 10 cpm. Even at high response frequencies, he never has to lag as much as 90° behind the error marker. When the man transfers to the position control system, he probably does not lag the full 90° behind which he should. Again it is not possible to check on the phase or time relationships, because they are not reported.

The results of the Searle (1951) experiment are probably due to a range effect. Searle (1951, Experiment 1) holds constant the ratio of the position and rate components of his control system at 1:4, and varies the acceleration component. His most different control systems have aiding ratios of 1:4:16, and 1:4:0 which is his pure rate aided control system. There are 2 intermediate control systems with ratios of 1:4:8 and 1:4:4. The 4 control systems are presented in a balanced treatment design which is repeated 6 times.

Tracking is reliably more accurate when using the control system with the intermediate aiding ratios of 1:4:8 than when using any of the other 3 control systems. The U shaped relationship between aiding ratios and accuracy corresponds to the U shaped relationship illustrated in Figure 16.7 (Helson, 1944). A U shaped relationship is reported also by Pearl and colleagues (1955) in the experiment listed in part A of Table 16.2. U shaped relationships are produced if people tend to respond always as if they have aiding ratios of intermediate size.

Searle's (1951) rate aided control system is one of his extreme conditions, with aiding ratios of 1:4:0. It would be likely to come off badly with a balanced treatment design which produces a range effect. Presumably the man does not lag as far behind the error marker as he should, when he changes to the rate aided control system from any of the acceleration aided control systems. Unfortunately Searle (1951) also does not report the phase or time relationships.

The results of the 3 experiments listed in part A of Table 16.4 are all suspect. They are likely to be due to transfer produced by the balanced treatment designs. The remaining experiments listed in the table all support the conclusion that a control system with an acceleration component is never better than a control system with only lower order components when the display is compensatory. If a control system has to have acceleration or higher order components, it can be improved by adding components of lower order.

The unfilled points in Figure 16.8 represent closed loop transfer functions for tracking sine waves with a compensatory display. The results are from the experiment of Allen and Jex (1968), which is listed in the top row of part **B** of the table. Over the unattenuated track frequencies up to 31 cpm there is little difference in the phase lag between the rate and the acceleration control systems when using the compensatory display. The main difference between the 2 control systems is the greater relative amplitude of the closed loop transfer function of the acceleration control system. The relative amplitude of the remnant is also considerably larger with the acceleration control system.

With the acceleration control system the pilot apparently makes great efforts to keep his phase lag small. This can be done by guessing what the next track movement is likely to be, and putting the corresponding control input into the acceleration control system. When the pilot predicts correctly, he reduces his phase lag. When he predicts incorrectly, he gets the amplitude of the output wrong. The figure indicates that he is more likely to overshoot than to undershoot when he predicts incorrectly with the acceleration control system.

Rate control systems, compensatory displays, and low frequency tracks

A compensatory display reduces the disadvantage of a rate control system. A rate control system is not very compatible with a pursuit display. In step tracking, a rate control is held stationary at its center when the response marker is stationary but displaced from its center. In tracking a constant velocity ramp, a rate control has to be held stationary in order to give the response marker a constant rate of movement. The left side of Table 9.4 shows that in copying a sine wave track movements of a rate control have to lead the movements of the track marker by 90°.

A rate control system is more compatible with a compensatory display. In step tracking, a rate control is held stationary at its center when the error marker is stationary and centered on the target. In tracking a constant velocity ramp, a rate control is held stationary when the error marker is stationary. The right side of Table 9.4 shows that in reproducing a sine wave track, movements of a rate control have simply to be more or less in phase with the movements of the error marker.

A rate control system produces less accurate tracking than a position control system. And a compensatory display produces less accurate tracking than a pursuit display (see Tables 9.2 and 9.3). But when a rate control system is paired with a compensatory display, at least the control system and the display are compatible with each other.

The reverse holds for a position control system. With a pursuit display, movements of a position control correspond directly to movements of the track marker. But with a compensatory display, the movements of a position control are not very compatible with the movements of the error marker. In step tracking, a position control is held stationary but displaced when the error marker is stationary and centered on the target. In tracking a constant velocity ramp, a position control has to be moved at a constant rate to hold the error marker stationary. The right side of Table 9.4 shows that in reproducing a sine wave track, movements of a position control have to lag about 90° behind the movements of the error marker.

It follows that the difference in difficulty between a position control system and a rate control system is likely to be smaller with a compensatory display than with a pursuit display. When the difference is reduced in size, a balanced treatment design which penalizes the position control system may actually reverse the direction of the difference. In the case of sine wave tracks, the point can be appreciated by comparing Table 16.3 for compensatory displays with Table 16.2 for pursuit displays. If anything, Table 16.3 is less favorable to a position control system than is Table 16.2.

A similar point is made for display modes in Chapter 9. The difference in difficulty between a pursuit display and a compensatory display is likely to be smaller with a rate control system than with a position control system.

The compatibility between a rate control system and a compensatory display helps only with tracks of low frequency. Irregular high frequencies cannot be tracked very well with a rate control system, because the man cannot achieve the 90° phase advance of his response over the track which a rate control system requires. With irregular high frequencies a position control system is always found to be the more accurate, even when using a compensatory display and a balanced treatment design which favor a rate control system.

Acceleration aiding with accelerating tracks

An acceleration aided control system has sometimes been thought to be appropriate for an accelerating track, such as the track of an approaching low flying aircraft. Figure 8.1 shows that an aircraft appears to accelerate as it approaches. It achieves its fastest angular rate when it is closest. It could be argued that up to this point acceleration aiding should help, although there is as yet no valid evidence for this.

Figure 7.6 (Garvey, 1960) shows that an unpracticed man can lag behind an accelerating target when he uses a pure rate control system. Unfortunately the results are probably due to transfer between tracks, produced by the balanced treatment design. The same criticism can be leveled at the earlier Garvey and Mitnick (1957) experiment with a position control system. It is not possible to conclude that people necessarily lag behind accelerating and delta accelerating ramps when they use a position or rate control system. The point needs to be investigated using a separate group experimental design.

The experiments of Speight and Bickerdike (1968) on aiming at a simulated approaching aircraft, also have balanced treatment designs. Speight and Bickerdike give groups of 12 soldiers various amounts of rate and acceleration aiding. From the results they calculate the optimum amount of rate and acceleration aiding. Presumably the optimum values fall rather nearer to the middle of the ranges than they should, because they are partly determined by the ranges, as in Figure 16.7. An experiment needs to be carried out using a separate group design. When this is done, the man may be found to track as well or better with a position control system, if he has not previously used higher order control systems.

The chief difficulty with acceleration aiding occurs once the aircraft passes and is flying away. Its angular rate is now decreasing, while the rate output of the acceleration aided control system is still increasing. The man has to move his control back to the other side of its zero position, in order to decelerate the output of the control system sufficiently quickly. His response corresponds to pushing against a heavy fly wheel in order to slow it up.

With a rate aided control system the man may have only to reverse the direction of movement of his control. With a position control system the man still moves his control in the same direction, but at a slower rate. When the aircraft is flying away, the man is therefore more likely to lose it from his sight if he has an acceleration aided control system. This point also has still to be investigated by experiment.

Adaptive training devices

In tracking, an adaptive or dynamic trainer is usually designed to teach people to control a system of high order. The adaptive trainer holds constant the difficulty of the man's task at a level which the experimenter believes will produce the quickest learning of the high order control system. This is done by measuring continuously a criterion of the man's success, such as his modulus mean error.

The experimenter chooses a level of error which indicates that the task is challenging, not too difficult yet not too easy. When the average error is smaller' than this value, the task is automatically made more difficult. The increase in difficulty depends upon how much better the man is tracking than the standard set by the experimenter. If the average level of the man's performance is below standard, the task is automatically made easier.

In designing an experiment on adaptive training, the experimenter has to make 3 fairly arbitrary choices or guesses (Kelley, 1969b). He has to select his criterion level of error. He has to decide what engineering variable or variables to change in order to hold constant the difficulty of the task. And he has to decide how the increases and decreases in the difficulty of the task are to be related to the average level of error below or above the criterion level.

Adaptive training devices which vary aiding

We have seen that there can be negative transfer between different orders of control system. The first experiments on adaptive training run into this problem, because the difficulty of the task is changed by changing the aiding of the control system. The man may start with an aided delta acceleration control system. If he tracks badly, the amount of aiding is increased. As the man improves with practice, the control system becomes more nearly a pure delta acceleration control system. A device of this kind is likely to produce interference between different orders of control, because different orders of control require different amounts of lead, and so different strategies.

Figure 16.5 suggests that the greatest amount of interference is likely to occur as the man improves, and the degree of aiding is reduced. But when the man happens to do badly, he may also run into interference. He finds himself tracking with a control system with more aiding. This may temporarily increase the difficulty of his task, instead of making his task easier. The lead strategies which he has just learned for the control system with less aiding, are no longer so appropriate. As a result, he may do still worse. As he does worse the aiding of the control system is increased still further, and he may run into additional interference.

Table 16.5 lists experiments on more than 1 or 2 people which vary the difficulty of the task by changing the aiding of the control system.

Table 16.5

Experiments on adaptive training which vary aiding

Author(s)	Year	N	Change produced by adaptation	Integration time constant (sec)	Criterion for adaptation	Other variables	Reference condition order of control	Reliably better
			Adaptive condition					
Chernikoff	1962	4 + 4	Amount of aiding	0	Error above or below 1 in	Aiding decreases 5 times as quickly as it increases	Delta acceleration	—
Hudson	1962	4 + 4	Amount of aiding	3	Size of mean error		Delta acceleration	—
	(Exp. 1)	+ 4		25				
	(Exp. 3)	5 + 5	Amount of aiding	75	Size of mean error above 2 in		Delta acceleration aided, ratio 1:4	Adaptive?
Hudson	1964	10 + 8	Amount of aiding	10 or 60	Size of mean error, or size of mean error above 2 in.	Large adaptation or adaptation only half as large	Delta acceleration	A group of moderately easy adaptive conditions
		+ 8	Stability of control system					
		+ 8	Control system gain					

Two methods are used to prevent the control system from changing too rapidly with every transient increase or decrease in error. In Chernikoff's (1962) experiment the direction of the change depends upon whether the error is greater or less than 1 in. The control system takes 150 sec to change from fully aided to pure delta acceleration. The change in the opposite direction can be completed in 30 sec.

In Hudson's (1962, 1964) experiments the amount of aiding depends directly upon the running average of the error over the last few seconds. In the table this is called the integration time constant. In some conditions 2 in is subtracted from all errors before they are summed. When the running average error is less than 2 in, the man automatically tracks with the pure, or almost pure, delta acceleration control system.

In Hudson's 1964 experiment there are 2 separate scales relating the size of the adaptation to the size of the running average error. With the half length scale, the control system adapts only half as much to a change in the running average error. Thus the easiest control system dynamics are excluded.

The right hand column of the table shows that changing the aiding of the control system is not a conspicuously successful method of adaptive training. Chernikoff (1962) reports no difference between his adaptive condition and his reference condition. In his 1962 experiments, Hudson reports that 1 of his 3 adaptive conditions is reliably better than the reference condition on a parametric statistical test. But when the more appropriate nonparametric test is used, the difference does not nearly reach statistical reliability (Poulton, 1966, page 193).

Hudson's 1964 experiment is more difficult to interpret. The 24 people who receive adaptive training, each work with a different adaptive condition. For 8 of them the gain of the control system is changed, not the amount of aiding. For another 8 the stability of the control system is changed.

Hudson divides the 24 conditions into 4 equal sized groups: very difficult, difficult, moderately easy and very easy, as indicated by the results of 5 additional practiced people who receive all 24 conditions. Only the average of the 6 conditions classed together as moderately easy is found to be reliably better than the reference condition. The 6 conditions include 1 with changing gain and 3 with changing stability. Only 2 of the conditions directly vary the amount of aiding.

The results of the experiments listed in Table 16.5 suggest that adaptive training devices are likely to work well only when they do not vary the aiding of the control system. It is better to change the difficulty of the task in some other way.

Adaptive training devices which vary
the amplitude of the track

Today adaptive training devices usually vary the amplitude of the
track. Ellis, Lowes, Norman and Matheny (1971) use separate groups,
each of 9 pilots. They report a reliable advantage in favor of adaptive
training. However Wood (1971) uses separate groups, each of 7 men
undergraduates, and finds a reliable advantage in favor of fixed training
with graded levels of difficulty.

The conflicting results reflect a difficulty of all experiments comparing
adaptive training with fixed training. When adaptive training is found
to be the better, it could be because the fixed training is partly inappropriate. This criticism can be leveled at the experiment of Ellis and his
colleagues (1971). When the fixed training is found to be the better,
it could be because the adaptive training is not optimal. This criticism
can be leveled at Wood's experiment.

Before adequate conclusions can be drawn about the value of adaptive
training, it is necessary to determine the best form of adaptive training.
It is also necessary to determine the best form of fixed training. Then
the 2 best forms can be compared. When this is eventually done, it
may well be found that there is little to choose between the best forms
of adaptive and fixed training.

Interference between simultaneous orders of control system

Probably the greatest interference between different orders of control
system is found when tracking in 2 dimensions with different dynamics
in the 2 dimensions. The interference is particularly marked when the
man has a single control stick, and is switched from one combination
of dynamics to another. This is illustrated in Table 16.6 (Chernikoff
and colleagues, 1960).

In the experiment the display is compensatory. The track comprises
a sine wave of 3.2 cpm in the vertical dimension, and a sine wave
of 1.9 cpm in the horizontal dimension. The single joystick is spring
centered. The 6 enlisted men track in 2 dimensions, using every pairing
of the 3 control systems with the 2 dimensions. The 9 pairs are presented
in balanced orders in each of 20 sessions. The table gives the average
modulus mean errors for the last 3 sessions.

Entries in each row of the table are for the control system indicated
on the left of the row. Reliably the largest average errors are in the
top right hand corner of the table and in the bottom left hand corner.
In both cases the results are for a zero order or position control system

Table 16.6
Interference between simultaneous orders of control system

Control system	Average modulus mean error when combined with:		
	Position	Rate	Acceleration
Position	**78**	91	160
Rate	38	**22**	40
Acceleration	152	53	**50**

The large bold entries in the diagonal represent tracking with the same dynamics in both dimensions. The results are biased by transfer in favor of the rate and acceleration control systems. (Results from Chernikoff and colleagues, 1960, Figure 2).

paired with a second order or acceleration control system. The difference in order between the 2 control systems is of size 2.

The average errors are not so large when a first order or rate control system is paired with a zero order or second order system. Here the difference in order between the 2 control systems is only of size 1. The large bold entries in the diagonal have the smallest values in each row. Here the control system is the same in both dimensions.

Table 11.4 (Chernikoff & Le May, 1963) shows a similar effect of pairing a position and an acceleration control system. The top and bottom rows of the table are for 1 error marker and 1 control stick, as in the experiment of Table 16.6. In the top row of Table 11.4, the error when 2 position control systems are paired is 42. The error is also 42 when 2 acceleration control systems are paired. In the bottom row of the table the position and acceleration control systems are paired. Here the errors are, respectively, 73 and 97 for the 2 control systems.

Increases in error also occur when an acceleration aided control system is paired with an acceleration control system (Duey & Chernikoff, 1959, Figure 2; Verdi and colleagues, 1965, displayed error in Tables 20 and 22).

The changes are due to crosscoupling (see Chapter 17) within the man. Strategies appropriate to the higher order control system affect the dimension with the lower order control system. Also strategies appropriate to the lower order control system affect the dimension with the higher order control system.

It is possible to reduce the crosscoupling within the man between different orders of control in the 2 dimensions. It is done by giving the man separate controls, one for each control system. This is illustrated by the results listed in row 6 of Table 11.4 (Chernikoff & Le May, 1963). It is discussed in Chapter 15.

Recommended orders of control system

The order of a control system should be as low as possible. A position control system should be used for changing the position of markers on an electronic display. A rate control system should be used for controlling a vehicle. If a control system has a naturally high order, step tracking is made easier by changing the control system to a lower order with a small exponential lag (see Table 17.4).

People should not be switched from a control system of one order to a control system of another order. Adaptive training devices should not vary the aiding of the control system. People should not be made to track in 2 dimensions with very different orders of control system in the 2 dimensions.

Chapter

17

Other control system variations

Summary

The relationship between acquisition time and the gain of a joystick or lever control is J shaped for all orders of control system, provided the maximum output of the control system is held constant.

Making a position control system nonlinear, stepping its input, and inserting a lag, all degrade tracking. The undamped oscillations of an acceleration control system also degrade tracking. A man can learn to compensate for fixed crosscoupling, but not for varying crosscoupling.

A sudden change in the relationship between the direction of control movements and the direction of display movements is sometimes adjusted to in a single instant. Other sudden changes in a control system are adjusted to more gradually.

Kinds of control system variation

Control gain and control system gain

The relationships between the gain of a control, the gain of the display, and the amplitude of the track, are illustrated in Figure 8.2. If the man himself supplies the power, he will have to exert a greater force when there is a high control gain. Reducing the gain of a control is a standard method of reducing the force needed to operate it. The force which a man can be expected to exert sets a limit to the gain of a control for which he supplies the power.

The maximum output of a power operated control system is also limited. If an experimenter uses an electrical analog of the control system, he may forget this. When he wishes to increase the gain of his control, he may increase the maximum output of the control system. This does increase the gain of the control. But it has a different effect upon the man's performance from increasing the gain of the control without altering the maximum output of the control system.

Nonlinear control systems

Figure 17.1 (Wortz and colleagues, 1965) illustrates 3 kinds of nonlinear control systems. The function labeled 1 is a common kind of nonlinearity. The control is not as sensitive in its extreme position as it is when it is moved less far. The gas pedal of an automobile may have a nonlinearity of this kind. Functions 2 and 4 resemble deadspace, which is discussed at the end of Chapter 15.

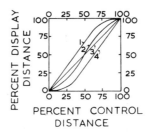

Figure 17.1. Nonlinear control systems.
In the experiment by Wortz and his colleagues (1965), the 4 control systems are each paired with transmission time lags of .5, .25 and 0 sec. The 12 combinations are used with both pursuit and compensatory displays on 3 different tracks. This makes a total of 72 different combinations of conditions. All 72 combinations are given to each of 24 engineers in different orders. Two of the tracks consist of multiple ramps. The third track consists of steps out and back of various sizes in various directions.

Tracking is in 2 dimensions. The joystick control is spring centered. In the pursuit condition a movement of the joystick makes the response marker move in the same direction. In the compensatory condition a movement of the joystick makes the error marker move in the opposite direction. This is not a compatible arrangement. It may increase the difficulty of tracking with the compensatory display. (After Wortz and colleagues 1965, Figure 6.)

Stepped inputs to control systems

In outer space, because there is no atmosphere, jets of gas have to be used for steering. A jet can be turned on a variable amount. But it is simpler to turn a jet full on or not on at all. This results in onoff control with only 3 possible inputs to the control system: full on one way, off, and full on the other way. Between onoff control and continuous control lie control devices with 2 or 3 sizes of input to the control system in each direction.

Control systems can sample the man's output at intervals of time. This happens when the man's response in tracking is fed directly into a digital computer. The rate of sampling depends upon the time taken by the computer to process each sample. The computer does not accept the next value from the man's control until it has processed the previous value.

Control system lags

The remote control of a vehicle in outer space involves a transmission time lag. This is the time which the message from the earth takes to reach the vehicle. There is an additional transmission time lag while the message which indicates the effect of the control action is returning to the earth.

An exponential control system lag may be used in manual control of a rocket, both in space and in the earth's atmosphere. The steering mechanism of a rocket is approximately an acceleration control system. The gas jet of the rocket can be made to turn rapidly through an angle which corresponds to the angle at which the man holds his control stick. The angle of the gas jet determines the rate at which the rocket turns. And the direction in which the rocket points determines the rate at which it moves in the vertical or the side to side dimension. The position of the rocket in the man's field of view is thus controlled by the man's joystick through approximately an acceleration control system.

The gas jet can be used to steer the rocket only if it does not roll round the long axis of the rocket. Rolling is prevented by a gyro system rather like the system used for the gyro horizon of an aircraft. The gyro system detects small angular deviations and corrects them automatically.

A gyro spins in 1 dimension, and can be used to detect angular changes in the 2 dimensions at right angles to this. In a rocket the gyro system can be fixed to detect angular changes in the side to side dimension, as well as to detect roll. It enables the design engineer to change the effective order of control in the side to side dimension from acceleration to rate with an exponential type of time lag.

With a lagged rate control system, the angular direction in which the rocket points gradually corresponds to the angle at which the man holds his control stick. When the man first moves his control, the gas jet of the rocket turns rapidly. The rocket itself then starts to turn. As the angle of the rocket approaches the angle of the man's control stick, the gas jet slowly turns back to its central position. It reaches the central position as the angular direction of the rocket corresponds to the angle of the man's control stick. The rocket is then moving across the man's field of view at a rate which corresponds to the angle at which he is holding his control stick.

Oscillating control systems

When the pilot of a high performance aircraft changes height, he may introduce oscillations. Frequencies of 20 to 60 cpm are often rapidly damped by the design of the aircraft. But low frequencies of 1 to 4 cpm may receive little damping. If the pilot attempts to track them, he may introduce additional low frequency oscillations which increase the overall amplitude of the oscillation.

Crosscoupled control systems

Flying an aircraft using a zero reader display like that illustrated in Figure 9.1, differs from simple compensatory tracking in 2 dimensions. In flying, the 2 dimensions are not independent. When an aircraft rolls in order to change position in the side to side dimension, it also loses height. The pilot has to move his control stick in both dimensions in order to change position in the side to side dimension without changing height.

A rocket can be controlled from an unstable platform such as a maneuvering aircraft or helicopter. When the platform tilts sideways in a roll, the world outside appears to tilt in the opposite direction. This is illustrated in Figure 9.2. The direction of the error between the rocket and the target tilts with the outside world. Yet the appropriate direction in its socket of the control which steers the rocket does not change. The tilting of the platform thus introduces a rotary or symmetrical crosscoupling between display and control.

Control system changes

The aerodynamic characteristics of an aircraft change as it climbs to heights where the air is less dense. There are also changes as the aircraft reaches the speed of sound. The control system of a sophisticated aircraft may change suddenly, as a result of a sudden failure. It may suddenly become less stable. The pilot may suddenly have to make control movements of a different size, perhaps in the opposite direction to usual. To avoid a crash, the pilot has to detect the failure, spot its nature, and compensate for it.

Many emergencies occur soon after take off. When the aircraft is in use for the first time after it has been repaired, the failure may be due to an error made during the repair. If the aircraft has not climbed very high, there may be only a few seconds before it will hit the ground. This does not allow the pilot much time for regaining control.

Optimum control gain and maximum output of a rate control system

Figure 5.10 shows that the time taken to acquire a target with a position control system depends upon the sensitivity or gain of the control. With a lever or joystick position control, travel time is almost constant. The theoretical U shaped relationship of Figure 5.10 becomes almost J shaped.

The J shaped rule for levers and joysticks probably applies to all orders of control system. But the rule will be found to apply only when the correct experimental procedure is used to determine the optimum gain. The maximum output of the control system must be held constant.

A design engineer may wish to determine the optimum gain for the gas pedal of an automobile. The maximum rate of the automobile is determined by the power of the engine. The design engineer does not alter this when he designs the gas pedal. He can change the gain of the pedal only by changing the distance which the pedal has to be depressed in order to give the full power.

The kind of relationship which he finds is illustrated by any one of the functions in Figure 17.2 (Hammerton, 1962). Each J shaped function is for a control system with a different maximum rate. The maximum is printed against the function. The functions level off on the left at different heights because travel to the target takes longer with the smaller maximum rates.

Optimum control gain determined with an electrical analog of a control system

An experimenter who works with an electrical analog in a laboratory, does not have to hold constant the maximum rate of the control system. He may start by using a control system with a large maximum rate, like the control system represented in the figure by the unfilled circles.

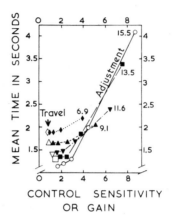

Figure 17.2 Travel and adjustment time with a joystick rate control.

The control sensitivity or gain shown on the abscissa represents the angular rate of the response marker at the man's eyes divided by the angular movement of the control. On the right of the figure a small control movement gives the response marker a large rate of movement. The numbers printed against each function indicate the maximum rate of movement of the response marker in degrees per second at the man's eyes.

The task is similar to the task described in the caption to Figure 15.2, except that tracking is in only the side to side dimension. The 10 men have a joystick 3.5 in long which they operate with the thumb, like the joystick illustrated in Figure 15.3A. The tip of the joystick moves a maximum distance of 13 mm. The gain is changed in 2 ways. One method is to increase the maximum rate which the joystick will give. The second method is to change the distance which the joystick has to be moved in order to give the maximum rate. Instead of moving the control the full distance, the control has to be moved only 80%, 60%, 40% or 20% of the distance. Larger movements than this do not increase the rate of the response marker.

The 5 functions in the figure are for 5 different maximum rates. The 5 points on the functions represent the 5 amounts of control movement which are required to give the maximum rates. Each man produces the results for a single function on any one day. (Results from Hammerton, 1962).

For the condition represented by the circle in the top right hand corner of the figure, a joystick deflection of 2.5 mm produces this full rate. The control is too sensitive, and the final adjustment therefore takes a long time.

The remaining circles in the figure represent smaller gains. For the circle at the bottom on the left, a full joystick deflection of 13 mm is required to produce the full rate. The final adjustment is therefore easier, and takes less time on average.

It is not possible to reduce the gain of the control any further without reducing the maximum rate which the control will give. This is because a joystick cannot be moved any further than its full range of movement. The unfilled square, triangles and diamond illustrate what happens if the experimenter does reduce both the gain and the maximum rate. Acquisition takes longer because it takes longer for the response marker to travel to the target. The function obtained by joining together all the unfilled points is U shaped, although all the individual functions are J shaped.

The results in Figure 17.2 illustrate a danger of experimenting with an electrical analog of a control system, instead of with the control system itself. Suppose the real control system has a maximum output of 6.9° per sec. The top function in the figure shows that the optimum control gain is produced by making the full range of movement of the control give the full output. The optimum control gain is .8.

But if the experimenter increases the gain of the control by increasing the maximum output of the control system, he will end up with a U shaped function like the one represented by the unfilled points. The bottom of the U represents the smallest control gain which can be obtained with the control system having the largest maximum output. In the figure the maximum output is 15.5, and the bottom of the U represents a control gain of 1.7. If a control system is used with twice this maximum output, 31, the bottom of the U may then represent a control gain twice as high, 3.4. The rule holds until the advantage of an increased maximum output becomes smaller than the disadvantage of the increased control gain.

By increasing the maximum gain of the control system, the experimenter finds an optimum gain which is a good deal larger than the true optimum. This will happen whether the man is tracking steps or sine waves. It seems likely that the gains of many controls, for example in aircraft, are higher than they should be because the optimum gain is measured in the laboratory using this incorrect procedure.

Experimenters in the laboratory appear to be unaware of this danger of experimenting with an electrical analog of a control system. Unless an experimenter states explicitly that he holds the maximum output of the control system constant, it should be assumed that he does not do so. With an electrical analog it is simpler to turn up the gain of the control system than to change the gain only of the control. The experimenter will do this unless he is aware of the danger of doing so. If he is aware of the danger, he is likely to state that he avoids it. If he does not state that he avoids the danger, it is probable that he is not aware of it and does not avoid it.

When the gain of a control system is increased, it means that the experimental results do not apply to a single physical control system.

The unfilled points in Figure 17.2 are taken from a total of 5 different physical control systems represented by the 5 functions. As we shall see in the next section when comparing pressure controls with moving controls, there can be difficulties of interpretation if changes in the control are confounded with changes in the maximum control system output.

Optimum control gain with sine wave tracks

The **J** shaped rule of Figure 17.2 may possibly have to be modified before it can be applied to the tracking of sine waves of relatively high frequency, using a rate or higher order control system. A sine wave track of high frequency stops only for an instant as it reverses direction. The marker controlled by the man spends most of the time moving. The man gets little opportunity for accurate adjustments. He may therefore be able to tolerate a higher control gain without his error increasing appreciably. If this is so, each **J** shaped function for control gain may possibly have an optimum region, instead of a single optimum point at the end on the left. The question has still to be investigated.

Part **A** of Table 15.3 suggests that the combination of a relatively high frequency track with a rate or higher order control system may favor a pressure control. A pressure control has an almost infinite gain. Unfortunately all except 2 of the reports listed in part **A** of the table probably run into the difficulty illustrated in Figure 17.2. In converting the moving control into a pressure control, the maximum output of the control system is increased. This gives the pressure control an unfair advantage.

Nonlinear control systems

Nonlinear control systems produce larger tracking errors than linear control systems do. Figure 10.6 shows that nonlinear control systems can be distinguished from nonlinear displays by the position at which the tracking error is measured. A nonlinear control system corresponds to the block diagram at the bottom of the figure, except that the track is unmodified, not modified as indicated in the figure. The man sees the error which is produced by the nonlinear output of the control system.

It might be thought that the nonlinearity of the function labeled 4 in Figure 17.1 would improve the accuracy of tracking. The man has a low control gain for small movements, which correspond to the adjustments of Figure 17.2. He has a relatively large control gain for large movements, which correspond to travel in Figure 17.2. But in practice nonlinearities of this kind always reduce the accuracy of tracking, just as an appreciable amount of deadspace does. This applies both with slow irregular sine wave tracks, and also with steps of equal or of unequal size (Vince, 1946).

Wortz and his colleagues (1965) report large differences between the nonlinearities illustrated in Figure 17.1, but some of the differences are difficult to interpret. When the track comprises multiple constant velocity ramps, the linear function labeled 3 and the nonlinear function labeled 1 give reliably the smallest average modulus mean errors. Function 1 is nonlinear only for displacements of the control from its center greater than about 65%. Probably displacements as large as this are not often used with the velocity ramps. The nonlinear function labeled 4 is reliably the worst. This is the kind of nonlinear function studied by Vince (1946), and always found to degrade tracking.

When the track comprises steps of irregular size, the linear function again gives the smallest average error. The S shaped nonlinearity labeled 2 is the next best. Function 2 reduces the effect of small control displacements, and exaggerates the effect of large displacements. This is the opposite of the range effect for sizes of step, which is illustrated in Figure 2.2. With a range effect, responses to small steps tend to be too large, and responses to large steps tend to be too small. Function 2 may produce relatively accurate tracking because it compensates for the range effect.

The nonlinear function labeled 1 is the worst with the step track. It is reliably worse than the linear function. For small and medium sized displacements, a range effect exaggerates the influence of this kind of nonlinearity, whereas it reduces the influence of the kind of nonlinearity labeled 4.

Unfortunately Wortz and his colleagues (1965) do not describe the man's strategies. Thus it is not possible to check on these points. The experiment needs to be repeated using a number of separate groups of people. It should then be possible to separate the main effects of the nonlinearities from the additional effects of transfer.

Stepped inputs to control systems

A stepped input can be regarded as a particular kind of control system nonlinearity. The 2 experiments by Bennett (1956), listed in part **A** of Table 17.1, use sampling rates of between 1 and 6 samples per sec. The remaining experiments in the table step the output of the man's control by amplitude instead of by time.

Table 17.1
Experiments on stepped inputs to control systems

Author(s)	Year	N	Display mode	Top track frequency (cpm)	Order of control	Other variables	Seconds between samples	Reliably better
A. Inputs stepped intermittently								
Bennett	1956	7	Compensatory	Steps	Rate	Control system gain	.5 to .17, continuous	Continuous
		7	Compensatory	Velocity ramps	Rate		1 to .2, continuous	.2 and continuous
B. Inputs stepped by amplitude							Number of positions	
Hammerton and Tickner (see Table 17.2)	1968	6 + 6	Pursuit	Step	Acceleration	Transfer between number of positions	5, continuous	—
Hunt	1966	8 + 8	Compensatory	Steps	Acceleration	Control system gain	3, 5, 7, continuous	—
Ziegler and Chernikoff	1968	5	Compensatory	7.3	Delta acceleration	Pressure control	3, continuous	Continuous (pressure control)

The experiments can be distinguished from experiments on stepped displays by the method illustrated in Figure 10.6.

Table 17.2
Asymmetrical transfer between continuous and
stepped inputs

	Average acquisition time (sec)	
Trial number	Group SC	Group CS
Training	Stepped	Continuous
1	34.6	27.8
60	10.0	8.5
Transfer	Continuous	Stepped
61	12.2*	32.2*
80	9.0	9.1

* Reliable difference between Groups SC and CS on trial 61 (results from Hammerton & Tickner, 1968).

There is another difference between the experiments in the 2 parts of the table. Bennett (1956) uses a rate control system. A single integrator is not sufficient to smooth out the steps in its input. Bennett finds intermittent stepping to be a reliable disadvantage. The remaining experiments use acceleration or higher order control systems. Two integrators considerably reduce the difference between short rapid pulses and a continuous input. It is pointed out in Chapter 10 that in compensatory tracking with an acceleration control system, onoff control is the optimal strategy provided the man knows how to use it.

Asymmetrical transfer between continuous and stepped inputs

Table 17.2 (Hammerton & Tickner, 1968) illustrates asymmetrical transfer between tracking with continuous and with stepped inputs. Group SC of 6 enlisted men practices on a condition with 5 amplitudes of input to the control system, and then transfers to a continuous input. The 6 enlisted men in Group CS receive the 2 conditions in the reverse order. The men in both groups have 10 trials daily for 6 days. They are then transferred to the other condition for 20 trials, spread over 2 days.

The task is similar to the task described in the caption to Figure 15.3, except that tracking is in only the side to side dimension. The men use a thumb joystick. The continuous joystick is spring centered. The stepped joystick is loaded so that it always remains in 1 of 5 positions. The extreme positions give the maximum output of the continuous joystick. The 2 intermediate positions give half the maximum output. The central position gives zero output.

The upper part of Table 17.2 shows that the continuous joystick gives if anything the shorter acquisition time at the start of training. But with only 6 men in each group, the difference is not marked enough to be reliable.

The 2 groups change controls on trial 61. Here there is a reliable difference in favor of the continuous joystick. Group SC practices with the stepped stick, and then transfers to the continuous stick. The average acquisition time increases by only about 2 sec, from 10 sec on trial 60 to 12 sec on trial 61. Group CS practices with the continuous stick, and then transfers to the stepped stick. The average time increases by about 24 sec, from 8 sec to 32 sec. By trial 80 there is virtually no difference between the 2 controls.

Table 17.2 shows that there need be little difference after practice between a continuous input to an acceleration control system and a stepped input. Yet transfer can produce a large and reliable difference. It seems likely that there can also be interference when changing between continuous control and 3 state or on off control.

Strategies with continuous and with onoff controls

An onoff control allows the man to use only either the full input to the control system or no input. With an acceleration control system, the man produces a rate of the required size in the output of the control system by holding the control in the on position for the corresponding length of time. He subsequently removes the rate by holding the control in the negative on position, on the other side of its center, for the same length of time. The man assesses the total input to the control system in terms of time. If the control system has a large gain, the on times are likely to be short.

A continuous control can be used in much the same way. The man can always hold the control either in an extreme position or in the center, and vary the holding time. The strategy is called onoff or bang-bang control. But a continuous control does not have to be used like this. Control movements can have a more or less fixed duration. The man then assesses the total input to the control system by the size of the displacement of the control from its center.

More likely the input will be assessed partly by the distance through which the control is moved, and partly by the time taken by the movement. The man learns the kind of out and back control movement which quickly puts on a rate of about the right size. This out and back movement produces a more prolonged input to the control system of smaller average amplitude than does the corresponding on response of the onoff control.

The strategy for continuous control and the strategy for onoff control are both suited to their particular kinds of control. But the strategies cannot be transferred successfully without modification to the alternative kind of control. There is likely to be interference when the 2 kinds of control are presented successively.

The result of the Ziegler and Chernikoff (1968) experiment in part B of Table 17.1 may be due to asymmetrical transfer favoring the continuous control, as happens immediately after transfer in the experiment of Table 17.2. But the experiment is complicated by the use of 2 continuous controls, 1 moving and 1 pressure. It is only the continuous pressure control which is reliably better than the onoff control. The pressure control has the greatest maximum output. Its maximum output is 8 times greater than the output of the onoff control. It is probably the greater maximum output which is largely responsible for the reliably more accurate tracking.

Control system lags

Three common kinds of control system lag are illustrated in Figure 11.9 for a step displacement of a position control. Experiments dealing with the 3 kinds of lag are listed in Table 17.3. All 3 kinds of lag increase the error in tracking. Large lags make tracking difficult or impossible. Even lags too small to be noticed by the man can degrade his performance.

A transmission time lag in a control system simply delays the effect of the man's response. Figure 11.5 shows that it is equivalent to a transmission time lag in a display The only difference is that a display time lag delays the time at which the man sees the track and responds to it. Transmission time lags are discussed in Chapter 11.

An exponential or first order lag distorts the output of the control system in the ways illustrated in Figure 11.10. For high frequencies, a position control system with an exponential lag behaves rather like a rate or first order control system. The high frequencies in the response have a phase lag of almost 90°. They are attenuated almost 6 dB per octave.

For low frequencies, a position control system with an exponential lag behaves more like a position control system with a transmission time lag. The phase lag is reduced, so that the lag in time is never quite as large as the time constant of the lowpass filter. The attenuation also is reduced.

Table 17.3
Experiments on control system lags

Author(s)	Year	N	Maximum lag (sec)	Display mode	Top track frequency (cpm)	Order of control	Other variables ¶
A. Transmission time lags							
Henry and colleagues (see Figure 11.7)	1967	4 + 4	3.2	Compensatory	0	Position	(Breath control)
Pew and colleagues (see Figure 11.8)	1967b	3	1.4	Compensatory	3 / 5.5	Position	
K. U. Smith and Putz	1970	6	1.6	Compensatory	10 / 0	Position	(Hand steadiness)
K. U. Smith and Sussman	1970	24	1.5	Pursuit	12.9	Position	
Wargo	1967	5	.84	Pursuit	17	Position	
		5		Compensatory	17	Position	
Warrick (see Figure 11.6)	1949	25	.32	Compensatory	30	Position	
		10	.32	Compensatory	6	Position	
		10	.16	Compensatory	12	Position	
Wortz and colleagues (see Figure 17.1)	1965	24	.5	Pursuit / Compensatory	Step track / Ramp 12.5‡ / 6.7‡	Position }	Nonlinear control systems
B. Exponential lags							
Conklin* (see Figure 17.5)	1957	3	16	Pursuit / Compensatory	30 / ?	Position	Sigmoid lags
Gibbs	1962	16	2	Pursuit	Step track	Position	Part of limb
		10	2	Pursuit	Step track	Rate	Control gain
Hammerton and Tickner (see Table 15.1)	1966	18	2	Pursuit	Step track	Rate	(Low gain)
		18	2	Pursuit	Step track	Rate	(High gain)
Helson	1944	8	.1	Compensatory	Variable ramp	Rate aided / Rate	Aiding time constant

				Pursuit (headup display of Figure 9.2)	Step track	Aircraft	Additional task
Huddleston and Wilson	1969	8	.5				
Levine	1953a	12	2.7	Compensatory	11	Position	
Levine	1953b	10 + 10	3	Compensatory	11	Position	
Rockway (see Figure 17.4)	1954	8	3	Compensatory	11	Position	Control gain
Tickner and Poulton (see Table 17.4)	1972	6 + 15	4	Pursuit	Step track	Rate	Acceleration control
Warrick	1955	20	1	Pursuit	Step track	Position	
C. Sigmoid lags							
Conklin* (see Figure 17.5)	1957	3	16	Pursuit Compensatory } { 30 ?		Position	Exponential lags
Garvey and colleagues (see Figure 11.11)	1958	8	.74	Compensatory	11	Position	Display lags

* Included in 2 parts of table.

† Half the number of reversals per minute.

¶ Bracketed items describe the task performed. Unbracketed items indicate other variables investigated.

The time constant of the filter determines which frequencies escape the almost full effect of integration and attenuation. The first part of the exponential function in Figure 11.9 is rather like the output of a rate control system. The later part of the function reflects the difference between an exponential lag and a true rate control system.

The simplest sigmoid lag is second order. It is produced by 2 lowpass filters connected in series, as illustrated in Figure 17.3 at the top on the right. The distortion is twice as great as with an exponential lag. For high frequencies, a position control system with a second order sigmoid lag behaves rather like an acceleration or second order control system. The high frequencies in the response have a phase lag of almost 180°. They are attenuated almost 12 dB per octave.

For low frequencies, a position control system with a second order sigmoid lag behaves more like a position control system with a transmission time lag. The phase lag is reduced, so that the lag in time is never quite as large as the sum of the time constants of the 2 lowpass filters. The attenuation also is reduced.

The time constants of the 2 filters together determine which frequencies escape the almost full effect of the double integration and attenuation. The first part of the sigmoid function in Figure 11.9 is rather like the output of an acceleration control system. The later part of the function reflects the difference between a sigmoid lag and an acceleration control system.

Exponential and sigmoid control system lags need to be distinguished from the corresponding filtered displays. This can be done by the method illustrated in Figure 10.6. A control system lag can be represented by the block diagram at the bottom of the figure, except that the track is unmodified, not modified as indicated in the figure. The man sees the error which is produced by the lag.

With a filtered display, the man does not see the error which is scored against him. He sees only the filtered version. This is represented by the block diagram at the top of Figure 10.6. Figure 11.11 shows that a sigmoid display lag can produce larger errors than a sigmoid control system lag, if a compensatory display is used with a balanced treatment design.

Exponential and sigmoid lags in step tracking with a position control system

Suppose a man is tracking a step using a position control system with an exponential lag. If the control system has sufficient gain, the man does not have to move his control a distance corresponding to the distance of the target and then wait for the response marker to

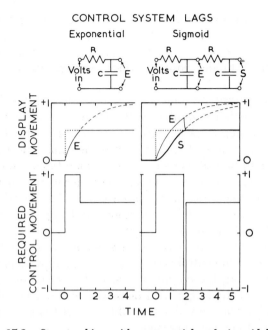

Figure 17.3.   **Step tracking with exponential and sigmoid lags.**
The theoretical responses illustrated below produce the display movements illustrated above. With the sigmoid lag on the right, the man does not see the output E of the first lowpass filter.

move to the target. The man can use the strategy illustrated on the left side of Figure 17.3.

The strategy corresponds to the strategy illustrated in Figure 16.1 for step tracking with a rate control system. The difference between the 2 strategies relates to the final position of the man's control. The rate control has to be moved back to its center in order to stop the response marker when it arrives at the target. The lagged position control has to be moved back only as far as the position which corresponds to the target.

The right side of Figure 17.3 shows the corresponding strategy for tracking a step with a position control system having a sigmoid lag of second order. The top function labeled **E** indicates the exponential output of the first lowpass filter. As the output **E** increases, the output **S** of the second filter starts to rise.

In order to stop the response marker on the target and to hold it there, both the outputs **E** and **S** have to be equated with the output corresponding to the position of the target. This can be done by waiting until the response marker has very nearly reached the target, and then moving the control hard across to the other side of its center. The value of **E** then drops rapidly to the value of **S**. At this stage the man moves his control back to the position which corresponds to the position of the target.

The man's control movements are illustrated at the bottom of the figure. They are fairly similar to the control movements illustrated in Figure 16.1 for step tracking with an acceleration control system. There are 2 main differences. The first control movement in the direction of the target has to be maintained for longer than the second control movement in the reverse direction. This is because the first control movement has to increase the value of **S**, the output of the second lowpass filter. Whereas the second control movement has to decrease only the value of **E**, the output of the first lowpass filter.

The second difference between controlling with a sigmoid lag and with an acceleration control system, is in the final position of the control. With a sigmoid lag the control has to end at a position corresponding to the position of the target, as it does with an exponential lag. Whereas with an acceleration control system the control has to end at its center, as it does with a rate control system.

The difficulty in acquiring a target with a sigmoid lag is to know when to make the second and third control movements. This is because the man does no see the value of **E**. He sees only the value of **S**. There is a similar difficulty in tracking with an acceleration control system. It is discussed in Chapter 10.

Reducing the effective order of control in step tracking by introducing an exponential lag

A design engineer may be able to reduce the effective order of a control system from acceleration to rate by introducing an approximately exponential lag. Table 17.4 shows that it may help the man, even if the lagged rate control system has a time constant as long as 4 sec. If the time constant can be reduced to 2 sec or less, the time taken to acquire a target after practice may be halved.

In the experiment the man has to move a spot of light on a CRT a distance of 3 cm to the left, and to hold it for 2 sec inside a circle with a diameter of 3 mm. The time taken to do this is measured automatically. The time which the man takes to hold the spot for 2 sec within a larger imaginary concentric circle with a diameter of 6 mm is also measured. When the 2 sec holding time is deducted, this last time is listed in column 5 of the table as the approach time.

The fine adjustment time in column 6 represents the difference between

Table 17.4
Performance with acceleration and lagged rate control systems

Order of control	Exponential lag (sec)	Maximum initial acceleration (cm per sec²)	N	Average time (sec)		Average size of first RMS error of approach (mm)	Average number of control movements
				Approach	Fine adjustment		
Acceleration (maximum 12 cm per sec²)	0	12	12(12)	5.3	6.6	6.7	10.0
Rate (maximum 11 cm per sec)	4	2.5	15(5)	4.5	3.4*	5.7	10.4
	2	5	11(6)	3.3*†	3.4*	2.4*	8.0
	.5	15	6(6)	2.8*†	2.4*	3.4*	5.1*†

The average times are for everyone in each group. The results in the 2 right hand columns are for only the numbers given in brackets in column 4.

* Lagged rate reliably different from acceleration.
† Lagged rate reliably different from rate with 4 sec lag.
(From Tickner & Poulton, 1972).

the time taken to stay inside the target circle, and the time taken to stay inside the larger imaginary concentric circle. The sum of the 2 times represents the total acquisition time.

The 12 men listed in the top row of the table track always with the unlagged acceleration control system. After practice, they take an average of 5.3 sec to remain near the target within the imaginary outer circle. The 3 lower rows of the table list the results of the 3 groups of men who track with one of the lagged rate control systems. The groups with the 2 sec and .5 sec exponential lags are reliably quicker at reaching and remaining within the imaginary outer circle. They take an average of only 3.3 and 2.8 sec respectively.

The third column of the table shows that the average approach timed does not depend much upon the effective gain of the control system. The rate control system with the 2 sec exponential lag has a maximum initial acceleration of 5 cm per sec^2. It is less than half the maximum acceleration of 12 cm per sec^2 of the acceleration control system. Yet the approach time is reliably shorter with the lagged rate control system. This is because the man learns not to approach the target at anywhere near the fastest rate which he can use. Fast rates of approach tend to give inaccurate approaches.

Column 6 of the table lists the average times taken to progress from remaining inside the imaginary outer circle to remaining inside the target circle. The group with the acceleration control system takes an average of 6.6 sec. The 3 groups with the lagged rate control systems are all reliably quicker than this. They take an average of 3.4 sec or less.

The 2 right hand columns of the table indicate why acquisition is slower with the unlagged acceleration control system. The initial approach to the target is reliably less accurate. It leaves an average RMS error of 6.7 mm, compared with the radii of the imaginary outer circle and target circle of 3 and 1.5 mm respectively.

The unlagged acceleration control system requires an average total of 10 control stick movements before the spot can be held within the target area for the required 2 sec. The rate control system with the long 4 sec lag is rather similar to the unlagged acceleration control system in these 2 respects.

In all conditions the man's difficulty is to get the spot to stay still inside the target circle. The major disadvantage of the unlagged acceration control system is that the man has to stop the response marker by a deliberate out and back movement. This may not be necessery when using a rate control system with a reasonably short lag. The man may need only to let the control return to its center. The rate will then soon fall to zero.

Exponential and sigmoid lags in tracking sine waves
with a position control system

In tracking sine waves, exponential and second order sigmoid lags with long time constants reduce considerably the effective gain of the control system at moderate and high frequencies. The reduced gain can be more detrimental than the phase lag. Figure 17.4 (Rockway, 1954) illustrates the effect which the reduced gain of an exponential lag can have upon the average time on target with a. position control system. The circles represent the smallest control system gain of 1. With the time constant of .3 sec on the left of the figure, the man can just keep up with the track at all times by using the full range of movement of his control.

At the track frequencies of 11, 5 and 3 cpm, a time constant of 3 sec reduces the output of the control system to about 30%, 50%, and 70%, respectively, of the full unfiltered output. The right side of the

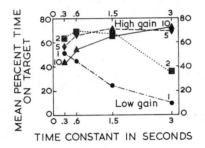

Fig. 17.4 **Performance with an exponential lag and a low gain.**
The gains of the position control system are printed against the functions. The display is compensatory. The track consists of 3 sine waves of equal amplitude with frequencies of 11, 5 and 3 cpm. With the smallest control system gain called 1, the full 10 in deflection of the man's joystick is just sufficient to match the maximum amplitude of the track when there is an exponential lag of .3 sec.
The 16 combinations of 4 control system gains and 4 time constants are presented in partly balanced orders to the 8 practiced people. In the analysis of variance there is a reliable interaction between control system gain and exponential time constant, as well as reliable main effects of control system gain and time constant. (After Rockway, 1954, Figure 2.)

For the .3 sec time constant on the left of the figure, average times on target are larger with gains of 2 and 5 than they are with gains of 1 and 10. This is probably due to a range effect. If the man always responds with sizes of movement which are a little more appropriate to the average gain than they should be, he produces a result like this. There is no need to put forward theoretical explanations of the result as Briggs (1966, page 417) does. Range effects can be prevented only by using separate groups of people for each condition.

figure shows how the reduced gain affects the man's time on target. With the smallest control system gain of 1, the average time on target falls to 10%. The man is unable to produce a large enough output fast enough to stay on target.

Increasing the gain to 2 is still not enough to enable the man to keep up with the track frequency of 11 cpm. The square on the right of the figure represents a time on target of only 36%. The man needs a control system gain 5 or 10 times the lowest gain in order to stay on target 70% of the time with the 3 sec time constant.

The large RMS errors in Figure 17.5 (Conklin, 1957) with long time constants are also caused by the reduction in the effective gain of the position control system. The 2 tracks represented by circles and triangles have top frequencies of 30 cpm. Part **A** is for exponential lags produced by a single lowpass filter. A time constant of 16 sec shifts the break

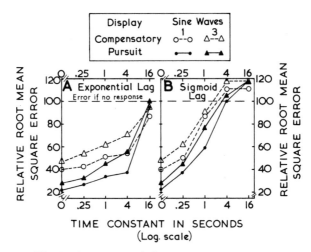

Figure 17.5. Performance with long exponential and sigmoid lags.
The circles are for a single sine wave track with an amplitude of 2 in and a frequency of 30 cpm. The triangles are for a track comprising 3 sine waves of equal amplitude with frequencies of 30, 20 and 5 cpm. The peak amplitude is 2 in. The man rests his forearm on a horizontal lever which is pivoted under his elbow joint. He has to rotate his forearm from side to side. A rotation of 5° moves the display marker 2 in.

There are 2 tracks in addition to the tracks whose results are illustrated in the figure. One of the tracks comprises 2 sine waves, the other consists of noise with an unspecified upper cutoff. All the conditions with the pursuit display are run before any of the conditions with the compensatory display. Unfortunately with only 3 highly practiced people, it is not possible to tell how representative the results are likely to be. (Results from Conklin, 1957.)

frequency of the filter illustrated in Figure 11.10 to .6 cpm. It reduces the amplitude of the output of the control system at 30 cpm to about 2% of the amplitude of the man's response.

In this condition the man cannot prevent his average error from practically reaching the no response level. To copy the sine wave of 30 cpm, the man would have to rotate the control through an angle of about 250°. The horizontal forearm cannot rotate this far. The experimental apparatus was not built to allow it.

Part **B** of Figure 17.5 shows the corresponding results for sigmoid lags produced by 2 lowpass filters in series. With each time constant, the attenuation for the conditions on the right side of the figure is the square of the attenuation for the conditions on the left side. The phase lag is doubled. The tracking errors are therefore reliably larger with the sigmoid lags on the right side.

At a frequency of 30 cpm, a time constant of 4 sec reduces the amplitude of the output of the control system to about .5% of the amplitude of the man's responses. With this time constant the man produces average errors which are as large as, or larger than, the no response error. A rotation of the control through about 1000° would be required to copy the sine wave of 30 cpm.

Oscillating control systems

An acceleration control system can be made to oscillate by changing the sign of its output and feeding it back as an additional input. This is what Muckler and his colleagues do. Figure 17.6 (Muckler & Obermayer, 1961; Muckler, Obermayer, Hanlon & Serio, 1961a, b; Muckler, Obermayer, Hanlon, Serio & Rockway, 1961) illustrates the output in response to a step movement of the control. The 3 control systems oscillate respectively at 60, 17 and 3.3 cpm.

A control movement of a certain size produces an oscillation with an amplitude of the corresponding size. Unfortunately, in order to keep this relationship the same for control systems with different frequencies of oscillation, it is necessary to change the gain of the control system. An acceleration control system which oscillates at a higher frequency needs a higher gain. This is because an acceleration control system attenuates high frequencies more than low frequencies. It means that results attributed to changes in the frequency of oscillation can be attributed equally well to changes in control system gain. The known effects of changes in gain can account for the results quite simply, without reference to the frequencies of oscillation.

In their experiment on control systems with high frequency oscillations,

Muckler and Obermayer (1961) practice their 6 people on a control system which oscillates at 10 cpm. It has a relatively low gain. They then test them on control systems with frequencies of oscillation which

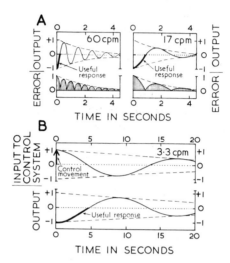

Figure 17.6.   Oscillating control systems.

The thick line labeled useful response represents the first $\frac{1}{4}$ cycle of the output of an oscillating acceleration control system used by Muckler and his colleagues (1961). The useful response and subsequent damped oscillation are produced by a step displacement of the control from its central position. The control movement is illustrated in the upper part of B on the left. The output of the acceleration control system in the lower part of B is changed in sign and fed back as the input to the control system. It is this which produces the oscillation. In B the low frequency oscillation is attenuated to half its amplitude in 17 sec. In A the high frequency oscillation is attenuated to half its amplitude in 1.5 sec.

The display is compensatory. The standard track is a sine wave with a frequency of 6 cpm and an amplitude on the display of .6 in. In the experiment with the high frequency oscillations illustrated in A, the 6 people first practice with an easier control system. The oscillations have a frequency of 10 cpm. They are attenuated to half amplitude in .2 sec. The 6 experimental control systems produce frequencies of oscillation of 60, 40, 30, 24, 20 and 17 cpm. Attenuation to half amplitude always takes 1.5 sec.

In the series of experiments with the low frequency oscillations illustrated in B, there are 9 basic control systems. They are produced by pairing each of 3 frequencies of oscillation with 3 amounts of attenuation. The frequencies of oscillation are 3.3, 1.7 and .85 cpm. The attenuation to half amplitude takes 17, 33 or 66 sec. A separate group of 10 men undergraduates performs with each control system. Unfortunately the only measure of performance is the time for which the man holds the error marker within a target area .4 in high. It is pointed out in Chapter 4 that this is not an easy measure to interpret.

range between 60 and 17 cpm, the 2 frequencies illustrated in Figure 17.6A. All the frequencies of oscillation are higher in the experiment than in the practice. Thus all the control system gains are higher.

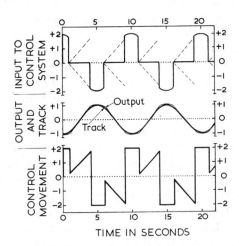

Figure 17.7.   Tracking a sine wave with an oscillating control system.
The sine wave has a frequency of 6 cpm. The oscillating control system has an output like that illustrated in Figure 17.6B. The man does not see the input to the control system. With the conventional compensatory display which Muckler and his colleagues (1961) use, the man sees only his error, the difference between the track and the output of the control system.

The theoretical control movements are shown at the bottom of the figure. The man starts by a quick step out and back. The middle part of the figure shows that this makes the control system put out a constant rate which more or less matches the average rate of the sine wave track around its point of inflection. The rate output of the control system is automatically inverted and fed back as the input to the control system. The inverted rate output is represented at the top of the figure by the first broken line on the left sloping downward.

To cancel the inverted rate output, the man has to move his control at the corresponding rate in the direction in which the track is moving. The input produced by the control movement is represented at the top of the figure by the first broken line on the left sloping upward. The inputs represented by the 2 sloping broken lines cancel each other. They leave the input represented by the thick line running horizontally at zero.

Just before the reversal of the track the man has to remove the rate output of the control system, and put on a rate output in the opposite direction. He does this by moving his control as far as possible over to the other side. He leaves it there until the rate output of the control system more or less matches the average rate of the track around its next point of inflection. The man then moves his control back almost to its center, in order to zero the input to the control system. The control has to be moved out again at a fixed rate to keep the input at zero. The whole sequence of control movements is repeated for each cycle of the track.

In the experiment the 6 people remain on target reliably less of the time with the high frequencies of oscillation and high gains, than with the lower frequencies of oscillation and lower gains. This could be due simply to transfer from the practice condition with the relatively low frequency oscillation and low gain. The strategies learned in the practice are more appropriate to control systems which resemble more closely the practice control system.

Except right at the end, transfer is excluded from the experiments on control systems with low frequency oscillations. Each group of 10 people tracks throughout training with only one control system. Muckler and his colleagues report that undergraduates can learn to track a sine wave of 6 cpm better than chance with oscillations of both 3.3 and 1.7 cpm. But with oscillations of .85 cpm, the time on target does not increase above the no response level. Even 2 groups each of 10 trained pilots cannot do better than chance. Variations in damping do not produce reliable differences in the average time on target.

Figure 17.6B shows that a movement of the control has 2 effects. First, it gradually changes the average value of the output of the control system. In the figure this is called the useful response. The useful response is followed by a low frequency oscillation around the new average value. In order to stay on target longer than by not responding, the man has to exploit the useful response while preventing the oscillation. It can be done by adopting a strategy like that illustrated in Figure 17.7. The strategy uses a constant rate output of the control system to copy the faster parts of the track around its points of inflection. The reversals of the track are copied by large amplitude movements which give the maximum acceleration.

If the control system does not have sufficient gain, the man can produce only a smaller amplitude version of the track. This is probably the difficulty in using the control system with the very low frequency oscillations of .85 cpm. It occurs because the experimenters reduce the gain of the output of the control system when they reduce the frequency of the oscillations, in order to hold constant the amplitude of the oscillations.

The results of 3 subsequent experiments by Muckler and his colleagues support this suggestion. In the first experiment the amplitude of the track is doubled. Only the group of undergraduates which track with the oscillations of 3.3 cpm. is able to do better than chance. The group with oscillations of 1.7 cpm probably does not have sufficient gain to deal with the larger amplitude track. The group tracks no better than the group with oscillations of .85 cpm.

In a second experiment the gain of the control system is doubled.

This enables the group with the oscillations of .85 cpm to do almost as well as the groups with the higher frequency oscillations.

In the third experiment Muckler and his colleagues equate the gain over the first .5 sec of a step input. This again enables the group with the oscillations of .85 cpm to do almost as well as the groups with the oscillations of 3.3 and 1.7 cpm. All these results suggest that the major determinant of the experiments must be the gain of the acceleration control system, not the frequency of the oscillations.

Crosscoupled control systems

Constant symmetrical crosscoupling

In constant symmetrical crosscoupling, the direction of a control movement has to be a constant number of degrees more clockwise or counterclockwise than the direction in which the man wishes the display marker to move. Bernotat (1970) reports that a rotation of 45° has only a small effect upon the accuracy of tracking of 10 people using a compensatory display. But a rotation of 90° has a marked effect upon their tracking. Similar results are reported by Smothergill, Martin and Pick (1971) for separate groups of 10 people tracking with preview.

Unfortunately in both experiments the people do not have very much practice with a single angle of rotation. Figure 17.8 shows that practice can overcome the detrimental effect of a single fixed crosscoupling angle.

For a group of another 10 people, Bernotat (1970) lays a crosswire over the front of the display. The angle of rotation of the crosswire indicates the crosscoupling angle. This almost halves the detrimental effect of the crosscoupling.

Bernotat (1970) almost eliminates the detrimental effect of crosscoupling by using a vector display, rather like Pew's (1966) velocity vector display discussed in Chapter 10. The vector shows the man the direction and magnitude of his control stick displacement in the rotated coordinates of movement of the error marker. The man has simply to keep the vector pointing always toward the target. Using this display, a group of another 5 people track almost as well with any crosscoupling angle as without crosscoupling. Thus people can compensate for a fixed crosscoupling angle without much practice, provided the display shows them their control movements in the rotated coordinates.

Constant asymmetrical crosscoupling

In asymmetrical crosscoupling, control movements in 1 of the 2 dimensions move the display marker in both dimensions. Control movements in the other dimension move the display marker only in the corresponding dimension. Figure 17.8 (Briggs & Waters, 1958) shows that a man can soon learn to compensate for a single constant asymmetrical crosscoupling angle.

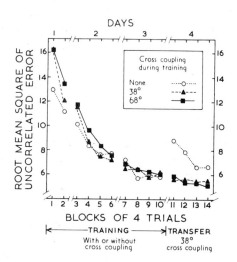

Figure 17.8. Performance with constant asymmetrical crosscoupling.

The functions represent the performance of separate groups of 16 USAF Reserve Officer Training Corps cadets. Each group practices for 3 days with only 1 amount of crosscoupling. For the conditions represented by the filled triangles and squares, a sideways movement of the control stick moves the aircraft symbol in a direction on the display respectively 38° and 68° below the horizontal. On the last day every group tracks with 38° of crosscoupling.

The center of a CRT is marked by a circle with a diameter of 1 in. The simulated aircraft is represented by a line about .8 in long and 1 mm thick. The track consists of visual noise with a peak amplitude at 3 cpm. The tracks in the 2 dimensions are statistically equivalent, but independent or uncorrelated. The control system is a simplified aircraft control system. A sideways movement of the control stick gives the display symbol representing the aircraft a rate of rotation. The symbol moves sideways at a rate which is proportional to its degree of rotation. A vertical movement of the control stick produces an upward or downward delta acceleration of the aircraft symbol with a damped oscillation like those illustrated in Figure 17.6A.

In addition to the 3 conditions illustrated in the figure, there are 3 groups of cadets with crosscouplings which move the aircraft symbol downward 8°, 23°, and 53° respectively. Curiously enough, the group with 53° of crosscoupling has a RMS error on transfer of about the same size as the group with only 8° of crosscoupling. Before tracking with crosscoupling, the man is told about it and has the amount of crosscoupling demonstrated to him. When the amount of crosscoupling is changed on the last day, the man is told the direction and size of the change. (After Briggs & Waters, 1958, Figure 4.)

The man has to fly a simulated aircraft so that the symbol representing the aircraft remains in the center of a CRT. Moving the control stick forward and backward changes the height of the aircraft on the display. Moving the control to the left or right moves the aircraft to the left or right, and also causes it to lose height. Separate groups of cadets fly the simulated aircraft with different constant amounts of cross-coupling. The figure illustrates the average RMS deviations from the flight path.

The unfilled circles represent a reference group which trains without any crosscoupling. With practice the average error is reduced to about half. The filled triangles and squares represent groups which train with respectively 38° and 68° of crosscoupling. At the start of training the average error is larger than with the uncrosscoupled control system. But after 40 trials there is little to choose between any of the control systems.

On the last day all 3 groups are transferred to the control system with the 38° of crosscoupling. This condition is used throughout by the group represented by the filled triangles. The men in the group represented by the filled squares find themselves with less crosscoupling than they are used to. They adjust to the change almost at once.

The men in the group represented by the unfilled circles have not met crosscoupling before. They are reliably worse than either of the other 2 groups on the first 4 trials after transfer. Briggs and Waters (1958) also train 2 groups with small amounts of crosscoupling. They are not shown in the figure. On transfer to the 38° of crosscoupling they track reliably better than the group which practices without cross-coupling. But they track reliably less well than the groups which practice with the 38° or 68° of crosscoupling.

The results in Figure 17.8 indicate that people can learn to track with constant asymmetrical crosscoupling. But a certain amount of prac-tice is necessary. People do not adjust at once to a constant amount of crosscoupling if they have not met as much crosscoupling before. The compensatory display used by Briggs and Waters (1958) may well conceal the crosscoupling. It may look simply as if the CRT has a variable downward drift.

Varying symmetrical crosscoupling

Figure 17.9 shows that a man does not learn to compensate fully for symmetrical crosscoupling when it is varying all the time. In McLeod's (1973b) experiment a small circle moves irregularly from side to side over the face of a CRT. The man has to keep a spot inside the circle. He has a lagged rate control system with a time constant

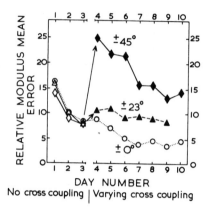

DAY NUMBER
No cross coupling | Varying cross coupling

Figure 17.9. Performance with varying symmetrical crosscoupling.
Each day there are 4 trials of 30 sec. An error score of zero indicates perfect performance. If the man does not touch the control, his error averages 100. The functions are from separate groups of 6 naval enlisted men. The groups represented by diamonds and by triangles have varying crosscoupling from day 4 onwards. The reference group represented by unfilled circles always tracks without crosscoupling. The average error with ±23° of crosscoupling is reliably different from the average error both with ±45° of crosscoupling, and with no crosscoupling.

The track moves only in the side to side dimension. It reverses direction irregularly on average once every 17 sec. The man uses an unloaded joystick. The joystick unit is mounted on a concealed turntable, which rotates back and forth following a sine wave with a frequency of 6 cpm. The man holds a circular knob which fits loosely over the end of the joystick. He is unable to see, feel or hear the crosscoupling vary. A similar result is obtained when the crosscoupling is produced electrically. (Results from McLeod, 1973b.)

of .8 sec. The difference in the angle between the direction of his control movements and the direction of the corresponding spot movements, varies at a frequency of 6 cpm.

For the group represented by the filled diamonds, the angle varies from 45° clockwise to 45° counterclockwise. One moment the man has to move his control 45° more clockwise than the direction in which he wants to move the response marker. After 2.5 sec the crosscoupling has disappeared. Another 2.5 sec later the man has to move his control 45° more counterclockwise than the direction in which he wants the response marker to go. The crosscoupling then disappears again, and so on. A separate group represented by triangles tracks with ±23° of crosscoupling. The results of a reference group without crosscoupling are represented by the unfilled circles. There is no crosscoupling for any group during the first 3 days.

The right side of the figure shows that after practice the average

error for the 2 crosscoupling conditions is well above the average error
for the reference condition. In this respect variable crosscoupling differs
from the fixed crosscoupling used by Briggs and Waters (1958). Figure
17.8 shows that with a single fixed crosscoupling angle the man can
learn to compensate fully.

A subsequent experiment indicates that changes in the frequency of
the variable crosscoupling between 2 and 12 cpm make little difference.
The average error depends principally upon the average amplitude of
the crosscoupling.

It is possible to predict fairly accurately the changes in the average
error produced by different angular amplitudes of variable crosscoupling.
The model assumes that the man responds always as if there were no
crosscoupling. He simply corrects the error produced by the hidden
crosscoupling when he makes his next response (McLeod, 1973b).

The man moves his control reliably further with the variable crosscoupling than he does without. This is because he corrects for the error
in the position of the response marker which is produced by the crosscoupling, as well as following the track marker. Figure 17.9 shows that
the modulus mean error becomes rather smaller during the first few
days with crosscoupling. This is accompanied by an increase in the
amount of control movement, as the man gradually learns to correct
for the error introduced by the variable crosscoupling.

The man behaves like this because tracking with a lagged rate control
system is partly a matter of trial and check. He never knows exactly
what his response marker is about to do. He moves his control around
until the response marker does what he wants it to. This strategy enables
him at the same time to correct the error introduced by the variable
crosscoupling.

In another experiment McLeod's (1973b) display has a gyro horizon
like that illustrated in Figure 9.2. The gyro horizon shows the man
how the crosscoupling angle varies. A vertical movement of the control
always moves the response marker at right angles to the gyro horizon.
The gyro horizon reduces the deterioration on day 4 when the crosscoupling is first introduced. But by the last day there is little difference
between groups tracking with and without the gyro horizon.

The difficulty with the gyro horizon display is that the gyro horizon
is not integrated with the track and response markers. The man has
first to note the direction of the error, and then to note the correction
which has to be made as a result of the rotation of the horizon. By
the time he has combined the two angles, the direction of the error
and the rotation of the horizon have changed somewhat. His computed
correction is no longer so appropriate. The man needs a single indication

of the direction in which to move his control, like the vector in Bernotat's (1970) vector display.

A range effect with constant symmetrical and asymmetrical crosscoupling

Figure 17.10 illustrates the 4 conditions of an experiment by Todosiev (1967) which compares constant symmetrical and asymmetrical cross-coupling. The filled arrowhead indicates a downward movement of the error marker. The unbroken arrow pointing upward indicates the direction of the control movement which produces this. The unfilled arrow-

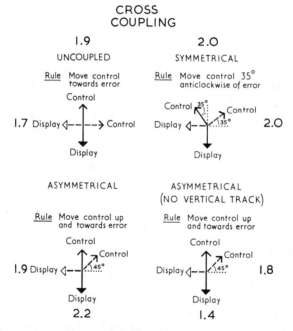

Figure 17.10. Performance with constant symmetrical and asymmetrical cross-coupling.

The figure shows the directional relationships between control and display, and the average RMS errors in each dimension. The display is compensatory. The track comprises random Gaussian noise with a cutoff at about 10 cpm. It is similar but independent for the vertical and horizontal dimensions. The control system represents a simplified version of an aircraft control system. An integrator is connected in series with a lowpass filter which has a time constant of .3 sec. The order of the 4 conditions is randomized for each of the 3 experienced trackers. The whole experiment is repeated 4 times in separate sessions. The results are from the last session. Unfortunately with only 3 people, it is not possible to tell how representative the results are likely to be. (Results from Todosiev, 1967.)

head and broken arrow indicate the corresponding directional relationships for sideways movement. Three experienced trackers change from condition to condition a number of times in an irregular order.

The numbers printed at the top and at the bottom of the figure represent the average RMS errors in the vertical dimension. The numbers on each side represent the average errors in the horizontal dimension. Unfortunately none of the differences is reliable statistically, because the 3 trackers vary too much from trial to trial.

More detailed analyses reveal a range effect. The man tracks in the control condition as if there is some asymmetrical crosscoupling. In the condition with symmetrical crosscoupling, he only fully compensates for the crosscoupling in the dimension of the asymmetrical crosscoupling. Thus the man tends to behave in all conditions as if there is asymmetrical crosscoupling. This is the optimal strategy if the man does not know which of the experimental conditions he is performing

The result is hardly surprising. During each session the man is given one condition of crosscoupling after another. The compensatory display and high order control system tend to conceal from him the new linkage between his control movements and the corresponding movements of the error marker. Range effects of this kind can be prevented only by using a separate group design.

Sudden changes in control systems

Sudden reversals of control direction

An experimenter may reverse the relationship between the direction of control and display movements without warning. When this happens, the man continues to respond as he has been doing until he sees that something is wrong (Chernikoff & Taylor, 1952; see Chapter 5). He then reverses the direction of his control movements. From then on interference is most likely to occur after the man temporarily stops responding. When the next error appears, he has to decide in which direction to move his control, and he may get it wrong (Vince, 1945, Figure 14). Interference is more marked with high frequency tracks which contain a lot of reversals in direction than it is with low frequency tracks (Andreas, Green and Spragg, 1954a, 1954b, 1955).

Sudden changes are easier to detect with a pursuit display because the response marker shows the man directly the output of his control system. Detecting a sudden change in a control system is more difficult with a compensatory display. It produces larger initial tracking errors (Christ & Newton, 1970).

Detection is rather easier if the track is predictable like Vince's (1945) multiple ramps, or like the steps in the experiment described by Chernikoff and Taylor (1952). A single sine wave track is also predictable, and so helps the man to detect a sudden change in the control system. Probably for this reason, most of the experiments on sudden changes have used compensatory displays and irregular sine wave tracks. They make detection more difficult.

Sudden changes in control direction and gain

Figure 17.11 (Elkind & Miller, 1966) illustrates the effect upon a practiced student of sudden changes in the gain and direction of a rate control system. The compensatory display which the student uses

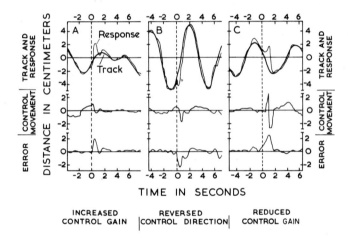

Figure 17.11.   Performance following sudden changes in a control system.
The vertical broken line indicates the time of the change. The display is compensatory. The quasirandom track has a top frequency of about 15 cpm, and a RMS amplitude of about 2 cm. During a trial lasting 4 to 8 min there are 18 sudden changes in the control system. Before the experiment the man practices with all the various control systems. He also has about 3 hr of practice with sudden changes between the control systems. The figure illustrates 3 selected paper records.

The error after the sudden changes is probably a little larger than it should be because the man has to signal with the other hand as soon as he detects a sudden change. Elkind and Miller (1966, Table 6) report for one student that signaling produces a reliable increase in mean squared error. Unfortunately only 3 students are used in the experiment. In the other experiments described by Elkind and Miller, there are only 2 students. Thus it is not possible to tell how representative the results are likely to be. (After Elkind & Miller, 1966, Figures 9a, b, c.)

corresponds to the error function in the lower part of the figure. The student does not have separate track and response markers corresponding to the 2 functions in the upper part of the figure.

All 3 sudden changes occur when the track is moving fast. When the track is stationary or is moving only slowly, the error which follows the change develops more slowly. The man then takes longer to detect the change and to adjust to it.

Part **A** of the figure illustrates a sudden 5 fold increase in the gain of the control system. When the track is moving fast, the output of the control system rapidly gets ahead of the track. The function half way down the figure shows that the man soon moves his rate control in the direction which is necessary to correct the error.

In correcting the error, the output of the control system overshoots. The overshoot is usually followed by a number of oscillations about the position of zero error, but they are not present in the figure. The overshoot and the subsequent oscillations indicate that the man first corrects the error which he sees. He only gradually adjusts to the increase in the gain of the control system.

Part **B** of the figure illustrates a sudden reversal in the relationship between the direction of control and display movements. When the track is moving fast, the output of the control system rapidly falls behind the track. The function half way down the figure shows that the man quickly moves his rate control in the direction which would previously have increased the error still further. He must guess that there is a reversal in direction.

A less practiced person first increases the size of his control movement in the direction of movement of the track, in an attempt to catch up with it. When he sees that this increases the error still further, he reverses the direction of his control movement.

Part **C** of the figure illustrates a sudden 5 fold reduction in the gain of the control system. This usually results in a more gradual increase in the error, like the increase in the figure. The man takes a longer average time to detect a reduction in gain than he does to detect an increase in gain or a reversal in direction. The output of the control system falls behind the track as it does with a reversal in direction.

In the example in the figure, the man at first reverses the direction of his rate control. This increases the size of the error. Presumably the man guesses that the relationship between the direction of control and display has changed. When he discovers that the error is increasing instead of decreasing, he hurriedly moves his control hard over the other way.

The man's strategy is different from the behavior of an unpracticed person. An unpracticed person usually moves the control further in the direction in which he has been moving it. He corrects the error more gradually than is illustrated in the figure.

As a general rule, the largest average error results from a change in direction which is accompanied by an increase in control system gain. A change in direction which is accompanied by a reduction in control system gain, produces a smaller average error than a change in direction without a change in gain.

A practiced man may adjust to a sudden change in direction in a single instant. A physical analogy is throwing a switch from positive to negative. Adjusting to a sudden change in the gain of the control system is generally slower. A physical analogy is rotating the knob of a volume control. If the gain is suddenly increased, the man usually overshoots and then oscillates around the position of zero error. If the gain is suddenly reduced, the man usually corrects the error only gradually.

The results in Figure 17.11 are for a rate control system. With an acceleration control system the average peak error is about twice as large. The man takes on average almost twice as long to recover from the sudden change in the control system, 2.8 sec compared with 1.5 sec.

With a position control system the average peak error is rather smaller than for a rate control system. The man recovers rather more quickly (Elkind & Miller, 1966, Table 14). The differences between orders of control system are due to the greater time lag which occurs with a higher order control system between a change in the position of the man's control and an appreciable change in the position output of the control system.

Sudden changes in the order of control

A change in the order of a control system between rate and acceleration can be compared with a change between position and rate. It follows from the results in the last 2 paragraphs that the change between rate and acceleration gives the larger average peak error. The man also takes longer to recover from a change between rate and acceleration than between position and rate (Elkind & Miller, 1966, Figures 20 and 21). These results also are due to the greater apparent time lags with the higher order control systems.

An increase in the order of a control system can be compared with the corresponding decrease. It might be predicted from the previous results that an increase in the order of a control system would give the larger average peak error, and that recovery would take longer. This is because the man has a higher order of control system after an increase than after a decrease. Elkind and Miller's (1966) 2 people do not behave consistently in this way. An experiment with a lot more people is needed to find out why this is.

Unexpected changes in control systems

In Elkind and Miller's (1966) experiments it takes the students only a few seconds on average to recover from a sudden change. This is because they are expecting the sudden changes, and are practiced at dealing with them. In order to obtain consistent experimental results in sufficient quantity, the students are given the same changes over and over again. They learn how to detect the changes and how to deal with them.

Expectancy is illustrated in Figure 17.11C. Here the student responds inappropriately, presumably because he is expecting a different sudden change. The student can be prevented from responding to a change before he is certain what the change is, by inserting catch tests at intervals (Elkind & Miller, 1966, Table 5). But catch tests do not make the task any more like tracking with an unexpected and unfamiliar change in a control system.

Sheridan (1960, Figures 4.27 and 4.28) finds longer recovery times by using unsuspecting students, who are not practiced at dealing with changes. But his changes are not so sudden. They take 8 sec.

Sheridan gives his 8 unwarned students a gradual change between a position control system with an exponential lag of .8 sec and a rate control system with the same exponential lag. The students first practice with both control systems, but they do not experience transitions. The display is pursuit. The track comprises 2 sine waves of 6.5 and 13 cpm.

On the very first transition the students take a median time of about 30 sec for their tracking error to recover fully from the change in the control system. The quickest student whose record is shown takes only about 5 sec. The slowest student takes about 5 min. These times do not include the 8 sec transition time of the control system.

The times are longer and more variable than the times reported by Elkind and Miller (1966) for students expecting changes and practiced at dealing with them. But unfortunately the longer recovery times can be due partly to the more gradual, and hence less noticeable, change in the control system. It is not possible to conclude that the longer recovery times occur simply because the students are not expecting the change, and are not practiced at dealing with changes.

Sudden changes with pilots in aircraft simulators

A failure in the control system of an aircraft can increase the order of control by 2. Sudden changes from a position control system to an acceleration control system are described by Weir and Johnson (1968) for 2 pilots. The pilots take on average about 6 sec to recover when the order of control is changed from position to acceleration, compared with about 5 sec when the change is from rate to acceleration.

When the pilot uses a position control system and expects a sudden change to an acceleration control system, he sometimes moves his control more than he should do if his aim is simply to track as accurately as possible. This may enable the pilot to detect the change in dynamics more rapidly. The finding reflects the difficulty of predicting from experiments with practiced pilots who are expecting a sudden change, to pilots on routine flights who are not expecting a sudden change.

The detection of a failure can be quicker in a simulator which moves because the man can feel that something unusual is happening. However if the failure inflicts a large acceleration on the man, or a large amplitude vibration, he may take longer to compensate for the failure. This is because too much acceleration or vibration reduces the man's efficiency (Poulton, 1970).

Sadoff (1962, Figures 8 and 9) simulates failures of the stability augmentation system of a high performance aircraft with and without cues of acceleration. The experiment follows on directly after the experiment of Figure 4.3. Unfortunately Sadoff gives results for only 2 pilots. The acceleration appears to help on about half the trials, and to hinder on the other half of the trials. Without more results on a lot more people, it is not possible to tell whether the differences are related in a systematic way to the kinds of failure investigated.

Sudden control system changes in the laboratory and in flight

The time required to recover from a sudden failure in a control system must depend upon the kind of failure, as in the experiments described by Elkind and Miller (1966). But Sheridan's (1960) experiment suggests that the average times reported by Elkind and Miller are too short. A similar criticism can be made of the average times reported by Weir and Johnson (1968) for pilots. An average of more than 5 or 6 sec is almost certainly required by a pilot to recover from a similar kind of failure when it is unexpected. But it is not yet possible to tell how much more.

The most valid experiment is one in which an unsuspecting pilot is asked to fly a simulator. When he settles down to his job, a single sudden change is introduced. Unfortunately the pilot may simply stop tracking and complain that the simulator has broken down. After this it is not possible to use him again as an unsuspecting pilot, because he will be on the look out for another sudden change.

If the pilot is flying an aircraft when the unexpected failure occurs, he will not stop. But an experiment of this kind involves a risk which is hard to justify. A more reasonable approach is to record the performance of pilots and aircraft, and to study the occasional spontaneous failures which are recorded. Records of this kind are now taken by commercial airlines.

Recommended variations for control systems

If a lever or joystick is used, the largest stick movement should produce the maximum output of the control system.

A position control system should have a linear output. Onoff controls and stepped controls are not recommended for use with position and rate control systems.

Lags in control systems should be minimized, unless they are used to reduce the effective order of control in tracking steps.

Control system oscillation, crosscoupling, and sudden control system changes should be prevented if possible.

References

Abbott, P. E., & Woodbury, J. R. Joint army-navy aircraft instrumentation research investigation of auditory displays. Douglas Aircraft Company Inc., Report LB 32125. Long Beach, California, 1965.

Adams, J. A. Some considerations in the design and use of dynamic flight simulators. In Sinaiko, H. W. (Ed.), *Selected papers on human factors in the design and use of control systems.* New York: Dover, 1961. Pp. 88–114.

Adams, J. A., & Chambers, R. W. Response to simultaneous stimulation of two sense modalities. *Journal of Experimental Psychology,* 1962, **63,** 198–206.

Adams, J. A., & Creamer, L. R. Anticipatory timing of continuous and discrete responses. *Journal of Experimental Psychology,* 1962, **63,** 84–90. a

Adams, J. A., & Creamer, L. R. Data processing capabilities of the human operator. *Journal of Engineering Psychology,* 1962, **1,** 150–158. b

Adams, J. A., & Creamer, L. R. Proprioception variables as determiners of anticipatory timing behavior. *Human Factors,* 1962, **4,** 217–222. c

Adams, J. A., & Xhignesse, L. V. Some determinants of two-dimensional visual tracking behavior. *Journal of Experimental Psychology,* 1960, **60,** 391–403.

Allen, R. W., & Jex, H. R. An experimental investigation of compensatory and pursuit tracking displays with rate and acceleration control dynamics and a disturbance input. U. S. National Aeronautics and Space Administration Report CR-1082. Washington, D.C., 1968.

Allnutt, M. F., Clifford, A. C., & Rolfe, J. M. Dynamic digital displays: a study of compensatory tracking with an acceleration order of control. UK RAF Institute of Aviation Medicine Report 374. Farnborough, Hants, 1966.

Ammons, R. B. Rotary pursuit apparatus: I. Survey of variables. *Psychological Bulletin*, 1955, **52**, 69–76.

Ammons, R. B., Farr, R. G., Bloch, E., Neumann, E., Dey, M., Marion, R., & Ammons, C. H. Long-term retention of perceptual-motor skills. *Journal of Experimental Psychology*, 1958, **55**, 318–328.

Andreas, B. G., Green, R. F., & Spragg, S. D. S. Transfer effects between performance on a following tracking task (modified SAM two-hand coordination test) and a compensatory tracking task (modified SAM two-hand pursuit test). *Journal of Psychology*, 1954, 37, 173–183. a

Andreas, B. G., Green, R. F., & Spragg, S. D. S. Transfer effects in following tracking (modified SAM two-hand coordination test) as a function of reversal of the display-control relationships on alternate blocks of trials. *Journal of Psychology*, 1954, 37, 185–197. b

Andreas, B. G., Green, R. F., & Spragg, S. D. S. Transfer effects in compensatory tracking (modified SAM two-hand pursuit test) as a function of reversal of the display-control relationships on alternate blocks of trials. *Journal of Psychology*, 1955, **40**, 421–430.

Angel, R. W., Garland, H., & Fischler, M. Tracking errors amended without visual feedback. *Journal of Experimental Psychology*, 1971, 89, 422–424.

Angel, R. W., & Higgins, J. R. Correction of false moves in pursuit tracking. *Journal of Experimental Psychology*, 1969, **82**, 185–187.

Annett, J., Golby, C. W., & Kay, H. The measurement of elements in an assembly task—the information output of the human motor system. *Quarterly Journal of Experimental Psychology*, 1958, **10**, 1–11.

Bahrick, H. P., Fitts, P. M., & Briggs, G. E. Learning curves—facts or artifacts? *Psychological Bulletin*, 1957, **54**, 256–268.

Bahrick, H. P., & Noble, M. E. Motor behavior. In Sidowski, J. B. (Ed.), *Experimental methods and instrumentation in psychology*. New York: McGraw-Hill, 1966. Pp. 645–675.

Bailey, A. W. Simplifying the operator's task as a controller. *Ergonomics*, 1958, **1**, 177–181.

Battig, W. F., Gregg, L. W., Nagel E. H., Small, A. M. Jr., & Brogden, W. J. Tracking and frequency of target intermittence. *Journal of Experimental Psychology*, 1954, **47**, 309–314.

Battig, W. F., Nagel, E. H., & Brogden, W. J. The effects of error-magnification and marker-size on bidimensional compensatory tracking. *American Journal of Psychology*, 1955, **68**, 585–594.

Battig, W. F., Nagel, E. H., Voss, J. F., & Brogden, W. J. Transfer and retention of bidimensional compensatory tracking after extended practice. *American Journal of Psychology* 1957, **70**, 75–80.

Battig, W. F., Voss, J. F., & Brogden, W. J. Effect of frequency of target intermittence upon tracking. *Journal of Experimental Psychology*, 1955, **49**, 244–248.

Bauerschmidt, D. K., & Roscoe, S. N. A comparative evaluation of a pursuit moving-airplane steering display. *IRE Transactions on Human Factors in Electronics*, 1960, **HFE-1**, 62–66.

Benepe, O. J., Narasimhan, R., & Ellson, D. G. An experimental evaluation of the application of harmonic analysis to the tracking behavior of the human operator. USAF Wright Air Development Center, Technical Report 53-384. Wright-Patterson Air Force Base, Ohio, 1954.

Bennett, C. A. Sampled-data tracking: sampling of the operator's output. *Journal of Experimental Psychology*, 1956, **51**, 429–438.

Benson, A. J., Huddleston, J. H. F., & Rolfe, J. M. A psychophysiological study of compensatory tracking on a digital display. *Human Factors*, 1965, **7**, 457–472.

Bergum, B. O., Klein, I. C., & Baldwin, R. D. The accuracy of two modes of radar tracking for two visual noise levels. Human Resources Research Office, Task Vigil 2. George Washington University, Washington, D.C., 1960.

Bernotat, R. K. Rotation of visual reference systems and its influence on control quality. *IEEE Transactions on Man-Machine Systems*, 1970, **MMS-11**, 129–131.

Birmingham, H. P. Comparison of a pressure and moving joystick: interim report on. U. S. Naval Research Laboratory Report 3297. Washington, D.C., 1950.

Birmingham, H. P., Kahn, A., & Taylor, F. V. A demonstration of the effects of quickening in multiple-coordinate control tasks. U. S. Naval Research Laboratory Report 4380. Washington, D.C., 1954.

Birmingham, H. P., & Taylor, F. V. A human engineering approach to the design of man-operated continuous control systems. U. S. Naval Research Laboratory Report 4333. Washington, D.C., 1954.

Birmingham, H. P., & Taylor, F. V. A design philosophy for man-machine control systems. In Sinaiko, H. W. (Ed.), *Selected papers on human factors in the design and use of control systems*. New York: Dover, 1961. Pp. 67–87.

Bowen, J. H., & Chernikoff, R. The relationships between magnification and course frequency in compensatory aided tracking. U. S. Naval Research Laboratory Report 4913. Washington, D.C., 1957.

Bowen, J. H., & Chernikoff, R. The effects of magnification and average course velocity on compensatory tracking. U. S. Naval Research Laboratory, Report 5186. Washington, D.C., 1958.

Briggs, G. E. Tracking behavior. Comments on Dr. Poulton's paper. In Bilodeau, E. A. (Ed.), *Acquisition of skill*. New York: Academic Press, 1966. Pp. 411–424.

Briggs, G. E. Transfer of training. In Bilodeau, E. A., and Bilodeau, I. McD. (Eds.), *Principles of skill acquisition*. New York: Academic Press, 1969. Pp. 205–234.

Briggs, G. E., Fitts, P. M., & Bahrick, H. P. Learning and performance in a complex tracking task as a function of visual noise. *Journal of Experimental Psychology*, 1957, **53**, 379–387. a

Briggs, G. E., Fitts, P. M., & Bahrick, H. P. Effects of force and amplitude cues on learning and performance in a complex tracking task. *Journal of Experimental Psychology*, 1957, **54**, 262–268. b

Briggs, G. E., & Howell, W. C. On the relative importance of time sharing at central and peripheral levels. U. S. Naval Training Device Center, Technical Report 508-2. Port Washington, New York, 1959.

Briggs, G. E., & Rockway, M. R. Learning and performance as a function of the percentage of pursuit component in a tracking display. *Journal of Experimental Psychology*, 1966, **71**, 165–169.

Briggs, G. E., & Waters, L. K. Training and transfer as a function of component interaction. *Journal of Experimental Psychology*, 1958, **56**, 492–500.

Briggs, G. E., & Wiener, E. L. Influence of time sharing and control loading on transfer of training. *Journal of Applied Psychology*, 1966, **50**, 201–203.

Broadbent, D. E. The bass cutting of frequency transposed speech. UK. MRC. Applied Psychology Research Unit Report 223. Cambridge, England, 1956.

Brown, I. D., Holmqvist, S. D., & Woodhouse, M. C. A laboratory comparison of tracking with four flight-director displays. *Ergonomics*, 1961, **4**, 229–251.

Buck, L. Performance data for the NRC stressalyzer. Canadian National Research Council, Division of Mechanical Engineering, Report 69. Ottawa, Ontario, 1972.

Burke, D., & Gibbs, C. B. A comparison of free-moving and pressure levers in a positional control system. *Ergonomics*, 1965, 8, 23–29.

Calvert, E. S. Manoeuvres to ensure the avoidance of collision. *Journal of the Institute of Navigation.* 1960, 13, 127–137.

Carriero, N. J. A note on "on simple methods of scoring tracking error." *Psychological Bulletin*, 1964, 61, 303.

Chase, R. A., Cullen, J. K., Jr., Openshaw, J. W., & Sullivan, S. A. Studies of sensory feedback: III. The effects of display gain on tracking performance. *Quarterly Journal of Experimental Psychology*, 1965, 17, 193–208.

Chernikoff, R. Human equalization: concept, machine and measurement. In Burrows, A. A., and Emery, J. A., (Eds.), *Complex vehicular controls.* Douglas Aircraft Company, Long Beach, California, 1962. Pp. 1–11.

Chernikoff, R., Birmingham, H. P., & Taylor, F. V. A comparison of pursuit and compensatory tracking under conditions of aiding and no aiding. *Journal of Experimental Psychology*, 1955, 49, 55–59.

Chernikoff, R., Birmingham, H. P., & Taylor, F. V. A comparison of pursuit and compensatory tracking in a simulated aircraft control loop. *Journal of Applied Psychology*, 1956, 40, 47–52.

Chernikoff, R., Bowen, J. H., & Birmingham, H. P. A comparison of zero-order and fourth-order aided compensatory systems as a function of course frequency. U. S. Naval Research Laboratory, Report 5262. Washington, D.C., 1959.

Chernikoff, R., Duey, J. W., & Taylor, F. V. Two-dimensional tracking with identical and different control dynamics in each coordinate. *Journal of Experimental Psychology*, 1960, 60, 318–322.

Chernikoff, R., & LeMay, M. Effect of various display-control configurations on tracking with identical and different coordinate dynamics. *Journal of Experimental Psychology*, 1963, 66, 95–99.

Chernikoff, R., & Taylor, F. V. Reaction time to kinesthetic stimulation resulting from sudden arm displacement. *Journal of Experimental Psychology*, 1952, 43, 1–8.

Chernikoff, R., & Taylor, F. V. Effects of course frequency and aided time constant on pursuit and compensatory tracking. *Journal of Experimental Psychology*, 1957, 53, 285–292.

Christ, R. E., & Newton, R. R. Relative effects of display mode and input function on tracking performance. *Journal of Experimental Psychology*, 1970, 85, 237–244.

Clutton-Baker, J. A comparison between combined and divided controls and one man and two man aiming. UK Royal Naval Personnel Research Committee Report 655. Medical Research Council, London, England, 1950.

Conklin, J. E. Effect of control lag on performance in a tracking task. *Journal of Experimental Psychology*, 1957, 53, 261–268.

Cooper, G. E. Understanding and interpreting pilot opinion. *Aeronautical Engineering Review*, 1957, 16, 47–51, 56.

Cooper, G. E., & Harper, R. P. The use of pilot rating in the evaluation of aircraft handling qualities. U. S. National Aeronautics and Space Administration Technical Note D-5153. Washington, D.C., 1969.

Corrigan, R. E., & Brogden, W. J. The effect of angle upon precision of linear pursuit movements. *American Journal of Psychology*, 1948, 61, 502–510.

Craig, D. R. Effect of amplitude range on duration of responses to step function displacements. USAF Air Material Command Technical Report 5913. Wright-Patterson Air Force Base, Dayton, Ohio, 1949.

Craik, K. J. W. Theory of the human operator in control systems. 1. The operator as an engineering system. *British Journal of Psychology*, 1947, 38, 56–61.

Craik, K. J. W. Theory of the human operator in control systems. II. Man as an element in a control system. *British Journal of Psychology*, 1948, 38, 142–148.

Craik, K. J. W., & Vince, M. A. Psychological and physiological aspects of control mechanisms with special reference to tank gunnery. Part I. UK MRC Military Personnel Research Committee Report, London, England, 1943. *Ergonomics*, 1963, 6, 1–33. a

Craik, K. J. W., & Vince, M. A. Psychological and physiological aspects of control mechanisms. Part II. UK MRC Military Personal Research Committee Report BPC 44/322, London, England, 1944. *Ergonomics*, 1963, 6, 419–440. b

✳ Day, R. H. The effect of one component of a task upon another during skilled performance. *Australian Journal of Psychology*, 1955, 7, 14–27.

Dooley, R. P., & Newton, J. M. Transfer of training between quickened and unquickened displays. *Perceptual & Motor Skills*, 1965, 21, 11–15.

Drew, G. C. Variations in reflex blink-rate during visual-motor tasks. *Quarterly Journal of Experimental Psychology*, 1951, 3, 73–88.

Drewell, N. H. The effect of preview on pilot describing functions in a simple tracking task. Institute for Aerospace Studies Technical Note 176. University of Toronto, 1972.

Duey, J. W., & Chernikoff, R. The use of quickening in one coordinate of a two-dimensional tracking system. U. S. Naval Research Laboratory Report 5428. Washington, D.C., 1959.

Elkind, J. I. Tracking response characteristics of the human operator. USAF Human Factors Operations Research Laboratories Memorandum 40. Air Research and Development Command, Washington, D.C., 1953.

Elkind, J. I. Characteristics of simple manual control systems. MIT Lincoln Laboratory Technical Report 111. Lexington, Massachusetts, 1956.

Elkind, J. I., & Miller, D. C. Adaptive characteristics of the human controller of time-varying systems. USAF Flight Dynamics Laboratory Technical Report 66-60. Wright-Patterson Air Force Base, Ohio, 1966.

Ellis, K. Track initiation and manual tracking using a rolling ball control. UK Ministry of Defence (Naval), Applied Psychology Unit, Note 3-67. London, 1967.

Ellis, N. C., Lowes, A. L., Matheny, W. G., & Norman, D. A. The feasibility of using an adaptive technique in flight simulator training. *Ergonomics*, 1971, 14, 381–390.

Ellis, W. H. B., & Allan, R. M. Pilots' eye movements during visual approaches and landings. UK RAF Flying Personnel Research Committee Report 888. Air Ministry, London, 1954.

Ellis, W. H. B., Burrows, A., & Jackson, K. F. Presentation of air speed while deck-landing: comparison of visual and auditory methods. UK RAF Flying Personnel Research Committee Report 841. Air Ministry, London, 1953.

Ellson, D. G., & Coppock, H. Further analysis of the psychological range effect. USAF Wright Air Development Center Technical Report 6012. Dayton, Ohio, 1951.

Ellson, D. G., & Gray, F. E. Frequency responses of human operators following a sine wave input. USAF Air Material Command, Memorandum Report MCREXD-694-2N. Wright-Patterson Air Force Base, Dayton, Ohio, 1948.

Ellson, D. G., & Hill, H. The interaction of responses to step function stimuli. 1. Opposed steps of constant amplitude. USAF Air Material Command, Memorandum Report MCREXD—694-2P. Wright-Patterson Air Force Base, Dayton, Ohio, 1948.

Ellson, D. G., Hill, H., & Gray, F. Wave length and amplitude characteristics of tracking error curves. USAF Air Material Command, Memorandum Report TSEAA 694-2D. Wright-Patterson Air Force Base, Dayton, Ohio, 1947.

Ellson, D. G., & Wheeler, L. The range effect. USAF Air Material Command Technical Report 5813. Wright-Patterson Air Force Base, Dayton, Ohio, 1949.

Eyman, R. K. The effect of sophistication on ratio- and discriminative scales. *American Journal of Psychology*, 1967, 80, 520–540.

Fenwick, C. Development of a peripheral vision command indicator for instrument flight. *Human Factors*, 1963, 5, 117–127.

Fitts, P. M. The information capacity of the human motor system in controlling the amplitude of movement. *Journal of Experimental Psychology*, 1954, 47, 381–391.

Fitts, P. M., Bennett, W. F., & Bahrick, H. P. Application of auto-correlation and cross-correlation analysis to the study of tracking behavior. In Finch, G., and Cameron, F. (Eds.), *Air Force human engineering, personnel, and training research*. Baltimore, Maryland: USAF Air Research and Development Command Technical Report 56-8, 1956. Pp. 125–141.

Fitts, P. M., & Jones, R. E. Analysis of factors contributing to 460 "pilot-error" experiences in operating aircraft controls. In Sinaiko, H. W. (Ed.), *Selected papers on human factors in the design and use of control systems*. New York: Dover, 1961. Pp. 332–358. a

Fitts, P. M., & Jones, R. E. Psychological aspects of instrument display. 1. Analysis of 270 "pilot-error" experiences in reading and interpreting aircraft instruments. In Sinaiko, H. W. (Ed.). *Selected papers on human factors in the design and use of control systems*. New York: Dover, 1961. Pp. 359–396. b

Fitts, P. M., Marlowe, E., & Noble, M. E. The interrelations of task variables in continuous pursuit tasks: I Visual-display scale, arm-control scale, and target frequency in pursuit tracking. USAF Human Resources Research Center Research Bulletin 53-34. Lackland Air Force Base, San Antonio, Texas, 1953.

Fitts, P. M., & Peterson, J. R. Information capacity of discrete motor responses. *Journal of Experimental Psychology*, 1964, 67, 103–112.

Fitts, P. M., & Simon, C. W. Some relations between stimulus patterns and performance in a continuous dual-pursuit task. *Journal of Experimental Psychology*, 1952, 43, 428–436.

Fleishman, E. A., & Parker, J. F., Jr. Factors in the retention and relearning of perceptual-motor skill. *Journal of Experimental Psychology*, 1962, 64, 215–226.

Forbes, T. W. Auditory signals for instrument flying. *Journal of Aeronautical Science*, 1946, 13, 255–258.

Frost, G. G. A comparison between tracking with "optimum" dynamics and tracking with a simple velocity control. USAF Aerospace Medical Research Laboratories Technical Documentary Report 62-150. Wright-Patterson Air Force Base, Ohio, 1962.

Fuchs, A. H. The progression-regression hypothesis in perceptual-motor skill learning. *Journal of Experimental Psychology*, 1962, 63, 177–182.

Garvey, W. D. A comparison of the effects of training and secondary tasks on tracking behavior. *Journal of Applied Psychology*, 1960, 44, 370–375.

Garvey, W. D. & Henson, J. B. Interactions between display gain and task-induced stress in manual tracking. *Journal of Applied Psychology*, 1959, 43, 205–208.

✳Garvey, W. D., Knowles, W. B., & Newlin, E. P. Prediction of future position of a target track on four types of displays. *Canadian Journal of Psychology*, 1957, 11, 93–103.

Garvey, W. D., & Mitnick, L. L. An analysis of tracking behavior in terms of lead-lag errors. *Journal of Experimental Psychology*, 1957, 53, 372–378.

Garvey, W. D., Sweeny, J. S., & Birmingham, H. P. Differential effects of "display lags" and "control lags" on the performance of manual tracking systems. *Journal of Experimental Psychology*, 1958, 56, 8–10.

Garvey, W. D., & Taylor, F. V. Interactions among operator variables, system dynamics, and task-induced stress. *Journal of Applied Psychology*, 1959, 43, 79–85.

Geldard, F. A. Some neglected possibilities of communication. *Science*, 1960, 131, 1583–1588.

Gerall, A. A., & Green, R. F. Effect of torque changes upon a two-handed coordination task. *Perceptual & Motor Skills*, 1958, 8, 287–290.

Gibbs, C. B. The continuous regulation of skilled response by kinaesthetic feed back. *British Journal of Psychology*, 1954, 45, 24–39.

Gibbs, C. B. Controller design: interactions of controlling limbs, time-lags and gains in positional and velocity systems. *Ergonomics*, 1962, 5, 385–402.

Gibbs, C. B. Probability learning in step-input tracking. *British Journal of Psychology*, 1965, 56, 233–242.

Gibson, J. J. Observations on active touch. *Psychological Review*, 1962, 69, 477–491.

Glencross, D. J. Temporal organization in a repetitive speed skill. *Ergonomics*, 1973, 16, 765–776.

Goldman, A. Sensory interaction and response capacity. U. S. Naval Training Device Center Technical Report 789-11-1. Port Washington, New York, 1959.

Goldstein, D. A. Linear quickening as guidance in training for manual control of complex systems. General Dynamics Corporation, Electric Boat Division Technical Report U411-61-053. Groton, Connecticut, 1961.

Gordon, N. B. Learning a motor task under varied display conditions. *Journal of Experimental Psychology*, 1959, 57, 65–73.

Gottsdanker, R. M. Prediction-motion with and without vision. *American Journal of Psychology*, 1952, 65, 533–543. a

Gottsdanker, R. M. The accuracy of prediction motion. *Journal of Experimental Psychology*, 1952, 43, 26–36. b

Gottsdanker, R. M. A further study of prediction-motion. *American Journal of Psychology*, 1955, 68, 432–437.

Gottsdanker, R. M. Prediction-span, speed of response, smoothness, and accuracy in tracking. *Perceptual & Motor Skills*, 1956, 6, 171–181. a

Gottsdanker, R. M. The ability of human operators to detect acceleration of target motion. *Psychological Bulletin*, 1956, 53, 477–487. b

Graham, D., & McRuer, D. *Analysis of nonlinear control systems*. New York: Wiley, 1961.

Griew, S. Set to respond and the effect of interrupting signals upon tracking performance. *Journal of Experimental Psychology*, 1959, **57**, 333–337.

Guercio, J. G., & Wall, R. L. Congruent and spurious motion in the learning and performance of a compensatory tracking task. *Human Factors*, 1972, **14**, 259–269.

Hahn, J. F. Unidimensional compensatory tracking with a vibrotactile display. *Perceptual & Motor Skills*, 1965, **21**, 699–702.

Hammerton, M. An investigation into the optimal gain of a velocity control system. *Ergonomics*, 1962, **5**, 539–543.

Hammerton, M. Transfer of training from a simulated to a real control situation. *Journal of Experimental Psychology*, 1963, **66**, 450–453.

Hammerton, M. Factors affecting the use of simulators for training. *Proceedings IEE*, 1966, **113**, 1881–1884.

Hammerton, M., & Tickner, A. H. Transfer of training between space-oriented and body-oriented control situations. *British Journal of Psychology*, 1964, **55**, 433–437.

Hammerton, M., & Tickner, A. H. An investigation into the comparative suitability of forearm, hand and thumb controls in acquisition tasks. *Ergonomics*, 1966, **9**, 125–130.

Hammerton, M., & Tickner, A. H. Visual factors affecting transfer of training from a simulated to a real control situation. *Journal of Applied Psychology*, 1967, **51**, 46–49.

Hammerton, M., & Tickner, A. H. Comparison of operator performance on a tracking task using discretely and continuously variable controls. *Journal of Applied Psychology*, 1968, **52**, 319–320.

Hammerton, M., & Tickner, A. H. Some factors affecting learning and transfer of training in visual-motor skills. *British Journal of Psychology*, 1969, **60**, 369–371.

Hammerton, M., & Tickner, A. H. Structural and blank backgrounds in a pursuit tracking task. *Ergonomics*, 1970, **13**, 719–722.

Harris, J. D., & Pikler, A. G. The stability of a standard of loudness as measured by compensatory tracking. *American Journal of Psychology*, 1960, **73**, 573–580.

Harris, J. D., Pikler, A. G., & Murphy, J. E. Compensatory and pursuit tracking of pitch. *Journal of the Acoustical Society of America*, 1963, **35**, 581–587.

Hartman, B. O. The effect of target frequency on compensatory tracking. U. S. Army Medical Research Laboratory Report 272. Fort Knox, Kentucky, 1957. a

Hartman, B. O. The effect of target frequency on pursuit tracking. U. S. Army Medical Research Laboratory Report 263. Fort Knox, Kentucky, 1957. b

Hartman, B. O., & Fitts, P. M. Relation of stimulus and response amplitude to tracking performance. *Journal of Experimental Psychology*, 1955, **49**, 82–92.

Hattler, K. W. Loudness display for accurate aerospace instrument flying. *Aerospace Medicine*, 1968, **39**, 688–692.

Hecker, D., Green, D., & Smith, K. U. Dimensional analysis of motion: X. Experimental evaluation of a time-study problem. *Journal of Applied Psychology*, 1956, **40**, 220–227.

Heinemann, R. F. D. The relationship between the difficulty level and kind of tracking problem and the type of tracking and type of control. U. S. Naval Training Device Center Technical Report 342-4. Port Washington, New York, 1961.

Helson, H. A study of aided and velocity tracking. Foxboro Company, Summary Report. Foxboro, Massachusetts, 1944.

Helson, H. Design of equipment and optimal human operation. *American Journal of Psychology*, 1949, **62**, 473–497.

Henry, J. P., Junas, R., & Smith, K. U. Experimental cybernetic analysis of delayed feedback of breath-pressure control. *American Journal of Physical Medicine*, 1967, **46**, 1317–1331.

Hershberger, M. L. An experimental study of image motion compensation tracking for earth reconnaisance from space. *Human Factors*, 1967, **9**, 105–118.

Hick, W. E. Friction in manual controls. UK MRC Applied Psychology Unit Report 18. Cambridge, England, 1945.

Hick, W. E. Reaction time for the amendment of a response. *Quarterly Journal of Experimental Psychology*, 1949, **1**, 175–179.

Hick, W . E., & Fraser, D. C. Speed and accuracy of plotting with a simulated P.P.I. marker strobe. Part 1. Comparison of joystick and pencil types of control. UK Royal Naval Personnel Research Committee Report 441. Medical Research Council, London, 1948.

Higgins, J. R., & Angel, R. W. Correction of tracking errors without sensory feedback. *Journal of Experimental Psychology*, 1970, **84**, 412–416.

Hoffeld, D. R., Seidenstein, S., & Brogden, W. J. Proficiency in finger-tracking as a function of number of fingers. *American Journal of Psychology*, 1961, **74**, 36–44.

Hofmann, M. A., & Heimstra, N. W. Tracking performance with visual, auditory, or electrocutaneous displays. *Human Factors*, 1972, **14**, 131–138.

Holding, D. H. Guidance in pursuit tracking. *Journal of Experimental Psychology*, 1959, **57**, 362–366.

Holland, J. G., & Henson, J. B. Transfer of training between quickened and unquickened tracking systems. *Journal of Applied Psychology*, 1956. **40**, 362–366.

Howell, W. C., & Briggs, G. E. The effects of visual noise and locus of perturbation on tracking performance. *Journal of Experimental Psychology*, 1959, **58**, 166–173.

Howland, D., & Noble, M. E. The effect of physical constants of a control on tracking performance. *Journal of Experimental Psychology*, 1955, **46**, 353–360.

Huddleston, H. F., & Wilson, R. V. An evaluation of the usefulness of four secondary tasks in assessing the effect of a lag in simulated aircraft dynamics. *Ergonomics*, 1971, **14**, 371–380.

Hudson, E. M. An adaptive tracking simulator. Otis Elevator Company, Brooklyn, New York, 1962.

Hudson, E. M. Adaptive training and nonverbal behavior. U.S. Naval Training Device Center Technical Report 1395-1. Port Washington, New York, 1964.

Humphrey, C. E., & Thompson, J. E. Auditory displays. II Comparison of auditory and visual tracking in one dimension. A. Discontinuous signals, simple course. Applied Physics Laboratory Report TG-146. Johns Hopkins University, Silver Spring, Maryland, 1952. a

Humphrey, C. E., & Thompson, J. E. Auditory displays. II Comparison of auditory tracking with visual tracking in one dimension. B. Discontinuous signals, complex course. Applied Physics Laboratory Report TG-147. Johns Hopkins University, Silver Spring, Maryland, 1952. b

Humphrey, C. E., & Thompson, J. E. Auditory displays. II Comparison of auditory tracking with visual tracking in one dimension. C. Continuous signals, simple, intermediate and complex courses. Applied Physics Laboratory Report TG-194. Johns Hopkins University, Silver Spring, Maryland, 1953.

Humphrey, C. E., Thompson, J. E., & Versace, J. Time-sharing and the tracking task. Applied Physics Laboratory Report TG-201. Johns Hopkins University, Silver Spring, Maryland, 1953.

Hunt, D. P. The effect of the precision of informational feedback on human tracking performance. *Human Factors*, 1961, 3, 77–85.

Hunt, D. P. Effects of nonlinear and discrete transformations of feedback information on human tracking performance. *Journal of Experimental Psychology*, 1964, 67, 486–494.

Hunt, D. P. Effects of discrete transformations of controller outputs on human tracking performance. *Journal of Applied Psychology*, 1966, 50, 35–40.

Ince, F., Williges, R. C., & Roscoe, S. N. Simulator motion and the frequency separation principle in attitude indicator/flight director displays. Aviation Research Laboratory Technical Report 73-2. Institute of Aviation, University of Illinois, Willard Airport, Savoy, Illinois, 1973.

Jackson, K. F. Behaviour in controlling a combination of systems. *Ergonomics*, 1958, 2, 52–62.

Jacobs, R. S., Williges, R. C., & Roscoe, S. N. Simulator motion as a factor in flight-director display evaluation. Aviation Research Laboratory Technical Report 72-1. Institute of Aviation, University of Illinois, Willard Airport, Savoy, Illinois, 1972.

Jenkins, W. L., & Connor, M. B. Some design factors in making settings on a linear scale. *Journal of Applied Psychology*, 1949, 33, 395–409.

Jenkins, W. L., Maas, L. O., & Olson, M. W. Influence of inertia in making settings on a linear scale. *Journal of Applied Psychology*, 1951, 35, 208–213.

Jenkins, W. L., Maas, L. O., & Rigler, D. Influence of friction in making settings on a linear scale. *Journal of Applied Psychology*, 1950, 34, 434–439.

Jenkins, W. L., & Olson, M. W. The use of levers in making settings on a linear scale. *Journal of Applied Psychology*, 1952, 36, 269–271.

Johnson, S. L., Williges, R. C., & Roscoe, S. N. A new approach to motion relations for flight director displays. Aviation Research Laboratory Technical Report 71-20. Institute of Aviation, University of Illinois, Willard Airport, Savoy, Illinois, 1971.

Johnston, W. A., Greenberg, S. N., Fisher, R. P., & Martin, D. W. Divided attention: a vehicle for monitoring memory processes. *Journal of Experimental Psychology*, 1970, 83, 164–171.

Katz, D., Emery, J. A., Gabriel, R. F., & Burrows, A. A. Experimental study of acoustic displays of flight parameters in a simulated aerospace vehicle. U. S. National Aeronautics and Space Administration Report CR-509. Washington, D.C., 1966.

Katz, M. S., & Spragg, S. D. S. Tracking performance as a function of frequency of course illumination. *Journal of Psychology*, 1955, 40, 181–191.

Keele, S. W., & Posner, M. I. Processing of visual feedback in rapid movements. *Journal of Experimental Psychology*, 1968, 77, 155–158.

Kelley, C. R. Predictor instruments look into the future. *Control Engineering*, 1962, 9, 86–90.

Kelley, C. R. *Manual and automatic control*. New York: Wiley, 1968.

Kelley, C. R. The measurement of tracking proficiency. *Human Factors*, 1969, **11**, 43–64. a

Kelley, C. R. What is adaptive training? *Human Factors*, 1969, **11**, 547–556. b

Kelley, C. R., Mitchell, M. B., & Strudwick, P. H. Applications of the predictor displays to the control of space vehicles. Dunlap and Associates Inc., Santa Monica, California, 1964.

Knowles, W. B., & Rose, D. J. Manned lunar landing simulation. Hughes Aircraft Company, Technical Memorandum 728. Culver City, California, 1962.

Lathrop, R. G. Measurement of analog sequential dependencies. *Human Factors*, 1964, **6**, 233–239.

Lawson, R. W. Blinking: its role in physical measurement. *Nature (London)* 1948, **161**, 154–157.

Levine, M. Tracking performance as a function of exponential delay between control and display. USAF Wright Air Development Center, Technical Report 53-236. Wright-Patterson Air Force Base, Ohio, 1953. a

Levine, M. Transfer of tracking performance as a function of a delay between the control and the display. USAF Wright Air Development Center, Technical Report 53-237. Wright-Patterson Air Force Base, Ohio, 1953. b

Levison, W. H., & Elkind, J. I. Studies of multi-variable manual control systems: two axis compensatory systems with compatible integrated display and control. U. S. National Aeronautics and Space Administration, Report CR-554. Washington, D.C., 1966.

Levison, W. H., & Elkind, J. I. Studies of multivariable manual control systems: two-axis compensatory systems with separated displays and controls. U. S. National Aeronautics and Space Administration Report CR-875. Washington, D.C., 1967. a

Levison, W. H., & Elkind, J. I. Two-dimensional manual control systems with separated displays. *IEEE Transactions on Human Factors in Electronics*, 1967, **HFE-8**, 202–209. b

Levison, W. H., Elkind, J. I., & Ward, J. L. Studies of multivariable manual control systems: a model for task interference. U. S. National Aeronautics and Space Administration, Report CR-1746. Washington, D.C., 1971.

Lewis, R. E. F. Consistency and car driving skill. *British Journal of Industrial Medicine*, 1956, **13**, 131–141.

Lincoln, R. S. Visual tracking: III. The instrumental dimension of motion in relation to tracking accuracy. *Journal of Applied Psychology*, 1953, **37**, 489–493.

Ludvigh, E., & Miller, J. W. Study of visual acuity during the ocular pursuit of moving test objects. 1. Introduction. *Journal of the Optical Society of America*, 1958, **48**, 799–802.

McConnell, D., & Shelley, M. W. Tracking performance on a sequence of step functions which approaches a continuous function as a limit. *Journal of Experimental Psychology*, 1960, **59**, 312–320.

McGee, D. H., & Christ, R. E. Effects of bimodal stimulus presentation on tracking performance. *Journal of Experimental Psychology*, 1971, **91**, 110–114.

Mackworth, J. F., & Mackworth, N. H. Eye fixations recorded on changing visual scenes by the television eye-marker. *Journal of the Optical Society of America*, 1958, **48**, 439–445.

McLane, R. C., & Wolf, J. D. Symbolic and pictorial displays for submarine control. *Proceedings of the Second Annual NASA—University Conference on*

Manual Control. U. S. National Aeronautics and Space Administration, Report SP-128, Washington, D.C., 1966. Pp. 213–228.

McLeod, P. D. Recovery startegy during temporary obscuration of a tracked target. *Ergonomics,* 1972, **15,** 57–64.

McLeod, P. D. Interference of "attend to and learn" tasks with tracking. *Journal of Experimental Psychology,* 1973, **99,** 330–333. a

McLeod, P. D. Response strategies with a cross-coupled control system. *Journal of Experimental Psychology,* 1973, **97,** 64–69. b

McLeod, P. D., & McCallum, I. R. Control strategies of experienced and novice controllers with a zero energy nuclear reactor. *Ergonomics,* 1975, **18,** in press.

Macrae, A. W., & Holding, D. H. Transfer of training after guidance or practice. *Quarterly Journal of Experimental Psychology,* 1966, **18,** 327–333.

McRuer, D. T., Graham, D., & Krendel, E. S. Manual control of single-loop systems. Part I. *Journal of the Franklin Institute,* 1967, **283,** 1–29. a

McRuer, D. T., Graham, D., & Krendel, E. S. Manual control of single-loop systems. Part II. *Journal of the Franklin Institute,* 1967, **283,** 145–168. b

McRuer, D., Graham, D., Krendel, E., & Reisener, W., Jr. Human pilot dynamics in compensatory systems. Theory, models, and experiments with controlled element and forcing function variations. U. S. Air Force Flight Dynamics Laboratory, Technical Report 65-15. Wright-Patterson Air Force Base, Ohio, 1965.

McRuer, D. T., & Krendel, E. S. Dynamic response of human operators. USAF Wright Air Development Center, Technical Report 56-524. Wright-Patterson Air Force Base, Ohio, 1957.

McRuer, D. T., & Krendel, E. S. The human operator as a servo system element. Part I. *Journal of the Franklin Institute,* 1959, **267,** 381–403. a

McRuer, D. T., & Krendel, E. S. The human operator as a servo system element. Part II. *Journal of the Franklin Institute,* 1959, **267,** 511–536. b

Martin, D. W. Residual processing capacity during verbal organization in memory. *Journal of Verbal Learning & Verbal Behavior,* 1970, **9,** 391–397.

Meiry, J. L. The vestibular system and human dynamic space orientation. MIT Man-Vehicle Control Laboratory Report T-65-1. Cambridge, Massachusetts, 1965.

Mengelkoch, R. F., Adams, J. A., & Gainer, C. A. The fogetting of instrument flying skills as a function of the level of initial proficiency. U. S. Naval Training Device Center, Technical Report 71-16-18 Port Washington, New York, 1958.

Mengelkoch, R. F., Adams, J. A., & Gainer, C. A. The forgetting of instrument flying skills. *Human Factors,* 1971, **13,** 397–405.

Michael, J. A., & Jones, G. M. Dependence of visual tracking capability upon stimulus predictability. *Vision Research,* 1966, **6,** 707–716.

Micheli, G. Augmented feedback and transfer of training. U. S. Naval Training Device Center, Report 1H-41. Port Washington, New York, 1966.

Miller, D. C. Behavioral sources of suboptimal human performance in discrete control tasks. MIT Engineering Projects Laboratory Report NsG-107-61, Cambridge, Massachusetts, 1969.

Milnes-Walker, N. A study of pursuit and compensatory tracking of auditory pitch. *Ergonomics,* 1971, **14,** 479–486.

Milton, J. L. Analysis of pilots' eye movements in flight. *Journal of Aviation Medicine,* 1952, **23,** 67–76.

Mirabella, A. Two-dimensional versus three-dimensional tracking under two modes of error feedback. *Human factors,* 1969, **11,** 9–12.

Monty, R. A., & Ruby, W. J. Effects of added work load on compensatory tracking for maximum terrain following. *Human Factors*, 1965, 7, 207–214.

Morgan, C. T., Cook, J. S., III, Chapanis, A., & Lund, M. W. *Human engineering guide to equpment design.* New York: McGraw-Hill, 1963.

Morgan, C. T., & Stellar, E. *Physiological psychology.* 2nd Ed. New York: McGraw-Hill, 1950.

Moss, S. M. Tracking with a differential brightness display: I. Acquisition and transfer. *Journal of Applied Psychology* 1964, 48, 115–122. a

Moss, S. M. Tracking with a differential brightness display: II. Peripheral tracking. *Journal of Applied Psychology*, 1964, 48, 249–254. b

Mowbray, G. H., & Gebhard, J. W. Man's senses as information channels. In Sinaiko, H. W. (Ed.), *Selected papers on human factors in the design and use of control systems.* New York: Dover, 1961. Pp. 115–149.

Muckler, F. A., & Matheny, W. G. Transfer of training in tracking as a function of control friction. *Journal of Applied Psychology*, 1954, 38, 364–367.

Muckler, F. A., & Obermayer, R. W. Compensatory tracking and oscillatory control system transients. *Perceptual & Motor Skills*, 1961, 13, 19–31.

Muckler, F. A., Obermayer, R. W., Hanlon, W. H., & Serio, F. P. Transfer of training with simulated aircraft dynamics: II. Variations in control gain and phugoid characteristics. USAF Aerospace Medical Research Laboratories, Technical Report WADD 60-615(II), Wright-Patterson Air Force Base, Ohio, 1961. a

Muckler, F. A., Obermayer, R. W., Hanlon, W. H., & Serio, F. P. Transfer of training with simulated aircraft dynamics: III. Variations in course complexity and amplitude. USAF Aerospace Medical Research Laboratories, Technical Report WADD 60-615(III), Wright-Patterson Air Force Base, Ohio, 1961. b

Muckler, F. A., Obermayer, R. W., Hanlon, W. H., Serio, F. P., & Rockway, M. R. Transfer of training with simulated aircraft dynamics: I. Variations in period and damping of the phugoid response. USAF Aerospace Medical Research Laboratories, Technical Report WADD 60-615(I), Wright-Patterson Air Force Base, Ohio, 1961.

Naish, J. M. Combination of information in superimposed visual fields. *Nature (London)* 1964, 202, 641–646.

Naish, J. M. Control gains in head-up presentation. *Proceedings of the Sixth Annual Conference on Manual Control.* U. S. Air Force Institute of Technology and U. S. Air Force Flight Dynamics Laboratory, Dayton, Ohio, 1970.

Newton, J. M. An investigation of tracking performance in the cold with two types of controls. U. S. Army Medical Research Laboratory Report 324. Fort Knox, Kentucky, 1958.

Noble, M. E., Fitts, P. M., & Marlowe, E. The interrelations of task variables in continuous pursuit tasks: II Visual-display scale, arm-control scale, and target frequency in compensatory tracking. USAF Human Resources Research Center, Research Bulletin 53-55. Lackland Air Force Base, San Antonio, Texas, 1953.

Noble, M., Fitts, P. M., & Warren, C. E. The frequency response of skilled subjects in a pursuit tracking task. *Journal of Experimental Psychology.* 1955, 49, 249–256.

Noble, M., & Trumbo, D. The organization of skilled response. *Organizational Behavior & Human Performance*, 1967, 2, 1–25.

Noble, M., Trumbo, D., & Fowler, F. Further evidence on secondary task interference in tracking. *Journal of Experimental Psychology*, 1967, 73, 146–149.

Noble, M., Trumbo, D., Ulrich, L., & Cross, K. Task predictability and the development of tracking skill under extended practice. *Journal of Experimental Psychology*, 1966, **72**, 85–94.

North, J. D., & Lomnicki, Z. A. Further experiments on human operators in compensatory tracking tasks. *Ergonomics*, 1961, **4**, 339–353.

Notterman, J. M., & Page, D. E. Evaluation of mathematically equivalent tracking systems. *Perceptual & Motor Skills*, 1962, **15**, 683–716.

Obermayer, R. W., Swartz, W. F., & Muckler, F. A. The interaction of information displays with control system dynamics in continuous tracking. *Journal of Applied Psychology*, 1961, **45**, 369–375.

Obermayer, R. W., Swartz, W. F., & Muckler, F. A. Interaction of information displays with control system dynamics and course frequency in continuous tracking. *Perceptual & Motor Skills*, 1962, **15**, 199–215.

Obermayer, R. W., Webster, R. B., & Muckler, F. A. Optimal control theory and manual control systems. Report submitted to U. S. National Aeronautics and Space Administration, Washington, D.C., 1967.

Pearl, B. E., Simon, J. R., & Smith, K. U. Visual tracking: IV. Interrelations of target speed and aided-tracking ratio in defining tracking accuracy. *Journal of Applied Psychology*, 1955, **39**, 209–214.

Pew, R. W. Performance of human operators in a three-state relay control system with velocity-augmented displays. *IEEE Transactions on Human Factors in Electronics*, 1966, HFE-7, 77–83.

Pew, R. W., Duffendack, J. C., & Fensch, L. K. Sine-wave tracking revisited. *IEEE Transactions on Human Factors in Electronics*, 1967, HFE-8, 130–134. a

Pew, R. W., Duffendack, J. C., & Fensch, L. K. Temporal limitations in human motor control. Paper presented at the Psychonomic Society, October, 1967. Human Performance Center, University of Michigan, 1967. b

Pikler, A. G & Harris, J. D. Compensatory and pursuit tracking of loudness. *Journal. of the Acoustical Society America*, 1960, **32**, 1129–1133.

Pitkin, E. T., & Vinje, E. W. Evaluation of human operator aural and visual delays with the critical tracking task. *Proceedings of the Eighth Conference on Manual Control.* U. S. Air Force Flight Dynamics Laboratory, Technical Report 72-92, Wright-Patterson Air Force Base, Ohio, 1973.

Platzer, H. L. A non-linear approach to human tracking. Franklin Institute, Laboratories for Research and Development, Interim technical report 2490-1. Philadelphia, Pennsylvania 1955.

Poulton, E. C. Perceptual anticipation and reaction time. *Quarterly Journal of Experimental Psychology*, 1950, **2**, 99–112. a

Poulton, E. C. Perceptual anticipation in tracking. UK MRC Applied Psychology Unit Report 118. Cambridge, England, 1950. b

Poulton, E. C. Two pointer and one pointer displays in tracking. UK MRC Applied Psychology Unit, Report 142. Cambridge, England, 1950. c

Poulton, E. C. Perceptual anticipation in tracking with two-pointer and one-pointer displays. *British Journal of Psychology*, 1952, **43**, 222–229. a

Poulton, E. C. The basis of perceptual anticipation in tracking. *British Journal of Psychology*, 1952, **43**, 295–302. b

Poulton, E. C. Eye-hand span in simple serial tasks. *Journal of Experimental Psychology*, 1954, **47**, 403–410.

Poulton, E. C. Learning the statistical properties of the input in pursuit tracking. *Journal of Experimental Psychology*, 1957, **54**, 28–32. a

Poulton, E. C. On prediction in skilled movements. *Psychological Bulletin,* 1957, **54,** 467–478. b

Poulton, E. C. On the stimulus and response in pursuit tracking. *Journal of Experimental Psychology,* 1957, **53,** 189–194. c

Poulton, E. C. Pursuit-tracking with partial control of the input. *American Journal of Psychology,* 1957, **70,** 631–633. d

Poulton, E. C. On simple methods of scoring tracking error. *Psychological Bulletin,* 1962, **59,** 320–328.

Poulton, E. C. Compensatory tracking with differentiating and integrating control systems. *Journal of Applied Psychology,* 1963, **47,** 398–402. a

Poulton, E. C. Pursuit tracking with differentiating and integrating control systems. *Journal of Applied Psychology,* 1963, **47,** 289–292. b

Poulton, E. C. Postview and preview in tracking with complex and simple inputs. *Ergonomics,* 1964, **7,** 257–266.

Poulton, E. C. Engineering psychology. *Annual Review of Psychology,* 1966, **17,** 177–200.

Poulton, E. C. A quantal model for human tracking. *Proceedings of the Third Annual NASA-University Conference on Manual Control,* U.S. National Aeronautics and Space Administration Report SP-144, Washington, D.C., 1967 Pp. 241–246. a

Poulton, E. C. Tracking a variable rate of movement. *Journal of Experimental Psychology,* 1967, **73,** 135–144. b

Poulton, E. C. The new psychophysics: six models for magnitude estimation. *Psychological Bulletin,* 1968, **69,** 1–19.

Poulton, E. C. Bias in experimental comparisons between equipments due to the order of testing. *Ergonomics,* 1969, **12,** 675–687.

Poulton, E. C. *Environment and human efficiency.* Springfield, Illinois: Thomas, 1970.

Poulton, E. C. Skilled performance. In Singer. R. N. (Ed.). *The psychomotor domain: movement behaviors.* Philadelphia, Pennsylvania: Lea & Febiger, 1972. Chapter 11. Pp. 267–284.

Poulton, E. C. Unwanted range effects from using within-subject experimental designs. *Psychological Bulletin,* 1973, **80,** 113–121.

Poulton, E. C., & Freeman, P. R. Unwanted asymmetrical transfer effects with balanced experimental designs. *Psychological Bulletin,* 1966, **66,** 1–8.

Poulton, E. C., & Gregory, R. L. Blinking during visual tracking. *Quarterly Journal of Experimental Psychology,* 1952, **4,** 57–65.

Provins, K. A. "Handedness" and skill. *Quarterly Journal of Experimental Psychology,* 1956, **8,** 79–95.

Regan, J. J. Tracking performance related to display control configurations. U. S. Naval Training Device Center, Technical Report 322-1-2. Port Washington, New York, 1959.

Regan, J. J. Tracking performance related to display-control configurations. *Journal of Applied Psychology,* 1960, **44,** 310–314.

Ritchie, M. L., & Bamford, H. E., Jr. Quickening and damping a feedback display. *Journal of Applied Psychology,* 1957, **41,** 395–402.

Robinson, G. H. The human controller as an adaptive, low pass filter. *Human Factors,* 1967, **9,** 141–147.

Rockway, M. R. The effect of variations in control-display ratio and exponential time delay on tracking performance. USAF Wright Air Development Center, Technical Report 54-618, Wright Patterson Air Force Base, Ohio, 1954.

Rockway, M. R. Effects of variations in control deadspace and gain on tracking performance. USAF Wright Air Development Center, Technical Report 57-326. Wright-Patterson Air Force Base, Ohio, 1957.

Rockway, M. R., & Franks, P. E. Effects of variations in control backlash and gain on tracking performance. USAF Wright Air Development Center, Technical Report 58-533, Wright-Patterson Air Force Base, Ohio, 1959.

Rogers, J. O. Discrete tracking performance with limited velocity resolution. *Human Factors*, 1970, **12**, 331–339.

Rolfe, J. M. A study of setting performance on a digital display. RAF. Institute of Aviation Medicine, Report 365, Farnsborough, Hants, UK, 1966.

Rolfe, J. M. Dynamic digital displays. A study of the effect of reward on the performance of a tracking task employing a digital display. RAF. Institute of Aviation Medicine, Report 395, Farnsborough, Hants, UK, 1967.

Rolfe, J. M., & Clifford, A. C. Compensatory tracking performance on a digital display. RAF. Institute of Aviation Medicine, Report 293, Farnsborough, Hants, UK, 1964.

Roscoe, S. N., & Williges, R. C. Motion relationships in aircraft attitude and guidance displays: a flight experiment. Aviation Research Laboratory, Technical Report 72-32. Institute of Aviation, University of Illinois—Willard Airport, Savoy, Illinois, 1972.

Rund, P. A., Birmingham, H. P., Tipton, C. L., & Garvey, W. D. The utility of quickening techniques in improving tracking performance with a binary display. U. S. Naval Research Laboratory Report 5013. Washington, D.C., 1957.

Runner, G. H., & Sweeney, J. S. A comparison of quickened and unquickened displays for the monitoring of vehicle performance under full automatic control. U. S. Naval Research Laboratory Report 5696. Washington, D.C., 1961.

Russell, R. W. Effects of variations in ambient temperature on certain measures of tracking skill and sensory sensitivity. U. S. Army Medical Research Laboratory Report 300. Fort Knox, Kentucky, 1957.

Sadoff, M. A study of a pilot's ability to control during simulated stability augmentation system failures. U. S. National Aeronautics and Space Administration, Technical Note D-1552. Washington, D.C., 1962.

Sadoff, M., McFadden, N. M., & Heinle, D. R. A study of longitudinal control problems at low and negative damping and stability with emphasis on effects of motion cues. U. S. National Aeronautics and Space Administration, Technical Note D-348. Washington, D.C., 1961.

Sampson, P. B., & Elkin, E. H. Level of display integration in compensatory tracking. *Perceptual & Motor Skills*, 1965, **20**, 59–62.

Schoeffler, M. S. The amount of information presented as a parameter of tracking performance. U. S. Army Medical Research Laboratory Report 197. Fort Knox, Kentucky, 1955.

Schori, T. R. Tracking performance as a funcion of precision of electrocutaneous feedback information. *Human Factors*, 1970, **12**, 447–452.

Searle, L. V. Psychological studies of tracking behavior: Part IV—The intermittency hypothesis as a basis for predicting optimum aided-tracking time constants. U. S. Naval Research Laboratory Report 3872. Washington, D.C., 1951.

Searle, L. V., & Taylor, F. V. Studies of tracking behavior. 1. Rate and time characteristics of simple corrective movements. *Journal of Experimental Psychology*, 1948, 38, 615–631.

Seidenstein, S., Chernikoff, R., & Taylor, F. V. The relationship of a retinal-gain index to system performance. U. S. Naval Research Laboratory Report 5548. Washington, D.C., 1960.

Senders, J. W. The influence of surround on tracking performance. Part 1. Tracking on combined pursuit and compensatory one-dimensional tasks with and without a structured surround. USAF Wright Air Development Center, Technical Report 52-229, Part 1. Wright-Patterson Air Force Base, Ohio, 1953.

Senders, J. W. Tracking with intermittently illuminated displays. USAF Wright Air Development Center, Technical Report 55-378. Wright-Patterson Air Force Base, Ohio, 1955.

Senders, J. W., & Bradley, J. V. Effect of backlash on manual control of pitch of a simulated aircraft. USAF Wright Air Development Center, Technical Report 56-107. Wright-Patterson Air Force Base, Ohio, 1956.

Senders, J. W., Carbonell, J. R., & Ward, J. L. Human visual sampling processes: a simulation validation study. U. S. National Aeronautics and Space Administration Report CR-1258 Washington, D.C.: 1969.

Senders, J. W., & Cruzen, M. Tracking performance on combined compensatory and pursuit tasks. USAF Wright Air Development Center, Technical Report 52-39. Wright-Patterson Air Force Base, Ohio, 1952.

Shackel, B. The human limbs in control. 1. Apparatus: optimum experimental conditions. UK MRC Applied Psychology Research Unit Report 214, Cambridge, England, 1954.

Shackel, B. Note on mobile eye viewpoint recording. *Journal of the Optical Society of America*, 1960, 50, 763–768.

Shelly, M. W. Some measures of continuous behavior. *Perceptual & Motor Skills*, 1963, 16, 239–245.

Sheridan, T. B. Time-variable dynamics of human operator systems. U. S. Air Force Cambridge Research Center, Technical Note 60-169. Bedford, Massachusetts, 1960.

Siegel, S. *Nonparametric statistics for the behavioral sciences*. New York: McGraw-Hill, 1956.

Slack, C. W. Learning in simple one-dimensional tracking. *American Journal of Psychology*, 1953, 66, 33–44. a

Slack, C. W. Some characteristics of the "range effect." *Journal of Experimental Psychology*, 1953, 46, 76–80. b

Smith, K. U., & Putz, V. Feedback factors in steering and tracking behavior. *Journal of Applied Psychology*, 1970, 54, 176–183.

Smith, K. U., & Sussman, H. M. Delayed feedback in steering during learning and transfer of learning. *Journal of Applied Psychology*, 1970, 54, 334–342.

Smith, M. C. Theories of the psychological refractory period. *Psychological Bulletin*, 1967, 67, 202–213.

Smith, R. L., Garfinkle, D. R., Groth, H., & Lyman, J. Effects of display magnification, proprioceptive cues, control dynamics and trajectory characteristics on compensatory tracking performance. *Human Factors*, 1966, 8, 427–434. a

Smith, R. L., Garfinkle, D. R., Groth, H., & Lyman, J. Performance studies on the NOTS-UCLA tracking simulator: Effects of selected controller configurations and transfer of training. Biotechnology Laboratory, Technical Report 33. Department of Engineering, UCLA. Los Angeles, California, 1966. b

Smith, R. L., Garfinkle, D. R., & Lyman, J. Independent effects of error magnification and field of view on compensatory tracking performance. *Human Factors,* 1966, **8,** 563–567.

Smith, S. Effects of control-display relationship on tracking in a dual-task setting. *Perceptual & Motor Skills,* 1963, **17,** 954.

Smothergill, D. W., Martin, R., & Pick, H. L., Jr. Perceptual-motor performance under rotation of the central field. *Journal of Experimental Psychology,* 1971, **87,** 64–70.

Speight, L. R. & Bickerdike J. S. Control law optimization in simulated visual tracking of aircraft. *Ergonomics,* 1968, **11,** 231–247.

Stark, L., Vossius, G., & Young, L. R. Predictive control of eye tracking movements. *IRE Transactions on Human Factors in Electronics,* 1962, **HFE-3,** 52–57.

Stephens, S. D. G. Personality and the slope of loudness function. *Quarterly Journal of Experimental Psychology,* 1970, **22,** 9–13.

Stevens, S. S., & Davis, H. *Hearing. Its psychology and physiology.* New York: Wiley, 1938.

Stone, M. Subjective discrimination as a statistical method. *British Journal of Statistical Psychology,* 1961, **14,** 25–28.

Sutton, G. G. The error power spectrum as a technique for assessing the performance of the human operator in a simple task. *Quarterly Journal of Experimental Psychology,* 1957, **9,** 42–51.

Sweeny, J. S., Bailey, A. W., & Dowd, J. F. Comparative evaluation of three approaches to helicopter instrumentation for hovering flight. U. S. Naval Research Laboratory Report 4954. Washington, D.C., 1957.

Taylor, F. V., & Birmingham, H. P. Studies of tracking behavior. II. The acceleration pattern of quick manual corrective responses. *Journal of Experimental Psychology,* 1948, **38,** 783–795.

Taylor, F. V., & Birmingham, H. P. Simplifying the pilot's task through display quickening. *Journal of Aviation Medicine,* 1956, **27,** 27–31.

Taylor, L. W., Jr. A look at pilot modeling techniques at low frequencies. *Proceedings of the Sixth Annual Conference on Manual Control.* U. S. Air Force Institute of Technology and U. S. Air Force Flight Dynamics Laboratory, Dayton, Ohio 1970. Pp. 871–896.

Thompson, R. F., Voss, J. F., & Brogden, W. J. The effect of target-velocity upon the trigonometric relationship of precision and angle of linear pursuit-movements. *American Journal of Psychology,* 1956, **69,** 258–263.

Thornton, G. B. Comparison of an experimental rolling-ball control and a conventional joystick in speed of tracking on a radar display. Defence Research Medical Laboratories Report 107-1. Toronto, Ontario, 1954.

Tickner, A. H., & Poulton, E. C. Acquiring a target with an unlagged acceleration control system and with 3 lagged rate control systems. *Ergonomics,* 1972, **15,** 49–56.

Tipton, C. L. Human vs filter as data extrapolator in a two-coordinate, sampled-data tracking system. U. S. Naval Research Laboratory Report 6323. Washington, D.C., 1965.

Todosiev, E. P. Human performance in a cross-coupled tracking system. *IEEE Transactions on Human Factors in Electronics,* 1967, **HFE-8,** 210–217.

Trumbo, D. Acquisition and performance as a function of uncertainty and structure in serial tracking tasks. *Acta Psychologica,* 1970, **33,** 252–266.

Trumbo, D., & Milone, F. Primary task performance as a function of encoding, retention and recall in a secondary task. *Journal of Experimental Psychology*, 1971, **91**, 273–279.

Trumbo, D., & Noble, M. Response uncertainty in dual-task performance. *Organizational Behavior & Human Performance*, 1972, **7**, 203–215.

Trumbo, D., Noble, M., Cross, K., & Ulrich, L. Task predictability in the organization, acquisition, and retention of tracking skill. *Journal of Experimental Psychology*, 1965, **70**, 252–263.

Trumbo, D., Noble, M., Fowler, F., & Porterfield, J. Motor performance on temporal tasks as a function of sequence length and coherence. *Journal of Experimental Psychology*, 1968, **77**, 397–406.

Trumbo, D., Noble, M., & Quigley, J. Sequential probabilities and the performance of serial tasks. *Journal of Experimental Psychology*, 1968, **76**, 364–372.

Trumbo, D., Noble, M., & Swink, J. Secondary task interference in the performance of tracking tasks. *Journal of Experimental Psychology*, 1967, **73**, 232–240.

Vallerie, L. L. Displays for seeing without looking. *Human Factors*, 1966, **8**, 507–513.

Vallerie, L. L. Peripheral vision displays. Dunlap and Associates Inc., Darien, Connecticut, 1968.

Verdi, A. P., Ornstein, G. N., Heydorn, R. P., & Frost, G. Effects of display quickening on human transfer functions during a dual-axis compensatory tracking task. USAF Aerospace Medical Research Laboratories, Technical Report 65-174. Wright-Patterson Air Force Base, Ohio, 1965.

Vince, M. A. Direction of movement of machine controls. UK Royal Naval Personnel Research Committee Report 233. Medical Research Council, London, 1945.

Vince, M. A. The psychological effect of a non-linear relation between control and display. UK Ministry of Supply, Servo Report 2. London, 1946.

Vince, M. A. Corrective movements in a pursuit task. *Quarterly Journal of Experimental Psychology*, 1948, **1**, 85–103. a

Vince M. A. The intermittency of control movements and the psychological refractory period. *British Journal of Psychology*, 1948, **38**, 149–157. b

Vince, M. A. Some exceptions to the psychological refractory period in unskilled manual responses. UK MRC Applied Psychology Unit Report 124. Cambridge, England, 1950.

Voss, J. F. Effect of target brightness and target speed upon tracking proficiency. *Journal of Experimental Psychology*, 1955, **49**, 237–243.

Walston, C. E., & Warren, C. E. A mathematical analysis of the human operator in a closed-loop control system. U. S. Air Force Personnel and Training Research Center, Research Bulletin 54-96. Lackland Air Force Base, San Antonio, Texas, 1954.

Wargo, M. J. Delayed sensory feedback in visual and auditory tracking. *Perceptual & Motor Skills*, 1967, **24**, 55–62.

Warrick, M. J. Effect of transmission-type control lags on tracking accuracy. USAF Air Material Command, Technical Report 5916. Wright-Patterson Air Force Base, Dayton, Ohio, 1949.

Warrick, M. J. Effect of exponential type control lags on the speed and accuracy of positioning a visual indicator. USAF Wright Air Development Center, Technical Note 55-348, Wright-Patterson Air Force Base, Ohio, 1955.

Webb, P. (Ed.) *Bioastronautics data book* (1st edition). U. S. National Aeronautics and Space Administration, Report SP-3006. Washington, D.C., 1964.

Weir, D. H., & Johnson, W. A. Pilot dynamic response to sudden flight control system failures and implications for design. U. S. National Aeronautics and Space Administration Report CR-1087. Washington, D.C., 1968.

Weir, D. H., & Klein, R. H. Measurement and analysis of pilot scanning behavior during simulated instrument approaches. *Proceedings of the Sixth Annual Conference on Manual Control.* U. S. Air Force Institute of Technology and U. S. Air Force Flight Dynamics Laboratory, Dayton, Ohio, 1970, Pp. 83–108.

Welford, A. T. The 'psychological refractory period' and the timing of high-speed performance—a review and a theory. *British Journal of Psychology,* 1952, **43**, 2–19.

Welford, A. T. *Ageing and human skill.* London and New York: Oxford University Press, 1958.

Welford, A. T. Single-channel operation in the brain. *Acta Psychologica,* 1967, **27**, 5–22.

Welford, A. T., Norris, A. H., & Shock, N. W. Speed and accuracy of movement and their changes with age. *Acta Psychologica,* 1969, **30**, 3–15.

Wheeless, L. L., Jr., Boynton, R. M., & Cohen, G. H. Eye-movement responses to step and pulse-step stimuli. *Journal of the Optical Society of America,* 1966, **56**, 956–960.

Wood, M. E. Flight training applications. In McGrath, J. J., and Harris, D. H. (Eds.). *Adaptive training.* Aviation Research Monographs, Vol. 1, no. 2, Session 2. Aviation Research Laboratory, University of Illinois, Urbana-Champaign, Illinois, 1971.

Wortz, E. C., McTee, A. C., Swartz, W. F., Rheinlander, T. W., & Dalhamer, W. A. Effects of control-display displacement functions on pursuit and compensatory tracking. *Aerospace Medicine,* 1965, **36**, 1042–1047.

Yasui, S., & Young, L. R. Manual time-optimal control for high-order plants. *Proceedings of the Third Annual NASA—University Conference on Manual Control* U.S. National Aeronautics and Space Administration Report SP-144, Washington, D.C., 1967, Pp. 351–370.

Young, L. R. Some effects of motion cues on manual tracking. *Journal of Spacecraft,* 1967, **4**, 1300–1303.

Young, M. L. Psychological studies of tracking behavior. Part III. The characteristics of quick manual corrective movements made in response to step-function velocity inputs. U. S. Naval Research Laboratory Report 3850. Washington, D.C., 1951.

Ziegler, P. N. Single and dual axis tracking as a function of system dynamics. *Human Factors,* 1968, **10**, 273–275.

Ziegler, P. N., & Chernikoff, R. A comparison of three types of manual controls on a third-order tracking task. *Ergonomics,* 1968, **11**, 369–374.

Ziegler, P. N., Reilly, R. E., & Chernikoff, R. The use of displacement, flash, and depth-of-flash coded displays for providing control system information. U. S. Naval Research Laboratory Report 6412. Washington, D.C., 1966.

Index

A 4
B 5
C 6
D 7
Γ 9
G 0
H 1
I 2
J 3